Go for DevOps

Learn how to use the Go language to automate servers, the cloud, Kubernetes, GitHub, Packer, and Terraform

John Doak

David Justice

BIRMINGHAM—MUMBAI

Go for DevOps

Copyright © 2022 Packt Publishing

All rights reserved. No part of this book may be reproduced, stored in a retrieval system, or transmitted in any form or by any means, without the prior written permission of the publisher, except in the case of brief quotations embedded in critical articles or reviews.

Every effort has been made in the preparation of this book to ensure the accuracy of the information presented. However, the information contained in this book is sold without warranty, either express or implied. Neither the authors, nor Packt Publishing or its dealers and distributors, will be held liable for any damages caused or alleged to have been caused directly or indirectly by this book.

Packt Publishing has endeavored to provide trademark information about all of the companies and products mentioned in this book by the appropriate use of capitals. However, Packt Publishing cannot guarantee the accuracy of this information.

Group Product Manager: Rahul Nair
Publishing Product Manager: Preet Ahuja
Senior Editor: Shazeen Iqbal
Content Development Editor: Romy Dias
Technical Editor: Shruthi Shetty
Copy Editor: Safis Editing
Project Coordinator: Ashwin Kharwa
Proofreader: Safis Editing
Indexer: Subalakshmi Govindhan
Production Designer: Joshua Misquitta
Marketing Coordinator: Sanjana Gupta

First published: June 2022
Production reference: 1010622

Published by Packt Publishing Ltd.
Livery Place
35 Livery Street
Birmingham
B3 2PB, UK.

ISBN 978-1-80181-889-6
www.packt.com

Monika, you are the North Star I guide my ship with and I love you with all my heart. I couldn't have done this without your support and guidance.

– *John Doak*

To Deya, Will, Thor, and Tron, without whom my days would be as muted and monotone as this page.

– *David Justice*

Contributors

About the authors

John Doak is the principal manager of Layer 1 Reliability Engineering at Microsoft. John led the development of the Azure Data Explorer and Microsoft Authentication Library Go SDKs. Previously, he was a Staff Site Reliability Engineer at Google. As part of network engineering, he created many of their first network automation systems. John led the migration of that group from Python to Go, developing Go training classes that have been taught around the world. He was a pivotal figure in transforming the network team to a network/systems group that integrated with SRE. Prior to that, he worked for Lucasfilm in video games and film. You can find his musings on Go/SRE topics and his Go classes on the web.

> *I'd like to thank Raleigh Mann who was my manager at both Lucasfilm and Google during most of my time there. His advice and steadfastness when standing beside me are why I still call him Boss today. Stephen Stuart, who gave me my initial foray into management, which I'm not sure I should thank or curse him for. Thanks to Less Lincoln, the man, the myth, the legend. I've worked with Less for four years, he's as much a mystery box as when I first met him (and I think he likes it that way). Of course, I would never have gotten here without the love and support of my parents, I love you both. Thanks to Sarah Murphy, who was an early contributor to the book. And thanks to David Justice. Without his hard work and enthusiasm, I would not have been able to do this.*

David Justice is the principal software engineer lead for the Azure K8s infrastructure and Steel Thread teams, which maintain a variety of CNCF and Bytecode Alliance projects. He is a maintainer of the Cluster API Provider Azure and a contributor to the Cluster API. Prior to that, David was the technical assistant to the Azure CTO, where he was responsible for Azure cross-group technical strategy and architecture. Early on at Microsoft, he was a program manager leading Azure SDKs and CLIs, where he transitioned all Azure services to describe them using OpenAPI specifications in GitHub and established automations to generate Azure reference docs, SDKs, and CLIs. Prior to working at Microsoft, David was the CTO of a mobile CI/CD SaaS called CISimple.

Thank you to my lovely, supportive wife, Deya, for encouraging me to pursue time-consuming activities such as writing a book, educational pursuits, start-ups, and her favorite, golf. Deya and Will, you will never know how much your love, hugs, and support powered me through late nights and droughts of creativity. This book would not be possible without the brilliance, reliability, and counter-perspectives of my coauthor, John, for whom the word example means a 30k-line robust application. Thank you to the whole Packt team and all the reviewers, but especially Romy Dias who edited my work into something more closely resembling English prose. Finally, thank you Dad and Papa for always believing in me.

About the reviewers

Trieu Pham is a software engineer with various technical ideas. His current focus and specialty are on API development, microservices, DevOps, and Golang. He has a bachelor's degree in mathematics and computer science, a master's degree in computer engineering, and a PhD in engineering.

Lukasz Sudol is a senior director of engineering at GumGum. He began working in the e-commerce industry by developing backend systems. During the past decade, his work has focused on developing high-availability application architectures for AdTech. He enjoys helping people to develop and working with interesting technologies.

> *I would like to thank my family, my fiancée Marcelina, and my friends who understand the time and commitment it takes to research and test engineering tools that are constantly changing. And to the reader, I hope my contribution will help you get through the book more easily.*

Table of Contents

Preface

Section 1: Getting Up and Running with Go

1
Go Language Basics

Technical requirements	5
Using the Go Playground	5
Utilizing Go packages	7
Declaring a package	7
Importing a package	8
Using a package	9
Package name conflicts	9
Packages must be used	10
A Go Hello World	11
Using Go's variable types	**12**
Go's types	14
Declaring variables	15
Variable scopes and shadowing	17
Function/statement variable must be used	20
Looping in Go	**21**
C style	21
Removing the init statement	21
Remove the post statement too and you have a while loop	22
Creating an infinite loop	22
Using conditionals	**24**
if statements	24
else	25
Learning about functions	**28**
Returning multiple values and named results	29
Variadic arguments	30
Anonymous functions	31
Defining public and private	**32**
Using arrays and slices	**34**
Arrays	34
Slices	35
Extracting all values	36
Understanding maps	37
Declaring a map	37
Accessing values	38
Adding new values	38
Extracting all values	39
Understanding Go pointers	**39**

Memory addresses	40	Changing a field's value in a method	47
Function arguments are copies	40	Constructors	48
Pointers to the rescue	41	**Comprehending Go interfaces**	**49**
Getting to know about structs	**43**	Defining an interface type	49
Declaring a struct	43	Important things about interfaces	50
Declaring a custom type	44	The blank interface – Go's universal value	51
Custom struct types	44	Type assertion	51
Adding methods to a type	45	**Summary**	**52**
Changing a field's value	46		

2
Go Language Essentials

Handling errors in Go	**54**	Channels	69
Creating an error	54	Sending/receiving	70
Using an error	55	select statements	71
Creating named errors	56	Channels as an event signal	72
Custom errors	57	Mutexes	74
Wrapping errors	58	RWMutex	75
Utilizing Go constants	**59**	**Understanding Go's Context type**	**75**
Declaring a constant	59	Using a Context to signal a timeout	76
Enumeration via constants	61	Honoring a context when receiving	77
Printing enumerators	62	Context in the standard library	78
Using defer, panic, and recover	**63**	Context to pass values	79
defer	63	Best practices	81
panic	64	**Utilizing Go's testing framework**	**81**
recover	64	Creating a basic test file	82
Utilizing goroutines for concurrency	**65**	Creating a simple test	83
Starting a goroutine	66	Table Driven Tests (TDT)	84
Synchronization	67		
WaitGroups	68		

| Creating fakes with interfaces | 86 | Type constraints with methods | 95 |
| Third-party testing packages | 90 | Adding type parameters to struct types | 96 |

Generics – the new kid on the block 91

Type parameters	91	Specifying the type when calling a generic function	98
Using type constraints	92	Gotchas to watch for	100
We could do better with constraints	93	When to use generics	101
Current built-in constraints	94	**Summary**	**102**

3

Setting Up Your Environment

Technical requirements	**103**	A note on Go compiler version compatibility	108
Installing Go on your machine	**104**	**Building code locally**	**108**
macOS installation using the package installer	104	Creating a module directory and go.mod file	109
macOS installation via Homebrew	104	Updating a module when adding dependencies	110
Windows installation using MSI	105	Adding a hello world	110
Linux	106	Running our first program	110
Other platforms	108	**Summary**	**111**

4

Filesystem Interactions

All I/O in Go are files	**114**	Stdin/Stdout/Stderr are just files	119
I/O interfaces	114	Reading data out of a stream	120
Reading and writing to files	**115**	Writing data into a stream	122
Reading local files	115	**OS-agnostic pathing**	**123**
Writing local files	116	What OS/platform am I running?	124
Reading remote files	117	Using filepath	124
Streaming file content	**119**		

Relative and absolute pathing	126	embed	128
		Walking our filesystem	129
OS-agnostic filesystems	126	The io/fs future	129
io.fs filesystems	127	Summary	131

5
Using Common Data Formats

Technical requirements	134	Popular encoding formats	149
CSV files	134		
Basic value separation using the strings package	135	The Go field tags	149
		JSON	150
Using the encoding/csv package	139	YAML encoding	158
		Summary	162
Using excelize when dealing with Excel	142		

6
Interacting with Remote Data Sources

Technical requirements	164	Developing REST services and clients	178
Accessing SQL databases	164		
Connecting to a Postgres database	165	REST for RPCs	178
		Developing gRPC services and clients	186
Querying a Postgres database	166		
Null values	169	Protocol buffers	187
Writing data to Postgres	170	Stating the prerequisites	189
Transactions	171	Generating your packages	189
Postgres-specific types	173	Writing a gRPC client	190
Other options	175	Writing a gRPC server	192
Storage abstractions	176	Creating a server binary	195
Case study – data migration of an orchestration system – Google	177	Creating a client binary	197
		Company-standard RPC clients and servers	199
		Summary	200

7
Writing Command-Line Tooling

Technical requirements	202	Using Cobra for advanced CLI applications	211
Implementing application I/O	202	Code organization	212
The flag package	203	The optional Cobra generator	213
Custom flags	205	The command package	215
Basic flag error handling	206	Handling OS signals	219
Shorthand flags	208	Capturing an OS signal	220
Accessing non-flag arguments	208	Using Context to cancel	221
Retrieving input from STDIN	209	Summary	228

8
Automating Command-Line Tasks

Technical requirements	230	change automations	248
Using os/exec to automate local changes	230	Components of a change	248
		Writing a concurrent job	249
Determining the availability of essential tools	231	Case study – Network rollouts	258
		Writing a system agent	259
Using SSH in Go to automate remote changes	240	Designing a system agent	259
		Implementing Install	262
Connecting to another system	241	Implementing SystemPerf	264
Designing safe, concurrent		Summary	267

Section 2: Instrumenting, Observing, and Responding

9
Observability with OpenTelemetry

Technical requirements	273	OpenTelemetry	273
An introduction to		Reference architecture for	

OpenTelemetry	274	Correlating traces and logs	295
OpenTelemetry components	275	Adding log entries to spans	296

Logging with context — 278

Our first log statement	278	**Instrumenting for metrics**	**297**
Structured and leveled logs with Zap	279	The life cycle of a metric	298
Ingesting, transforming, and exporting logs using OpenTelemetry	281	Client/server metrics with OpenTelemetry	299

Instrumenting for distributed tracing — 286

		Alerting on metrics abnormalities	**308**
		Adding and configuring Alertmanager	308
The life cycle of a distributed trace	286	**Summary**	**313**

10
Automating Workflows with GitHub Actions

Technical requirements	**316**	**Creating a custom GitHub Action using Go**	**345**
Understanding the basics of GitHub Actions	**316**	Basics of custom actions	345
Exploring the components of a GitHub Action	317	Goals for the tweeter custom GitHub Action	348
How to build and trigger your first GitHub Action	323	Creating the tweeter action	349
Building a continuous integration workflow	**328**	**Publishing a custom Go GitHub Action**	**360**
Introducing the tweeter command-line tool	328	The basics of publishing actions	360
Goals of the tweeter continuous integration workflow	329	Goals for publishing the tweeter custom action	361
Continuous integration workflow for tweeter	330	Managing action semantic versioning	361
Building a release workflow	**334**	Publishing the tweeter action to the GitHub Marketplace	364
GitHub releases	334	**Summary**	**364**
Release automation for tweeter	335		

11
Using ChatOps to Increase Efficiency

Technical requirements	368	Case Study – Regexes versus Lexer and Parser	378
Environment architecture	368		
Using an Ops service	370	Creating our Slack application	386
Building a basic chatbot	371		
Creating event handlers	377	Running the applications	391
		Summary	395

Section 3: Cloud ready Go

12
Creating Immutable Infrastructure Using Packer

Technical requirements	400	Creating a spec file	413
Building an Amazon Machine Image	403	Adding a Packer provisioner	416
Setting up an AWS source	404	Customizing Packer with plugins	419
Defining a build block and adding some provisioners	406	Writing your own plugin	420
		Releasing a plugin	431
Executing a Packer build	411	Using our plugin in a build	433
Validating images with Goss	413	Debugging a Packer plugin	435
		Summary	436

13
Infrastructure as Code with Terraform

Technical requirements	438	Understanding the basics of Terraform providers	447
An introduction to IaC	439		
Understanding the basics of Terraform	439	Defining and provisioning cloud resources	448
Initializing and applying infrastructure specs using Terraform	440	Building a pet store Terraform provider	458

Resources for building custom providers	458	Publishing custom providers	474
The pet store provider	459	Summary	475

14

Deploying and Building Applications in Kubernetes

Technical requirements	**479**	Creating an ingress to expose our application on a local host port	492
Interacting with the Kubernetes API	**479**	Streaming pod logs for the NGINX application	494
Creating a KinD cluster	479		
Using kubectl to interact with the API	480	**Extending Kubernetes with custom resources and operators**	**495**
Deploying a load-balanced HTTP application using Go	**483**	Custom Resource Definitions	497
It all starts with main	485	Controllers	500
Creating a ClientSet	486	Standing on the shoulders of giants	500
Creating a namespace	487		
Deploying the application into the namespace	488	**Building a pet store operator**	**501**
Creating the NGINX deployment	488	Initializing the new operator	501
Waiting for ready replicas to match desired replicas	490	**Summary**	**515**
Creating a Service to load-balance	491		

15

Programming the Cloud

Technical requirements	**518**	Creating an Azure account and accessing the API	522
What is the cloud?	**518**		
Learning the basics of the Azure APIs	**519**	**Building infrastructure using Azure Resource Manager**	**524**
A background on cloud APIs and SDKs	520	Azure SDK for Go	525
Microsoft Azure identity, RBAC, and resource hierarchy	521	Setting up your local environment	525

| Building an Azure virtual machine | 526 | Building an Azure Storage account | 539 |
| Using provisioned Azure infrastructure | 539 | Summary | 546 |

16
Designing for Chaos

Technical requirements	550	Using three-way handshakes to prevent workflow loss	566
Using overload prevention mechanisms	551	Using policies to restrict tools	568
Case study – AWS client requests overwhelm the network	552	Defining a gRPC workflow service	568
Using circuit breakers	552	Creating a policy engine	570
Using backoff implementations	555	Writing a policy	573
Combining circuit breakers with backoff	557	Cautions on policy engines	577
Using rate limiters to prevent runaway workflows	558	Building systems with an emergency stop	578
Case study – Google satellite disk erase	558	Understanding emergency stops	578
Channel-based rate limiter	559	Building an emergency-stop package	579
Token-bucket rate limiter	561	Using the emergency-stop package	582
Building workflows that are repeatable and never lost	563	Case study – Google's network backbone emergency stop	584
Building idempotent workflows	564	Summary	585

Index
Other Books You May Enjoy

Preface

When you get older it seems to me that most people reflect on their lives. How they got where they are, where they succeeded, and where they failed. I can say in all honesty that I've failed in my career. I know it is abnormal to start a book with an admission of failure, but I figure why start the book off with lies about succeeding beyond my wildest dreams?

My aspirations align more with Jimmy Buffet than Warren Buffet. Keeping my interest in anything for more than a few years is a challenge and my idea of a hard day's work is sipping a piña colada on a Hawaiian beach. Alas, I have failed in my ambitions. The closest to that dream I've gotten is working for a boss who always wore Hawaiian shirts and I don't think that counts.

This whole "expertise" in automation came out of my need to do as little work as possible. When I was a desktop support technician, I needed ways to build a lot of machines in a few hours instead of manually installing Windows and applications. I wanted to spend my days in the office playing video games, reading books, or walking around and talking to people. When I was a network engineer, I wanted people to stop paging me when I was comfortably sleeping in the switch closets around campus. So I wrote tools that allowed others to switch VLAN ports or clear security parameters from a network port without calling me. Why manually balance BGP traffic every week when I could write a program that used SFLOW data to do it?

It was going so well until I got ambitious and went to Google. I wrote a few tools to help make the job easier for myself, such as figuring out whether on-call pages were really caused by ongoing scheduled work or programs to provision all load balancers in a data center. Back in those days, Google had plenty of massage chairs and other amenities I'd rather have been taking advantage of instead of migrating links on a data center router while on the phone with an overworked hardware ops technician in Atlanta and typing into an IRC channel on why my network drains were still in place.

But then people started wanting to use my tools. My friend Adel would ask whether I could make something to program facility routers or validate that Force10 routers were set up right. And he was such a nice person, you just couldn't say no. Or Kirk would come over and ask how we could automate edge router turnups because his team was getting overworked. Instead of making my job easier, I ended up working more hours to make other people's jobs easier!

Hopefully my failures can help you in your success (my father used to say that no one is completely useless; they can always be used as a bad example).

This book is filled with many of the methodologies I've used in my career and lessons on what I believe to be the best language for DevOps at this time, Go.

David (my coauthor who will introduce himself in a moment) and I come from two different extremes of the DevOps world. I come from a school of thought where almost no commercial or standard open source software is used. All DevOps tools are developed internally and are form-fitted to work in a specific environment. David comes from the school where you use as much open source software such as Kubernetes, GitHub, Docker, Terraform, and so on... as you can. This allows you to leverage a collection of available and popular tools that may not be exactly what you want, but come with support networks and lots of options. It is easier to hire engineers who already know how to work on industry-standard tools than those who work with custom toolsets. In this book, you will find a mix of these ideas and methodologies that encompass both schools of thought. It is our belief that a mixture of readymade and custom tools will give you the biggest bang for your buck.

Our sincere hope is that this book will offer you not only a guide in using Go for your DevOps needs but also the ability to write your own tools or modify existing ones to leverage the power of Go to scale your operational needs at any company. And if nothing else, both David and I will be giving our proceeds away to Doctors Without Borders, so if you bought this book and nothing else comes of it, you will be helping a good cause.

But maybe you will one day be sitting on the beach, collecting your paycheck while your automations take care of the day-to-day. I'll keep working on that goal, so if you get there first, have a drink for me.

With that said, I'd like to introduce my esteemed coauthor, David Justice.

As John mentioned, we come from different origins, but find ourselves approaching similar problem spaces. My background is in software development and software engineering spanning everything from mobile application development, web development, and database optimization to machine learning and distributed systems. My focus has never really been DevOps. I'm what you might call an accidental practitioner of DevOps. My DevOps skills have come from the necessity to provide ever-increasing business value, which required me to automate all of the things that were not related to delivering new features and defect resolutions. My secondary motivation for developing DevOps skills is my desire to consistently deploy code and sleep through the night. There is no motivation quite like running a start-up and being the only person around to service a high-severity issue at 3 a.m. to encourage you to build resilient systems and automations.

The motivations I described here should provide the basis for why I tend to choose solutions that are quickly applied and have considerable support in the open source community. If I can find an open source solution with great documentation that can do the vast majority of what I need pretty well, then I can glue and tape the rest together as needed (if you get down deep enough, at the bottom of nearly every solution is some dirty Bash script). For me or my teams to invest a great deal of time and effort into building bespoke tooling, I would need to have a considerable return on investment. Furthermore, when I think of bespoke tooling, I also consider the cost of ongoing maintenance and education of new team members. It's simple to point new team members to a project such as Terraform and ask them to learn it. There's great documentation and endless blog posts detailing every imaginable scenario. There's also a good chance the new team member already knows Terraform because they were using it at a previous job. This reasoning drives me to require a significant burden of proof to approve a project to build bespoke tooling. For these reasons, I've spent quite a bit of time using open source DevOps tooling, and I've made it my business to be as good at extending that tooling as I can be.

In this book, you will find a variety of bespoke tools for accomplishing tasks using only Go and the standard library. However, you will also find several examples of how to use existing open source tools to accomplish tasks that would otherwise take a vast amount of custom code to achieve. I believe our different approaches add to the value of the content and provide you with the tools needed for understanding the trade-offs involved in inventing your own solutions or extending existing solutions to solve common DevOps tasks.

As John left off, I too hope that this book will help you reach a Zen-like state of automation mastery so that you can follow in John's steps and live more like Jimmy Buffet than Warren Buffet.

Who this book is for

This book is for anyone who would like to use Go to develop their own DevOps tooling or to integrate custom features with DevOps tools such as Kubernetes, GitHub Actions, HashiCorp Packer, and Terraform. You should have experience with some type of programming language, but not necessarily Go.

What this book covers

Chapter 1, Go Language Basics, introduces the basics of the Go language.

Chapter 2, Go Language Essentials, covers essential features of the Go language.

Chapter 3, Setting Up Your Environment, explains setting up the Go environment.

Chapter 4, Filesystem Interactions, explores using Go to interact with the local filesystem.

Chapter 5, Using Common Data Formats, looks at using Go to read and write common file formats.

Chapter 6, Interacting with Remote Data Sources, explores using Go to interact with gRPC and REST services.

Chapter 7, Writing Command-Line Tools, shows how to write command-line tools in Go.

Chapter 8, Automating Command-Line Tasks, addresses leveraging Go's exec and SSH packages to automate work.

Chapter 9, Observability with OpenTelemetry, looks at using OpenTelemetry with Go for better instrumentation and alerting.

Chapter 10, Automating Workflows with GitHub Actions, shows how to use GitHub for continuous integration, release automation, and custom actions using Go.

Chapter 11, Using ChatOps to Increase Efficiency, covers how to write ChatOps services using Go to provide operational insights and manage incidents effectively.

Chapter 12, Creating Immutable Infrastructure Using Packer, explains customizing HashiCorp's Packer to automate virtual machine image creation on AWS.

Chapter 13, Infrastructure as Code with Terraform, shows how to define your own custom Terraform provider.

Chapter 14, *Deploying and Building Applications in Kubernetes*, looks at how to program and extend the Kubernetes APIs.

Chapter 15, *Programming the Cloud*, explains using Go to provision and interact with cloud resources.

Chapter 16, *Designing for Chaos*, discusses using rate limiters, centralized workflow engines, and policies to reduce blast radiuses.

To get the most out of this book

You will need to have some programming experience, but not necessarily with Go. A basic understanding of command-line tools for any of the supported operating systems will be required. It will also be helpful to have some DevOps experience.

Software covered in the book	Operating system requirements
Go 1.18 (https://go.dev)	Windows, macOS, or Linux
Packer (https://www.packer.io)	Windows, macOS, or Linux
Terraform (https://www.terraform.io)	Windows, macOS, or Linux
Kubernetes (https://kubernetes.io)	Windows, macOS, or Linux
Docker (https://www.docker.com)	Windows, macOS, or Linux
Tilt (https://tilt.dev)	Windows, macOS, or Linux
Protocol Buffers (https://developers.google.com/protocol-buffers)	Windows, macOS, or Linux
gPRC (https://grpc.io)	Windows, macOS, or Linux
Buf CLI (https://buf.build)	Windows, macOS, or Linux
Azure CLI (https://docs.microsoft.com/en-us/cli/azure/)	Windows, macOS, or Linux
KinD (https://kind.sigs.k8s.io/#installation-and-usage)	Windows, macOS, or Linux
Operator SDK (https://sdk.operatorframework.io/docs/installation/)	Windows, macOS, or Linux
ctlptl (https://github.com/tilt-dev/ctlptl#how-do-i-install-it)	Windows, macOS, or Linux

If you are using the digital version of this book, we advise you to type the code yourself or access the code from the book's GitHub repository (a link is available in the next section). Doing so will help you avoid any potential errors related to the copying and pasting of code.

This book heavily relies on Docker and Docker Compose to allow you to set up cluster configurations that work natively on Linux. It is possible to use Windows for this book using **Windows Subsystem for Linux** (**WSL**), but the authors have not tested this. Additionally, many of the exercises may be done on other operating systems that are POSIX GNU compliant. The *Chapter 12*, Creating Immutable Infrastructure Using Packer, requires an AWS account running Linux virtual machines and the *Chapter 13*, *Infrastructure as Code with Terraform*, and *Chapter 15*, *Programming the Cloud*, require an Azure account.

Download the example code files

You can download the example code files for this book from GitHub at `https://github.com/PacktPublishing/Go-for-DevOps`. If there's an update to the code, it will be updated in the GitHub repository.

We also have other code bundles from our rich catalog of books and videos available at `https://github.com/PacktPublishing/`. Check them out!

Download the color images

We also provide a PDF file that has color images of the screenshots and diagrams used in this book. You can download it here: `https://static.packt-cdn.com/downloads/9781801818896_ColorImages.pdf`.

Conventions used

There are a number of text conventions used throughout this book.

`Code in text`: Indicates code words in text, database table names, folder names, filenames, file extensions, pathnames, dummy URLs, user input, and Twitter handles. Here is an example: "Set up a directory called `packer` in your user's home directory."

A block of code is set as follows:

```
packer {
  required_plugins {
    amazon = {
      version = ">= 0.0.1"
```

When we wish to draw your attention to a particular part of a code block, the relevant lines or items are set in bold:

```
source "amazon-ebs" "ubuntu" {
  access_key = "your key"
  secret_key = "your secret"
  ami_name        = "ubuntu-amd64"
  instance_type = "t2.micro"
```

Any command-line input or output is written as follows:

```
sudo yum install -y yum-utils
sudo yum-config-manager --add-repo https://rpm.releases.hashicorp.com/AmazonLinux/hashicorp.repo
sudo yum -y install packer
```

Bold: Indicates a new term, an important word, or words that you see onscreen. For instance, words in menus or dialog boxes appear in **bold**. Here is an example: "You will need to go to **Settings | Secrets** in your GitHub repository. Click the provided button, **New Repository Secret**."

> Tips or Important Notes
> Appear like this.

Get in touch

Feedback from our readers is always welcome.

General feedback: If you have questions about any aspect of this book, email us at customercare@packtpub.com and mention the book title in the subject of your message.

Errata: Although we have taken every care to ensure the accuracy of our content, mistakes do happen. If you have found a mistake in this book, we would be grateful if you would report this to us. Please visit www.packtpub.com/support/errata and fill in the form.

Piracy: If you come across any illegal copies of our works in any form on the internet, we would be grateful if you would provide us with the location address or website name. Please contact us at `copyright@packt.com` with a link to the material.

If you are interested in becoming an author: If there is a topic that you have expertise in and you are interested in either writing or contributing to a book, please visit `authors.packtpub.com`.

Share your thoughts

Once you've read *Go for DevOps*, we'd love to hear your thoughts! Scan the QR code below to go straight to the Amazon review page for this book and share your feedback.

`https://packt.link/r/1801818894`

Your review is important to us and the tech community and will help us make sure we're delivering excellent quality content.

Download a free PDF copy of this book

Thanks for purchasing this book!

Do you like to read on the go but are unable to carry your print books everywhere?

Is your eBook purchase not compatible with the device of your choice?

Don't worry, now with every Packt book you get a DRM-free PDF version of that book at no cost.

Read anywhere, any place, on any device. Search, copy, and paste code from your favorite technical books directly into your application.

The perks don't stop there, you can get exclusive access to discounts, newsletters, and great free content in your inbox daily

Follow these simple steps to get the benefits:

1. Scan the QR code or visit the link below

`https://packt.link/free-ebook/9781801818896`

2. Submit your proof of purchase
3. That's it! We'll send your free PDF and other benefits to your email directly

Section 1: Getting Up and Running with Go

Go is a type-safe concurrent language that is easy to develop with while being extremely performant. In this section, we will start by learning the basics of the Go language such as types, variable creation, functions, and other basic language constructs. We will continue teaching essential topics that include concurrency, the `context` package, testing, and other necessary skills. You will learn how to set up a Go environment for your operating system, interact with the local filesystem, use common data formats, and communicate with remote data sources using methods such as REST and gRPC. Finally, we will dive into automation by writing command-line tools with popular packages that issue commands to local and remote resources.

The following chapters will be covered in this section:

- *Chapter 1, Go Language Basics*
- *Chapter 2, Go Language Essentials*
- *Chapter 3, Setting Up Your Environment*
- *Chapter 4, Filesystem Interactions*
- *Chapter 5, Using Common Data Formats*
- *Chapter 6, Interacting with Remote Data Sources*
- *Chapter 7, Writing Command-Line Tooling*
- *Chapter 8, Automating Command-Line Tasks*

1
Go Language Basics

DevOps is a concept that has been floating around since the early 2000s. It is a popularization of an operations discipline that relies on programming skills with *development psychology* popularized by Agile.

Site reliability engineering (SRE) is now considered a subdiscipline of DevOps, though it is likely the precursor to DevOps and relies more heavily on software skills and **Service - Level Obligation (SLO)/Service - Level Agreement (SLA)** modeling.

During my early time at Google, like many of today's DevOps shops, we used Python heavily. I think C++ was too painful for many SREs, and we had Python celebrities in *Guido van Rossum* and *Alex Martelli*.

But, as time wore on, many of the groups working in Python started having scaling issues. This included everything from Python running out of memory (requiring us to hack in our own `malloc`) to the **Global Interpreter Lock (GIL)** preventing us from true multithreading. At scale, we found that the lack of static types was giving us an abundance of errors that should have been caught at compile time. This mirrored what production services had seen years before.

But, Python came with more than compile-time and service-scaling issues. Simply moving to a new version of Python in the fleet might cause a service to stop working. The Python version run on Google machines would often get upgraded and expose bugs in your code that the previous version did not. Unlike a compiled binary, you could not just roll back to an old version.

Several of us in different organizations were looking to solve these types of problems without having to use C++. For my personal journey, I heard about **Go** from my colleagues in our Sydney office (*Hey, Ross!*). It was the pre-1.0 days, but they said it was already showing a lot of promise. I can't say I was even remotely convinced that what we needed was another language.

About 6 months later, however, I had bought Go *hook, line, and sinker*. It had everything we needed without everything we didn't. Now, it was still pre-1.0 days, so there was a certain amount of churn back then that was unpleasant (such as finding that Russ Cox had changed the `time` package over the weekend, so I had to rewrite a bunch of code). But, the benefits after writing my first service were undeniable.

I spent the next 4 years moving my department from a complete Python shop to almost a complete Go shop. I started teaching classes in Go across the world, targeted at operations engineers, rewriting core libraries for Go, and evangelizing to what was probably an annoying amount. Just because Go was invented at Google, it didn't mean that the engineers wanted to throw away their Python code and learn something new; there was more than a little resistance.

Now, Go has become the *de facto* language for cloud orchestration and software in the larger world (from Kubernetes to Docker). Go comes with all the tools you need to make huge strides in the reliability of your tooling and ability to scale.

Because many of these cloud services are written in Go, their parts are available to you by accessing their packages for your own tooling needs. This can make writing tooling for the cloud an easier experience.

For the next two chapters, I will be sharing my 10+ years' experience of teaching Go to engineers around the world to give you the basics and essentials of the Go language. Much of what you will read here is based on my free Go basics video training course, `https://www.golangbasics.com`. This course will differ slightly from that one in that it is more condensed. As you work your way through the book, we will continue to extend your knowledge of the Go language's standard library and third-party packages.

This chapter will cover the following main topics:

- Using the Go Playground
- Utilizing Go packages
- Using Go's variable types
- Looping in Go
- Using conditionals

- Learning about functions
- Defining public and private
- Using arrays and slices
- Getting to know about structs
- Understanding Go pointers
- Comprehending Go interfaces

Now, let's get the basics down and get you on your way!

Technical requirements

The only technical requirement for this chapter is a modern web browser for using the **Go Playground**.

Using the Go Playground

The Go Playground, which you can find at `https://play.golang.org/`, is an online code editor and compiler that allows you to run Go code without installing Go on your machine. This is the perfect tool for our introductory chapters, allowing you to save your work online without the initial fuss of installing the Go tooling, or finding a code editor, for example.

There are four important parts of the Go Playground:

- The code editing pane
- The console window
- The **Run** button
- The **Share** button

The code editing pane, which is the yellow portion of the page, allows you to type in the Go code for your program. When you hit the **Run** button, the code will be compiled and then run with the output sent to the console, which is the white portion of the page below the code editor.

The following screen shows a glimpse of what the Go Playground does:

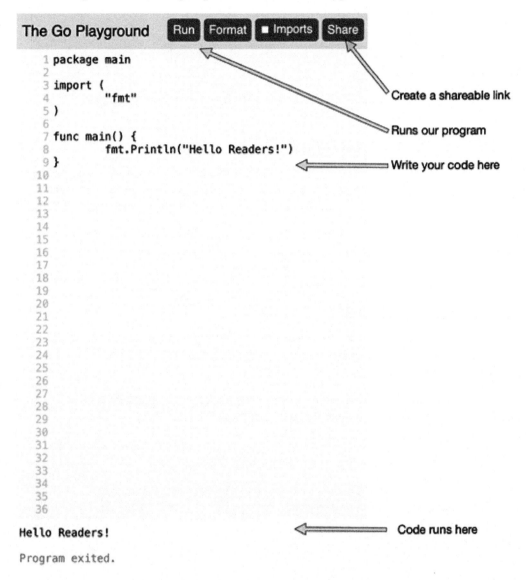

Figure 1.1 – Go Playground code editor

Clicking the **Share** button will store an immutable copy of the code and will change the URL from play.golang.org into a shareable link, such as play.golang.org/p/HmnNoBf0p1z. This link is a unique URL that you can bookmark and share with others. The code in this link cannot be changed, but if you hit the **Share** button again, it will create a new link with any changes.

Later chapters, starting with *Chapter 4*, *Filesystem Interaction*, will require installing the Go tooling for your platform.

This section taught you about the Go Playground and how to use it to write, view, share, and run your Go code. The Playground will be used extensively throughout the book to share runnable code examples.

Now, let's jump into writing Go code, starting with how Go defines packages.

Utilizing Go packages

Go provides reusable blocks of code that can be imported into other code using packages. Packages in Go are synonymous with libraries or modules in other languages. Packages are the building blocks of Go programs that divide the content into understandable parts.

This section will cover how to declare and import a package. We will discuss how to deal with package name conflicts, explore rules around packages, and we will write our first main package.

Declaring a package

Go divides programs into **packages**, sometimes called *modules* or *libraries* in other languages. Packages live on a path, and the path is made to look like a path to a directory on a Unix-like filesystem.

All Go files in a directory must belong to the same package. The package is most commonly named the same as the directory it lives in.

Declaring a package happens at the top of the file, and should only be preceded by a comment. Declaring a package is as simple as the following:

```
// Package main is the entrance point for our binary.
// The double slashes provides a comment until the end of the
line.
/*
This is a comment that lasts until the closing star slash.
*/
package main
```

`package main` is special. All other package names declare a package that must be imported into another package to be used. `package main` will declare `func main()`, which is the starting point for a binary to run.

All Go files in a directory must have the same package header (compiler-enforced). These files, for most practical purposes, act as if they are concatenated together.

Let's say you have a directory structure as follows:

```
mypackage/
    file1.go
    file2.go
```

Then, `file1.go` and `file2.go` should have the following:

```
package mypackage
```

When `mypackage` is imported by another package, it will include everything declared in all files in the `mypackage` directory.

Importing a package

There are two general types of packages:

- The **standard library** (**stdlib**) packages
- All other packages

Standard library packages stand out because they don't list some repository information in their path, such as the following:

```
"fmt"
"encoding/json"
"archive/zip"
```

All other packages generally have repository information preceding them, as follows:

```
"github.com/johnsiilver/golib/lru"
"github.com/kylelemons/godebug/pretty"
```

> **Note**
>
> A complete listing of `stdlib` packages can be found at the following link: https://golang.org/pkg/.

To import packages, we use the `import` keyword. So, let's import the standard library `fmt` package and the `mypackage` package, which lives at `github.com/devopsforgo/mypackage`:

```
package main
import (
    "fmt"
    "github.com/devopsforgo/mypackage"
)
```

It is important to note that the filenames are not part of the package path, but simply the directory path.

Using a package

Once you've imported a package, you can start accessing functions, types, or variables declared in the package by prefacing what you want to access with the name of the package and a period.

For example, the `fmt` package has a function called `Println()` that can be used to print a line to *stdout*. If we want to use it, it is as simple as the following:

```
fmt.Println("Hello!")
```

Package name conflicts

Let's say you have two packages named `mypackage`. They both have the same name, so our program won't be able to tell which one we are referring to. You can rename a package import into whatever name you want:

```
import(
    "github.com/devopsforgo/mypackage"
    jpackage "github.com/johnsiilver/mypackage"
)
```

`jpackage` declares that in this package, we will refer to `github.com/johnsiilver/mypackage` as `jpackage`.

This ability allows us to use two similarly named packages as follows:

```
mypackage.Print()
jpackage.Send()
```

Now, we will look at an important rule around packages that improves compile-time and binary size.

Packages must be used

Let's introduce you to the following rule: *If you import a package, you must use it.*

One of the things that the Go authors noticed about many of the other programming languages being used at Google was that they often had unused imports.

This was leading to compile times that were longer than needed and, in some cases, binary sizes that were much bigger than required. Python files were packaged in a proprietary format to ship around production, and some of these unused imports were adding hundreds of megabytes to the files.

To prevent these types of problems, Go will not compile a program that imports a package but doesn't use it, as shown here:

```
package main
import (
    "fmt"
    "sync"
)
func main() {
    fmt.Println("Hello, playground")
}
```

The preceding code outputs the following:

```
./prog.go:5:2: imported and not used: "sync"
```

In certain rare circumstances, you may need to do a *side effects* import, in which just loading the package causes something to happen, but you don't use the package. This should *always* be done in `package main` and requires prepending with an underscore (`_`):

```
package main
import (
    "fmt"
    _ "sync" //Just an example
)
func main() {
    fmt.Println("Hello, playground")
}
```

Next, we will declare a main package and discuss the basics of writing a Go program that imports a package.

A Go Hello World

Let's write a simple **hello world** program that is similar to the default program in the Go Playground. This example will demonstrate the following:

- Declaring a package
- Importing the `fmt` package from the standard library, which can print to our screen
- Declaring the `main()` function of a program
- Declaring a string variable using the `:=` operator
- Printing the variable to the screen

Let's see what this looks like:

```
1  package main
2
3  import "fmt"
4
5  func main() {
6      hello := "Hello World!" fmt.Println(hello)
7
8  }
```

In our first line, we declared the name of our package using the `package` keyword. The entrance point for any Go binary is a package named `main` that has a function called `main()`.

In our third line, we import the `fmt` package. `fmt` has functions for doing string formatting and writing to various outputs.

On our fifth line, we declare a function called `main` that takes no arguments and returns no values. `main()` is special, as when a binary is run, it starts by running the `main()` function.

Go uses `{}` to show where a function starts and where a function ends (similar to C).

The sixth line declares a variable named `hello` using the `:=` operator. This operator indicates that we wish to create a new variable and assign it a value in a single line. This is the most common, but not the only, way to declare a variable.

As Go is typed, so `:=` will assign the type based on the value. In this case, it will be a string, but if the value was an **integer** (such as 3), it would be the `int` type, and if a **floating-point** (such as 2.4), it would be the `float64` type. If we wanted to declare a specific type, such as `int8` or `float32`, we would need some modifications (which we will talk about later).

On the seventh line, we call a function that is in the `fmt` package called `Println`. `Println()` will print the contents of the `hello` variable to `stdout` followed by a new line character (`\n`).

You will notice that the way to use a function declared in another package is to use the *package name (without quotes) + a period + the name of the function*. In this case, `fmt.Println()`.

In this section, you have learned how to declare a package, import a package, what the function of the `main` package is, and how to write a basic Go program with a variable declaration. In the next section, we will go into some depth on declaring and using variables.

Using Go's variable types

Modern programming languages are built with primitives called **types**. When you hear that a variable is a *string* or *integer*, you are talking about the variable's type.

With today's programming languages, there are two common type systems used:

- **Dynamic types** (also called duck typing)
- **Static types**

Go is a **statically typed** language. For many of you who might be coming from languages such as Python, Perl, and PHP, then those languages are **dynamically typed**.

In a dynamically typed language, you can create a variable and store anything in it. In those languages, the type simply indicates what is stored in the variable. Here is an example in Python:

```
v = "hello"
v = 8
v = 2.5
```

In this case, v can store anything, and the type held by v is unknown without using some runtime checks (*runtime* meaning that it can't be checked at compile time).

In a statically typed language, the type of the variable is set when it is created. That type cannot change. In this type of language, the type is both what *is* stored in the variable and what *can* be stored in the variable. Here is a Go example:

```
v := "hello" // also can do: var v string = "hello"
```

The v value cannot be set to any other type than a string.

It might seem like Python is superior because it can store anything in its variable. But in practice, this lack of being specific means that Python must wait until a program is running before it can find out there is a problem (what we call a **runtime error**). It is better to find the problem when the software is compiled than when it is deployed.

Let's take a look at a function to add two numbers together as an example.

Here is the Python version:

```
def add(a, b):
    return a+b
```

Here is the Go version:

```
func add(a int, b int) int {
    return a + b
}
```

In the Python version, we can see that a and b will be added together. But, what types are a and b? What is the result type? What happens if I pass an integer and a float or an integer and a string?

In some cases, two types cannot be added together in Python, which will cause a runtime exception, and you can never be sure of what the result type will be.

> **Note**
> Python has added **type hints** to the language to help avoid these problems. But, practical experience has taught us with JavaScript/Dart/TypeScript/Closure that while it can help, optional type support means that a lot of problems fall through the cracks.

Our Go version defines the exact types for our arguments and our result. You cannot pass an integer and a float or an integer and a string. You will only ever receive an integer as a return. This allows our compiler to find any errors with variable types when the program is compiled. In Python, this error could show up at any time, from the instant it ran to 6 months later when a certain code path was executed.

> **Note**
>
> A few years ago, there was a study done on the *Rosetta Code* repository for some of the top languages in use to see how they fared in processing time, memory use, and runtime failures. For runtime failures, Go had the least failures, with Python towards the bottom of the ranking. Static typing would have certainly played into that.
>
> The study can be found here: `https://arxiv.org/pdf/1409.0252.pdf`.

Go's types

Go has a rich type system that not only specifies that a type might be an integer but also the size of the integer. This allows a Go programmer to reduce the size of a variable both in memory and when encoding for network transport.

The following table shows the most common types used in Go:

Type	Description
`int`	A 64-bit signed integer on 64-bit systems, 32 on 32-bit systems
`bool`	A Boolean, either true or false
`string`	A string of UTF-8 characters
`float64`	A 64-bit floating-point number
`slice`	A growable list of items
`map`	Key-value pairs, similar to Python's dictionaries
`struct`	A collection of named attributes (variables), similar to Python objects
`interface`	A type that holds a value with specifically defined methods
`pointers`	A type that stores the memory address of a variable, not the variable
`channels`	A buffered or non-buffered pipe for sending data asynchronously

Table 1.1 – Common types used in Go and their descriptions

We will be keeping our discussion mostly to the preceding types; however, the following table is the full list of types that can be used:

Type	Description
uint8	The set of all unsigned 8-bit integers (0 to 255)
uint16	The set of all unsigned 16-bit integers (0 to 65,535)
uint32	The set of all unsigned 32-bit integers (0 to 4,294,967,295)
uint64	The set of all unsigned 64-bit integers (0 to 18,446,744,073,709,551,615)
int8	The set of all signed 8-bit integers (-128 to 127)
int16	The set of all signed 16-bit integers (-32,768 to 32,767)
int32	The set of all signed 32-bit integers (-2,147,483,648 to 2,147,483,647)
int64	The set of all signed 64-bit integers (-9,223,372,036,854,775,808 to 9,223,372,036,854,775,807)
float32	The set of all IEEE-754 32-bit floating-point numbers
complex64	The set of all complex numbers with float32 real and imaginary parts
complex12	The set of all complex numbers with float64 real and imaginary parts
byte	Alias for uint8
rune	Alias for int32
uint	An unsigned integer, either 32- or 64-bit
uintptr	An unsigned integer large enough to store the uninterpreted bits of a pointer value
array	A non-growable list of items
function	A function that can be stored in a variable, not just defined and called

Table 1.2 – Full list of types that you can use in Go

Go doesn't just provide these types; you can also create new types based on these basic types. These custom types become their own type and can have methods attached to them.

Declaring a custom type is done with the type keyword and will be discussed during the section on the struct type. For now, we are going to move on to the basics of declaring variables.

Now that we've talked about our variable types, let's have a look at how we can create them.

Declaring variables

As in most languages, declaring a variable allocates storage that will hold some type of data. In Go, that data is typed so that only that type can be stored in the allocated storage. As Go has multiple ways to declare a variable, the next parts will talk about the different ways this can be done.

The long way to declare a variable

The most specific way to declare a variable is using the `var` keyword. You can use `var` to declare a variable both at the package level (meaning not inside a function) and within a function. Let's look at some examples of ways to declare variables using `var`:

```
var i int64
```

This declares an `i` variable that can hold an `int64` type. No value is assigned, so the value is assigned the *zero value* of an integer, which is 0:

```
var i int = 3
```

This declares an `i` variable that can hold an `int` type. The value 3 is assigned to `i`.

Note that the `int` and `int64` types are distinct. You cannot use an `int` type as an `int64` type, and vice versa. However, you can do type conversions to allow interchanging these types. This is discussed later:

```
var (
    i int
    word = "hello"
)
```

Using `()`, we group together a set of declarations. `i` can hold an `int` type and has the integer zero value, 0. `word` doesn't declare the type, but it is inferred by the string value on the right side of the equal (=) operator.

The shorter way

In the previous example, we used the `var` keyword to create a variable and the = operator to assign values. If we do not have an = operator, the compiler assigns the *zero value* for the type (more on this later).

The important concept is as follows:

- `var` created the variable but did not make an assignment.
- = assigned a value to the variable.

Within a function (not at the package level), we can do a *create and assign* by using the `:=` operator. This both creates a new variable and assigns a value to it:

```
i := 1                  // i is the int type
word := "hello"         // word is the string type
f := 3.2                // f is the float64 type
```

The important thing to remember when using := is that it means *create and assign*. If the variable already exists, you cannot use :=, but must use =, which just does an assignment.

Variable scopes and shadowing

A **scope** is the part of the program in which a variable can be seen. In Go, we have the following variable scopes:

- **Package scoped**: Can be seen by the entire package and is declared outside a function
- **Function scoped**: Can be seen within { } which defines the function
- **Statement scoped**: Can be seen within { } of a statement in a function (`for` loop, `if`/`else`)

In the following program, the `word` variable is declared at the package level. It can be used by any function defined in the package:

```
package main

import "fmt"

var word = "hello"

func main() {
    fmt.Println(word)
}
```

In the following program, the `word` variable is defined inside the `main()` function and can only be used inside { } which defines `main`. Outside, it is undefined:

```
package main

import "fmt"

func main() {
    var word string = "hello"
    fmt.Println(word)
}
```

Finally, in this program, i is statement scoped. It can be used on the line starting our `for` loop and inside { } of the loop, but it doesn't exist outside the loop:

```
package main

import "fmt"

func main() {
    for i := 0; i < 10; i++ {
        fmt.Println(i)
    }
}
```

The best way to think of this is that if your variable is declared on a line that has { or within a set of { }, it can only be seen within those { }.

Cannot redeclare a variable in the same scope

The rule for this, *You cannot declare two variables with the same name within the same scope.*

This means that no two variables within the same scope can have the same name:

```
func main() {
    var word = "hello"
    var word = "world"
    fmt.Println(word)
}
```

This program is invalid and will generate a compile error. Once you have declared the `word` variable, you cannot recreate it within the same scope. You can change the value to a new value, but you cannot create a second variable with the same name.

To assign `word` a new value, simply remove `var` from the line. `var` says *create variable* where we want to only do an assignment:

```
func main() {
    var word = "hello"
    word = "world"
    fmt.Println(word)
}
```

Next, we will look at what happens when you declare two variables with the same name in the same scope, but within separate code blocks.

Variable shadowing

Variable shadowing occurs when a variable that is within your variable scope, but not in your local scope, is redeclared. This causes the local scope to lose access to the **outer scoped variable**:

```go
package main

import "fmt"

var word = "hello"

func main() {
    var word = "world"
    fmt.Println("inside main(): ", word)
    printOutter()
}

func printOutter() {
    fmt.Println("the package level 'word' var: ", word)
}
```

As you can see, word is declared at the package level. But inside main, we define a new word variable, which overshadows the package level variable. When we refer to word now, we are using the one defined inside main().

printOutter() is called, but it doesn't have a locally shadowed word variable (one declared between its {}), so it used the one at the package level.

Here's the output of this program:

```
inside main():  world
the package level 'word' var:  hello
```

This is one of the more common bugs for Go developers.

Zero values

In some older languages, a variable declaration without an assignment has an unknown value. This is because the program creates a place in memory to store the value but doesn't put anything in it. So, the bits representing the value are set to whatever happened to be in that memory space before you created the variable.

This has led to many unfortunate bugs. So, in Go, declaring a variable without an assignment automatically assigns a value called the *zero value*. Here is a list of the zero values for Go types:

Type	Description
`(u)int/8/16/32/64`	The integer 0
`string`	The empty string, `""`
`bool`	false
`float32/64`	0.0
`slice`	The nil value
`map`	The nil value
`struct`	An empty struct, `{}`, with all attributes having zero values
`interface`	The nil value
`pointers`	The nil value
`channels`	The nil value
`byte`	The integer 0
`rune`	The integer 0
`array`	A zero-length array
`function`	The `nil` value

Table 1.3 – Zero values for Go types

Now that we understand what zero values are, let's see how Go prevents unused variables in our code.

Function/statement variable must be used

The rule here is that if you create a variable within a function or statement, it must be used. This is much for the same reason as package imports; declaring a variable that isn't used is almost always a mistake.

This can be relaxed in much the same way as an import, using `_`, but is far less common. This assigns the value stored in `someVar` to nothing:

```
_ = someVar
```

This assigns the value returned by `someFunc()` to nothing:

```
_ = someFunc()
```

The most common use for this is when a function returns multiple values, but you only need one:

```
needed, _ := someFunc()
```

Here, we create and assign to the `needed` variable, but the second value isn't something we use, so we drop it.

This section has provided the knowledge of Go's basic types, the different ways to declare a variable, the rules around variable scopes and shadows, and Go's *zero values*.

Looping in Go

Most languages have a few different types of loop statements: `for`, `while`, and `do while`.

Go differs in that there is a single loop type, `for`, that can implement the functionality of all the loop types in other languages.

In this section, we will discuss the `for` loop and its many uses.

C style

The most basic form of a loop is similar to C syntax:

```
for i := 0; i < 10; i++ {
    fmt.Println(i)
}
```

This declares an `i` variable that is an integer scoped to live only for this loop statement. `i := 0;` is the loop initialization statement; it only happens once before the loop starts. `i < 10;` is the conditional statement; it happens at the start of each loop and must evaluate to `true` or the loop ends.

`i++` is the `post` statement; it occurs at the end of every loop. `i++` says to increment the `i` variable by 1. Go also has common statements, such as `i += 1` and `i--`.

Removing the init statement

We don't need to have an `init` statement, as shown in this example:

```
var i int
for ;i < 10;i++ {
    fmt.Println(i)
```

```
}
fmt.Println("i's final value: ", i)
```

In this, we declared `i` outside the loop. This means that `i` will be accessible outside the loop once the loop is finished, unlike our previous example.

Remove the post statement too and you have a while loop

Many languages have a `while` loop that simply evaluates whether a statement is true or not. We can do the same by eliminating our `init` and `post` statements:

```
var i int
for i < 10 {
    i++
}
b := true
for b { // This will loop forever
    fmt.Println("hello")
}
```

You might be asking, *how do we make a loop that runs forever?* The `for` loop has you covered.

Creating an infinite loop

Sometimes you want a **loop** to run forever or until some internal condition inside the loop occurs. Creating an infinite loop is as simple as removing all statements:

```
for {
    fmt.Println("Hello World")
}
```

This is usually useful for things such as servers that need to process some incoming stream forever.

Loop control

With loops, you occasionally need to control the execution of the loop from within the loop. This could be because you want to exit the loop or stop the execution of this iteration of the loop and start from the top.

Here's an example of a loop where we call a function called doSomething() that returns an error if the loop should end. What doSomething() does is not important for this example:

```go
for {
    if err := doSomething(); err != nil {
        break
    }
    fmt.Println("keep going")
}
```

The break function here will break out of the loop. break is also used to break out of other statements, such as select or switch, so it's important to know that break breaks out of the first statement it is nested inside of.

If we want to stop the loop on a condition and continue with the next loop, we can use the continue statement:

```go
for i := 0; i < 10; i++ {
    if i % 2 == 0 { // Only 0 for even numbers
        continue
    }
    fmt.Println("Odd number: ", i)
}
```

This loop will print out the odd numbers from zero to nine. i % 2 means *i modulus 2*. Modulus divides the first number by the second number and returns the remainder.

Loop braces

Here is the introduction of this rule: A for loop's open brace must be on the same line as the for keyword.

With many languages, there are arguments about where to put the braces for loops/conditionals. With Go, the authors decided to pre-empt those arguments with compiler checks. In Go, you can do the following:

```go
for {
    fmt.Println("hello world")
}
```

However, the following is incorrect as the opening brace of the `for` loop is on its own line:

```
for
{
    fmt.Println("hello world")
}
```

In this section we learned to use `for` loops as C style loops, as `while` loops.

Using conditionals

Go supports two types of conditionals, as follows:

- `if/else` blocks
- `switch` blocks

The standard `if` statement is similar to other languages with the addition of an optional `init` statement borrowed from the standard C-style `for` loop syntax.

`switch` statements provide a sometimes-cleaner alternative to `if`. So, let's jump into the `if` conditional.

if statements

`if` statements start with a familiar format that is recognizable in most languages:

```
if [expression that evaluates to boolean] {
    ...
}
```

Here's a simple example:

```
if x > 2 {
    fmt.Println("x is greater than 2")
}
```

The statements within { } in `if` will execute if x has a value greater than 2.

Unlike most languages, Go has the ability to execute a statement within the `if` scope before the evaluation is made:

```
if [init statement];[statement that evaluates to boolean] {
    ...
}
```

Here is a simple example that is similar to the init statement in a `for` loop:

```
if err := someFunction(); err != nil {
    fmt.Println(err)
}
```

Here, we initialize a variable called `err`. It has a scope of the `if` block. If the `err` variable does not equal the `nil` value (a special value that indicates certain types are not set – more on this later), it will print the error.

else

If you need to execute something when the condition of an `if` statement is not met, you can use the `else` keyword:

```
if condition {
    function1()
}else {
    function2()
}
```

In this example, if the `if` condition is true, `function1` will be executed. Otherwise, `function2` occurs.

It should be noted that most uses of `else` can generally be eliminated for cleaner code. If your `if` condition results in returning from a function using the `return` keyword, you can eliminate `else`.

An example is as follows:

```
if v, err := someFunc(); err != nil {
    return err
}else{
    fmt.Println(v)
    return nil
}
```

This can be simplified to the following:

```go
v, err := someFunc()
if err != nil {
    return err
}
fmt.Println(v)
return nil
```

Sometimes, you want to only execute code if the `if` condition is not met and another condition is. Let's look at that next.

else if

An `if` block can also contain `else if`, providing multiple levels of execution. The first `if` or `else if` that is matched in order is executed.

Note that often Go developers choose the `switch` statement as a cleaner version of this type of conditional.

An example is as follows:

```go
if x > 0 {
    fmt.Println("x is greater than 0")
} else if x < 0 {
    fmt.Println("x is less than 0")
} else{
    fmt.Println("x is equal to 0")
}
```

Now that we have seen the basics of this conditional, we need to talk about brace style.

if/else braces

It's time to introduce this rule: Opening braces for `if/else` must be on the line with the associated keyword. If there is another statement in the chain, it must start on the same line as the previous close brace.

With many languages, there are arguments about where to put the braces for loops/conditionals.

With Go, the authors decided to pre-empt those arguments with compiler checks. In Go, you can't do the following:

```
if x > 0
{ // This must go up on the previous line
    fmt.Println("hello")
}
else { // This line must start on the previous line
    fmt.Println("world")
}
```

So, with the arguments on bracing style in Go settled, let's look at an alternative to `if/else`, the `switch` statement.

The switch statement

`switch` statements are more elegant `if/else` blocks that are very flexible in their use. They can be used for doing exact matching and multiple true/false evaluations.

Exact match switch

The following is an exact match `switch`:

```
switch [value] {
case [match]:
    [statement]
case [match], [match]:
    [statement]
default:
    [statement]
}
```

`[value]` is matched against each `case` statement. If it matches, the `case` statement executes. Unlike some languages, once a match occurs, no other case is considered. If no match occurs, the `default` statement executes. The `default` statement is optional.

This has a nicer syntax than `if/else` for handling cases where your value can be several values:

```
switch x {
case 3:
```

```
        fmt.Println("x is 3")
case 4, 5:    // executes if x is 4 or 5
    fmt.Println("x is 4 or 5")
default:
    fmt.Println("x is unknown")
}
```

switch can also have an `init` statement, similar to `if`:

```
switch x := someFunc(); x {
case 3:
    fmt.Println("x is 3")
}
```

True/false evaluation switch

We can also eliminate [match] so that each `case` statement isn't an exact match, but a true/false evaluation (as with `if` statements):

```
switch {
case x > 0:
    fmt.Println("x is greater than 0")
case x < 0:
    fmt.Println("x is less than 0")
default:
    fmt.Println("x must be 0")
}
```

At the end of this section, you should be able to use Go's conditional statements to branch code execution in your program based on some criteria and handle cases where no statement was matched. As conditionals are one of the standard building blocks of software, we will use these in many of the remaining sections.

Learning about functions

Functions in Go are what you'd expect from a modern programming language. There are only a few things that make Go functions different:

- Multiple return values are supported
- Variadic arguments
- Named return values

The basic function signature is as follows:

```
func functionName([varName] [varType], ...) ([return value],
[return value], ...){
}
```

Let's make a basic function that adds two numbers together and returns the result:

```
func add(x int, y int) int {
    return x + y
}
```

As you can see, this takes in two integers, x and y, adds them together, and returns the result (which is an integer). Let's show how we can call this function and print its output:

```
result := add(2, 2)
fmt.Println(result)
```

We can simplify this function signature by declaring both x and y types with a single `int` keyword:

```
func add(x, y int) int {
    return x + y
}
```

This is equivalent to the previous one.

Returning multiple values and named results

In Go, we can **return multiple values**. For example, consider a function that divides two integers and returns two variables, the result and the remainder, as follows:

```
func divide(num, div int) (res, rem int) {
    result = num / div
    remainder = num % div
    return res, rem
}
```

This code demonstrates a few new features in our function:

- Argument `num` is the number to be divided
- Argument `div` is the number to divide by

- Return value `res` is the result of the division
- Return value `rem` is the remainder of the division

First is **named returns** (`res` and `rem`). These variables are automatically created and ready for use inside the function.

Notice I use = and not := when doing assignments to those variables. This is because the variable already exists, and we want to assign a value (=). := means **create and assign**. You can only create a new variable that doesn't exist. You will also notice that now the return type is in parenthesis. You will need to use parenthesis if you use more than one return value or named returns (or in this case, both).

Calling this function is just as simple as calling `add()` before, as shown here:

```
result, remainder := divide(3, 2)
fmt.Printf("Result: %d, Remainder %d", result, remainder)
```

Strickly speaking, you don't have to use `return` to return the values. However, doing so will prevent some ugly bugs that you will eventually encounter.

Next, we will look at how we can have a variable number of arguments as function input that allows us to create functions such as `fmt.Println()`, which you have been using in this chapter.

Variadic arguments

A **variadic argument** is when you want to provide 0 to infinite arguments. A good example would be calculating a sum of integers. Without variadic arguments, you might use a slice (a *growable array type*, which we will talk about later), as follows:

```
func sum(numbers []int) int {
    sum := 0
    for _, n := range numbers {
        sum += n
    }
    return sum
}
```

While this is fine, using it is cumbersome:

```
args := []int{1,2,3,4,5}
fmt.Println(sum(args))
```

We can accomplish this same thing by using the variadic (...) notation:

```
func sum(numbers ...int) int {
    // Same code
}
```

`numbers` is still `[]int`, but has a different calling convention that is more elegant:

```
fmt.Println(sum(1,2,3,4,5))
```

> **Note**
>
> You can use variadic arguments with other arguments, but it must be the last argument in the function.

Anonymous functions

Go has a concept of **anonymous functions**, which means a function without a name (also called a **function closure**).

This can be useful to take advantage of special statements that honor function boundaries, such as `defer`, or in `goroutines`. We will show how to take advantage of these for `goroutines` later, but for now let's show how to execute an anonymous function. This is a contrived example that is only useful in teaching the concept:

```
func main() {
    result := func(word1, word2 string) string {
        return word1 + " " + word2
    }("hello", "world")
    fmt.Println(result)
}
```

This code does the following:

- Defines a single-use function (`func(word1, word2 string) string`)
- Executes the function with the `hello` and `world` arguments
- Assigns the `string` return value to the `result` variable
- Prints `result`

Now that we have arrived at the end of this section, we have learned about how Go functions are declared, the use of multiple return values, variadic arguments for simplified function calling, and anonymous functions. Multiple return values will be important in future chapters where we deal with errors, and anonymous functions are key components of our future `defer` statements and for use with concurrency.

In the next section, we will explore public and private types.

Defining public and private

Many modern languages provide a set of options when declaring constants/variables/functions/methods that detail when a method can be called.

Go simplifies these *visibility* choices down to two types:

- **Public** (exported)
- **Private** (not exported)

Public types are types that can be referred to outside of the package. **Private types** can only be referred to inside the package. To be public, the constant/variable/function/method must simply start with an uppercase letter. If it starts with a lowercase letter, it is private.

There is a third type of visibility that we don't cover here: **internally exported**. This occurs when a type is public but in a package, located within a directory called `internal/`. Those packages can only be used by packages within a parent directory. You can read about this here: `https://golang.org/doc/go1.4#internalpackages`.

Let's declare a package and create some public and private methods:

```go
package say

import "fmt"

func PrintHello() {
    fmt.Println("Hello")
}

func printWorld() {
    fmt.Println("World")
}

func PrintHelloWorld() {
    PrintHello()
```

```
        printWorld()
}
```

We have three function calls, two public (`PrintHello()` and `PrintHelloWorld()`) and one private (`printWorld()`). Now, let's create `package main`, import the `say` package, and call our functions:

```
package main

import "github.com/repo/examples/say"

func main() {
    say.PrintHello()
    say.PrintHelloWorld()
}
```

Now, let's compile and run it:

```
$ go run main.go
Hello
Hello
World
```

These work because `PrintHello()` and `PrintHelloWorld()` are both **exported** (public) functions. `PrintHelloWorld()` calls the private `printWorld()`, but that is legal because they are in the same package.

If we try to add `say.printWorld()` to `func main()` and run it, we will get the following:

```
./main.go:8:2: cannot refer to unexported name say.printWorld
```

Public and private apply to variables declared outside functions/methods and type declarations.

By the end of this short and sweet section, you've acquired the knowledge of Go's public and private types. This will be useful in code where you do not want to expose types in your public API. Next, we will look at arrays and slices.

Using arrays and slices

Languages require more than the basic types to hold data. The `array` type is one of the core building blocks in lower-level languages, providing the base sequential data type. For most day-to-day use, Go's `slice` type provides a flexible **array** that can grow as data needs grow and can be sliced into sections in order to share views of the data.

In this section, we will talk about arrays as the building blocks of **slices**, the difference between the two, and how to utilize them in your code.

Arrays

The base sequential type in Go is the array (important to know, but rarely used). Arrays are statically sized (if you create one that holds 10 `int` types, it will always hold exactly 10 `int` types).

Go provides an `array` type designated by putting `[size]` before the type you wish to create an array of. For example, `var x [5]int` or `x := [5]int{}` creates an array holding five integers, indexed from 0 to 4.

An assignment into an array is as easy as choosing the index. `x[0] = 3` assigns 3 to index 0. Retrieving that value is as simple as referring to the index; `fmt.Println(x[0] + 2)` will output 5.

Arrays, unlike slices, are *not* pointer wrapper types. Passing an array as a function argument passes a copy:

```go
func changeValueAtZeroIndex(array [2]int) {
    array[0] = 3
    fmt.Println("inside: ", array[0]) // Will print 3
}
func main() {
    x := [2]int{}
    changeValueAtZeroIndex(x)
    fmt.Println(x) // Will print 0
}
```

Arrays present the following two problems in Go:

- Arrays are typed by size – `[2]int` is distinct from `[3]int`. You cannot use `[3]int` where `[2]int` is required.
- Arrays are a set size. If you need more room, you must make a new array.

While it is important to know what arrays are, the most common sequential type used in Go is the slice.

Slices

The easiest way to understand a slice is to see it as a type that is built on top of arrays. A slice is a *view* into an array. Changing what you can see in your slice's view changes the underlying array's value. The most basic use of slices acts like arrays, with two exceptions:

- A slice is not statically sized.
- A slice can grow to accommodate new values.

A slice tracks its array, and when it needs more room, it will create a new array that can accommodate the new values and copies the values from the current array into the new array. This happens invisibly to the user.

Creating a slice can be done similarly to an array, `var x = []int` or `x := []int{}`. This creates a slice of integers with a length of 0 (which has no room to store values). You can retrieve the size of the slice using `len(x)`.

We can create a slice with initial values easily: `x := []int{8,4,5,6}`. Now, we have `len(x) == 4`, indexed from 0 to 3.

Similar to arrays, we can change a value at an index by simply referencing the index. `x[2] = 12` will change the preceding slice to `[]int{8,4,12,6}`.

Unlike arrays, we can add a new value to the slice using the append command. `x = append(x, 2)` will cause the underlying x array references to be copied to a new array and assigns the new view of the array back to x. The new value is `[]int{8,4,12,6,2}`. You may append multiple values by just putting more comma-delimited values in `append` (that is, `x = append(x, 2, 3, 4, 5)`).

Remember that slices are simply *views* into a trackable array. We can create new limited views of the array. `y := x[1:3]` creates a view (y) of the array, yielding `[]int{4, 12}` (1 is inclusive and 3 is exclusive in `[1:3]`). Changing the value at `y[0]` will change `x[1]`. Appending a single value to y via `y = append(y, 10)` will change `x[3]`, yielding `[]int{8,4,12,10,2}`.

This kind of use isn't common (and is confusing), but the important part is to understand that slices are simply views into an array.

While slices are a pointer-wrapped type (values in a slice passed to a function that are changed will change in the caller as well), a slice's view will not change.

```go
func doAppend(sl []int) {
    sl = append(sl, 100)
    fmt.Println("inside: ", sl) // inside:   [1 2 3 100]
}

func main() {
    x := []int{1, 2, 3}
    doAppend(x)
    fmt.Println("outside: ", x) // outside:   [1 2 3]
}
```

In this example, the `sl` and x variables both use the same underlying array (which has changed in both), but the view for x does not get updated in `doAppend()`. To update x to see the addition to the slice would require passing a pointer to the slice (pointers are covered in a future chapter) or returning the new slice as seen here:

```go
func doAppend(sl []int) []int {
    return append(sl, 100)
}

func main() {
    x := []int{1, 2, 3}
    x = doAppend(x)
    fmt.Println("outside: ", x) // outside:   [1 2 3 100]
}
```

Now that you see how to create and add to a slice, let's look at how to extract the values.

Extracting all values

To extract values from a slice, we can use the older C-type `for` loop or the more common for...range syntax.

The older C style is as follows:

```go
for i := 0; i < len(someSlice); i++{
    fmt.Printf("slice entry %d: %s\n", i, someSlice[i])
}
```

The more common approach in Go uses `range`:

```
for index, val := range someSlice {
    fmt.Printf("slice entry %d: %s\n", index, val)
}
```

With `range`, we often want to use only the value, but not the index. In Go, you must use variables that are declared in a function, or the compiler will complain with the following:

`index declared but not used`

To only extract the values, we can use `_`, (which tells the compiler not to store the output), as follows:

```
for _, val := range someSlice {
    fmt.Printf("slice entry: %s\n", val)
}
```

On very rare occasions, you may want to only print out indexes and not values. This is uncommon because it will simply count from zero to the number of items. However, this can be achieved by simply removing `val` from the `for` statement: `for index := range someSlice`.

In this section, you have discovered what arrays are, how to create them, and how they relate to slices. In addition, you've acquired the skills to create slices, add data to slices, and extract data from slices. Let's move on to learning about maps next.

Understanding maps

Maps are a collection of key-value pairs that a user can use to store some data and retrieve it with a key. In some languages, these are called **dictionaries** (*Python*) or **hashes** (*Perl*). In contrast to an array/slice, finding an entry in a map requires a single lookup versus iterating over the entire slice comparing values. With a large set of items, this can give you significant time savings.

Declaring a map

There are several ways to declare a map. Let's first look at using `make`:

```
var counters = make(map[string]int, 10)
```

The example just shared creates a map with `string` keys and stores data that is an `int` type. `10` signifies that we want to pre-size for 10 entries. The map can grow beyond 10 entries and the `10` can be omitted.

Another way of declaring a map is by using a **composite literal**:

```
modelToMake := map[string]string{
    "prius": "toyota",
    "chevelle": "chevy",
}
```

This creates a map with `string` keys and stores the `string` data. We also pre-populate the entry with two key-value entries. You can omit the entries to have an empty map.

Accessing values

You can retrieve a value as follows:

```
carMake := modelToMake["chevelle"]
fmt.Println(carMake) // Prints "chevy"
```

This assigns the `chevy` value to `carMake`.

But what happens if the key isn't in the map? In that case, we will receive the zero value of the data type:

```
carMake := modelToMake["outback"]
fmt.Println(carMake)
```

The preceding code will print an empty string, which is the zero value of the string type that is used as values in our map.

We can also detect if the value is in the map:

```
if carMake, ok := modelToMake["outback"]; ok {
    fmt.Printf("car model \"outback\" has make %q", carMake)
}else{
    fmt.Printf("car model \"outback\" has an unknown make")
}
```

Here we assign two values. The first (`carMake`) is the data stored in the key (or zero value if not set), and the second (`ok`) is a Boolean that indicates if the key was found.

Adding new values

Adding a new key-value pair or updating a key's value, is done the same way:

```
modelToMake["outback"] = "subaru"
counters["pageHits"] = 10
```

Now that we can change a key-value pair, let's look at extracting values from a map.

Extracting all values

To extract values from a map, we can use the `for...range` syntax that we used for slices. There are a few key differences with maps:

- Instead of an index, you will get the map's key.
- Maps have a non-deterministic order.

Non-deterministic order means that iterating over the data will return the same data but not in the same order.

Let's print out all the values in our `carMake` map:

```
for key, val := range modelToMake {
    fmt.Printf("car model %q has make %q\n", key, val)
}
```

This will yield the following, but maybe not in the same order:

```
car model "prius" has make "toyota"
car model "chevelle" has make "chevy"
car model "outback" has make "subaru"
```

> **Note**
> Similar to a slice, if you don't need the key, you may use _ instead. If you simply want the keys, you can omit the value `val` variable, such as `for key := range modelToMake`.

In this section, you have learned about the `map` type, how to declare them, add values to them, and finally how to extract values from them. Let's dive into learning about pointers.

Understanding Go pointers

Pointers are another essential tool for programming languages for efficient memory use. Some readers may have not encountered pointers in their current language, instead having used its cousin, the reference type. In Python, for example, the `dict`, `list`, and `object` types are reference types.

In this section, we will cover what pointers are, how to declare them, and how to use them.

Memory addresses

In an earlier chapter, we talked about variables for storing data of some type. For example, if we want to create a variable called x that stores an int type with a value of 23, we can write var x int = 23.

Under the hood, the memory allocator allocates us space to store the value. The space is referenced by a unique memory address that looks like 0xc000122020. This is similar to how a home address is used; it is the reference to where the data lives.

We can see the memory address where a variable is stored by prepending & to a variable name:

```
fmt.Println(&x)
```

This would print 0xc000122020, the memory address of where x is stored.

This leads to an important concept: functions always make a copy of the arguments passed.

Function arguments are copies

When we call a function and pass a variable as a function argument, inside the function you get a copy of that variable. This is important because when you change the variable, you are only affecting the copy inside the function.

```
func changeValue(word string) {
    word += "world"
}
```

In this code, word is a copy of the value that was passed. word will stop existing at the end of this function call.

```
func main() {
    say := "hello"
    changeValue(say)
    fmt.Println(say)
}
```

This prints "hello". Passing the string and changing it in the function doesn't work, because inside the function we are working with a copy. Think of every *function call* as making a copy of the variable with a copy machine. Editing the copy that came out of the copy machine does not affect the original.

Pointers to the rescue

Pointers in Go are types that store the address of a value, not the value. So, instead of storing `23`, it would store `0xc000122020`, which is where in memory `23` is stored.

A pointer type can be declared by prepending the type name with `*`. If we want to create an `intPtr` variable that stores a pointer to `int`, we can do the following:

```
var intPtr *int
```

You cannot store `int` in `intPtr`; you can only store the address of `int`. To get the address of an existing `int`, you can use the `&` symbol on a variable representing `int`.

Let's assign `intPtr` the address of our x variable from previously:

```
intPtr = &x
intPtr now stores 0xc000122020.
```

Now for the big question, *how is this useful?* This lets us refer to a value in memory and change that value. We do that through what is called **dereferencing** the pointer. This is done with the `*` operator on the variable.

We can view or change the value held at x by dereferencing the pointer. The following is an example:

```
fmt.Println(x)           // Will print 23
fmt.Println(*intPtr)     // Will print 23, the value at x
*intPtr = 80             // Changes the value at x to 80
fmt.Println(x)           // Will print 80
```

This also works across functions. Let's alter `changeValue()` to work with pointers:

```
func changeValue(word *string) {
    // Add "world" to the string pointed to by 'word'
    *word += "world"
}
func main() {
    say := "hello"
    changeValue(&say) // Pass a pointer
    fmt.Println(say) // Prints "helloworld"
}
```

Note that operators such as * are called **overloaded operators**. Their meaning depends on the context in which they are used. When declaring a variable, * indicates a pointer type, `var intPtr *int`. When used on a variable, * means dereference, `fmt.Println(*intPtr)`. When used between two numbers, it means multiply, `y := 10 * 2`. It takes time to remember what a symbol means when used in certain contexts.

But, didn't you say every argument is a copy?!

I did indeed. When you pass a pointer to a function, a copy of the pointer is made, but the copy still holds the same memory address. Therefore, it still refers to the same piece of memory. It is a lot like making a copy of a treasure map on the copy machine; the copy still points to the place in the world where you will find the treasure. Some of you are probably thinking, *But maps and slices can have their values changed, what gives?*

They are a special type called a **pointer-wrapped** type. A pointer-wrapped type hides internal pointers.

Don't go crazy with pointers

While in our examples we used pointers for basic types, typically pointers are used on long-lived objects or for storage of large data that is expensive to copy. Go's memory model uses the stack/heap model. **Stack** memory is created for exclusive use by a function/method call. Allocation on the stack is significantly faster than on the **heap**.

Heap allocation occurs in Go when a reference or pointer cannot be determined to live exclusively within a function's call stack. This is determined by the compiler doing **escape analysis**.

Generally, it is much cheaper to pass copies into a function via an argument and another copy in the return value than it is to use a pointer. Finally, be careful with the number of pointers. Unlike C, it is uncommon in Go to see pointers to pointers, such as `**someType`, and, in over 10 years of coding Go, I have only once seen a single use for `***someType` that was valid. Unlike in the movie *Inception*, there is no reason to go deeper.

To sum up this section, you have gained an understanding of pointers, how to declare them, how to use them in your code, and where you should probably use them. You will use them on long-lived objects or types holding large amounts of data where copies are expensive. Next, let's explore structs.

Getting to know about structs

Structs represent a **collection of variables**. In the real world, we work with data all the time that would be well represented by a struct. For example, any form that is filled out in a job application or a vaccine card is a collection of variables (for example, last name, first name, and government ID number) that each has types (for example, `string`, `int`, and `float64`) and are grouped together. That grouping would be a struct in Go.

Declaring a struct

There are two methods for declaring a struct. The first way is uncommon except in tests, as it doesn't allow us to reuse the struct's definition to create more variables. But, as we will see it later in tests, we will cover it here:

```go
var record = struct{
    Name string
    Age int
}{
    Name: "John Doak",
    Age: 100, // Yeah, not publishing the real one
}
```

Here, we created a struct that contains two fields:

- `Name (string)`
- `Age (int)`

We then created an instance of that struct that has those values set. To access those fields, we can use the dot `.` operator:

```go
fmt.Printf("%s is %d years old\n", record.Name, record.Age)
```

This prints `"John Doak is 100 years old"`.

Declaring single-use structs, as we have here, is rarely done. Structs become more useful when they are used to create custom types in Go that are reusable. Let's have a look at how we can do that next.

Declaring a custom type

So far, we have created a single-use struct, which generally is not useful. Before we talk about the more common way to do this, let's talk about creating **custom types**.

Up until this point, we've seen the basic and pointer-wrapped types that are defined by the language: `string`, `bool`, `map`, and `slice`, for example. We can create our own types based on these basic types using the `type` keyword. Let's create a new type called `CarModel` that is based on the `string` type:

```
type CarModel string
```

`CarModel` is now its own type, just like `string`. While `CarModel` is based on a `string` type, it is a distinct type. You cannot use `CarModel` in place of a string or vice versa.

Creating a variable of `CarModel` can be done similar to a `string` type:

```
var myCar CarModel = "Chevelle"
```

Or, by using type conversion, as shown here:

```
myCar = CarModel("Chevelle")
```

Because `CarModel` is based on `string`, we can convert `CarModel` back to `string` with type conversion:

```
myCarAsString := string(myCar)
```

We can create new types based on any other type, including maps, slices, and functions. This can be useful for naming purposes or adding custom methods to a type (we will talk about this in a moment).

Custom struct types

The most common way to declare a struct is using the `type` keyword. Let's create that record again, but this time let's make it reusable by declaring a type:

```
type Record struct{
    Name string
    Age int
}

func main() {
    david := Record{Name: "David Justice", Age: 28}
    sarah := Record{Name: "Sarah Murphy", Age: 28}
```

```
            fmt.Printf("%+v\n", david)
            fmt.Printf("%+v\n", sarah)
}
```

By using `type`, we have made a new type called `Record` that we can use again and again to create variables holding `Name` and `Age`.

> **Note**
> Similar to how you may define two variables with the same type on a single line, you may do the same within a `struct` type, such as `First, Last string`.

Adding methods to a type

A method is similar to a function, but instead of being independent, it is bound to a type. For example, we have been using the `fmt.Println()` function. That function is independent of any variable that has been declared.

A method is a function that is attached to a variable. It can only be used on a variable of a type. Let's create a method that returns a string representation of the `Record` type we created earlier:

```
type Record struct{
      Name string
      Age int
}
// String returns a csv representing our record.
func (r Record) String() string {
      return fmt.Sprintf("%s,%d", r.Name, r.Age)
}
```

Notice `func (r Record)`, which attaches the function as a method onto the `Record` struct. You can access the fields of `Record` within this method by using `r.<field>`, such as `r.Name` or `r.Age`.

This method cannot be used outside of a `Record` object. Here's an example of using it:

```
john := Record{Name: "John Doak", Age: 100}
fmt.Println(john.String())
```

Let's look at how we change a field's value.

Changing a field's value

Struct values can be changed by using the variable attribute followed by = and the new value. Here is an example:

```
myRecord.Name = "Peter Griffin"
fmt.Println(myRecord.Name) // Prints: Peter Griffin
```

It is important to remember that a struct is not a reference type. If you pass a variable representing a struct to a function and change a field in the function, it will not change on the outside. Here is an example:

```
func changeName(r Record) {
    r.Name = "Peter"
    fmt.Println("inside changeName: ", r.Name)
}

func main() {
    rec := Record{Name: "John"}
    changeName(rec)
    fmt.Println("main: ", rec.Name)
}
```

This will output the following:

```
Inside changeName: Peter
Main: John
```

As we learned in the section on **pointers**, this is because the variable is copied, and we are changing the copy. For struct types that need to have fields that change, we normally pass in a pointer. Let's try this again, using pointers:

```
func changeName(r *Record) {
    r.Name = "Peter"
    fmt.Println("inside changeName: ", r.Name)
}

func main() {
    // Create a pointer to a Record
    rec := &Record{Name: "John"}
    changeName(rec)
    fmt.Println("main: ", rec.Name)
}
```

```
Inside changeName: Peter
Main: Peter
```

This will output the following:

```
Inside changeName: Peter
Main: Peter
```

Note that `.` is a *magic* operator that works on `struct` or `*struct`.

When I declared the `rec` variable, I did not set the `age`. Non-set fields are set to the zero value of the type. In the case of `Age`, which is `int`, this would be `0`.

Changing a field's value in a method

In the same way that a function cannot alter a non-pointer struct, neither can a method. If we had a method called `IncrAge()` that increased the age on the record by one, this would not do what you wanted:

```
func (r Record) IncrAge() {
    r.Age++
}
```

The preceding code passes a copy of `Record`, adds one to the copy's `Age`, and returns.

To actually increment the age, simple make `Record` a pointer, as follows:

```
func (r *Record) IncrAge() {
    r.Age++
}
```

This will work as expected.

> **Tip**
> Here is a basic rule that will keep you out of trouble, especially when you are new to the language. If the `struct` type should be a pointer, then make all methods pointer methods. If it shouldn't be, then make them all non-pointers. Don't mix and match.

Constructors

In many languages, **constructors** are specially-declared methods or syntax that are used to initialize fields in an object and sometimes run internal methods as setup. Go doesn't provide any specialized code for that, instead, we use a **constructor pattern** using simple functions.

Constructors are commonly either called `New()` or `New[Type]()` when declaring a public constructor. Use `New()` if there are no other types in the package (and most likely won't be in the future).

If we wanted to create a constructor that made our `Record` from the previous section, it might look like the following:

```go
func NewRecord(name string, age int) (*Record, error) {
    if name == "" {
        return nil, fmt.Errorf("name cannot be the empty string")
    }
    if age <= 0 {
        return nil, fmt.Errorf("age cannot be <= 0")
    }
    return &Record{Name: name, Age: age}, nil
}
```

This constructor takes in a `name` and `age` argument and returns a pointer to `Record` with those fields set. If we pass bad values for those fields, it instead returns the pointer's zero value (`nil`) and an error. Using this looks like the following:

```go
    rec, err := NewRecord("John Doak", 100)
    if err != nil {
        return err
    }
```

Don't worry about the error, as we will discuss it in the course of the book's journey.

By now, you have learned how to use `struct`, Go's base object type. This included creating a struct, creating custom structs, adding methods, changing field values, and creating constructor functions. Now, let's look at using Go interfaces to abstract types.

Comprehending Go interfaces

Go provides a type called an **interface** that stores any value that declares a set of methods. The implementing value must have declared this set of methods to implement the interface. The value may also have other methods besides the set declared in the interface type.

If you are new to interfaces, understand that they can be a little confusing. Therefore, we will take it one step at a time.

Defining an interface type

Interfaces are most commonly defined using the `type` keyword that we discussed in the earlier section on structs. The following defines an interface that returns a string representing the data:

```
type Stringer interface {
        String() string
}
```

> **Note**
>
> `Stringer` is a real type defined in the standard library's `fmt` package. Types that implement `Stringer` will have their `String()` method called when passed to `print` functions in the `fmt` package. Don't let the similar names confuse you; `Stringer` is the interface type's name, and it defines a method called `String()` (which is uppercase to distinguish it from the `string` type, which is lowercase). That method returns a `string` type that should provide some human-readable representation of your data.

Now, we have a new type called `Stringer`. Any variable that has the `String() string` method can be stored in a variable of type `Stringer`. The following is an example:

```
type Person struct {
    First, Last string
}
func (p Person) String() string {
    return fmt.Sprintf("%s,%s", p.Last, p.First)
}
```

Person represents a record of a person, first and last name. We define `String()` string on it, so `Person` implements `Stringer`:

```
type StrList []string
func (s StrList) String() string {
    return strings.Join(s, ",")
}
```

`StrList` is a slice of strings. It also implements `Stringer`. The `strings.Join()` function used here takes a slice of strings and creates a single string with each entry from the slice separated by a comma:

```
// PrintStringer prints the value of a Stringer to stdout.
func PrintStringer(s Stringer) {
    fmt.Println(s.String())
}
```

`PrintStringer()` allows us to print the output of `Stringer.String()` of any type that implements `Stringer`. Both the types we created above implement `Stringer`.

Let's see this in action:

```
func main() {
    john := Person{First: "John", Last: "Doak"}
    var nameList Stringer = StrList{"David", "Sarah"}

    PrintStringer(john)     // Prints: Doak,John
    PrintStringer(nameList) // Prints: David,Sarah
}
```

Without interfaces, we would have to write a separate `Print[Type]` function for every type we wanted to print. Interfaces allow us to pass values that can do common operations defined by their methods.

Important things about interfaces

The first thing to note about interfaces is that values *must* implement every method defined in the interface. Your value can have methods not defined for the interface, but it doesn't work the other way.

Another common issue new Go developers encounter is that once the type is stored in an interface, you cannot access its fields, or any methods not defined on the interface.

The blank interface – Go's universal value

Let's define a blank interface variable: `var i interface{}`. `i` is an interface with no defined methods. So, what can you store in that?

That's right, you can store *anything*.

`interface{}` is Go's universal value container that can be used to pass any value to a function and then figure out what it is and what to do with it later. Let's put some things in `i`:

```
i = 3
i = "hello world"
i = 3.4
i = Person{First: "John"}
```

This is all legal because each of those values has types that define all the methods that the interface defined (which were no methods). This allows us to pass around values in a universal container. This is actually how `fmt.Printf()` and `fmt.Println()` work. Here are their definitions from the `fmt` package:

```
func Println(a ...interface{}) (n int, err error)
func Printf(format string, a ...interface{}) (n int, err error)
```

However, as the interface did not define any methods, `i` is not useful in this form. So, this is great for passing around values, but not using them.

> **Note about interface{} in 1.18:**
>
> Go 1.18 has introduced an alias for the blank `interface{}`, called `any`. The Go standard library now uses `any` in place of `interface{}`. However, all packages prior to 1.18 will still use `interface{}`. Both are equivalent and can be used interchangeably.

Type assertion

Interfaces can have their values *asserted* to either another interface type or to their original type. This is different than **type conversion**, where you change the type from one to another. In this case, we are saying *it already is this type*.

Type assertion allows us to change an `interface{}` value into a value that we can do something with.

There are two common ways to do this. The first uses the `if` syntax, as follows:

```
if v, ok := i.(string); ok {
    fmt.Println(v)
}
```

`i.(string)` is asserting that `i` is a `string` value. If it is not, `ok == false`. If `ok == true`, then `v` will be the `string` value.

The more common way is with a `switch` statement and another use of the `type` keyword:

```
switch v := i.(type) {
case int:
    fmt.Printf("i was %d\n", i)
case string:
    fmt.Printf("i was %s\n", i)
case float:
    fmt.Printf("i was %v\n", i)
case Person, *Person:
    fmt.Printf("i was %v\n", i)
default:
    // %T will print i's underlying type out
    fmt.Printf("i was an unsupported type %T\n", i)
}
```

Our `default` statement prints out the underlying type of `i` if it did not match any of the other cases. `%T` is used to print the type information.

In this section, we learned about Go's `interface` type, how it can be used to provide type abstraction, and converting an interface into its concrete type for use.

Summary

In this chapter, you have learned the basics of the Go language. This includes variable types, functions, loops, methods, pointers, and interfaces. The skills acquired in this chapter provide the basic foundation needed to explore more advanced features of the Go language in our next chapter.

Next, we will be looking at essential capabilities of the Go language, such as handling errors, using concurrency, and Go's testing framework.

2
Go Language Essentials

In the previous chapter, we covered the basics of the Go language. While some of the syntax is new in relation to other languages, most of the concepts in that chapter are familiar to programmers coming from other languages.

This isn't to say that the way Go uses those concepts doesn't lead to code that is easier to read and reason about—it's just that most of it doesn't stand out from other languages.

In this chapter, we will be discussing the essential parts of Go that make it stand out from other languages, from Go's more pragmatic error handling to its core concurrency concept, the goroutine, and the newest feature of the Go language, generics.

Here are the main topics that will be covered:

- Handling errors in Go
- Utilizing Go constants
- Using `defer`, `panic`, and `recover`
- Utilizing goroutines for concurrency
- Understanding Go's `Context` type
- Utilizing Go's testing framework
- Generics—the new kid on the block

Now, let's get the essentials down and get you on your way!

Handling errors in Go

Many of you will come from languages that handle *errors* using *exceptions*. Go took a different approach, treating errors like our other data types. This prevents common problems that exception-based models have, such as exceptions escaping up the stack.

Go has a built-in error type called `error`. `error` is based on the `interface` type, with the following definition:

```
type error interface {
    Error() string
}
```

Now, let's look at how we can create an error.

Creating an error

The most common way to create errors is using either the `errors` package's `New()` method or the `fmt` package's `Errorf()` method. Use `errors.New()` when you don't need to do variable substitution and `fmt.Errorf()` when you do. You can see both methods in the following code snippet:

```
err := errors.New("this is an error")
err := fmt.Errorf("user %s had an error: %s", user, msg)
```

In both the preceding examples, `err` will be of type `error`.

Using an error

The most common way to use an error is as the last return value on a function or method call. The caller can then test if the returned error is `nil`, indicating there is no error.

Let's say we want a function that divides a number, and we want to detect if the divisor is zero. In that case, we want to return an error because a computer cannot divide a number by zero. This is how it might look:

```go
func Divide(num int, div int) (int, error) {
    if div == 0 {
        // We return the zero value of int (0) and an error.
        return 0, errors.New("cannot divide by 0")

    }
    return num / div, nil

}

func main() {
    divideBy := []int{0, 1, 2, 3, 4, 5, 6, 7, 8, 9}

    for _, div := range divideBy {
        res, err := Divide(100, div)
        if err != nil {
            fmt.Printf("100 by %d error: %s\n", div, err)
            continue
        }
        fmt.Printf("100 divided by %d = %d\n", div, res)
    }
}
```

The preceding example uses Go's multiple return ability to return two values: **the result** and **the error**.

In our `main` package, we can now divide our numbers and check the returned `error` type to see if it is not `nil`. If it is, we know we had an error and should ignore the return value. If not, we know the operation completed successfully.

Creating named errors

Sometimes, you want to create errors that indicate a specific type of error—say, a network error versus an incorrect argument. This can be done by creating specific types of errors using the `var` keyword and `errors.New()` or `fmt.Errorf()`, as illustrated in the following code snippet:

```
var (
    ErrNetwork = errors.New("network error")
    ErrInput   = errors.New("input error")
)
```

We can use the `errors` package's `Is()` function to detect the error type and retry on `ErrNetwork` and not on other errors, as follows:

```
// The loop is for retrying if we have an ErrNetwork.
for {
    err := someFunc("data")
    if err == nil {
        // Success so exit the loop
        break
    }
    if errors.Is(err, ErrNetwork) {
        log.Println("recoverable network error")
        time.Sleep(1 * time.Second)
        continue
    }
    log.Println("unrecoverable error")
    break // exit loop, as retrying is useless
}
```

`someFunc()` is not defined here. You can view a full example here:

`https://play.golang.org/p/iPwwwmIBcAG`

Custom errors

Because the `error` type is simply an interface, you can implement your own custom errors. Here is a more in-depth network error that we could use:

```
const (
      UnknownCode = 0
      UnreachableCode = 1
      AuthFailureCode = 2
)
type ErrNetwork struct {
      Code int
      Msg string
}
func (e ErrNetwork) Error() string {
    return fmt.Sprintf("network error(%d): %s", e.Code, e.msg)
}
```

We can now return a custom network error for something such as an authentication failure, as follows:

```
return ErrNetwork{
      Code: AuthFailureCode,
      Msg: "user unrecognized",
}
```

When we receive an error from a call, we can detect if it was a network error using the `errors.As()` function, as follows:

```
var netErr ErrNetwork
if errors.As(err, &netErr) {
      if netErr.Code == AuthFailureCode {
            log.Println("unrecoverable auth failure: ", err)
            break
      }
      log.Println("recoverable error: %s", netErr)
}
log.Println("unrecoverable error: %s", err)
break
```

You can also view this here: https://play.golang.org/p/gZ5AK8-o4zA.

The preceding code detects if the network error is unrecoverable, such as an authentication failure. Any other network error is recoverable. If it is not a network error, it is unrecoverable.

Wrapping errors

Many times, there is an error chain where we want to **wrap an error** received by a lower-level package with information from an upper layer package. For example, you might be making a **REpresentational State Transfer (REST)** call that sends some data and you receive an error from the net/http package. In that case, you might want to put information about which REST call you were making with the underlying error.

We can **wrap errors** so that not only can we include more specific information, but we can also keep the underlying error for extraction later.

We do this using fmt.Errorf() with %w for variable substitution of our error type. Let's say we want to call someFunc() from another function called restCall() and add more information, as illustrated in the following code snippet:

```
func restCall(data) error {
    if err := someFunc(data); err != nil {
        return fmt.Errorf("restCall(%s) had an error: %w", data, err)
    }
    return nil
}
```

Someone using restCall() can detect and extract an ErrNetwork using errors.As(), just as we did before. The following code snippet provides an illustration of this:

```
for {
    if err := restCall(data); err != nil {
        var netErr ErrNetwork
        if errors.As(err, &netErr) {
            log.Println("network error: ", err)
            time.Sleep(1 * time.Second)
            continue
        }
        log.Println("unrecoverable: ", err)
    }
}
```

The preceding code extracts the `ErrNetwork` from the wrapped `error` it was contained in. This will work no matter how many layers of wrapping the error was contained in.

In this section, you have learned how Go handles errors and about Go's `error` type and how to create basic errors, how to create custom errors, how to detect specific error types, and how to wrap/unwrap errors. As good `error` handling is the basis of reliable software, this knowledge will be useful in every Go program you write.

Utilizing Go constants

Constants provide values that are set at compile time and cannot change. This is in contrast to variables, which store values that can be set at runtime and can be altered. This provides types that cannot accidentally be changed by a user and are allocated for use in the software on startup, providing some speed advantages and safety over variable declarations.

Constants can be used to store the following:

- Booleans
- Runes
- Integer types (`int`, `int8`, `uint16`, and so on)
- Floating-point types (`float32`/`float64`)
- Complex data types
- Strings

In this section, we will discuss how to **declare constants** and common use in your code.

Declaring a constant

Constants are declared using the `const` keyword, as illustrated in the following code snippet:

```
const str = "hello world"
const num = 3
const num64 int64 = 3
```

Constants are different from variable types in that they come in two flavors, as follows:

- **Untyped constants**
- **Typed constants**

This is going to seem a little weird because constants store a typed value. But if you don't declare the exact type (as in the third example, num64, where we declared it to be an int64 type), the constant can be used for any type that has the same base type or family of types (such as integers). This is called an **untyped constant**.

For example, num can be used to set the value of an int8, int16, int32, int64, uint8, uint16, uint32, or uint64 type. So, the following will work:

```
func add(x, y int8) int8 {
    return x + y
}
func main() {
    fmt.Println(add(num, num))   // Print: 6
}
```

While we didn't discuss it earlier, that is what happens when we wrote code such as add (3, 3)—3 is actually an untyped constant. If the signature of add changed to add (x, y int64), add (3, 3) works because of this property of an untyped constant.

This extends to any type based on that basic type. Have a look at the following example:

```
type specialStr string
func printSpecial(str specialStr)
    fmt.Println(string(str))
}

func main() {
    const constHelloWorld = "hello world"
    var varHelloWorld = "hello world"

    printSpecial(varHelloWorld)   // Won't compile
    printSpecial(constHelloWorld) // Will compile
    printSpecial("hello world")   // Will compile
}
```

From the preceding code, you will receive the following output:

```
./prog.go:18:14: cannot use varHelloWorld (type string) as type
specialStr in argument to printSpecial
```

This is because varHelloWorld is a string type and not a specialStr type. But the unique properties of an untyped constant allow for constHelloWorld to satisfy any type based on string.

Enumeration via constants

Many languages provide an **enumerated type** that gives a readable name to some value that cannot be changed. This is most commonly done for integer constants, though you can do this for any type of constant.

For integer constants specifically, there is a special `iota` keyword that can be used to generate constants. It increments the value by 1 for each constant defined in the grouping, as illustrated in the following code snippet:

```
const (
    a = iota // 0
    b = iota // 1
    d = iota // 2
)
```

This can also be shortened to have only the first value use `iota`, and the following values would also automatically be set. The value can also be set to a formula in which `iota` uses a multiplier or other mathematical operation. Here is an example of both those concepts:

```
const (
    a = iota *2 // 0
    b // 2
    d // 4
)
```

Enumeration with `iota` is great, as long as the values will never be stored on disk or sent to another process that is local or remote. The value of constants is controlled by the order of the constants in the code. Here, look what happens if we insert c into our first example:

```
const (
    a = iota // 0
    b        // 1
    c        // 2
    d        // 3
)
```

Notice that d now has the value of 3? This would cause serious errors if the code needed to read back values that were written to disk and needed to be read back in. In cases where these values could be used by another process, it is best practice to statically define enumeration values.

Enumerators in Go can be hard to interpret when printed. Maybe you are using them for error codes and would prefer to have the constant's name printed when printing the *value* to logs or **standard output** (**stdout**). Let's have a look at how we can get better output.

Printing enumerators

Enumerators are much easier to use when displaying a value as the enumerated name instead of the value. This can be done easily when the constant is a string such as `const toyota = "toyota"`, but for other more efficient enumerator types such as integers, printing the value simply outputs a number.

Go has the concept of code generation built into the tooling. This is a more far-reaching subject than we will cover here (read about it here: `https://blog.golang.org/generate`).

However, we will borrow from the linked document to show how this can be used to set up an enumerator to a string value for printing automatically, as follows:

```
//go:generate stringer -type=Pill
type Pill int
const (
    Placebo Pill = iota
    Aspirin
    Ibuprofen
    Paracetamol
    Acetaminophen = Paracetamol
)
```

> **Note**
> This requires the Go `stringer` binary to be installed.

`//go:generate stringer -type=Pill` is a special syntax that indicates that when the `go generate` command is run for this package, it should call the `stringer` tool and pass it the `-type=Pill` flag, which indicates to read our package code and generate a method that reverses the constants based on type `Pill` to a string. This will be placed in a file called `pill_string.go`.

Before running the command, `fmt.Println(Aspirin)` would print 1; after, it would print `Aspirin`.

In this section, you have learned how constants can provide non-changeable values for use in your code, how you can create enumerators with them, and finally, how you can generate textual printed output for enumerators for better logging. In the next section, we will explore how to use `defer`, `panic`, and `recover` methods.

Using defer, panic, and recover

Modern programming languages have a need to provide some method of running routines when a section of code ends. This is useful when you need to guarantee a file closure or unlock a mutex. In addition, there are times when a program needs to stop execution and exit. This can be caused by loss of access to a critical resource, a security issue, or another need.

We also require the ability to recover from a premature program exit caused by a package that contains code we do not control. This section will cover each of the abilities in Go and their interrelations.

defer

The `defer` keyword allows you to execute a function when the function that contains `defer` exits. If there are multiple `defer` statements, they execute last to first.

This can be useful for debugging, unlocking mutexes, decrementing counters, and so on. Here's an example:

```
func printStuff() (value string) {
    defer fmt.Println("exiting")
    defer func() {
        value = "we returned this"
    }()
    fmt.Println("I am printing stuff")
    return ""
}

func main() {
    v := printStuff()
    fmt.Println(v)
}
```

This outputs the following:

```
I am printing stuff
exiting
we returned this
```

You can also see it at the following link:

https://play.golang.org/p/DaoP9M79E_J

If you run this example, you will notice that our `defer` statements execute after the rest of `printStuff()` has run. We use a deferred anonymous function to set our named return `value` before exiting. You will see `defer` used frequently in future chapters.

panic

The `panic` keyword is used to cause the execution of the program to stop and exit while displaying some text and a stack trace.

Using `panic` is as simple as calling the following:

```
panic("ran into some bug")
```

`panic` is intended to be used when a program cannot or should not continue to execute. This might be because there is a security issue, or on startup, you cannot connect to a required data source.

In most circumstances, a user should return an `error` and not `panic`.

As a general rule, only use `panic` in the `main` package.

recover

There are rare circumstances in which a program might panic due to an unforeseen bug or a package that unnecessarily panics. After more than 10 years of programming in Go, I can count on my fingers the number of times I have needed to recover from a panic.

Remote Procedure Call (**RPC**) frameworks such as **Google RPC** (**gRPC**) (https://grpc.io/docs/what-is-grpc/) use `recover` to prevent a server crash when an RPC call panics and then signals the caller of the issue.

If, like the RPC framework, you need to catch a panic that is occurring or protect against potential panics, you can use the `recover` keyword with the `defer` keyword. Here is an example of this:

```go
func someFunc() {
    defer func() {
        if r := recover(); r != nil {
            log.Printf("called recover, panic was: %q", r)
        }
    }()
    panic("oh no!!!")
}
```

You can also see this here: https://play.golang.org/p/J8RfjOe1dMh.

This has similarities to other languages' exception types, but you should not confuse the two. Go does not intend for you to use `panic`/`defer`/`recover` in that way—it will simply cause you problems in the future.

Now that you have completed this section, you have learned how to defer the execution of a function, cause a panic within the `main` package, how to recover from a misbehaving package, and when these should be used. Let's hop onto the next topic relevant to this chapter: *goroutines*.

Utilizing goroutines for concurrency

In the modern era of computers, **concurrency** is the name of the game. In the years before 2005 or so, computers used Moore's law to double the speed of a single **central processing unit** (**CPU**) every 18 months. Multiple CPU consumer systems were rare and there was one core per CPU in the system. Software that utilized multiple cores efficiently was rare.

Over time, it became more expensive to increase single-core speed and multi-core CPUs have become the norm. Each core on a CPU supports a number of hardware threads and **operating systems** (**OSs**) provide OS threads that are mapped to hardware threads that are then shared between processes.

Languages can utilize these OS threads to run functions in their language *concurrently* instead of *serially* as we have been doing in all of our code so far.

Starting an OS thread is an expensive operation and to fully utilize the thread's time requires paying a lot of attention to what you are doing.

Go takes this to another level than most languages with **goroutines**. Go has built a runtime scheduler that maps these goroutines onto OS threads and switches which routine is running on which thread to optimize CPU utilization.

This produces concurrency that is easy and cheap to use, requiring less mental burden on the developer.

Starting a goroutine

Go gets its name from the go keyword that is used to spawn a goroutine. By applying go before a function call, you can cause that function to execute concurrently with the rest of the code. Here is an example that causes 10 goroutines to be created, with each printing out a number:

```
for i := 0; i < 10; i++ {
    go fmt.Println(x) // This happens concurrently
}
fmt.Println("hello")
// This is used to prevent the program from exiting
// before our goroutines above run. We will talk about
// this later in the chapter.
select{}
```

The output will look similar to, but not necessarily in the same order as, what is shown next. . . . indicates more numbers follow, but have been omitted for brevity:

```
Hello
2
0
5
3
...
fatal error: all goroutines are asleep - deadlock!
```

You can see the preceding example here:

https://play.golang.org/p/RBD3yuBA3Gd

> **Note**
> You will also notice that this panics with an error after running. This is because the program will have no running goroutines, which means the program is effectively dead. It is killed by Go's deadlock detector. We will handle this more gracefully in the next chapter.

Running this will print out the numbers in random order. Why random? Once you are running concurrently, you cannot be sure when a scheduled function will execute. At any given moment, there will be between 0 and 10 goroutines executing `fmt.Println(x)`, and another one executing `fmt.Println("hello")`. That's right—the `main()` function is its own goroutine.

Once the `for` loop ends, `fmt.Println("hello")` will execute. `hello` might be printed out before any of the numbers, somewhere in the middle, or after all the numbers. This is because they are all executing at the same time like horses on a racetrack. We know all the horses will reach the end, but we don't know which one will be first.

Synchronization

When doing **concurrent programming**, there is a simple rule: *You can read a variable concurrently without synchronization, but a single writer requires synchronization.*

These are the most common methods of synchronization in Go:

- The `channel` data type to exchange data between goroutines
- `Mutex` and `RWMutex` from the `sync` package to lock data access
- `WaitGroup` from the `sync` package to track access

These can be used to prevent multiple goroutines from reading and writing to variables at the same time. It is undefined what happens if you try to read and write to the same variable from multiple goroutines simultaneously (in other words, *that is a bad idea*).

Reading and writing to the same variable concurrently is called a **data race**. Go has a data race detector not covered in this book to uncover these types of problems. You can read about it here: https://golang.org/doc/articles/race_detector.

WaitGroups

A `WaitGroup` is a synchronization counter that only has positive values starting at 0. It is most often used to indicate when some set of tasks is finished before executing code that relies on those tasks.

A `WaitGroup` has a few methods, as outlined here:

- `.Add(int)`: Used to add some number to the `WaitGroup`
- `.Done()`: Subtract 1 from the `WaitGroup`
- `.Wait()`: Block until `WaitGroup` is 0

In our previous section on goroutines, we had an example that *panicked* after running. This was due to having all goroutines stopped. We used a `select` statement (covered in this chapter) to block forever to prevent the program from exiting before the goroutines could run, but we can use a `WaitGroup` to wait for our goroutines to end and exit gracefully.

Let's do it again, as follows:

```go
func main() {
    wg := sync.WaitGroup{}
    for i := 0; i < 10; i++ {
        wg.Add(1)
        go func(n int) {
            defer wg.Done()
            fmt.Println(n)
        }(i)
    }
    wg.Wait()
    fmt.Println("All work done")
}
```

You can also see this here: https://play.golang.org/p/cwA3kC-d3F6.

This example uses a `WaitGroup` to track the number of goroutines that are outstanding. We add 1 to wg before we launch our goroutine (*do not add it inside the goroutine*). When the goroutine exits, the `defer` statement is called, which subtracts 1 from the counter.

> **Important Note**
>
> A `WaitGroup` can only have positive values. If you call `.Done()` when the `WaitGroup` is at 0, it will cause a panic. Because of the way they are used, the creators knew that any attempt to reach a negative value would be a critical bug that needs to be caught early.

`wg.Wait()` waits for all the goroutines to finish, and calling `defer wg.Done()` causes our counter to decrement until it reaches 0. At that point, `Wait()` stops blocking and the program exits the `main()` function.

> **Important Note**
>
> If passing a `WaitGroup` in a function or method call, you need to use a `wg := &sync.WaitGroup{}` pointer. Otherwise, each function is operating on a copy, not the same value. If used in a struct, either the struct or the field holding the `WaitGroup` must be a pointer.

Channels

Channels provide a synchronization primitive in which data is inserted into a channel by a goroutine and removed by another goroutine. A channel can be buffered, meaning it can hold a certain amount of data before blocking, or unbuffered, where a sender and receiver must both be present for the data to transfer between goroutines.

A common analogy for a channel is a pipe in which water flows. Water is inserted into a pipe and flows out the far side. The amount of water that can be held in the pipe is the buffer. Here, you can see a representation of goroutine communication using a channel:

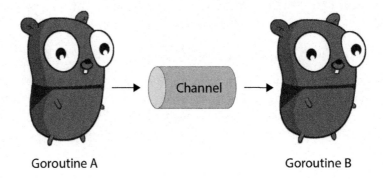

Figure 2.1 – Goroutine communication using a channel

Channels are used to pass data from one goroutine to another, where the goroutine that passed the data stops using it. This allows you to pass *control* from one goroutine to another, giving access to a single goroutine at a time. This provides synchronization.

Channels are typed, so only data of that type can go into the channel. Because channels are a pointer-scoped type such as map and `slice`, we use `make()` to create them, as follows:

```
ch := make(chan string, 1)
```

The preceding statement creates a channel called `ch` that holds a `string` type with a buffer of 1. Leaving ", 1" off will make it an unbuffered channel.

Sending/receiving

Sending to a channel is done with the `<-` syntax. To send a `string` type to the preceding channel, we could do the following: `ch <- "word"`. This attempts to put the "word" string into the `ch` channel. If the channel has an available buffer, we continue execution in this goroutine. If the buffer is full, this blocks until either buffer becomes available or—in the case of unbuffered channels—a goroutine tries to pull from the channel.

Receiving is similar using the same syntax but on the opposite side of the channel. The goroutine trying to pull from the channel would do this: `str := <-ch`. This assigns the next value on the channel to the `str` variable.

More commonly when receiving variables, the `for range` syntax is used. This allows us to pull all values out of a channel. An example using our preceding channel might look like this:

```
for val := range ch {  // Acts like a <-ch
    fmt.Println(val)
}
```

Channels can be closed so that no more data will be sent to them. This is done with the `close` keyword. To close the preceding channel, we could do `close(ch)`. This should *always* be done by the sender. Closing a channel will cause a `for range` loop to exit once all values on the channel have been removed.

Let's use a channel to send words from one goroutine to another, as follows:

```
func main() {
    ch := make(chan string, 1)
    go func() {
        for _, word := range []string{"hello", "world"} {
```

```
            ch <- word
            close(ch)
        }
    }()
    for word := range ch {
        fmt.Println(word)
    }
}
```

You can also see the preceding example here:

https://go.dev/play/p/9km80Jz6f26

> **Important Note**
> After a channel is closed, sending a value on a channel will cause a panic.
>
> Receiving from a closed channel will return the zero value of the type the channel holds.
>
> A channel can be `nil`. Sending or receiving from a `nil` channel can block forever. It is a common bug for developers to forget to initialize channels in a struct.

select statements

A `select` statement is similar to a `switch` statement but is geared toward listening to multiple channels. This allows us to receive and act on multiple inputs at the same time.

The following example will listen to several channels and execute a `case` statement whenever it receives a value on one of them. In the example cases, we spin off a goroutine to do something with the value so that we can continue the execution of our loop for the next value. If no value is present on the channel, this blocks until one is. If values are on more than one channel, `select` uses a pseudo-random method to select which case to execute:

```
for {
    select {
    case v := <-inCh1:
        go fmt.Println("received(inCh1): ", v)
    case v := <-inCh2:
        go fmt.Println("received(inCh2): ", v)
    }
}
```

With a `select` statement, we sometimes only want to check if a value is on a channel, but if it is not, then we want to move on. In those cases, we can use a `default` statement. `default` executes if no other case statement can execute (versus the previous behavior of waiting for channel data indefinitely). You can see an example of this in the following code snippet:

```
select {
case s := <-ch:
      fmt.Printf("had a string(%s) on the channel\n", s)
default:
      fmt.Println("channel was empty")
}
```

`select` has one more use we saw before but it wasn't explained. `select{}` has no case statements and no default statement; therefore, it blocks forever. This is often used by servers that want to run forever to prevent the `main()` function from exiting, which stops the execution of the program.

Channels as an event signal

One common use of channels is to use them to send a signal to another goroutine. Often, this is an indication to exit a loop or some other execution.

In the `select` example from before where we used the `for` loop, the loop will continue forever, but we can use a channel to signal that we want to exit, as follows:

```
func printWords(in1, in2 chan string, exit chan struct{}, wg
*sync.WaitGroup) {
      defer wg.Done()
      for {
            select{
            case <-exit:
                  fmt.Println("exiting")
                  return
            case str := <-in1:
                  fmt.Println("in1: ", str)
            case str := <-in2:
                  fmt.Println("in2: ", str)
            }
      }
}
```

`printWords()` reads input off of three channels. If the input is on `in1` or `in2`, it prints the channel name and what string was sent on the channel. If it is the `exit` channel, it prints that it is exiting and returns. When returning, wg will have `.Done()` called on it, which will decrement the it by 1:

```go
func main() {
    in1 := make(chan string)
    in2 := make(chan string)
    wg := &sync.WaitGroup{}
    exit := make(chan struct{})

    wg.Add(1)
    go printWords(in1, in2, exit, wg)

    in1 <- "hello"
    in2 <- "world"
    close(exit)

    wg.Wait()
}
```

Here we create all the channels required for `printWords()` and spin `printWords` off in a goroutine. We then send input on our input channels and once that is completed, we close the `exit` channel to signal there is no further input to `printWords`. The `wg.Wait()` call prevents `main()` from exiting until `printWords` has exited.

The output looks like this:

```
in1:   hello
in2:   world
exiting
```

You can also see the preceding example at the following link:

https://play.golang.org/p/go7Klf5JNQn

`exit` is used in this example to signal to `printWords()` that we want to exit the `for` loop. This is made possible because receiving on a closed channel returns the zero value of the type that the channel holds. We use a blank `struct{}` instance because it doesn't cost memory. We do not store the returned value in a variable because it is the signal that the channel closed that is important.

Mutexes

A **mutex** is a **synchronization primitive** (also known as a **lock**) that can only be locked by one owner at a time. If another would-be owner attempts to lock a mutex while it is locked by another owner, the code blocks until the mutex is unlocked and the new owner can take possession. Go provides a mutex type in the `sync` package called `Mutex`.

This is used to protect a variable or set of variables from being accessed by multiple goroutines. Remember—if one goroutine tries to write to a value at the same time another wants to read or write to that value, the variable must be protected by a synchronization primitive.

In the following example, we will spin off 10 goroutines to add a number to a `sum` value. The `sum` value must be protected as we are reading and writing from multiple goroutines:

```go
type sum struct {
    mu   sync.Mutex
    sum  int
}
func (s *sum) get() int {
    s.mu.Lock()
    defer s.mu.Unlock()
    return s.sum
}
func (s *sum) add(n int) {
    s.mu.Lock()
    defer s.mu.Unlock()
    s.sum += n
}
func main() {
    mySum := &sum{}
    wg := sync.WaitGroup{}
    for i := 0; i < 100; i++ {
        wg.Add(1)
        go func(x int) {
            defer wg.Done()
            mySum.add(x)
        }(i)
    }
    wg.Wait()
    fmt.Println("final sum: ", mySum.get())
}
```

You can also see this example at the following link:

https://play.golang.org/p/mXUk8PCzBI7

This code uses a Mutex named `mu` that is part of the `sum` struct to control access to the `get()` and `add()` methods. As each is locked, only one of those may execute at a time. We use the `defer` statement to unlock the Mutex when the function exits. This protects us from forgetting to unlock the Mutex when a function gets long.

RWMutex

Along with `sync.Mutex` is `sync.RWMutex`. This distinguishes itself by providing a read and write lock. Any number of `mu.RLock()` read locks may be held at a time, but a single `mu.Lock()` write lock waits for all existing read locks to complete (new `Rlock()` attempts block) and then provides the writer with exclusive access.

This proves to be faster when there are lots of concurrent readers and writing happens infrequently. However, the standard `Mutex` is faster in the generalized case because its implementation is less complicated.

In this section, you have gained basic skills in using goroutines for concurrent operations, learned what synchronization is and when you must use it, and learned about Go's various methods for synchronization and signaling. Let's dive into understanding another type, known as `context`.

Understanding Go's Context type

Go provides a package called `context` that is useful for two purposes, as outlined here:

- Canceling a chain of function calls after some event (such as a timeout)
- Passing information through a chain of function calls (such as user information)

A `Context` object is usually created in either `main()` or at the point of ingestion of some request (such as an RPC or **HyperText Transfer Protocol** (**HTTP**) request). A basic `Context` object is created from our background `Context` object, as follows:

```
import "context"

func main() {
    ctx := context.Background()
}
```

The `context` package and the `Context` type is an advanced subject, but I want to introduce it here as you will see it used throughout the Go ecosystem.

Using a Context to signal a timeout

`Context` is often used to communicate a timer state or to terminate a wait condition—for example, when your program is waiting for a network response.

Let's say we want to call a function to get some data, but we don't want to wait longer than 5 seconds for the call to complete. We can signal this via a `Context`, as follows:

```
ctx, cancel := context.WithTimeout(context.Background(), 5 *
time.Second)
data, err := GatherData(ctx, args)
cancel()
if err != nil {
    return err
}
```

`context.WithTimeout()` creates a new `Context` that will automatically be canceled after 5 seconds and a function that will cancel the `Context` (`context.CancelFunc`) when called.

Every `Context` is said to be derived from another `Context`. Here, we derive our `ctx` object from `context.Background()`. `context.Background()` is our parent `Context`. New `context` objects can be derived from `ctx` forming a chain, and those new `Context` objects can have different timeouts.

Canceling a `Context` either directly via `cancel()` or with a timeout or deadline causes that `Context` and its children to also be canceled.

The preceding code does the following:

- Creates a `Context` that is canceled after 5 seconds.
- Calls `GatherData()` and passes the `Context`.
- Once the call is complete, we cancel the `Context` if not already canceled.

Now, we need to set up `GatherData()` to honor our `Context` cancellation.

Honoring a context when receiving

If we are executing the `GatherData()` function, we need to honor this context. There are a few ways to do that with a basic call to `ctx.Err()`, as follows:

```go
func GatherData(ctx context.Context, args Args) ([]file, error) {
    if ctx.Err() != nil {
        return nil, err
    }

    localCtx, localCancel := context.WithTimeout(ctx, 2 * time.Second)
    local, err := getFilesLocal(localCtx, args.local)
    localCancel()
    if err != nil {
        return nil, err
    }

    remoteCtx, remoteCancel := context.WithTimeout(ctx, 3 * time.Second)
    remote, err := getFilesRemote(remoteCtx, args.remote)
    remoteCancel()
    if err != nil {
        return nil, err
    }
    return append(local, remote), nil
}
```

`GatherData()` looks at `ctx.Err()` and checks the value to see if it returns an error. If so, we know the `Context` has been canceled and simply return.

In this example, we derive two new `Context` objects that share the parent of `ctx`. If `ctx` is canceled, `localCtx` and `remoteCtx` are canceled. Canceling `localCtx` or `remoteCtx` has no effect on `ctx`. In most circumstances, passing `ctx` instead of deriving new `Context` objects is done, but we wanted to show how you derive new `Context` objects.

`Context` also supports a `.Done()` method in case you need to check for cancellation inside a `select` statement. `.Done()` returns a channel that, if closed, indicates cancellation. Using it is simple, as we can see here:

```
select {
case <-ctx.Done():
    return ctx.Err()
case data := <-ch:
    return date, nil
}
```

Now that we have shown you how you should add `Context` to your functions, let's talk about how this works in the standard library and why it is not the same as the examples we have shown.

Context in the standard library

The `context` package was added in **Go 1.7**, well after the introduction of Go's standard library. Unfortunately, this meant that it had to be hacked into the standard library packages in order to avoid breaking Go's version 1.0-compatibility promise.

This is the one thing added to Go that has added some real ugliness. Previously, we showed you how when using `Context` it should be the first argument of a function called `ctx`. However, the standard library cannot do this.

A common pattern you will see when using `Context` in the standard library will be to add it via a method. Here is an example of using `Context` for `http.Client` to fetch `www.golang.org` and print it to the screen:

```
client := &http.Client{}
req, err := http.NewRequest("GET", "http://www.golang.org", nil)
if err != nil {
        fmt.Println("error: ", err)
        return
}

ctx, cancel := context.WithTimeout(context.Background(), 3 * time.Second)
```

```go
// Attach it to our request.
req = req.WithContext(ctx)

// Get our resp.
resp, err := client.Do(req)
cancel()
if err != nil {
        fmt.Println("error: ", err)
        return
}

// Print the page to stdout
io.Copy(os.Stdout, resp.Body)
```

In this code we do the following:

- Create an HTTP client
- Create a `*http.Request` (req) to get the page at www.golang.org
- Create Context (ctx) and CancelFunc (cancel) where the Context is cancelled after 3 seconds
- Attach ctx to req to prevent `*http.Request` from taking longer than 3 seconds
- Uses `cancel()` to cancel the Context's internal goroutine that is tracking the timeout once the `client.Do()` call has completed

So far, we have talked about how to use Context for cancellation. Now let's talk about another use of Context—passing values through a call chain.

Context to pass values

A Context's other main use is to pass a value through a **call chain**. You should only use a Context to pass values that are useful on a per-call basis, not as generalized storage.

These are the two best uses for passing values on a Context:

- Security information about a user making a call.
- Telemetry information such as the data types used with *OpenTelemetry*.

In the case of security information, you are informing the system who the user is, probably with **OpenID Connect (OIDC)** information. This allows the call stack to make authorization checks.

For telemetry, this allows a service to record information related to this specific call to track function execution times, database latency, input, and errors. This can be dialed up or down to debug service issues. We discuss telemetry in future chapters.

Passing a value to a Context requires a little care. Values stored in a context are key-value pairs, and to prevent overwriting of keys between multiple packages, we need to create our own custom key type that can only be implemented by our package. In this way, keys from different packages will have different types. The code to achieve this is shown in the following snippet:

```go
type key int
const claimsKey key = 0

func NewContext(ctx context.Context, claims Claims) context.Context {
    return context.WithValue(ctx, claimsKey, claims)
}

func ClaimsFromContext(ctx context.Context) (Claims, bool) {
    // ctx.Value returns nil if ctx has no value for the key;
    // the Claims type assertion returns ok=false for nil.
    claims, ok := ctx.Value(userIPKey).(Claims)
    return claims, ok
}
```

This code does the following:

- Defines a type called key that is private, which prevents other packages from implementing it
- Defines a claimsKey constant of type key. This is used as the key for a value that holds an OIDC IDToken claim
- NewContext() provides a function that attaches a Claim to our Context
- ClaimsFromContext() provides a function that extracts Claims from a Context and indicates if Claims were found

The preceding code might exist in a security package for **Open Authorization (OAuth)/ OIDC** (a widely used authentication system). `Claims` would represent user data we have validated. `NewContext()` would allow us to add this information to a context in some middleware, and `ClaimsFromContext()` would allow us to extract it anywhere in the call chain that was required.

Best practices

I recommend that all public functions and methods have an initial argument of `ctx context.Context`. This allows you to add future-proofing to your public functions/methods/interfaces if you need to add capabilities that `Context` provides at a later date, even if you aren't using it now.

> **Important Note**
> Future-proofing methods/functions/interfaces is a practice of adding arguments and return values that are not used at the moment in order to prevent breaking them (and users) at some future date—for example, adding a returned `error` for a constructor that cannot currently return an error, but might in the future.

Maybe you won't need to handle cancellations (execution is too fast or can't be canceled), but something such as adding telemetry might come in handy later.

In this section, you learned about Go's `Context` object and how it is used to signal cancellation and to pass values through the call stack. You will see this used in many of the third-party packages you will use in your code. The final topic of this chapter will be about *Go's testing package*. Let's dive right into it.

Utilizing Go's testing framework

Testing is one of the most important and least loved parts of any language. Testing provides a developer with the knowledge that something works as expected. I cannot count the times that writing unit tests has proven that a function or method did not work the way I expected. This saved countless hours of debugging.

To this end, tests need to have the following attributes:

- Easy to write
- Fast to execute

- Simple to refactor
- Effortless to understand

To satisfy these needs, Go tackles tests by doing the following:

- Breaking tests into their own files
- Providing a simple `testing` package
- Using a testing methodology called **table-driven tests** (**TDTs**)

In this section, we will cover how to write basic tests, Go's standard TDT methodology, creating fakes with interfaces, and—finally—some third-party packages that I used and others that are popular, but I don't necessarily recommend.

Creating a basic test file

Go tests are contained in package files with a `_test.go` suffix. These files have the same package name, and you can include as many test files as needed. The usual rule is to write a test file per package file you want to test so that there is a 1:1 association for clarity.

Each test in a test file is a function whose name is prefixed with `Test` and has a single argument, `t *testing.T`, with no returns. This is how it looks:

```
func TestFuncName(t *testing.T) {
}
```

`t` is passed by the `go test` command and provides the necessary utilities for our tests. The primary methods used are listed here:

- `t.Error()`
- `t.Errorf()`
- `t.Fatalf()`
- `t.Log()`
- `t.Logf()`

When a test is executed, if the test ends without `panic/Error/Errorf/Fatal/Fatalf` called, the test is considered passed. If any of these are called, then the test fails. With `Error/Errorf`, the test continues executing and accumulates these error messages for the test. With `Fatal/Fatalf`, the test fails immediately.

`Log()/Logf()` calls are informative and are only displayed on failure or when other flags are passed for a test.

Creating a simple test

Borrowing from `golang.org` tutorials (https://golang.org/doc/tutorial/add-a-test), let's create a simple test for a function called `Greeter()` that takes a name as an argument and returns `"Hello [name]"`. The code is illustrated in the following snippet:

```go
package greetings

import (
"testing"
)

func TestGreet(t *testing.T) {
    name := "Bob"
    want := "Hello Bob"
    got, err := Greet(name)
    if got != want || err != nil {
        t.Fatalf("TestGreet(%s): got %q/%v, want %q/nil", name, got, err, want)
    }
}
```

You can also see this example here: https://play.golang.org/p/vjAhW0hfwHq.

To run the test, we need to simply run `go test` inside the package directory. If the test is successful, we should see the following:

```
=== RUN   TestGreet
--- PASS: TestGreet (0.00s)
PASS
```

To show what a failure looks like, I changed want to be `Hello Sarah` while leaving the name `Bob`, as illustrated here:

```
=== RUN   TestGreet
    prog.go:21: TestGreet(Bob): got "Hello Bob"/<nil>, want "Hello Sarah"/nil
--- FAIL: TestGreet (0.00s)
FAIL
```

It is important to include enough information to debug your test. I like to include the following:

- The name of the test
- If table-driven, the description of the table row executed
- What I received (called `got`)
- What I wanted (called `want`)

Now, let's talk about Go's preferred style of testing—TDTs.

Table Driven Tests (TDT)

For very simple tests, the preceding methodology works fine, but often, you need to test a function for multiple types of success and failure, such as in the following scenarios:

- What if they send a bad argument?
- What if the network has a problem and returns an error?
- What if the data isn't on disk?

Writing a test per condition creates a lot of churns in a test file that is harder to read and understand. TDTs to the rescue! A TDT uses the non-named struct concept we talked about in *Chapter 1, Go Language Basics*. This is the one place where it is common to see them.

The concept is to create a list of structs where each struct entry represents a set of test conditions and results that we want to see. We execute each struct entry one at a time to test the function.

Let's convert our preceding test to a TDT. In this case, there are only two expected ways for our `Greet()` function to react, as outlined here:

- We pass an empty string for `name`, which results in an error
- Anything else results in `"Hello"` and the name

Let's write a TDT that handles both these cases, as follows:

```go
func TestGreet(t *testing.T) {
    tests := []struct{
        desc string // What we are testing
        name string // The name we will pass
        want string // What we expect to be returned
```

```go
                expectErr bool // Do we expect an error
    }{
        {
            desc: "Error: name is an empty string",
            expectErr: true,
            // name and want are "", the zero value for string
        },
        {
            desc: "Success",
            name: "John",
            want: "Hello John",
            // expectErr is set to the zero value, false
        },
    }

    // Executes each test.
    for _, test := range tests {
        got, err := Greet(test.name)
        switch {
        // We did not get an error, but expected one
        case err == nil && test.expectErr:
            t.Errorf("TestGreet(%s): got err == nil, want err != nil", test.desc)
            continue
        // We got an error but did not expect one
        case err != nil && !test.expectErr:
            t.Errorf("TestGreet(%s): got err == %s, want err == nil", test.desc, err)
            continue
        // We got an error we expected, so just go to the next test
        case err != nil:
            continue
        }
        // We did not get the result we expected
        if got != test.want {
            t.Errorf("TestGreet(%s): got result %q, want %q", test.desc, got, test.want)
        }
    }
}
```

This example can also be found at the following link:
https://play.golang.org/p/vYWW-GiyT-M.

As you can see, TDT tests are longer but have clearly defined test parameters and clear error output.

Unlike the previous example, this tests that our error condition occurs when `name == ""`. Using a TDT is overkill for something so simple but becomes a powerful tool in the toolbox when writing tests against more complicated functions in Go.

Creating fakes with interfaces

Tests should generally be hermetic, meaning that tests should not use resources that are not located locally on a machine.

If we are testing a client to a REST service, it should not actually call out to the REST service. There are integration tests that should test the basic connectivity to a test version of a service, but those should be small and rare tests that we are not going to cover here.

To test the behaviors of remote resources, we create what are called **fakes** using interfaces. Let's write a client that talks to a service via a network client to get a user record. We don't want to test the logic of the server (the kind of logic we tested previously), but instead, want to test what happens if the REST client has an error or we get back the wrong record from the service.

First, let's say we use a `Fetch` client in a `client` package that looks like this:

```go
type Fetch struct{
    // Some internals, like an http.Client
}

func (f *Fetch) Record(name string) (Record, error){
    // Some code to talk to the server
}
```

We use `Fetch` in a function called `Greeter()` to get information we might use to change our responses to the person, as follows:

```go
func Greeter(name string, fetch *client.Fetch) (string, error) {
    rec, err := fetch.Record(name)
    if err != nil {
        return "", err
    }

    if rec.Name != name {
        return "", fmt.Errorf("server returned record for %s, not %s", rec.Name, name)
    }
    if rec.Age < 18 {
        return "Greetings young one", nil
    }
    return fmt.Sprintf("Greetings %s", name), nil
}
```

This is hard to test hermetically because `Fetch` is a concrete type that talks to a service. However, we can change this to an interface that `Fetch` implements and then use a fake. Firstly, let's add the interface and change the `Greeter` argument, as follows:

```go
type recorder interface {
    Record(name string) (Record, error)
}

func Greeter(name string, fetch recorder) (string, error) {
```

Now, we can pass a `*client.Fetch` instance or we can pass anything else that implements `recorder`. Let's create a fake that implements `recorder` that we can cause to return results useful for testing, as follows:

```go
type fakeRecorder struct {
    data Record
    err  bool
}
func (f fakeRecorder) Record(name string) (Record, error) {
    if f.err {
        return "", errors.New("error")
    }
```

```
        return f.data, nil
}
```

Now, let's integrate this into a TDT, like this:

```
func TestGreeter(t *testing.T) {
    tests := []struct{
        desc string
        name string
        recorder recorder
        want string
        expectErr bool
    }{
        {
            desc: "Error: recorder had some server error",
            name: "John",
            recorder: fakeRecorder{err: true},
            expectErr: true,
        },
        {
            desc: "Error: server returned wrong name",
            name: "John",
            recorder: fakeRecorder{
                Record: Record{Name: "Bob", Age: 20},
            },
            expectErr: true,
        },
        {
            desc: "Success",
            name: "John",
            recorder: fakeRecorder{
                Record: Record{Name: "John", Age: 20},
            },
            want: "Greetings John",
        },
```

```
        }

        for _, test := range tests {
                got, err := Greeter(test.name)
                switch {
                case err == nil && test.expectErr:
                        t.Errorf("TestGreet(%s): got err == nil, want err != nil", test.desc)
                        continue
                case err != nil && !test.expectErr:
                        t.Errorf("TestGreet(%s): got err == %s, want err == nil", test.desc, err)
                        continue
                case err != nil:
                        continue
                }

                if got != test.want {
                        t.Errorf("TestGreet(%s): got result %q, want %q", test.desc, got, want)
                }
        }
}
```

This example can be found here: https://play.golang.org/p/fjj2WrbG1KY.

We now are simply faking the response that would come from our real client, `Fetch`. In code using `Greeter()`, they can simply pass the real client and in our tests, we pass our `fakeRecorder` instance. This allows us to control our environment to test that our function handles each type of response in the way we expect. This test is missing a test that checks the result when a `Record` instance is returned where the `Age` value is set to < 18. We leave this as an exercise for you.

Third-party testing packages

When I'm writing tests, there is really only one tool I reach for: `https://pkg.go.dev/github.com/kylelemons/godebug/pretty?utm_source=godoc`.

`pretty` allows me to easily test if two complicated structs/maps/slices are equivalent. Using it in a test is simple, as illustrated here:

```
if diff := pretty.Compare(want, got); diff != "" {
    t.Errorf("TestSomeFunc(%s): -want/+got:\n%s", diff)
}
```

This outputs a readable format showing what is missing (prepended with -) and what was received (prepended with +). For more control over what is compared, the package offers a `Config` type that can be customized.

This code doesn't get updated often because it just works, but Kyle does answer bug requests, so the project is still alive.

Many in the Go community use the `github.com/stretchr/testify` set of packages, specifically the `assert` and `mock` packages.

I list them here because they are popular in the Go community; however, I would give the following warnings:

- Using asserts in Go for many years was considered bad practice
- Mocking frameworks in Go often have terrible corner cases

The original authors of Go thought that using asserts was a bad practice for the language and unneeded. The current Go team has relaxed this stance. Mocking frameworks in Go tend to rely heavily on `interface{}` and have some sharp corner cases. I find using mocks results in testing behavior that is not important (call order or which calls were executed) versus testing that a given input causes an expected output. This is less burdensome and fragile to code changes.

The original mocking framework (`https://github.com/golang/mock`) was considered unsafe at Google and its use was restricted.

To sum this section up, we have learned about Go's `testing` package, how to use that package to write tests, the TDT methodology, and my (*John Doak's*) thoughts on third-party testing packages.

Now that you have an understanding of how to do testing, we are going to look at a major addition to Go that was added in version 1.18—generics.

Generics – the new kid on the block

Generics are a new feature in Go 1.18 that looks to have vast ramifications for Go's future. Generics provide a way to represent multiple types with a new feature called a `type` parameter to allow functions to operate on multiple types.

This differs from the standard `interface{}` where these types of operations always happen at runtime and where you must convert `interface{}` to the concrete type to do work.

Generics are a new feature, so we are only going to give a very general overview. The Go community and Go authors at this time do not have a set of best practices that have been rigorously tested. This comes with experience in using a feature, and we are only at the early stages of generics at this time, with more features around generics coming in the future.

Type parameters

Type parameters can be added to functions or `struct` types to support a generic type. However, a key gotcha is that they cannot be used on methods! This is the most requested feature; however, it poses certain challenges to the language that the language authors are not sure how to deal with (or if they can be dealt with).

Type parameters are defined after the function name within brackets. Let's look at a basic one here:

```
func sortInts[I int8 |int16 |int32 |int64](slice []I) {
```

This creates a function that can sort any of our signed integer types. `I` is the type parameter and it is limited to the types listed in the bracket. The `|` pipe character acts as an `or` statement saying `I` can be an `int8` or an `int16` type, and so on.

Once `I` is defined, we can use it as a type in our arguments. Our function will operate on a slice type of `I`. It should be noted that all values in `I` must be the same type; it cannot be a mix of say `int8` and `int64` values.

Let's look at how that might work with a simple bubble-sort implementation, as follows:

```
func sortInts[I int8 |int16 |int32 |int64](slice []I) {
    sorted := false
    for !sorted {
        sorted = true
        for i := range slice[:len(slice)-1] {
            if slice[i] > slice[i+1] {
```

```
                    sorted = false
                    slice[i], slice[i+1] = slice[i+1], slice[i]
                }
            }
        }
    }
}
```

You can see this example here: `https://go.dev/play/p/jly7i9hz0YT`.

We now have a function that can be used to sort any type of signed integer. If we were to do this without generics, it would require an argument of `interface{}` that would need to be type switched on the slice type. Then, we would need to write functions to handle each type. You can see an example of what that would look like here: `https://go.dev/play/p/lqVUk9GQFPX`.

The other option would be to use runtime reflection using the `reflect` package, which is slow and unwieldy. `reflect` is an advanced package that has lots of gotchas and should be avoided unless absolutely necessary. Here is an example of this method: `https://go.dev/play/p/3euBYL9dcsU`.

As you can see, the generic version is much simpler to implement and can significantly reduce your code base.

Let's have a look at how we could make this slightly easier to read using type constraints.

Using type constraints

In our last example, `int8 |int16 |int32 |int64` was our type constraint. It limited the types that we could use for our `I` value type parameter, but typing that all the time is burdensome, so we can also define named type constraints.

This is where the addition of generics is likely to create some confusion. Type constraints are made using the `interface` type. Here's an example of a type constraint containing what we had previously:

```
type SignedInt interface {
    int8 |int16 |int32 |int64
}
```

We can now use that in our previous code, as follows:

```
func sortInts[I SignedInt](slice []I) {
```

This reduces the amount of boilerplate we need. It is important to note that `SignedInt` is a type constraint and not a type. `I` is a defined type parameter that acts as a type. I've often found myself writing code like this:

```
func sortInts[I SignedInt](slice []SignedInt) {
```

However, that syntax is incorrect. `SignedInt` here is simply the definition of a constraint, not a type to be used. `I` is the type to be used in the generic function.

Another gotcha is that `SignedInt` can only be used on the exact basic types defined here. You might create your own type, like this:

```
type myInt8 int8
```

If you do so, you cannot use this as a `SignedInt` type constraint. But not to worry—if we want this to work on any type based on signed integers, we can change this to the following:

```
type SignedInt interface {
    ~int8 |~int16 |~int32 |~int64
}
```

~ signals that we want to allow any type based on this type.

Now, let's look at how we can write our sort function to handle more than just signed integers.

We could do better with constraints

What we are doing here can be applied to more than just signed integers. We could make changes to which types we support, and our function would work exactly the same on a larger set of slice types.

The only thing that a type must have for our function to work is that the type must be able to use > on two variables that share the same type. That is what allows the `if slice[i] > slice[i+1]` statement to work.

The current Go version, as of this writing, does not define a few basic type constraints that are planned for a future release. This future package, which will likely be called `constraints`, is being developed here: https://pkg.go.dev/golang.org/x/exp/constraints.

It includes a type constraint that looks like this:

```
type Ordered interface {
      ~int | ~int8 | ~int16 | ~int32 | ~int64 |
         ~uint | ~uint8 | ~uint16 | ~uint32 | ~uint64 |
~uintptr |
         ~float32 | ~float64 |
         ~string
}
```

We will borrow that here and change our function signature, as follows:

```
func sortSlice[O constraints.Ordered](slice[]O) {
```

Now, our function can sort any type of slice that can be compared using > <. See it at work here: https://go.dev/play/p/PwrXXLk5rOT.

Current built-in constraints

Go has two constraints that are currently built in, as follows:

- comparable
- any

comparable contains all types that support == or != operators. This is particularly useful when writing generics that use map types. The key to a map type is always the comparable type.

any is an alias for interface{}. The Go team has changed all references to interface{} in the Go standard library to any. You may use them interchangeably, and any as a type constraint allows any type.

Here is an example of a function that extracts all keys from a map type using these constraints:

```
func ExtractMapKeys[K comparable, V any](m map[K]V) []K {
    var keys = make([]K, 0, len(m))
    for k := range m {
```

```
            keys = append(keys, k)
    }
    return keys
}
```

Here it is running in the playground, so give it a try: https://go.dev/play/p/h8aKwoTaOLj.

Let's look at what happens if we do type constraining and we constrain a type such as a standard interface by requiring a method.

Type constraints with methods

A type constraint can act like a standard interface in that it can require methods to be attached to the type. Here is an example:

```
type StringPrinter interface {
    ~string
    Print()
}
```

This type constraint can only be satisfied by a type based on `string` and that has the `Print()` method defined.

A key requirement here is that we use `~string` and not `string`. A standard `string` type can never have the `Print()` method, and therefore this type constraint could never be satisfied.

Here is a simple use of this constraint:

```
func PrintStrings[S StringPrinter](slice []S) {
    for _, s := range slice {
        s.Print()
    }
}
```

Now, let's take a look at why you might want to add type parameters to struct types.

Adding type parameters to struct types

Earlier, we wrote a generic function for sorting slices called `SortSlice()`, but that has some limitations in that it can only handle slices that are based on types that meet the constraints in `constraints.Ordered`. Oftentimes, we might want to handle slices that might contain types based on `struct`—say, for example, this type:

```
type Record struct {
    First, Last string
}
```

Our `SortSlice()` function could not handle a `[]Record`, so we need to do something different to handle these types of cases.

For this example, we want to use Go's built-in `sort.Sort()` function. This is a highly optimized sort that uses multiple sorting algorithms, depending on slice size.

To use it, you need a type that implements the `sort.Interface` type. That `interface` type is defined as follows:

```
type Interface interface {
    Len() int
    Less(i, j int) bool
    Swap(i, j int)
}
```

Before Go generics, you would have needed to implement an adapter type to implement these for every type you wanted to sort. For example, here is an adapter to sort `[]int`:

```
type intAdapter struct {
    sl []int
}

func (in intAdapter) Len() int {
    return len(in.sl)
}

func (in intAdapter) Swap(i, j int) {
    in.sl[i], in.sl[j] = in.sl[j], in.sl[i]
}
func (in intAdapter) Less(i, j int) bool {
    return in.sl[i] < in.sl[j]
}
```

And you could use it like so:

```
ints := []int{5, 3, 7, 1}
sort.Sort(intAdapter{ints})
```

You can see that running here: https://go.dev/play/p/Yl6Al9ylEhd.

You would then need to do this for every other signed type or other types you wanted to sort. Imagine doing this for all `int8`, `int16`, `int32`, and `int64` signed integer types. You would also need to do that for every other type you want to sort.

So, what we want to do is use generics to give us a single adapter type that can be used for a slice with any element type.

Let's use a `type` parameter on a struct to allow us to create a generic adapter so that we can adapt any slice to the `sort.Interface` type, as follows:

```
type sortableSlice[T any] struct {
    slice []T
    less func(T, T) bool
}

func (s sortableSlice[T]) Len() int {
    return len(s.slice)
}

func (s sortableSlice[T]) Swap(i, j int) {
    s.slice[i], s.slice[j] = s.slice[j], s.slice[i]
}

func (s sortableSlice[T]) Less(i, j int) bool {
    return s.less(s.slice[i], s.slice[j])
}
```

This is very similar to `intAdapter` from before, with two distinctions, as follows:

- The slice elements are a `T` type parameter that can be any value
- We added a `less` field, which is a function that does the comparison when `Less()` is called

Let's create a function that can implement `func(T, T) bool` for our `Record` type. This compares the full name with the last name being considered first. The code is illustrated in the following snippet:

```
func recordLess(a, b Record) bool {
    aCmp := a.Last + a.First
    bCmp := b.Last + b.First

    return aCmp < bCmp
}
```

Finally, we can use `sortableSlice` to write a generic sort function that uses the existing `sort.Sort()` function to sort any slice that we can do comparisons on. Here's the code we need to execute:

```
func SortSlice[T any](slice []T, less func(T, T) bool) {
    sort.Sort(sortableSlice[T]{slice: slice, less: less})
}
```

Here is this in action: https://go.dev/play/p/6Gd7DLgVQ_y.

You will notice that when we create our `sortableSlice` instance, we have `[T]` in the syntax. This is used to tell Go what type `T` will be, which in this case is the generic `T` type passed in `SortSlice`. If you try to remove `[T]`, you will get the following message:

```
cannot use generic type sortableSlice[T any] without
instantiation
```

We will talk about this in our next section.

Of course, if you want to do a generic sort without using the `sort.Sort()` function, this can be done with less complication. Here is a generic version of the quicksort algorithm that uses generics: https://go.dev/play/p/gvPl9jHtAS4.

Now, we will look at calling a generic function when Go cannot infer a type for the generic function to use.

Specifying the type when calling a generic function

So far, all the generic cases up until the `sortableSlice` function have allowed the Go compiler to infer which type would be used and therefore how to deal with invoking the function.

But Go cannot always infer which type it needs to use. We can see in our last section where we told `sortableSlice` it would be using the `T` generic type we defined.

Let's create a function that can be used with `SortSlice()` to do our less comparison whenever the types are of type `constraints.Ordered`. The code is illustrated in the following snippet:

```go
func orderedCmp[O constraints.Ordered](a O, b O) bool {
    return a < b
}
```

With this, we can call `SortSlice()` and pass in any slice of types contained in `constraints.Ordered` and our new `orderedCmp` generic function to sort a slice.

Let's give it a try, as follows:

```go
strings := []string{"hello", "I", "must", "be", "going"}
SortSlice(strings, orderedCmp)
```

Uh oh—Go can't seem to get that to work, as we receive the following message:

cannot use generic function orderedCmp without instantiation

This is because we are passing the function and not invoking the function. Go's inference only currently happens by looking at the call types it receives. It doesn't infer inside `SortSlice()` where `orderedCmp()` will be called and passed a `string` type. So, to use it, we need to tell it which type it will be working on when it is called.

In contrast, `SortSlice()` doesn't require this because it is being invoked directly and can infer that `T` will be a `string` type from looking at the passed argument, `strings`.

By using `[string]`, we can give `orderedCmp` a little more information for this to work, as follows:

```go
SortSlice(strings, orderedCmp[string])
```

Now that it knows that we will be comparing `string` types, it is ready to rock and roll, as you can see here: https://go.dev/play/p/kd6sy1V17Jz.

If we wanted to be very verbose, we could do the following:

```go
SortSlice[string](strings, orderedCmp[string])
```

Now, let's take a look at some common gotchas you might run into when trying to use generics.

Gotchas to watch for

When you are playing with generics, there are a lot of gotchas where the error messages are not yet clear. So, let's talk about some of them so that you can avoid the mistakes that I've made.

First up, impossible type constraints. See if you can spot the problem in the following code:

```
type Values interface {
    int8 | int16 | int32 |int64
    string | []byte
}
func Print[V Values](v V) {
    fmt.Println(v)
}
func main() {
    Print[string]("hello")
}
```

If you were to run this, you would get the following:

```
cannot implement Values (empty type set)
```

This is because `Values` is incorrectly defined. I forgot to put `|` after `int64`. Without that, the constraint says the value must be `int8` or `int16` or `int32` or `int64` **AND** a `string` or `[]byte` type. That is an impossible type, which means nothing can implement it. You can see this here: https://go.dev/play/p/Nxsz4HKxdc4.

The next gotcha is instantiation when returning `struct` types that implement type parameters. Here's an example of this:

```
type ValueType interface {
    string | bool | int
}

type Value[T ValueType] struct {
    val T
}

func New[T ValueType](v T) Value {
    return Value[T]{val: v}
}
func (v Value[T]) Value() T {
```

```
        return v.val
}
```

An attempt to compile this code will give you the following message:

```
cannot use generic type Value[T ValueType] without
instantiation
```

It was not clear to me what the problem was here for a while. It turns out that I needed to add the `type` parameter on the return value as well. Here is the change:

```
func New[T ValueType](v T) Value[T] {
```

With this change, everything works fine. Try the broken version (https://go.dev/play/p/EGTr2zd7qZW) and fix it with the aforementioned change to familiarize yourself.

I expect that we will see better error messages and better detection in our development tools in the near future.

Now that we have covered the basics of generics, let's talk about when you should consider using generics.

When to use generics

The only guideline at this time is taken from the creator of Go's generics feature, Ian Taylor, as presented here:

"If you find yourself writing the exact same code multiple times where the only difference between the copies is that the code uses different types, consider whether you can use a type parameter."

I have found this translates to the following:

If your function needs a switch statement on the generic type, you should probably be using standard interfaces instead of generics.

To close out on generics, I would leave you with the thought that this is a new language feature, and the jury is still out on the best ways for this to be used. The best advice I can give is to be reserved in your use of this feature.

Summary

In this chapter, you have learned the essential parts of the **Go** language. This has included handling errors, using Go concurrency, taking advantage of Go's testing framework, and an introduction to Go's newest feature, generics. The skills acquired in this chapter are essential for all future chapters.

You should now possess the ability to read Go code contained in the rest of the book. In addition, this chapter has given you the necessary skills to write your own Go code. We will use these skills to manipulate files in the filesystem, execute commands on remote machines, and build RPC services that can do a myriad of tasks. You will build chatbots in order to do **chat-based operations** (**ChatOps**) and write software to extend Kubernetes. The learnings here are truly foundational.

Next, we will look at how to setup your Go environment to compile code locally on your machine. Let's get started!

3
Setting Up Your Environment

In this chapter, we are going to talk about setting up your **Go** environment for use in *our future chapters* and for developing your own Go software in the future.

We're going to cover the following main topics:

- Installing Go on your machine
- Building code locally

Before we begin, let's have a brief walk-through of the technical requirements you need to be aware of before reading on.

Technical requirements

The only technical requirements for this chapter are as follows:

- A computer with an OS supported by the Go tools
- An internet connection and web browser to download the Go tools

Installing Go on your machine

The **Go compiler** and toolset can be found at `https://golang.org/dl/`. Here, you will find releases for the macOS, Windows, and Linux platforms for a multitude of computing platforms.

The most common platform is the **AMD64** architecture, which should be used for any x86 system. For macOS, it is important to note that if you are using a machine with a non-Intel-based CPU, such as an Apple M1, you will want to use the **arm64 builds**.

In the next sections, we will describe methods of installing Go for the major OSs. You should skip to the OS you plan to install on.

macOS installation using the package installer

The easiest way to install the Go tooling for macOS is to use a `.pkg` installer. The download page offers `.tar.gz` builds and `.pkg`. With the tarballs, you must unpack the files in a location and add that location to your path. It also means you will have to manually handle upgrades. You should only do this if you have advanced needs.

The `.pkg` file makes installation and upgrading simple. Simply double-click the `.pkg` file and follow the onscreen prompts to install. This may require entering in your credentials at a prompt.

Once installation is finished, open the `Applications/Utilities/terminal.app` terminal and type `go version`, which should yield something similar to the following:

```
$ go version
go version go1.17.5 linux/amd64
```

Note that the **version output** will depend on the version of Go that you have downloaded and the platform you are running on.

macOS installation via Homebrew

Many developers on macOS prefer to use the popular **Homebrew** (`https://brew.sh`) to install Go. If you are a Homebrew user, there is a simple two-step process for installing Go, as explained in the following sections.

Installing Xcode

Go has some reliance on Apple's **Xcode**, and it needs to be installed in order to work correctly. To see whether you have Xcode installed, type the following:

```
$ xcode-select -p
```

This should output something like this:

```
$ /Library/Developer/CommandLineTools
```

If it gives an error, you need to install Xcode by following this link on the App Store: https://itunes.apple.com/us/app/xcode/id497799835?mt=12&ign-mpt=uo%3D2.

Once installed, you can install the separate command-line tools with the following:

```
$ xcode-select --install
```

Now, let's look at the next step.

Homebrew update and Go installation

Update Homebrew and install the latest Go tools with the following:

```
$ brew update
$ brew install golang
```

You can verify the Go version with `$ go version`.

Next, we will look at installation on Windows.

Windows installation using MSI

Windows installation is similar to other Windows application installations using a **Microsoft Installer** (**MSI**) file. Simply download the MSI file and follow the onscreen instructions. By default, this will install the Go tooling at **Program Files** or **Program Files (x86)**.

To verify that Go was installed correctly, click the *Start* menu, type `cmd` into the search box, and the Command Prompt shell should appear. Type `go version`, and it should display the installed version of Go.

Next, we will look at installation on Linux.

Linux

Linux package management could be the subject of its own series of books and, as Linus points out, it is one of the reasons why Linux as a desktop system has failed so spectacularly.

If you are using Linux for development, chances are you have some knowledge on how to install packages for your distribution. As we can't cover all possible methods of installation on Linux, we are going to cover installation using `apt`, Snap, and via `tarball`.

Linux installation via APT on Ubuntu

APT is a package installation manager used in various distributions. Installing Go via APT is pretty straightforward.

Update and upgrade APT to the latest version, as follows:

```
$ sudo apt update
$ sudo apt upgrade
```

Install the Go package as follows:

```
sudo apt install golang-go
```

Now, type `go version` into the terminal, and it should display the installed version of Go.

Linux installation via Snap on Ubuntu

Snap is a universal package manager meant to make the installation of a package easy across multiple distributions or versions by including all the necessary files in the package.

If you have Snap installed, you can simply use `snap info go` to locate a version of Go to install:

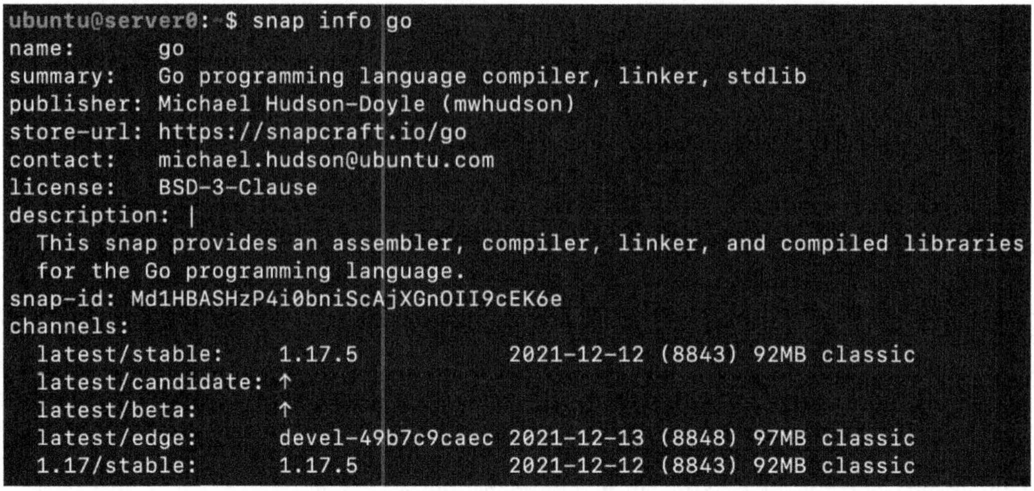

```
ubuntu@server0:~$ snap info go
name:      go
summary:   Go programming language compiler, linker, stdlib
publisher: Michael Hudson-Doyle (mwhudson)
store-url: https://snapcraft.io/go
contact:   michael.hudson@ubuntu.com
license:   BSD-3-Clause
description: |
  This snap provides an assembler, compiler, linker, and compiled libraries
  for the Go programming language.
snap-id: Md1HBASHzP4i0bniScAjXGnOII9cEK6e
channels:
  latest/stable:    1.17.5              2021-12-12 (8843) 92MB classic
  latest/candidate: ↑
  latest/beta:      ↑
  latest/edge:      devel-49b7c9caec 2021-12-13 (8848) 97MB classic
  1.17/stable:      1.17.5              2021-12-12 (8843) 92MB classic
```

Figure 3.1 – Screenshot showing the snap info go command output

You can choose to install the latest stable version of Go by typing the following:

```
sudo snap install go
```

Now, type `go version` into the terminal, and it should display the installed version of Go.

Note that you may receive a warning about the Go package being built on a revision of Snap with classic confinement. In that case, to install using Snap, you may need to append `--classic` as follows:

```
sudo snap install go --classic
```

Linux installation via tarball

In order to do this, you need to download the package for Linux and your platform. Our example will use `go1.16.5.linux-amd64.tar.gz`. You will notice that the name gives the Go version (*1.16.5*), the OS (Linux), and the architecture (*AMD64*). You will need to download the current version of Go and your architecture into a directory.

The rest of these instructions will use the terminal.

We want to install our version into `/usr/local/go` and remove any previous installation. This can be achieved with the following:

```
rm -rf /usr/local/go && tar -C /usr/local -xzf go1.16.5.linux-amd64.tar.gz
```

Now, let's add our directory to our `PATH` so that we can find our Go tools. This can be accomplished with the following:

```
export PATH=$PATH:/usr/local/go/bin
```

With most shells, this change will not happen immediately. The easiest way to cause `PATH` to update is simply to open a new shell. You may also use the `source` command to reload your shell's profile if you know the name/location of your shell's profile – `source $HOME/.profile`, for example.

To test if your `PATH` was updated correctly, type `go version`, which should yield the following:

```
$ go version
go version go1.16.5 linux/amd64
```

What about installing Go on other platforms?

Other platforms

Go can certainly be installed on other platforms, such as **FreeBSD**, but those are not covered here. See the Go *installation documentation* for these other platforms.

A note on Go compiler version compatibility

The Go project is governed by the Go compatibility promise: `https://golang.org/doc/go1compat`. The gist is that Go will be backward compatible unless there is a major semantic version number change (**1.x.x** to **2.x.x**). While you might hear people talk about Go 2.0, the authors have been very clear that they have no plans to leave version 1.

This means software written for **Go 1.0.0** works in the latest **Go 1.17.5** version. This has been a major win for the Go community in stability. This book will be using Go 1.17.5 for its revision.

By the end of this section, you should have installed the Go tooling and tested that the tooling is working for your OS of choice. In the next section, we will discuss how to build code on your machine.

Building code locally

The current Go ecosystem (Go 1.13 onward) and toolchain allow you to write Go code from any location in the filesystem. Most users choose to set up a local Git repository for their package(s) and develop within that directory.

This is accomplished using Go modules that the Go team describes as *"a collection of Go packages stored in a file tree with a go.mod file at its root."* A Go module most often represents a GitHub repository, such as `github.com/user/repository`.

Most Go developers will use the command line to move around the filesystem environment and for interacting with the Go toolchain. In this section, we will concentrate on using Unix commands for accessing the filesystem and using Go compiler tools. The Go compiler commands will be the same between each OS, but filesystem commands may not be, and the file paths may also differ, such as Windows using \ instead of / as path separators.

Creating a module directory and go.mod file

The directory can be anywhere on the filesystem you have access. `godev/` is a good directory name to use, and putting it in your home directory, which is OS-dependent, is a logical place to make it easy to find.

Within that directory, I will create a new directory for my package. For this example, I will create a directory called `hello/` that will represent my Go module:

```
$ cd ~
$ mkdir -p ~/godev/hello
$ cd ~/godev/hello
```

To create our module, we simply need to create a `go.mod` file that contains our module name. Module names are typically the Git path, such as `github.com/johnsiilver/fs`.

If you have a GitHub repository that you wish to store this example in, you can substitute it in our command:

```
$ go mod init example.com/hello
go: creating new go.mod: module example.com/hello
```

This `go.mod` file will contain a few key sections worth noting:

```
module example.com/hello
go 1.17
```

The first line defines our module, which is the path to the root of the Git repository. The second defines the minimum version of Go that can be used to compile this module. Depending on what features you use, your module may be compatible with previous versions of Go, and you can modify this to have a lower version number.

While this example will not have any third-party packages, it is worth noting that most `go.mod` files will have a *require* section that lists packages and their versions that your module imports.

Updating a module when adding dependencies

When adding a third-party package, your `go.mod` file will need to be modified to contain the dependency information. This would be a tedious task, but Go has you covered with the `go mod tidy` command.

Running `go mod tidy` will look at all your package imports and add them to your `go.mod` file automatically. Remember to run this after adding any external dependencies.

Adding a hello world

To learn how to compile and run Go code, we are going to create a *hello world* application. In Go, all Go source files end with the `.go` extension.

Create a file in the directory called `hello.go` using your favorite text editor and insert the following code:

```go
package main

import "fmt"

func main() {
    fmt.Println("Hello World")
}
```

Next, let's run our first program.

Running our first program

Once you have that file saved, let's try compiling and running that code:

```
$ go run hello.go
Hello World
$
```

This compiled our source file and ran it as a binary. You may only use `go run` for a package called `main`.

If we want to create a binary for this OS and architecture, we can simply run the following:

```
$ go build hello.go  # Builds a program called hello
$ ./hello            # Executes the hello binary
Hello World
```

There is now a binary called `hello` that can be run on any OS/architecture of the same type. If our package was not called `main`, this would compile the package and emit any errors encountered, but it would not create a binary.

Summary

You have now created your first Go module, initialized your first `go.mod` file, created a Go program, run the Go program with `go run`, and built a Go executable for your OS. This chapter has left you with the necessary skills to create a basic Go module and the basic knowledge of the Go command-line tool required to both run a Go package and build a Go program. These are used every day in the life of a Go developer.

In the next chapter, we're going to cover the basics of the Go language, including how packages work, testing, and many more essentials.

4
Filesystem Interactions

A fundamental part of any developer's life is interacting with **files**. They represent data that must be processed and configured for our systems, cached items can be served, and many other uses.

One of Go's strongest features is its abstraction of **file interfaces**, which allows a common set of tools to interact with streams of data from disks and networks. These interfaces set a common standard that all major packages use to export their data streams. Moving from one to another just becomes an exercise in accessing the **filesystem** with the necessary credentials.

Packages related to specific data formats, such as CSV, JSON, YAML, TOML, and XML, build on these common file interfaces. These packages use the interfaces defined by the standard library to read these types of files from disk or HTTP streams.

Because Go is multiplatform, you may want to write software that can work on different OSs. Go provides packages that allow you to detect the OS and its packages to handle differences in OS pathing.

In this chapter, we are going to cover the following topics:

- All I/O in Go are files
- Reading and writing to files
- Streaming file content
- OS-agnostic pathing
- OS-agnostic filesystems

After completing this chapter, you should have a set of skills for interacting with data that's stored in a wide variety of mediums, which will be useful in your everyday life as a DevOps engineer.

All I/O in Go are files

Go provides an **input-output** (**I/O**) system based on files. This should come as no surprise since Go is the brainchild of two prominent engineers, Rob Pike and Ken Thompson, who, while at *Bell Labs*, designed the UNIX and Plan 9 operating systems – both of which treat (almost) everything as a file.

Go provides the `io` package, which contains interfaces to interact with I/O primitives such as disk files, remote files, and network services.

I/O interfaces

The basic block of I/O is `byte`, an 8-bit value. I/O uses streams of bytes to allow you to read and write. With some I/Os, you can only read from beginning to end as you process the stream (such as network I/O). Some I/Os, such as disks, allow you to *seek* something in the file.

Some common operations that we perform when we interact with a byte stream include reading, writing, seeking a location in a byte stream, and closing a stream when we have finished our work.

Go provides the following interfaces for these basic operations:

```
// Read from an I/O stream.
type Reader interface {
    Read(p []byte) (n int, err error)
}
// Write to an I/O stream.
```

```
type Writer interface {
    Write(p []byte) (n int, err error)
}
// Seek to a certain spot in the I/O stream.
type Seeker interface {
    Seek(offset int64, whence int) (int64, error)
}
// Close the I/O stream.
type Closer interface {
    Close() error
}
```

The `io` package also contains composite interfaces such as `ReadWriter` and `ReadWriteCloser`. These interfaces are common in packages that allow you to interact with files or networks. These interfaces allow you to use common tooling that uses these interfaces, regardless of what is underneath (such as a local filesystem, remote filesystem, or an HTTP connection).

In this section, we have learned that Go file interaction is based on the `[]byte` type and introduced the basic interfaces for I/O. Next, we will learn about reading and writing files using methods that utilize these interfaces.

Reading and writing to files

The most common scenario in DevOps tooling is the need to manipulate files: *reading*, *writing*, *reformatting*, or *analyzing* the data in those files. These files could be in many formats – JSON, YAML, XML, CSV, and others that are probably familiar to you. They are used to configure both local services and to interact with your cloud network provider.

In this section, we will cover the basics of reading and writing entire files.

Reading local files

Let's start by reading a configuration file on a local disk by using the `os.Readfile()` function:

```
data, err := os.ReadFile("path/to/file")
```

The `ReadFile()` method reads the location from its function parameter and returns that file's content. That return value is then stored in the data variable. An error is returned if the file cannot be read. For a refresher on errors, see the *Handling errors in Go* section in *Chapter 2, Go Language Essentials*.

`ReadFile()` is a helper function that calls `os.Open()` and retrieves an `io.Reader`. The `io.ReadAll()` function is used to read the entire content of `io.Reader`.

`data` is of the `[]byte` type, so if you would like to use it as a `string`, you can simply convert it into one by using `s := string(data)`. This is called *type conversion*, where we convert from one type into another. In Go, you can only convert certain types from one into another. The full list of conversion rules can be found at https://golang.org/ref/spec#Conversions. strings can be converted back into bytes with `b := []byte(s)`. Most other types require a package called `strconv` to be converted into strings (https://pkg.go.dev/strconv).

If the data that's represented in the file is of a common format such as JSON or YAML, then we can retrieve and write that data efficiently.

Writing local files

The most common way to write to local disk is by using `os.Writefile()`. This writes a complete file to disk. `WriteFile` will create the file if necessary and truncate the file if it exists:

```
if err := os.WriteFile("path/to/fi", data, 0644); err != nil {
    return err
}
```

The preceding code writes data to `path/to/fi` with Unix-like permissions, `0644`. If you have not seen Unix-like permissions before, a quick internet search will help you with these.

If your data is stored in a `string`, you can simply convert it into `[]byte` by doing `[]byte(data)`. `WriteFile()` is a wrapper around `os.OpenFile()` that handles file flags and modes for you while closing the file after the write is complete.

Reading remote files

The way the remote file is read is going to be implementation-dependent. However, these concepts will still be built on the `io` interfaces we discussed earlier.

For example, let's say that we want to connect to a text file that is stored on an HTTP server, to collect common text-formatted information such as application metrics. We can connect to that server and retrieve the file in a way that's very similar to what was shown in the preceding example:

```
client := &http.Client{}
req, err := http.NewRequest("GET", "http://myserver.mydomain/myfile", nil)
if err != nil {
        return err
}
req = req.WithContext(ctx)

resp, err := client.Do(req)
cancel()
if err != nil {
        return err
}

// resp contains an io.ReadCloser that we can read as a file.
// Let's use io.ReadAll() to read the entire content to data.
data, err := io.ReadAll(resp.Body)
```

As you can see, the setup to get our `io.ReadCloser` depends on our I/O target, but what it returns is just an interface from the `io` package that we can use with any function that supports those interfaces.

Because it uses `io` interfaces, we can do slick things such as stream the content directly to a local file instead of copying the entire file into memory and writing it to disk. This is faster and more memory efficient as each chunk that is read is then immediately written to disk.

Let's use `os.OpenFile()` to open a file for writing and stream the content from the web server into the file:

```
flags := os.O_CREATE|os.O_WRONLY|os.O_TRUNC
f, err := os.OpenFile("path/to/file", flags, 0644)
if err != nil {
    return err
}
defer f.Close()

if err := io.Copy(f, resp.Body); err != nil {
    return err
}
```

`OpenFile()` is the more complex method of opening a file when you need to either write to a file or be more specific with how you interact with it. You should use `os.Open()` when you just want to read from a local file. Our flags here are the standard Unix-like bitmasks that do the following:

- Create the file if it doesn't exist: `os.O_CREATE`.
- Write to a file: `os.O_WRONLY`.
- If the file exists, truncate it versus append to it: `os.O_TRUNC`.

A list of flags can be found here: `https://pkg.go.dev/os#pkg-constants`.

`io.Copy()` reads from `io.Reader` and writes to `io.Writer` until `Reader` is empty. This copies the file from the HTTP server to the local disk.

In this section, you learned how to read an entire file using `os.ReadFile()`, how to type convert a `[]byte` into a `string`, and how to write an entire file to disk using `os.WriteFile()`. We also learned about the differences between `os.Open()` and `os.OpenFile()` and showed you how to use utility functions such as `io.Copy()` and `io.ReadAll()`. Finally, we learned how HTTP clients expose their data streams as `io` interfaces that can be read using these same tools.

Next, we will look at interacting with these file interfaces as streams instead of reading and writing entire files.

Streaming file content

In the previous sections, we learned how to read and write in large blocks using `os.ReadFile()` and `os.WriteFile()`.

This works well when the files are small, which is usually the case when you're doing DevOps automation. However, sometimes, the files we want to read are very large – in most cases, you wouldn't want to read a 2 GiB file into memory. In those cases, we want to stream the contents of the file in manageable chunks that we can operate on while keeping memory usage low.

The most basic version of this was shown in the previous section. There, we used two streams to copy a file: `io.ReadCloser` from the HTTP client and `io.WriteCloser` for writing to local disk. We used the `io.Copy()` function to copy from the network file to the disk file.

Go's `io` interfaces also allow us to stream files to copy content, search for content, manipulate input to output, and more.

Stdin/Stdout/Stderr are just files

Throughout this book, you will see us writing to the console using `fmt.Println()` or `fmt.Printf()`, two functions from the `fmt` package. Those functions are reading and writing to files that represent the terminal.

Those functions use an `io.Writer` called `os.Stdout`. When we use the same functions in the `log` package, we are usually writing to `os.Stderr`.

You can use the same interfaces we've been using to read/write to other files to also read/write to these files. When we want to copy a file and output its content to the terminal, we can do the following:

```
f, err := os.Open("path/to/file")
if err != nil {
    return err
}
if err := io.Copy(os.Stdout, f); err != nil {
    return err
}
```

While we won't go into the details, `os.Stdin` is simply an `io.Reader`. You can read from it using the `io` and `bufio` packages.

Reading data out of a stream

What if we wanted to read a stream that represented user records and return them on a channel?

Let's say the records are simple `<user>:<id>` text and each record was delimited by the new line character (\n). These records might be stored on an HTTP server or a local disk. This doesn't matter to us because it is simply a stream behind an interface. Let's assume that we receive this as an `io.Reader`.

First, we will define a `User` struct:

```
type User struct{
  Name string
   ID int
}
```

Next, let's define a function that can split a line we receive:

```
func getUser(s string) (User, error) {
    sp := strings.Split(s, ":")
    if len(sp) != 2 {
        return User{}, fmt.Errorf("record(%s) was not in the correct format", s)
    }

   id, err := strconv.Atoi(sp[1])
    if err != nil {
        return User{}, fmt.Errorf("record(%s) had non-numeric ID", s)
    }
    return User{Name: strings.TrimSpace(sp[0]), ID: id}, nil
}
```

`getUser()` takes a string and returns a `User`. We use the `strings` package's `Split()` function to split the string into a `[]string` while using `:` as the divider.

`Split()` should return two values; if not, then we return an error.

Since we are splitting a string, our user ID is stored as a `string`. But we want to use the integer value in our `User` record. Here, we can use the `strconv` package's `Atoi()` method to convert the string version of the number into an integer. If it is not an integer, then the entry is bad, and we return an error.

Now, let's create a function that reads in the stream and writes the `User` records to a channel:

```
func decodeUsers(ctx context.Context, r io.Reader) chan User {
    ch := make(chan User, 1)
    go func() {
        defer close(ch)
        scanner := bufio.NewScanner(r)
        for scanner.Scan() {
            if ctx.Err() != nil {
                ch <- User{err: ctx.Err()}
                return
            }
            u, err := getUser(scanner.Text())
            if err != nil {
                u.err = err
                ch <- u
                return
            }
            ch <- u
        }
    }()
    return ch
}
```

Here, we are using the `bufio` package's `Scanner` type. `Scanner` allows us to take an `io.Reader` and scan it until we find a delimiter. By default, this is \n, though you can change this using the `.Split()` method. `Scan()` will return `true` until we reach the end of the Reader's output. Note that `io.Reader` returns an error, `io.EOF`, when it reaches the end of the stream.

After each `Scan()` call, the scanner stores the bytes read, which you can retrieve as a string using `.Text()`. The content in `.Text()` changes each time `.Scan()` is called. Also, note that we check our `Context` object and stop its execution if it's canceled.

We pass the content of that `string` to our previously defined `getUser()`. If we receive an `error`, we return it in the `User` record to inform the caller of the error. Otherwise, we return our `User` record with all the information.

Now, let's invoke this against a file:

```
f, err := os.Open("path/to/file/with/users")
if err != nil {
    return err
}
defer f.Close()
for user := range decodeUsers(ctx, f) {
    if user.err != nil {
        fmt.Println("Error: ", user.err)
        return err
    }
    fmt.Println(user)
}
```

Here, we open our file on disk and pass it to `decodeUsers()`. We receive a `User` record from the *output channel* and we print the user to the screen concurrently while reading the file stream.

Instead of using `os.Open()`, we could have opened the file via `http.Client` and passed it to `decodeUsers()`. The complete code can be found here: `https://play.golang.org/p/OxehTsHT6Qj`.

Writing data into a stream

Writing to a stream is even simpler – we just convert our `User` into a `string` and write it to an `io.Writer`. This looks as follows:

```
func writeUser(ctx context.Context, w io.Writer, u User) error {
    if ctx.Err() != nil {
        return ctx.Err()
    }
    if _, err := w.Write([]byte(user.String())); err != nil {
        return err
    }
    return nil
}
```

Here, we have taken in an `io.Writer` that represents the place to write to and a `User` record that we want to write into that output. We can use this to write to a file on disk:

```
f, err := os.OpenFile("file", flags, 0644); err != nil{
    return err
}
defer f.Close()

for i, u := range users {
    // Write a carriage return before the next entry, except
    // the first entry.
    if i != 0 {
        if err := w.Write([]byte("\n")); err != nil {
            return err
        }
    }
    if err := writeUser(ctx, w, u); err != nil {
        return err
    }
}
```

Here, we opened a file on our local disk. When our containing function (not shown) returns, the file will be closed. Then, we wrote the `User` records stored in variable users (`[]Users`) one at a time to the file. Finally, we wrote a carriage return, (`"\n"`), before every record except the first one.

You can see this in action here: https://play.golang.org/p/bxuFyPT5nSk. We have provided a streaming version of this using channels that you can find here: https://play.golang.org/p/njuE1n7dyOM.

In the next section, we'll learn how to use the `path/filepath` package to write software that works on multiple OSs that use different path delimiters.

OS-agnostic pathing

One of Go's greatest strengths lies in its multiplatform support. A developer can develop on a Linux workstation and run the same Go program, recompiled into native code, on a Windows server.

One of the areas of difficulty when developing software that runs on multiple OSs is *accessing files*. Path formats are slightly different for each operating system. The most obvious example is the different file separators for OSs: \ on Windows and / on Unix-like systems. Less obvious would be how to escape special characters on a particular OS, which can differ even between Unix-based OSs.

The path/filepath package provides access to functions that will allow you to handle pathing for the native OS. This should not be confused with the root path package, which looks similar but handles a more general URL-style pathing.

What OS/platform am I running?

While we will discuss how to gain file access and perform pathing using agnostic functions, it is still important to understand what OS you are running on. You may use different locations for files based on the OS you are running.

Using the runtime package, you can detect the OS and platform you are running on:

```
fmt.Println(runtime.GOOS)   // linux, darwin, ...
fmt.Println(runtime.GOARCH) // amd64, arm64, ...
```

This gives you the running OS. We can print out the current list of OS types and hardware architecture that's supported by Go with **go tool dist list**.

Using filepath

With **filepath**, you can be ignorant of the pathing rules for the OS you are running on when manipulating a path. Paths are divided into the following areas:

- The **directories** in the path
- The **file** in the path

A file path's final directory or file is called the **base**. The path your binary is running in is called the **working directory**.

Joining a file path

Let's say we want to access a configuration file, config.json, that is stored in the config/ directory, which is in the same directory as our binary. Let's use os and path/filepath to read that file in a way that works on all OSs:

```
wd, err := os.Getwd()
if err != nil {
    return err
```

```
}
content, err := os.ReadFile(filepath.Join(wd, "config",
"config.json"))
```

In this example, the first thing we do is get the working directory. This allows us to make calls relative to where our binary is running.

`filepath.Join()` allows us to join the components of our path into a single path. This fills in the OS-specific directory separators for you and uses the native pathing rules. On a Unix-like system, this might be `/home/jdoak/bin/config/config.json`, while on Windows, this might be `C:\Documents and Settings\jdoak\go\bin\config\config.json`.

Splitting a file path

In some circumstances, it is important to split filepaths along their path separators in different ways. `filepath` provides the following:

- `Base()`: Returns the last element of the path
- `Ext()`: Returns the file extension, if it has one
- `Split()`: Returns the split directory and file

We can use these to get various parts of a path. This can be useful when we wish to copy a file into another directory while retaining the file's name.

Let's copy a file from its location to our OS's **TMPDIR**:

```
fileName := filepath.Base(fp)
if fileName == "." {
    // Path is empty
    return nil
}

newPath := filepath.Join(os.TempDir(), fileName)

r, err := os.Open(fp)
if err != nil {
    return err
}
defer r.Close()

w, err := os.OpenFile(newPath, O_WRONLY | O_CREATE, 0644)
if err != nil {
```

```
        return err
}
defer w.Close()
// Copies the file to the temporary file.
_, err := io.Copy(w, r)
return err
```

Now, it's time to look at the different pathing options you can use to reference files and how the `filepath` package can help.

Relative and absolute pathing

There are two types of pathing when it comes to accessing a filesystem:

- **Absolute pathing**: Pathing from the root directory to the file
- **Relative pathing**: Pathing from your current location in the filesystem

During development, it is often handy to convert a relative path into an absolute path and vice versa.

`filepath` provides a few functions to help with this:

- `Abs()`: Returns the absolute path. If it's not an absolute path, return the working directory, as well as the path.
- `Rel()`: Returns the relative path of a path to a base.

We will leave it as an exercise for you to experiment with using these.

In this section, we learned how to use the `path/filepath` and `runtime` packages to handle file pathing for different OSs. We introduced `runtime.GOOS` to help you detect the OS your user is using and `os.Getwd()` to determine where in the filesystem your program is. `os.TempDir()` was introduced to locate your OS's location for temporary files. Finally, we learned about the functions in `path/filepath` that allow you to combine and split file paths agnostically to you but with an output specific to the OS.

Next, we will look at Go's new `io/fs` package, which was introduced in version 1.16. It introduces new interfaces to abstract filesystems in the same way `io` does for files.

OS-agnostic filesystems

One of the newest and more exciting developments in the latest Go releases is the new `io/fs` and `embed` packages, which were introduced in **Go 1.16**.

While we have shown agnostic access to our local filesystem via the `os` package, as well as agnostic file pathing manipulation through `filepath`, we haven't seen an agnostic way of accessing an entire filesystem.

In the cloud era, files are just as likely to be in filesystems that exist in remote data centers such as Microsoft Azure's Blob Storage, Google Cloud's Filestore, or Amazon AWS's EFS as they are on local disk.

Each of these filesystems comes with a client for accessing the files in Go, but they are specific to that network service. We can't treat each of these in the same way as I treat my local filesystem. `io/fs` is meant to provide a foundation to help solve this problem.

Another problem is that many files must be packaged with that binary, often in a container definition. Those files do not change during the lifetime of the program. It would be easier to include them in the binary and access them with a filesystem interface. A simple web application that needs image, HTML, and CSS files is a good example of this use case. The new `embed` package aims to fix this issue.

io.fs filesystems

Our new `io/fs` filesystem exports interfaces that can be implemented by filesystem providers. The root interface, `FS`, has the simplest definition:

```
type FS interface {
    Open(name string) (File, error)
}
```

This lets you open any file, where `File` is defined as follows:

```
type File interface {
    Stat() (FileInfo, error)
    Read([]byte) (int, error)
    Close() error
}
```

This provides the simplest of filesystems. You can open a file at a path and either get information about the file or read it. As filesystems tend to differ in functionality, this is the only shared functionality between all the given filesystems.

A **filesystem** can have other capabilities, all of which are defined as supersets of `FS` (such as `ReadDirFS` and `StatFS`) to allow for file walking and to provide directory information. There is a noticeable lack of writability for FS objects. You must provide your own since the Go authors haven't defined one as part of the standard library.

embed

The `embed` package allows you to embed files directly into the binary using a `//go:embed` directive.

`embed` can embed files in three ways, as follows:

- As bytes
- As a string
- Into an `embed.FS` (which implements `fs.FS`)

The first two are done by putting a directive over the specific variable type:

```
import _ "embed"

//go:embed hello.txt
var s string
//go:embed world.txt
var b []byte
```

`//go:embed hello.txt` represents a Go directive instructing the compiler to take a file called `hello.txt` and store it in variables.

`_` on the `import` line instructs the compiler to ignore the fact that we don't directly use `embed`. This is called an *anonymous import*, where we need a package to be loaded but don't use its functionality directly. Without `_`, we would receive a compile error for not using the imported package.

The final method of using `embed.FS` is useful when you wish to embed several files in the filesystem:

```
// The lines beginning with //go: are not comments, but
compiler directives
//go:embed image/*
//go:embed index.html
var content embed.FS
```

We now have an `fs.FS` that's storing all the files in our `image` directory and our `index.html` file. These files no longer need to be included in a container filesystem when we ship our binary.

Walking our filesystem

The `io/fs` package offers a filesystem-agnostic method of walking a filesystem *if the filesystem supports that capability*. In the previous example, we had a directory in our embedded filesystem holding image files. We can print out any `.jpg` files using a directory walker:

```
err := fs.WalkDir(
    content,
    ".",
    func(path string, d fs.DirEntry, err error) error {
        if err != nil {
            return err
        }
        if !d.IsDir() && filepath.Ext(path) == ".jpg" {
            fmt.Println("jpeg file: ", path)
        }
        return nil
    },
)
```

The preceding function walks the directory structure of our embedded filesystem (content) from the root (".") and calls the function that was defined, passing it the path of the file, its directory entry, and an error, if there was one.

In our function, we simply print the path of the file if the file is not a directory and has the `.jpg` extension.

But what about packages that are using `io/fs` to access other types of filesystems?

The io/fs future

At the time of writing, the major user of `io/fs` is `embed`. However, we are starting to see third-party packages implementing this interface.

`absfs` provides an `io.FS` hook for their `boltfs/memfs/os` filesystem packages (https://github.com/absfs). Several of these packages have wrappers around the popular `afero` filesystem package (https://github.com/spf13/afero). Azure has a non-official package that supports Blob storage (https://github.com/element-of-surprise/azfs).

There are also packages for accessing **Redis**, **GroupCache**, **memfs**, local filesystems, and tooling support at `https://github.com/gopherfs/fs`.

> **Note**
> `github.com/element-of-surprise` and `https://github.com/gopherfs` are owned by the author.

In this section, you learned about Go's `io/fs` package and how it is becoming a standard for interacting with filesystems. You also learned how to use the `embed` package to embed files into a binary and access them via the `io/fs` interfaces.

We've only scratched the surface

I highly encourage you to read the standard library's **GoDoc** pages to become familiar with its capabilities. The following are the GoDocs that were covered in this chapter. Here, you can find many useful utilities for dealing with files:

- File interfaces and basic I/O functions: `https://pkg.go.dev/io`
- Buffered I/O package: `https://pkg.go.dev/bufio`
- Converting to/from strings into other types: `https://pkg.go.dev/strconv`
- Package for manipulating strings: `https://pkg.go.dev/strings`
- Package for manipulating bytes: `https://pkg.go.dev/bytes`
- Package for OS interaction: `https://pkg.go.dev/os`
- Package for forward slash paths, like URLs: `https://pkg.go.dev/path`
- Package for file paths: `https://pkg.go.dev/path/filepath`
- Filesystem interfaces: `https://pkg.go.dev/io/fs`
- Embedded filesystem: `https://pkg.go.dev/embed`

In this section, we learned how to use `io` interfaces to stream data in and out of files, as well as about the `os` package's `Stdin`/`Stdout`/`Stderr` implementations for reading and writing to a program's input/output. We also learned how to read data by delimiter using the `bufio` package and how to split string content up using the `strings` package.

Summary

This chapter has provided you with a foundation for working with file I/O in the Go language. You learned about the `io` package and its file abstractions and how to read and write files to disk. Then, you learned how to stream file content so that you can work with the network and be more efficient with memory. After that, you learned about the `path/filepath` package, which can help you deal with multiple OSs. Finally, you learned about Go's filesystem-agnostic interfaces for interacting with any filesystem, starting with the new `embed` filesystem.

In the next chapter, you will learn how to interact with common data types and storage using popular Go packages. There, you will need to rely on the file and filesystem packages from this chapter to interact with data types.

Interacting with data and storage systems is critical to DevOps work. It allows us to read and change software configurations, store data and make it searchable, ask systems to do work on our behalf, and generate reporting.

So, let's dive in!

5
Using Common Data Formats

One of the key skills that a DevOps engineer requires is the ability to manipulate data across a variety of storage mediums.

In the last chapter, we interacted with the local filesystem to read and stream files. That is foundational for the skills we will be learning in this chapter.

This chapter will focus on how to manipulate common data formats that engineers commonly use. These formats are used to configure services, structure log data, and to export metrics, among the many other uses.

In this chapter, you will learn how to use **comma-separated values** (**CSV**) files to read and store data and encode/decode the popular JSON and YAML formats. You will discover how Go uses `struct` field tags to store metadata about fields. Also, you will learn how to stream these formats efficiently when working with large amounts of data.

Unlocking these skills will allow you to engage with services by manipulating configuration files, searching through records that might include logs or metrics, and outputting data into Excel for reporting purposes.

In this chapter, we will cover the following topics:

- CSV files
- Popular encoding formats

In the next section, we will dive into the process of utilizing data in one of the oldest formats, CSV.

Let's get started!

Technical requirements

The code files for this chapter can be downloaded from `https://github.com/PacktPublishing/Go-for-DevOps/tree/rev0/chapter/5`

CSV files

CSV is one of the most common data sources that a DevOps engineer can encounter.

This simple format has long been a mainstay in the corporate world as one of the easiest ways to export data out of a system for manipulation and back into a data store.

Many critical systems at large cloud providers, such as Google's GCP and Microsoft's Azure, have critical data sources and systems based on the CSV format. We have seen systems such as network modeling and critical data reporting stored in CSV.

Data scientists love CSV for its easy searching and streaming capabilities. The added quality of being able to quickly visualize the data in software has only added to its appeal.

And, like many other formats, it is human-readable, which allows the data to be manipulated by hand.

In this section, we are going to focus on importing and exporting CSV data using the following:

- The `strings` package and the `bytes` package
- The `encoding/csv` package

Additionally, we are going to look at importing and exporting data to the popular Excel spreadsheet format using `excelize`, which is a popular package for Microsoft Excel.

Now, let's discuss how we can use simple string/byte manipulation packages to read/write CSV files.

Basic value separation using the strings package

Go provides several packages that you will find useful in the manipulation of the `string` and `[]byte` types:

- `strings`
- `bytes`

These packages offer similar functionality such as the following:

- Functions to split data such as `strings.Split()`
- Functions to merge data with separators such as `strings.Join()`
- Buffer types that implement the `io` package's interfaces, such as `bytes.Buffer` and `strings.Builder`

When dealing with CSV files, a developer either streams the data or reads the whole file.

Many developers prefer to read an entire file into memory and convert it from a `[]byte` type into a `string` type. Strings are easier for developers to understand the join and split rules.

However, this causes a copy to be created during conversion, which can be inefficient because you have to double the amount of memory used and dedicate some CPU to doing the copy. When that is a problem, developers reach for the `bytes` and `bufio` packages. These are slightly more difficult to use, but they prevent any unnecessary conversion cost.

Let's look at how we can read an entire file and covert the entries into a structured record.

Conversion after reading the whole file

When doing basic CSV manipulation, sometimes, it is easier to simply split data using a carriage return and then split the line based on a comma or other separator. Let's say we have a CSV file representing first and last names and break that CSV file into records:

```
type record []string
func (r record) validate() error {
    if len(r) != 2 {
        return errors.New("data format is incorrect")
    }
    return nil
}
func (r record) first() string {
```

```
        return r[0]
}

func (r record) last() string {
        return r[1]
}

func readRecs() ([]record, error) {
        b, err := os.ReadFile("data.csv")
        if err != nil {
                return nil, err
        }
        content := string(b)
        lines := strings.Split(content, "\n") // Split by line
        var records []record
        for i, line := range lines {
                // Skip empty lines
                if strings.Trimspace(line) == "" {
                        continue
                }
                var rec record = strings.Split(line, ",")
                if err := rec.validate(); err != nil {
                        return nil, fmt.Errorf("entry at line %d was invalid: %w", i, err)
                }
                records = append(records, rec)
        }
        return records, nil
}
```

The preceding code does the following:

1. It defines a `record` type based on a slice of strings, `[]string`.
2. We can check whether a `record` type was valid by calling its `validate()` method.
3. The record's first name can be retrieved using `first()`.
4. The record's last name can be retrieved using `last()`.
5. It defines a `readRecs()` function to read a file, called `data.csv`.
6. It reads the entire file into memory and converts it into a string called `content`.
7. `content` is split by the new line character, `\n`, with each entry representing a line.

8. It loops through the lines, splitting each line with a comma, ,.
9. It assigns each return from Split, which is a [] string type to a record type.
10. It compiles all records to a slice of records, [] record.

You can view this code in action at https://play.golang.org/p/CVgQZzScO8Z.

Converting line by line

If the file is large and we want to be efficient, we can use the bufio and bytes packages:

```
func readRecs() ([]record, error) {
    file, err := os.Open("data.csv")
    if err != nil {
        return nil, err
    }
    defer file.Close()

    scanner := bufio.NewScanner(fakeFile)
    var records []record
    lineNum := 0
    for scanner.Scan() {
        line := scanner.Text()
        if strings.TrimSpace(line) == "" {
            continue
        }
        var rec record = strings.Split(line, ",")
        if err := rec.validate(); err != nil {
            return nil, fmt.Errorf("entry at line %d was invalid: %w", lineNum, err)
        }
        records = append(records, rec)
        lineNum++
    }
    return records, scanner.Err()

}
```

This differs from the previous code in that the following occurs:

- We read each line, one by one, using `bufio.Scanner` instead of the entire file.
- `scanner.Scan()` reads the next set of content until it sees `\n`.
- That content can be retrieved using `scanner.Text()`.

You can view this code in action at `https://play.golang.org/p/2JPaNTchaKV`.

With this version, we are still doing a `[]byte` conversion on each line into a `string` type. If you are interested in a version that does not do this, please refer to `https://play.golang.org/p/RwsTHzM2dPC`.

Writing records

Writing records to CSV is fairly simple using the methods that we played with earlier. If after reading our records, we wanted to sort them and write them back to a file, we could accomplish this with the following code:

```go
func writeRecs(recs []record) error {
    file, err := os.OpenFile("data-sorted.csv", os.O_CREATE|os.O_TRUNC|os.O_WRONLY, 0644)
    if err != nil {
        return err
    }

    defer file.Close()
    // Sort by last name
    sort.Slice(
        recs,
        func(i, j int) bool {
            return recs[i].last() < recs[j].last()
        },
    )

    for _, rec := range recs {
        _, err := file.Write(rec.csv())
        if err != nil {
            return err
        }
    }
    return nil
}
```

We can also modify the `record` type to have this new method:

```
// csv outputs the data in CSV format.
func (r record) csv() []byte {
    b := bytes.Buffer{}
    for _, field := range r {
        b.WriteString(field + ",")
    }
    b.WriteString("\n")
    return b.Bytes()
}
```

You can see this running at `https://play.golang.org/p/qBCDAsOSgS6`.

The `writeRecs()` function does the following:

- It opens `data-sorted.csv` for writing.
- It sorts the records using `sort.Slice()` from the `sort` package.
- It loops over the records and writes out the CSV file, as generated by the new `csv()` method.

The `csv()` method does the following:

- It creates a `bytes.Buffer` interface, which acts similar to an in-memory file.
- It loops through each field in the record and writes the field value followed by a comma.
- It writes a carriage return after the content on the CSV line.
- It returns the buffer as a `[]bytes` type that now represents a single line.

Using the encoding/csv package

To handle CSV encodings that conform to the RFC 4180 standard, `https://www.rfc-editor.org/rfc/rfc4180.html`, the standard library provides the `encoding/csv` package.

Developers should opt to use this package for CSV handling when the CSV conforms to this specification.

This package provides two types for handling CSVs:

- `Reader` for reading in CSVs
- `Writer` for writing CSVs

In this section, we will tackle the same problem as before, but we will utilize the `Reader` and `Writer` types.

Reading line by line

In the same way as before, we want to read each CSV entry from the file one at a time and process it to a `record` type:

```go
func readRecs() ([]record, error) {
    file, err := os.Open("data.csv")
    if err != nil {
        return nil, err
    }
    defer file.Close()

    reader := csv.NewReader(file)
    reader.FieldsPerRecord = 2
    reader.TrimLeadingSpace = true

    var recs []record
    for {
        data, err := reader.Read()
        if err != nil {
            if err == io.EOF{
                break
            }
            return nil, err
        }
        rec := record(data)
        recs = append(recs, rec)
    }
    return recs, nil
}
```

You can view this code in action at https://go.dev/play/p/Sf6A1AbbQAq.

This function utilizes our reader to perform the following:

- Pass the file to our `NewReader()` constructor.
- Set the reader to require two fields per record.
- Remove any leading space in a line.
- Read each record and store it in a `[]record` slice.

The `Reader` type has other fields that can change how data is read in. For more information, please refer to https://pkg.go.dev/encoding/csv.

In addition, `Reader` provides a `ReadAll()` method that reads all of the records in a single call.

Writing line by line

The companion of the CSV `Reader` type, `Writer`, makes it simple to write to a file. Let's replace the writing part of our previous `writeRecs()` function:

```go
w := csv.NewWriter(file)
defer w.Flush()

for _, rec := range recs {
    if err := w.Write(rec); err != nil {
        return err
    }
}
return nil
```

Here is the runnable code: https://play.golang.org/p/7-dLDzI4b3M

The preceding code does the following:

- It spawns a new `Writer` type that writes to our file.
- It flushes our content to the file on function exit.
- It writes each record out as a CSV file, one per line.

Using excelize when dealing with Excel

Microsoft's Excel has been a popular tool for visualizing data since the 1980s. While the power of the program has grown, its simplicity has helped to make spreadsheets a common tool in most businesses.

While Excel is not CSV, it can import and export data in CSV. For basic usage, you can use the `encoding/csv` package detailed earlier in this chapter.

However, if your organization uses Excel, it can be more helpful to use its native format to write the data and supply visual representations of the data. `excelize` is a third-party Go package that can help you do that.

The package can be found at https://github.com/qax-os/excelize/tree/v2. Additionally, the official documentation can be found at https://xuri.me/excelize/.

There is also an online version of Excel that is part of Microsoft's Office 365. You can manipulate spreadsheets directly there; however, I find it easier to manipulate the spreadsheet offline and then import it.

If you are interested in the REST API, you can read about it at https://docs.microsoft.com/en-us/sharepoint/dev/general-development/excel-services-rest-api.

Creating a .xlsx file and adding some data

Excel has a few characteristics that are helpful to understand:

- An Excel file has the `.xlsx` extension.
- Each `.xlsx` file contains **sheets**.
- Each sheet includes a set of rows and columns.
- A `.xlsx` file has a default sheet, called **Sheet1**.
- The intersection of a row and column is called a **cell**.
- Columns start with the letter A.
- Rows start with the number 1.

We are going to add some data that represents server data for a fictional fleet of devices. This includes the name of the server, the hardware generation, when it was acquired, and the CPU vendor:

```
func main() {
    const sheet = "Sheet1"
    xlsx := excelize.NewFile()
    xlsx.SetCellValue(sheet, "A1", "Server Name")
    xlsx.SetCellValue(sheet, "B1", "Generation")
    xlsx.SetCellValue(sheet, "C1", "Acquisition Date")
    xlsx.SetCellValue(sheet, "D1", "CPU Vendor")

    xlsx.SetCellValue(sheet, "A2", "svlaa01")
    xlsx.SetCellValue(sheet, "B2", 12)
    xlsx.SetCellValue(sheet, "C2", mustParse("10/27/2021"))
    xlsx.SetCellValue(sheet, "D2", "Intel")

    xlsx.SetCellValue(sheet, "A3", "svlac14")
    xlsx.SetCellValue(sheet, "B3", 13)
    xlsx.SetCellValue(sheet, "C3", mustParse("12/13/2021"))
    xlsx.SetCellValue(sheet, "D3", "AMD")

    if err := xlsx.SaveAs("./Book1.xlsx"); err != nil {
        panic(err)
    }
}
```

The preceding code does the following:

- It creates an Excel spreadsheet.
- It adds column labels.
- It adds two servers, `slvaa01` and `slvac14`.
- It saves the Excel file.

There is a `mustParse()` function (used, but not defined above) that converts a string representing a date into
`time.Time`. In Go, when you see `must` proceeding a function name, by convention if the function encounters an error, it will panic.

You can find the runnable code in the repository at `https://github.com/PacktPublishing/Go-for-DevOps/blob/rev0/chapter/5/excel/simple/excel.go`.

This example is the simplest way to add data to a sheet. However, it is not very scalable. Let's create one that is:

```go
type serverSheet struct {
    mu sync.Mutex
    sheetName string
    xlsx *excelize.File
    nextRow int
}
func newServerSheet() (*serverSheet, error) {
    s := &serverSheet{
        sheetName: "Sheet1",
        xlsx: excelize.NewFile(),
        nextRow: 2,
    }
    s.xlsx.SetCellValue(s.sheetName, "A1", "Server Name")
    s.xlsx.SetCellValue(s.sheetName, "B1", "Generation")
    s.xlsx.SetCellValue(s.sheetName, "C1", "Acquisition")
    s.xlsx.SetCellValue(s.sheetName, "D1", "CPU Vendor")
    return s, nil
}
```

The preceding code does the following:

- It creates a `serverSheet` type for managing our Excel sheet.
- It has a constructor that adds our column labels.

Now we need something to add the data:

```go
func (s *serverSheet) add(name string, gen int, acquisition time.Time, vendor CPUVendor) error {
    s.mu.Lock()
    defer s.mu.Unlock()

    if name == "" {
            return errors.New("name cannot be blank")
    }
    if gen < 1 || gen > 13 {
            return errors.New("gen was not in range")
    }
    if acquisition.IsZero() {
            return errors.New("acquisition must be set")
    }
```

```
    if !validCPUVendors[vendor] {
            return errors.New("vendor is not valid )
    }

    s.xlsx.SetCellValue(s.sheetName, "A" +
strconv.Itoa(s.nextRow), name)
    s.xlsx.SetCellValue(s.sheetName, "B" + strconv.Itoa(s.
nextRow), gen)
    s.xlsx.SetCellValue(s.sheetName, "C" + strconv.Itoa(s.
nextRow), acquisition)
    s.xlsx.SetCellValue(s.sheetName, "D" + strconv.Itoa(s.
nextRow), vendor)
    s.nextRow++
    return nil
}
```

This code does the following:

- It uses a lock to prevent multiple calls.
- It performs very basic data validation checks.
- It adds a row and then increments our internal `nextRow` counter.

Now we have a more scalable way to add data to our sheet. Next, let's discuss how to summarize data.

Data summarization

There are two ways to summarize data that is added:

- Tracking summaries in our object
- Excel pivot tables

For our example, I am going to use the first method. This method comes with several advantages:

- It is easier to implement.
- It performs faster calculations.
- It removes complex calculations from the spreadsheet.

However, it comes with a distinctive disadvantage:

- Data changes do not affect the summary.

To track our data summary, let's add a `struct` type:

```
type summaries struct {
      cpuVendor cpuVendorSum
}

type cpuVendorSum struct {
      unknown, intel, amd int
}
```

Let's modify the `add()` method that we wrote earlier to summarize our table:

```
      ...
      s.xlsx.SetCellValue(s.sheetName, "D" + strconv.Itoa(s.nextRow), vendor)
      switch vendor {
      case Intel:
            s.sum.cpuVendor.intel++
      case AMD:
            s.sum.cpuVendor.amd++
      default:
            s.sum.cpuVndor.unknown++
      }
      s.nextRow++
      return nil
}

func (s *serverSheet) writeSummaries() {
    s.xlsx.SetCellValue(s.sheetName, "F1", "Vendor Summary")
    s.xlsx.SetCellValue(s.sheetName, "F2", "Vendor")
    s.xlsx.SetCellValue(s.sheetName, "G2", "Total")

    s.xlsx.SetCellValue(s.sheetName, "F3", Intel)
    s.xlsx.SetCellValue(s.sheetName, "G3", s.summaries.cpuVendor.intel)
    s.xlsx.SetCellValue(s.sheetName, "F4", AMD)
    s.xlsx.SetCellValue(s.sheetName, "G4", s.summaries.cpuVendor.amd)
}
```

The preceding code does the following:

- It looks at our vendor and adds to our summary counters.
- It adds a method to write our summaries to the sheet.

Next, let's discuss how we can add visualizations using this data.

Adding visualizations

One of the reasons for using Excel over CSV for output is to add visualization elements. This allows you to quickly generate reports that users can look at that are more appealing than CSV and less intensive to write than web pages.

Adding a chart is done via the `AddChart()` method. `AddChart()` takes in a string representing JSON that indicates how to build the chart. In our example, you will see a package, called `chart`, that extracts private types from `excelize` used to represent the charts and makes them public types. In this way, we can use a typed data structure instead of JSON that has been converted into that structure. This also allows for the easier discovery of values that you might wish to set:

```
func (s *serverSheet) createCPUChart() error {
    c := chart.New()

    c.Type = "pie3D"
    c.Dimension = chart.FormatChartDimension{640, 480}
    c.Title = chart.FormatChartTitle{Name: "Server CPU Vendor Breakdown"}
    c.Format = chart.FormatPicture{
        FPrintsWithSheet: true,
        NoChangeAspect: false,
        FLocksWithSheet: false,
        OffsetX: 15,
        OffsetY: 10,
        XScale: 1.0,
        YScale: 1.0,
    }
    c.Legend = chart.FormatChartLegend{
        Position: "bottom",
        ShowLegendKey: true,
    }
    c.Plotarea.ShowBubbleSize = true
    c.Plotarea.ShowCatName = true
    c.Plotarea.ShowLeaderLines = false
```

```go
        c.Plotarea.ShowPercent = true
        c.Plotarea.ShowSerName = true
        c.ShowBlanksAs = "zero"

        c.Series = append(
                c.Series,
                chart.FormatChartSeries{
                        Name: `%s!$F$1`,
                        Categories: fmt.Sprintf(`%s!$F$3:$F$4`, s.sheetName),
                        Values: fmt.Sprintf(`%s!$G$3:$G$4`, s.sheetName),
                },
        )

        b, err := json.Marshal(c)
        if err != nil {
                return err
        }
        if err := s.xlsx.AddChart(s.sheetName, "I1", string(b)); err != nil {
                return err
        }

        return nil
}
```

This code does the following:

- It creates a new 3D pie chart type.
- It sets the dimensions, title, and legend.
- It applies the chart values and categories.
- It marshals the chart's instructions to JSON.
- It calls AddChart to insert the chart into the sheet.

You can find the runnable code in the following repository: https://github.com/PacktPublishing/Go-for-DevOps/tree/rev0/chapter/5/excel/visualization

So, we have covered the base minimum of using Excel for outputting reports. There are many other options, including inserting pictures, pivot tables, and advanced formatting directives. And while we wouldn't recommend Excel for data input into a system or a data storage format, it can be a useful data output system for summaries and viewing data.

Popular encoding formats

CSV is one of the more basic human-readable encodings that DevOps engineers will encounter, but it is by no means the only one. Within the last two decades, several new formats have emerged that are used to transfer information or provide configuration to applications.

JavaScript Object Notation (JSON) is a data serialization format that was designed to convert JavaScript objects into a textual representation so that they could be saved or transferred. This notation, due to its simplicity and clarity, has been adopted by almost every language to transfer data.

Yet Another Markup Language (YAML) is another data serialization format that is often used to store configuration information for a service. YAML is the primary configuration language in Kubernetes clusters.

In this section, we will look at the ways to marshal and unmarshal data from Go types into these formats and back into the Go type.

The Go field tags

Go has a feature called field tags that allow a developer to add string tags to `struct` fields. This allows a Go program to inspect the extra metadata regarding a field before performing an operation. Tags are key/value pairs:

```go
type Record struct {
    Last string `json:"last_name"`
}
```

In the preceding code snippet, you can see a `struct` type with a field called `Last` that has a field tag. The field tag is an inline raw string. Raw strings are denoted by backticks. This will produce a tag with a key of `"json"` and a value of `"last_name"`.

Go packages can use the `reflect` package to read these tags. These tags allow a package to change the behavior of an operation based on the tag data. In this example, it tells our JSON encoder package to use `last_name` instead of `Last` when writing data to JSON and the reverse when reading data.

This feature is key for packages that handle data marshaling.

JSON

Over the past decade, the JSON format has become the de facto format for data encoding to disk and for communicating via RPC to services. No language in the cloud space can be successful without supporting JSON.

A developer might encounter JSON as an application configuration language, but it is poorly suited for this task due to the following reasons:

- The lack of multiline strings
- The inability to have comments
- The pickiness regarding its punctuation (that is, good for machines, and bad for humans)

For the interchange of data, JSON can be quite useful with only a few downsides, such as the following:

- Schemaless
- Non-binary format
- Lack of byte array support

A schema is a definition of a message's content that lives outside code.

Schemaless means there is no strict definition of what a message contains. This means that, for every language that is supported, we must create definitions for our messages in that language. Formats such as protocol buffers have entered into this space to provide a schema that can be used to generate code for any language.

JSON is also a human-readable format. These types of formats are not as efficient as binary formats in terms of size and speed. This generally matters when trying to scale large services. However, many prefer human-readable formats due to their ability to be easily debugged.

JSON's lack of support for byte arrays is also a failing. JSON can still transfer raw bytes, but it requires encoding and decoding the bytes using `base64` encoding and storing them in JSON's `string` type. This requires an extra level of encoding that should be unnecessary. There are several supersets of JSON that are not widely supported (such as Binary JSON, or BSON for short) that contain a byte array type.

JSON is delivered to a user in one of several ways:

- As a single message that can contain sub-messages
- As an array of JSON messages
- As a stream of JSON messages

JSON's origins started as a format for simply encoding a JavaScript object for transfer. However, as its uses have grown, the need for sending large messages or streams of messages became a use case.

Single, large messages can be hard to decode. Generally, JSON decoders are written to read the entire message into memory and validate the message's content.

To simplify large sets of messages or streaming content, you might encounter a message with brackets, [], surrounding a set of messages or individual messages separated with carriage returns. These are not valid JSON as intended, but have become de facto standards for handling large sets of data as small, individual messages that make up part of a whole stream.

Because JSON is a standard part of the cloud ecosystem, Go has built-in language support in the standard library's encoding/json package. In the upcoming sections, we will detail the most common ways to use the JSON package.

Marshaling and unmarshaling to maps

Because JSON is schemaless, it is possible to have messages of different types in a stream or in files. This is usually undesirable, and it is better to have a top-level message that holds these types of messages.

When you need to handle multiple message types or do discovery on a message, Go allows you to decode messages into map[string]interface{}, where the string key represents the field name and interface{} represents the value.

Let's examine an example of unmarshaling a file into a map:

```go
b, err := os.ReadFile("data.json")
if err != nil {
    return "",
        err
}

data := map[string]interface{}{}
if err := json.Unmarshal(b, &data); err != nil {
    return "", err
}

v, ok := data["user"]
if !ok {
    return "", errors.New("json does not contain key 'user'")
}
```

```
switch user := v.(type) {
case string:
    return user, nil
}
return "", fmt.Errorf("key 'user' is not a string, was %T", v)
```

The preceding example does the following:

- It reads the content of the data.json file into variable b.
- It creates a map, called data, to store our JSON content.
- It unmarshals the raw bytes representing the JSON into data.
- It looks up the user key in data.
- If user does not exist, we return an error.
- If it does exist, we type assert to determine what the value type is.
- If the value is a string, we return the content.
- If the value is not a string, we return an error.

Using the map, we can explore the values in the data to discover a message type, type assert the interface{} value to a concrete type, and then use the concrete value. Remember that type assertion converts an interface variable into another interface variable or a concrete type such as string or int64.

Using a map is the hardest method of data decoding for JSON. It is only recommended in cases where the JSON is unpredictable, and there is no control of the data provider. It is usually better to have whatever is providing the data change its behavior than decoding in this way.

Marshalling a map into JSON is simple:

```
if err := json.Marshal(data); err != nil {
    return err
}
```

json.Marshal will read our map and output valid JSON for the contents. []byte fields are automatically base64 encoded into JSON's string type.

Marshaling and unmarshaling to structs

The preferred method of JSON decoding is doing so in a Go `struct` type that represents the data. Here is an example of how to create a user record struct, which we will use to decode a JSON stream:

```go
type Record struct {
    Name string `json:"user_name"`
    User string `json:"user"`
    ID int
    Age int `json:"-"`
}

func main() {
    rec := Record{
        Name: "John Doak",
        User: "jdoak",
        ID: 23,
    }

    b, err := json.Marshal(rec)
    if err != nil {
        panic(err)
    }
    fmt.Printf("%s\n", b)
}
```

The preceding code outputs `{"user_name":"John Doak","user":"jdoak","ID":23}`. You can find the runnable code at https://play.golang.org/p/LzoUpOeEN9y.

This code does the following:

- It defines a `Record` type.
- It uses field tags to tell JSON what the output field mapping should be.
- It uses a field tag of - on `Age` so that it will not be marshaled.
- It creates a `Record` type called `rec`.
- It marshals `rec` to JSON.
- It prints the JSON.

Notice that the Name field was translated to user_name and User to user. The ID field was unchanged in the output because we did not use a field tag. Age was not output because we used a field tag of -.

Fields that are private because they start with a lowercase letter cannot be exported. This is because the JSON marshaler is in a different package and cannot see the private type in this package.

You can read about the field tags that JSON supports in the encoding/json GoDoc, located under Marshal() (https://pkg.go.dev/encoding/json#Marshal).

The JSON package also includes MarshalIndent(), which can be used to output more readable JSON with line separators between the fields and indentions.

Decoding data into a struct type, such as Record earlier, can be done as follows:

```
rec := Record{}

if err := json.Unmarshal(b, &rec); err != nil {
    return err
}
```

This transforms text that represents the JSON into a Record type stored in the rec variable. You can find the runnable code at https://play.golang.org/p/DD8TrKgTUwE.

Marshaling and unmarshaling large messages

Sometimes, we might receive a stream of JSON messages or a file that contains a list of JSON messages.

Go provides json.Decoder to handle a series of messages. Here is an example borrowed from the GoDoc, where each message is separated by a carriage return:

```
const jsonStream = `
    {"Name": "Ed", "Text": "Knock knock."}
    {"Name": "Sam", "Text": "Who's there?"}
`

type Message struct {
    Name, Text string
}

reader := strings.NewReader(jsonStream)
```

```go
dec := json.NewDecoder(reader)
msgs := make(chan Message, 1)
errs := make(chan error, 1)

// Parse the messages concurrently with printing the message.
go func() {
    defer close(msgs)
    defer close(errs)
    for {
        var m Message
        if err := dec.Decode(&m); err == io.EOF {
            break
        } else if err != nil {
            errs <- err
            return
        }
        msgs <- m
    }
}()

// This will print the messages as we decode them.
for m := range msgs {
    fmt.Printf("%+v\n", m)
}

if err := <-errs; err != nil {
    fmt.Println("stream error: ", err)
}
```

You can view this running code at https://play.golang.org/p/kqmSvfdK4EG.

This example does the following:

- It defines a Message struct.
- It wraps the jsonStream raw output in an io.Reader via strings.NewReader().
- It starts a goroutine that decodes the messages as they are read and puts them on a channel.
- It reads all messages that are sent until the output channel is closed.
- It prints out any errors that are encountered.

Sometimes, this format of streaming will have brackets, [], around the messages and use commas as separators between the entries.

In this case, we can utilize another feature of the decoder, dec.Token(), to remove them safely:

```go
const jsonStream = `[
    {"Name": "Ed", "Text": "Knock knock."},
    {"Name": "Sam", "Text": "Who's there?"}
]`

dec := json.NewDecoder(reader)

_, err := dec.Token() // Reads [
if err != nil {
    return fmt.Errorf(`outer [ is missing`))
}

for dec.More() {
    var m Message
    // decode an array value (Message)
    err := dec.Decode(&m)
    if err != nil {
        return err
    }

    fmt.Printf("%+v\n", m)
}

_, err = dec.Token() // Reads ]
if err != nil {
    return fmt.Errorf(`final ] is missing`)
}
```

You can view this running code at https://play.golang.org/p/_PrUVUy4zRv.

This code works in the same way, except it removes the outer brackets and requires a comma-delimited list instead.

Encoding data in a stream is very similar to decoding. We can write JSON messages into `io.Writer` to output to a stream. Here's an example:

```
func encodeMsgs(in chan Message, output io.Writer) chan error {
    errs := make(chan error, 1)
    go func() {
        defer close(errs)
        enc := json.NewEncoder(output)
        for msg := range in {
            if err := enc.Encode(msg); err != nil {
                errs <- err
                return
            }
        }
    }()
    return errs
}
```

You can see this code running at `https://play.golang.org/p/ELICEC41cax`.

This code does the following:

- It reads from a `channel` of `Message`.
- It writes to an `io.Writer`.
- It returns a channel that signals when the encoder is done processing.
- If an error is returned, it means that the encoder had a problem.

This outputs the JSON as separated values without brackets.

JSON final thoughts

The `encoding/json` package has support for other methods of decoding that are not covered here. You can mix `map[string]interace{}` into your `struct` types and vice versa, or you can decode each field and value individually.

However, the best use cases are those that are straightforward `struct` types as a single value or stream of values.

This is why `encoding/json` is my first choice when encoding or decoding JSON values. It is not the fastest method, but it is the most flexible.

There are other third-party libraries that can increase your throughput while sacrificing some flexibility. Here is just a small list of packages that you might want to consider:

- `https://github.com/francoispqt/gojay`
- `https://github.com/goccy/go-json`
- `https://pkg.go.dev/github.com/json-iterator/go`
- `https://pkg.go.dev/github.com/valyala/fastjson`

YAML encoding

YAML (yet another markup language/YAML Ain't Markup Language) is a language that is commonly used to write configurations.

YAML is the default language of services such as Kubernetes to hold configurations, and as a DevOps engineer, you are likely to come across it in a variety of applications.

YAML has a few advantages over JSON for use in configurations:

- Support for comments
- More flexible for humans, such as unquoted strings and quoted strings
- Multiline strings
- Anchors and references to avoid repetition of the same text data

YAML is often cited as having the following flaws:

- It is schemaless.
- The standard is large and some features are confusing.
- Large files can have indention errors that go unnoticed.
- Implementations in some languages can accidentally execute code embedded in YAML. This can lead to a few security patches in software projects.

Go does not have support in the standard library, but it has a third-party library that has become the de facto package for YAML serialization, called `go-yaml` (`https://github.com/go-yaml/yaml`).

Next, let's discuss how we can read these YAML files to read our configurations.

Marshaling and unmarshaling to maps

YAML, like JSON, is schemaless and suffers from the same drawbacks. However, unlike JSON, YAML is intended to represent a configuration, so we don't have the same need to stream content.

For YAML, the general use case would entail encoding/decoding to a `struct` type instead of a `map`. However, if you have a need for message discovery, YAML can handle a `map` decode in the same way that we can handle it for JSON.

Let's look at an example of unmarshaling a file into a `map`:

```
data := map[string]interface{}{}

if err := yaml.Unmarshal(yamlContent, &data); err != nil {
    return "", err
}

v, ok := data["user"]
if !ok {
    return "", errors.New("'user' key not found")
}
```

The preceding example does the following:

- It creates a `map` called `data` to store our YAML content.
- It unmarshals the raw bytes representing the YAML into `data`.
- It looks up the `user` key in `data`.
- If `user` does not exist, we return an error.

For a more complete example, please refer to https://play.golang.org/p/wkHkmu47e6V.

Marshalling a map into YAML is simple:

```
if err := yaml.Marshal(data); err != nil {
    return err
}
```

Here, `yaml.Marshal()` will read our `map` and output valid YAML for the contents.

Marshaling and unmarshaling to structs

The `struct` serialization is the preferred way to handle YAML. As YAML is a configuration language, programs must know what fields are available ahead of time to set program parameters.

YAML serialization works in a similar way to JSON serialization, and you will find that similarity across most data serialization packages:

```go
type Config struct {
      Jobs []Job
}

type Job struct {
      Name     string
      Interval time.Duration
      Cmd      string
}

func main() {
      c := Config{
            Jobs: []Job{
                  {
                        Name:     "Clear tmp",
                        Interval: 24 * time.Hour,
                        Cmd:      "rm -rf " + os.TempDir(),
                  },
            },
      }

      b, err := yaml.Marshal(c)
      if err != nil {
            panic(err)
      }
      fmt.Printf("%s\n", b)
}
```

You can see this running code at https://play.golang.org/p/SvJHLKBsdUP.

This outputs the following:

```
jobs:
- name: Clear tmp dir
  interval: 24h0m0s
  cmd: rm -rf /tmp
```

The preceding code does the following:

- It creates a top-level configuration called `Config`.
- It creates a list of sub-messages called `Job`.
- It marshals an example into the text representation.

Unmarshaling is just as easy:

```
        data := []byte(`
jobs:
  - name: Clear tmp
    interval: 24h0m0s
    whatever: is not in the Job type
    cmd: rm -rf /tmp
`)

        c := Config{}

        if err := yaml.Unmarshal(data, &c); err != nil {
            panic(err)
        }
        for _, job := range c.Jobs {
            fmt.Println("Name: ", job.Name)
            fmt.Println("Interval: ", job.Interval)
        }
```

The preceding code does the following:

- It takes a YAML config that is represented by data.
- It converts it into the `Config` type.
- It prints out contained `Job` information.
- It ignores the `whatever` field.

This code will ignore the unknown `whatever` field. However, in many cases, you do not want to ignore a field that could potentially be misspelled. In those cases, we can use `UnmarshalStrict()`.

That would cause this code to fail with the following message:

```
line 5: field whaterver not found in type main.Job
```

When using `UnmarshalStrict()`, you must add new field support to your programs and deploy them before adding them to your configs, or you will cause old binaries to fail.

YAML final thoughts

The `github.com/go-yaml/yaml` package has support for other methods of serialization that we are not going to cover here. One that is used most often is decoding into a `yaml.Node` object in order to preserve comments, then changing the content and writing the configuration back out. However, this is relatively uncommon.

In this section, you have learned how to use JSON and YAML to read and write data in their respective data formats. In the next section, we will look at how to interact with SQL data sources that are used to commonly store data.

Summary

This also ends our chapter on using common data formats. We have covered how to read and write with CSV files and Excel reports. Additionally, we have learned how to encode and decode data in JSON and YAML formats. This chapter has shown how we can decode data in streams while reinforcing ways to concurrently read and use data with goroutines.

Your newly acquired skills for JSON will be immediately useful in our next chapter. In that chapter, we will look at how to connect to SQL databases and interact with RPC services. As REST RPC services and databases such as Postgres can use JSON, this skill will come in handy.

So, let's jump in!

6
Interacting with Remote Data Sources

In the last chapter, we talked about dealing with common data formats and showed how we can read and write data in those formats. But in that chapter, we were simply dealing with data that was accessible through a filesystem.

While the filesystem may actually have files that exist on remote devices through services such as the **Network File System (NFS)** or the **Server Message Block (SMB)**, other remote data sources exist.

In this chapter, we will look at some common ways to send and receive data in remote data sources. This will focus on accessing data on remote systems using the **Structured Query Language (SQL)**, **REpresentational State Transfer (REST)**, and **Google Remote Procedure Call (gRPC)**. You will learn how to access common SQL data stores, with a focus on PostgreSQL. We will also explore how **Remote Procedure Call (RPC)** services are created and queried using REST- and gRPC-style RPC methodologies.

With the skills you gain here, you will be able to connect and query data in a SQL database, add new entries to the database, request a remote action from a service, and gather information from a remote service.

We will cover the following topics in this chapter:

- Accessing SQL databases
- Developing REST services and clients
- Developing gRPC services and clients

In the next section, we will dive into utilizing data in one of the oldest formats, **Comma-Separated Values (CSV)**.

Let's get started!

Technical requirements

The code files for this chapter can be downloaded from `https://github.com/PacktPublishing/Go-for-DevOps/tree/rev0/chapter/6/grpc`

Accessing SQL databases

DevOps engineers commonly have a need to access data stored in database systems. **SQL** is a standard for communicating with database systems that a DevOps engineer will encounter in their day-to-day lives.

Go provides a standard library for interacting with SQL-based systems called `database/sql`. The interfaces provided by that package, with the addition of a database driver, allow a user to work with several different SQL databases.

In this section, we will look at how we can access a Postgres database to perform basic SQL operations using Go.

> **Important Note**
> Examples in this section will require you to set up a Postgres database. This is beyond the scope of this book. This will not be a guide to SQL. Some basic SQL knowledge is required.

You can find information regarding how to install Postgres for your OS at `https://www.postgresql.org/download/`. If you prefer to run Postgres in a local Docker container, you can find that information at `https://hub.docker.com/_/postgres`.

Connecting to a Postgres database

To connect to a Postgres database will require using a database driver for Postgres. The currently recommended third-party package is `github.com/jackc/pgx`. This package implements a SQL driver for `database/sql` and provides its own methods/types for Postgres-specific features.

The choice to use `database/sql` or Postgres-specific types will depend on whether you need to ensure compatibility between different databases. Using `database/sql` allows you to write functions that work on any SQL database, while using Postgres-specific features removes compatibility and makes migration to another database more difficult. We will discuss how to perform our examples using both methods.

Here is how to connect using a standard SQL package without extra Postgres features:

```go
/*
dbURL might look like:
"postgres://username:password@localhost:5432/database_name"
*/
conn, err := sql.Open("pgx", dbURL)
if err != nil {
    return fmt.Errorf("connect to db error: %s\n", err)
}
defer conn.Close()

ctx, cancel := context.WithTimeout(
    context.Background(),
    2 * time.Second
)

if err := conn.PingContext(ctx); err != nil {
  return err
}
cancel()
```

Here, we open a connection to Postgres using the `pgx` driver that will be registered when you import the following package:

```go
_ "github.com/jackc/pgx/v4/stdlib"
```

This is an anonymous import, meaning we are not using `stdlib` directly. This is done when we want a *side effect*, such as when registering a driver with the `database/sql` package.

The `Open()` call doesn't test our connection. You will see `conn.PingContext()` to test that we will be able to make calls to the database.

When you want to use `pgx-specific` types for Postgres, the setup is slightly different, starting with a different package import:

```
"github.com/jackc/pgx/v4/pgxpool"
```

To create that connection, type the following:

```
conn, err := pgxpool.Connect(ctx, dbURL)
if err != nil {
    return fmt.Errorf("connect to db error: %s\n", err)
}
defer conn.Close(ctx)
```

This uses a connection pool to connect to the database for performance. You will notice that we don't have a `PingContext()` call, as the native connection tests the connection as part of `Connect()`.

Now that you know how to connect to Postgres, let's look at how we can make queries.

Querying a Postgres database

Let's consider making a call to your SQL database to fetch some information about a user that is held in a table.

Using the standard library, type the following:

```
type UserRec struct {
    User string
    DisplayName string
    ID int
}

func GetUser(ctx context.Context, conn *sql.DB, id int) (UserRec, error) {
    const query = `SELECT "User","DisplayName" FROM users WHERE "ID" = $1`
    u := UserRec{ID: id}
    err := conn.QueryRowContext(ctx, query, id).Scan(&u)
    return u, err
}
```

This example does the following:

- Creates `UserRec` to store SQL data for a user
- Creates a query statement called `query`
- Queries our database for a user with the requested ID
- Returns `UserRec` and an error if we had one

We can increase the efficiency of this example by using a prepared statement in an object instead of just a function:

```go
type Storage struct {
    conn *sql.DB
    getUserStmt *sql.Stmt
}

func NewStorage(ctx context.Context, conn *sql.DB) *Storage {
    return &Storage{
        getUserStmt: conn.PrepareContext(
            ctx,
            `SELECT "User","DisplayName" FROM users WHERE "ID" = $1`,
        )
    }
}

func (s *Storage) GetUser(ctx context.Context, id int) (UserRec, error) {
    u := UserRec{ID: id}
    err := s.getUserStmt.QueryRow(id).Scan(&u)
    return u, err
}
```

This example does the following:

- Creates a reusable object
- Stores `*sql.Stmt`, which increases the efficiency when doing repeated queries
- Defines a `NewStorage` constructor that creates our object

Because of the generic nature of using the standard library, in these examples, any implementation of `*sql.DB` could be used. Switching Postgres for MariaDB would work as long as MariaDB had the same table names and format.

If we use the Postgres-specific library, the same code is written like so:

```
err = conn.QueryRow(ctx, query).Scan(&u)
return u, err
```

This implementation looks and works in a similar way to the standard library. But the `conn` object here is a different, non-interface `pgxpool.Conn` type and not `sql.Conn`. And while the functionality looks similar, the `pgxpool.Conn` object supports queries with Postgres-specific types and syntax, such as `jsonb`, that `sql.Conn` does not.

There is no need to use a prepared statement for non-transactions when using Postgres-specific calls. The call information is automatically cached.

The preceding example was simplistic in that we were pulling a specific entry. What if we wanted to also have a method to retrieve all users with IDs between two numbers? We could define this using the standard library:

```
/*
stmt contains `SELECT "User","DisplayName","ID" FROM users
WHERE "ID" >= $1 AND "ID" < $2`
*/
func (s *Storage) UsersBetween(ctx context.Context, start, end int) ([]UserRec, error) {
    recs := []UserRec{}
    rows, err := s.usersBetweenStmt(ctx, start, end)
    defer rows.Close()

    for rows.Next() {
        rec := UserRec{}
        if err := rows.Scan(&rec); err != nil {
            return nil, err
        }
        recs = append(recs, rec)
    }
    return recs, nil
}
```

The Postgres-specific syntax is the same; it just switches `s.usersBetweenStmt()` for `conn.QueryRow()`.

Null values

SQL has a concept of null values for basic types such as Booleans, strings, and int32. Go doesn't have the convention; instead, it provides zero values for those types.

When SQL allows a column to have a null value, the standard library provides special null types in `database/sql`:

- `sql.NullBool`
- `sql.NullByte`
- `sql.NullFloat64`
- `sql.NullInt16`
- `sql.NullInt32`
- `sql.NullInt64`
- `sql.NullString`
- `sql.NullTime`

When you design your schema, it is better to use zero values instead of null values. But sometimes, you need to tell the difference between a value being set and the zero value. In those cases, you can use these special types in place of the standard type.

For example, if our `UserRec` could have a null `DisplayName`, we can change the `string` type to `sql.NullString`:

```
type UserRec struct {
    User string
    DisplayName sql.NullString
    ID int
}
```

You can see an example of how the server sets these values depending on the value that the column holds for `DisplayName` here: https://go.dev/play/p/KOkYdhcjhdf.

Writing data to Postgres

Writing data into a database is simple but requires some consideration of the syntax. The two major operations that a user wants when writing data are as follows:

- Updating an existing entry
- Inserting a new entry

In standard SQL, you cannot do an *update entry if it exists; insert if not*. As this is a common operation, each database offers some way to do this with its own special syntax. When using the standard library, you must choose between doing an update or an insert. If you do not know whether the entry exists, you will need to use a transaction, which we will detail in a bit.

Doing an update or insert is simply using a different SQL syntax and the `ExecContext()` call:

```
func (s *Storage) AddUser(ctx context.Context, u UserRec) error {
    _, err := s.addUserStmt.ExecContext(
        ctx,
        u.User,
        u.DisplayName,
        u.ID,
    )
    return err
}

func (s *Storage) UpdateDisplayName(ctx context.Context, id int, name string) error {
    _, err := s.updateDisplayName.ExecContext(
        ctx,
        name,
        id,
    )
    return err
}
```

In this example, we have added two methods:

- `AddUser()` adds a new user into the system.
- `UpdateDisplayName()` updates the display name of a user with a specific ID.
- Both use the `sql.Stmt` type, which would be a field in the object, similar to `getUserStmt`.

The major difference when implementing using the Postgres-native package is the method name that is called and the lack of a prepared statement. Implementing `AddUser()` would look like the following:

```
func (s *Storage) AddUser(ctx context.Context, u UserRec) error {
    const stmt = `INSERT INTO users (User,DisplayName,ID)
    VALUES ($1, $2, $3)`
    _, err := s.conn.Exec(
        ctx,
        stmt,
        u.User,
        u.DisplayName,
        u.ID,
    )
    return err
}
```

Sometimes, it is not enough to just do a read or a write to the database. Sometimes, we need to do multiple actions atomically and treat them as a single action. So, in the next section, we will talk about how to do this with transactions.

Transactions

Transactions provide a sequence of SQL operations that are executed on the server as one piece of work. This is commonly used to provide some type of atomic operation where a read and a write are required or to extract data on a read before doing a write.

Transactions are easy to create in Go. Let's create an `AddOrUpdateUser()` call that will look to see whether a user exists before adding or updating our data:

```
func (s *Storage) AddOrUpdateUser(ctx context.Context, u
UserRec) (err error) {
    const (
```

```go
            getStmt = `SELECT "ID" FROM users WHERE "User" = $1`
            insertStmt = `INSERT INTO users (User,DisplayName,ID)
            VALUES ($1, $2, $3)`
            updateStmt = `UPDATE "users" SET "User" = $1,
            "DisplayName" = $2 WHERE "ID" = 3`
    )

    tx, err := s.conn.BeginTx(ctx, &sql.TxOptions{Isolation: sql.LevelSerializable})
    if err != nil {
        return err
    }
    defer func() {
        if err != nil {
            tx.Rollback()
            return
        }
        err = tx.Commit()
    }()

    _, err := tx.QueryRowContext(ctx, getStmt, u.User)
    if err != nil {
        if err == sql.ErrNoRows {
            _, err = tx.ExecContext(ctx, insertStmt, u.User, u.DisplayName, u.ID)
            if err != nil {
                return err
            }
        }
        return err
    }

    _, err = tx.ExecContext(ctx, updateStmt, u.User, u.DisplayName, u.ID))
    return err
}
```

This code does the following:

- Creates a transaction with an isolation level of `LevelSerializable`
- Uses a `defer` statement to determine whether we had an error:
  - If we did, we roll back the entire transaction.
  - If not, we attempt to commit the transaction.
- Queries to find whether the user exists:
  - It determines this by checking the error type.
  - If the error is `sql.ErrNoRows`, we did not find the user.
  - If the error is anything else, it was a system error.
- Executes an insert statement if we didn't find the user
- Executes an update statement if we did find the user

The keys to a transaction are the following:

- `conn.BeginTx`, which starts the transaction
- `tx.Commit()`, which commits our changes
- `tx.Rollback()`, which reverts our changes

A `defer` statement is an excellent way to handle either `Commit()` or `Rollback()` once the transaction has been created. It ensures that when the function ends, either one or the other is executed.

The isolation level is important for a transaction as it affects the performance and reliability of your system. Go provides multiple levels of isolation; however, not all database systems will support all levels of isolation.

You can read more about isolation levels here: https://en.wikipedia.org/wiki/Isolation_(database_systems)#Isolation_levels.

Postgres-specific types

So far in our examples, we have shown you how to use both the standard library and Postgres-specific objects to interact with Postgres. But we haven't really shown a compelling reason to use Postgres objects.

Postgres objects shine when you need to use types or capabilities that aren't a part of the SQL standard. Let's rewrite our transaction example, but instead of storing data across standard columns, let's have our Postgres database only have two columns:

- An ID of the int type
- Data of the jsonb type

jsonb is not part of the SQL standard and cannot be implemented with the standard SQL library. jsonb can greatly simplify your life, as it allows you to store JSON data while querying using JSON fields:

```go
func (s *Storage) AddOrUpdateUser(ctx context.Context, u UserRec) (err error) {
    const (
        getStmt = `SELECT "ID" FROM "users" WHERE "ID" = $1`
        updateStmt = `UPDATE "users" SET "Data" = $1 WHERE "ID" = $2`
        addStmt = `INSERT INTO "users" (ID,Data) VALUES ($1, $2)`
    )
    tx, err := conn.BeginTx(
        ctx,
        pgx.TxOptions{
            IsoLevel: pgx.Serializable,
            AccessMode: pgx.ReadWrite,
            DeferableMode: pgx.NotDeferrable,
        },
    )
    defer func() {
        if err != nil {
            tx.Rollback()
            return
        }
        err = tx.Commit()
    }()

    _, err := tx.QueryRow(ctx, getUserStmt, u.ID)
    if err != nil {
```

```
                if err == sql.ErrNoRows {
                        _, err = tx.ExecContext(ctx, insertStmt, u.ID,
u)
                        if err != nil {
                            return err
                        }
                }
                return err
        }
        _, err = tx.Exec(ctx, updateStmt, u.ID, u)
        return err
}
```

This example is different in a few ways:

- It has additional `AccessMode` and `DeferableMode` parameters.
- We can pass our object, `UserRec`, as our `Data jsonb` column.

The access and deferable modes add extra constraints that are not available directly with the standard library.

Using `jsonb` is a boon. Now, we can do searches on our tables with `WHERE` clauses that can filter on the `jsonb` field values.

You will also notice that `pgx` is smart enough to know our column type and automatically convert our `UserRec` into JSON.

If you'd like to know more about Postgres value types, you can visit `https://www.postgresql.org/docs/9.5/datatype.html`.

If you'd like to know more about `jsonb` and functions to access its values, visit `https://www.postgresql.org/docs/9.5/functions-json.html`.

Other options

Besides the standard library and database-specific packages are **Object-Relational Mappings** (**ORMs**). ORMs are a popular model for managing data between your services and data storage.

Go's most popular ORM is called **GORM**, which can be found here: `https://gorm.io/index.html`.

Another popular framework that also includes support for REST and web services is Beego, which you can find here: `https://github.com/beego/beego`.

Storage abstractions

Many developers are tempted to use storage systems directly in their code, passing around a connection to a database. This is not optimal in that it can cause problems when you need to do the following:

- Add caching layers before storage access.
- Migrate to a new storage system for your service.

Abstracting storage behind an internal **Application Programming Interface (API)** of interfaces will allow you to change storage layers later by simply implementing the interfaces with the new backend. You can then plug in the new backend at any time.

A simple example of this might be adding an interface for getting user data:

```
type UserStorage interface {
    User(ctx context.Context, id string) (UserRec, error)
    AddUser(ctx context.Context, u UserRec) error
    UpdateDisplayName(ctx context.Context, id string, name string) error
}
```

This interface allows you to implement your storage backend using Postgres, local files, SQLite, Azure Cosmos DB, in-memory data structures, or any other storage medium.

This has the benefit of allowing migration from one storage medium to another by plugging in a new implementation. As a side benefit, you can decouple tests from using a database. Instead, most tests can use an in-memory data structure. This allows you to test your functionality without bringing up and tearing down infrastructure, which would be necessary with a real database.

Adding a cache layer becomes a simple exercise of writing a `UserStorage` implementation that calls the cache on reads and when not found calls your data store implementation. You can replace the original and everything keeps working.

Note that everything described here for abstraction behind an interface applies to access to service data. A SQL API should only be used for your application to store and read data. Other services should use a stable RPC interface. This provides the same type of abstraction, allowing you to move data backends without migrating users.

Case study – data migration of an orchestration system – Google

One of the systems I was involved with during my tenure at Google was an orchestration system for automating network changes. The system received automation instructions and executed them against various targets. These operations might involve pushing files via **Secure File Transfer Protocol (SFTP)**, interacting with network routers, updating authoritative data stores, or running state verifications.

With operations, it is critical that data representing the state of a workflow is always up to date. This includes not only the currently running workflows but also the states of previous workflows, which are used to create new workflows.

To ease our operational burden, we wanted to move the storage system for workflows from Bigtable to Spanner. Bigtable required a more complicated setup to handle failover to a backup cell when problems occurred, while Spanner was designed to handle this as part of the system design. This removed the need for us to intervene when cells had problems.

The storage layer was hidden behind a storage interface. Storage was initialized in our `main()` and passed around to other modules that required it. This meant that we could replace the storage layer with a new implementation.

We implemented a new storage interface that wrote data to both Bigtable and Spanner while reading from them both, using the latest data stamp and updating the records if needed.

This allowed us to operate using both data stores while our historical data was being transferred. Once synchronization was complete, we moved our binaries to a version that only had a Spanner implementation. Our migration was complete with no service downtime while thousands of critical operations were running.

So far in this chapter, we have learned about how to use `database/sql` to access generic data stores and Postgres specifically. We learned how to read and write to Postgres and implement transactions. The benefits of using `database/sql` versus a database-specific library such as `pgx` were discussed. And finally, we showed how hiding your implementations behind interface abstractions can allow you to change storage backends more easily and test code relying on storage hermetically.

Next, we will look into accessing RPC services using REST or gRPC.

Developing REST services and clients

Before the web and distributed systems that now permeate the cloud space, standards for communicating between systems were not in widespread use. This communication is often called an RPC. This simply means that a program on one machine has a method to call a function running on a different machine and receive any output.

Monolithic applications were the norm and servers tended to either be silo'd per application and vertically scaled or were run as jobs on larger, more specialized hardware from companies such as IBM, Sun, SGI, or Cray. When systems did need to communicate with each other, they tended to use their own custom wire formats, such as what you would see with Microsoft SQL Server.

With the web defining the internet of the 2000s, large monolithic systems could not provide the compute power behind services such as Google Search or Facebook at any reasonable cost point. To power these services, companies needed to treat large collections of standard PCs as a single system. Where a single system could communicate between processes using Unix sockets or shared memory calls, companies needed common and secure ways to communicate between processes running on different machines.

As HTTP became the de facto standard for communication between systems, RPC mechanisms of today use some form of HTTP for data transport. This allows the RPC to transit systems more easily, such as load balancers, and easily utilize security standards, such as **Transport Layer Security** (**TLS**). It also means that as the HTTP transport is upgraded, these RPC frameworks can leverage the hard work of hundreds if not thousands of engineers.

In this section, we are going to talk about one of the most popular RPC mechanisms, REST. REST uses HTTP calls and whatever messaging format you want, although the majority of cases use JSON for messaging.

REST for RPCs

Writing REST clients in Go is fairly simple. Chances are that if you have been developing applications in the last 10 years, you have either used a REST client or written one. Cloud APIs for services such as Google Cloud Platform's Cloud Spanner, Microsoft's Azure Data Explorer, or Amazon DynamoDB use REST to communicate with the services via their client libraries.

REST clients can do the following:

- Use `GET`, `POST`, `PATCH`, or any other type of HTTP method.
- Support any serialization format (although this is normally JSON).
- Allow for data streaming.
- Support query variables.
- Support multiple versions of an API using URL standards.

REST in Go also has the luxury of not requiring any framework to implement on the server side. Everything that is required lives in the standard library.

Writing a REST client

Let's write a simple REST client that accesses a server and receives a **Quote of the Day** (**QOTD**). To do this, the server has the following endpoint using POST - `/v1/qotd`.

First, let's define the message we need to send to the server:

```
type getReq struct {
    Author string `json:"author"`
}
type getResp struct {
    Quote string `json:"quote"`
    Error *Error `json:"error"`
}
```

Let's talk about what each of these does:

- `getReq` details the arguments to the server's `/v1/qotd` function call.
- `getResp` is what we expect as a return from the server's function call.

We are using field tags to allow conversion from lowercase keys into our public variables that are capitalized. For the `encoding/json` package to see these values for serialization, they must be public. Private fields will not be serializable:

```
type Error struct {
    Code ErrCode
    Msg string
}
func (e *Error) Error() string {
```

```
        return fmt.Errorf("(code %v): %s", e.Code, e.Msg)
}
```

This defines a custom error type. This way, we can store error codes to return to the user. This code is defined next to our response object, but it isn't used until much later in the code we are defining.

Let's now define a QOTD client and a constructor that does some basic checks on the address and creates an HTTP client to allow us to send data to the server:

```
type QOTD struct {
    addr string
    client *http.Client
}
func New(addr string) (*QOTD, error) {
    if _, _, err := net.SplitHostPort(addr); err != nil {
        return nil, err
    }
    return &QOTD{addr: addr, client: &http.Client{}}
}
```

The next step is to make a generic function for making REST calls. Because REST is so open-ended, it is hard to make one that can handle any type of REST call. A best practice to use when writing REST servers is to only support the POST method; never use query variables and simple URLs. However, in practice, you will deal with a wide variety of REST call types if you don't control the service:

```
func (q *QOTD) restCall(ctx context.Context, endpoint string, req, resp interface{}) error {
    if _, ok := ctx.Deadline(); !ok {
        var cancel context.CancelFunc
        ctx, cancel = context.WithDeadline(ctx, 2 * time.Second)
        defer cancel()
    }

    b, err := json.Marshal(req)
    if err != nil {
        return err
    }
    hReq, err := http.NewRequestWithContext(
```

```
            ctx,
            http.POST,
            endpoint,
            bytes.NewBuffer(b),
        )
        if err != nil {
            return err
        }
        resp, err := q.client.Do(hReq)
        if err != nil {
            return err
        }
        b, err := io.ReadAll(resp.Body)
        if err != nil {
            return err
        }
        return json.Unmarshal(b, resp)
}
```

This code does the following:

- Checks our context for a deadline:
  - If it has one, it is honored
  - If not, a default one is set
  - `cancel()` is called after the call is done
- Marshals a request into JSON.
- Creates a new `*http.Request` that does the following:
  - Uses the `POST` method
  - Talks to an endpoint
  - Has `io.Reader` storing the JSON request
- Uses the client to send a request and get a response.
- Retrieves the response from the body of `http.Response`.
- Unmarshals JSON into the response object.

You will notice that `req` and `resp` are both `interface{}`. This allows us to use this routine with any struct that will represent a JSON request or response.

Now, we will use that in a method that gets a QOTD by an author:

```
func (q *QOTD) Get(ctx context.Context, author string) (string,
error) {
    const endpoint = `/v1/qotd`
    resp := getResp{}
    err := q.restCall(ctx, path.Join(q.addr, endpoint),
getReq{Author: author}), &resp)
    switch {
    case err != nil:
        return "", err
    case resp.Error != nil:
        return "", resp.Error
    }
    return resp.Quote, nil
}
```

This code does the following:

- Defines an endpoint for our `get` function on the server.
- Calls our `restCall()` method, which does the following:
  - Uses `path.Join()` to unite our server address and URL endpoint.
  - Creates a `getReq` object as the `req` argument of `restCall()`.
  - Reads the response into our `resp` response object.
  - If `*http.Client` returns an error, we return that error.
  - If `resp.Error` is set, we return it.
- Returns the response's quote.

To see this running now, you can go here: `https://play.golang.org/p/Th0PxpglnXw`.

We have shown how to make a base REST client here using HTTP `POST` calls and JSON. However, we have only scratched the surface of making a REST client. You may need to add authentication to the header in the form of a **JSON Web Token (JWT)**. This used HTTP and not HTTPS, so there was no transport security. We did not try to use compression such as Deflate or Gzip.

While using `http.Client` is easy to do, you may want a more intelligent wrapper that handles many of these features for you. One that is worth looking at would be `resty`, which can be found here: https://github.com/go-resty/resty.

Writing a REST service

Now that we have a client written, let's write a REST service endpoint that can receive the request and send the user the output:

```go
type server struct {
    serv *http.Server
    quotes map[string][]string
}
```

This code does the following:

- Creates the server `struct`, which will act as our server
- Uses `*http.Server` to server HTTP content
- Has `quotes`, which stores authors as keys and values that are a slice of quotes

Now, we need a constructor:

```go
func newServer(port int) (*server, error) {
    s := &server{
        serv: &http.Server{
            Addr: ":" + strconv.Itoa(port),
        },
        quotes: map[string][]string{
            // Add quotes here
        },
    }
    mux := http.NewServeMux()
    mux.HandleFunc(`/qotd/v1/get`, s.qotdGet)
    // The muxer implements http.Handler
```

```
        // and we assign it for our server's URL handling.
        s.serv.Handler = mux
        return s, nil
}

func (s *server) start() error {
        return s.serv.ListenAndServe()
}
```

This code does the following:

- Creates a `newServer` constructor:
  - This has an argument of `port`, which is the port to run the server on.
- Creates a `server` instance:
  - Makes an instance of `*http.Server` running at :[port]
  - Populates our `quotes map`
- Adds `*http.ServeMux` to map URLs to methods.

> **Note**
> We will create the `qotdGet` method in a moment.

- Creates a method called `start()` that will start our HTTP server.

`*http.ServeMux` implements the `http.Handler` interface that is used by `*http.Server`. ServeMux uses pattern matching to determine which method is called for which URL. You can read about pattern-matching syntax here: https://pkg.go.dev/net/http#ServeMux.

Now, let's create the method to answer our REST endpoint:

```
func (s *server) qotdGet(w http.ResponseWriter, r *http.Request) {
        req := getReq{}
        if err := req.fromReader(r.Body); err != nil {
                http.Error(w, err.Error(), http.StatusBadRequest)
                return
        }
```

```go
        var quotes []string

        if req.Author == "" {
            // Map access is random, this will randomly choose a
            // set of quotes from an author.
            for _, quotes = range s.quotes {
                break
            }
        } else {
            var ok bool
            quotes, ok = s.quotes[req.Author]
            if !ok {
                b, err := json.Marshal(
                    getResp{
                        Error: &Error{
                            Code: UnknownAuthor,
                            Msg: fmt.Sprintf("Author %q was not found", req.Author),
                        },
                    },
                )
                if err != nil {
                    http.Error(w, err.Error(), http.StatusBadRequest)
                    return
                }
                w.Write(b)
                return
            }
        }

        i := rand.Intn(len(quotes))
        b, err := json.Marshal(getResp{Quote: quotes[i]})
        if err != nil {
            http.Error(w, err.Error(), http.StatusBadRequest)
            return
        }
        w.Write(b)
        return
```

This code does the following:

- Implements the `http.Handler` interface.
- Reads the HTTP request body and marshals it to our `getReq`:
  - This uses HTTP error codes with `http.Error()` if the request was bad
- If the request did not contain an "author," randomly chooses an author's quotes.
- Otherwise, finds the author and retrieves their quotes:
  - If that author did not exist, responds with `getResp` containing an error
- Randomly chooses a quote and returns it to the client.

Now, we have a REST endpoint that can answer our client's RPCs. You can see this code running here: `https://play.golang.org/p/Th0PxpglnXw`.

This just scratches the surface of building a REST service. You can build authentication and compression on top of this, performance tracing, and so on

To help with bootstrapping features and removing some boilerplate, here are a few third-party packages that might be helpful:

- Gin: `https://github.com/gin-gonic/gin`:
  - A REST example: `https://golang.org/doc/tutorial/web-service-gin`
- Revel: `https://revel.github.io`

Now that we have talked about using REST for RPCs, let's take a look at the faster alternative that is being adopted by large companies everywhere, gRPC.

Developing gRPC services and clients

gRPC provides an entire framework for RPCs based on HTTP and utilizing Google's protocol buffer format, a binary format that can convert into JSON but provides both a schema and, in many cases, a 10x performance improvement over JSON.

There are other formats in this space, such as Apache's Thrift, Cap'n Proto, and Google's FlatBuffers. However, these are not as popular and well supported, or satisfy a particular niche, while also being hard to use.

gRPC, like REST, is a client/server framework for making RPC calls. Where gRPC differs is that it prefers a binary message format called **protocol buffers** (**proto** for short).

This format has a schema stored in a `.proto` file that is used to generate the client, server, and messages in a native library for the language of your choice using a compiler. When a proto message is marshaled for transport on the wire, the binary representation will be the same for all languages.

Let's talk more about protocol buffers, gRPC's message format of choice.

Protocol buffers

Protocol buffers define RPC messages and services in one location and can generate a library for every language with the proto compiler. Protocol buffers have the following advantages:

- They write once and generate for every language.
- Messages can be converted to JSON as well as binary.
- gRPC can use a reverse proxy to provide REST endpoints, which is great for web apps.
- Binary protocol buffers are smaller and can encode/decode at 10x the rate of JSON.

However, protocol buffers do have some negatives:

- You must regenerate the messages on any change to the `.proto` file to get the changes.
- Google's standard proto compiler is painful and confusing to use.
- JavaScript does not have native support for gRPC, even though it supports protocol buffers.

Tooling can help with some of the negatives, and we will be using the new **Buf** tools, `https://buf.build`, to help with proto generation.

Let's take a look at what a protocol buffer .proto file looks like for a QOTD service:

```
syntax = "proto3";
package qotd;
option go_package = "github.com/[repo]/proto/qotd";

message GetReq {
        string author = 1;
}
message GetResp {
        string author = 1;
        string quote = 2;
}

service QOTD {
   rpc GetQOTD(GetReq) returns (GetResp) {};
}
```

The `syntax` keyword defines which version of the proto language we are using. The most common version is `proto3`, the third iteration of the language. All three have the same wire format but have different feature sets and generate different language packages.

`package` defines the proto package name, which allows this protocol buffer to be imported by another package. We have put `[repo]` as a placeholder to represent the GitHub repository.

`go_package` defines the package name specifically when generating Go files. While this is marked as `option`, it is not optional when compiling for Go.

`message` defines a new message type, which in Go is generated as `struct`. Entries inside `message` detail the fields. `string author = 1` creates a field in `struct` `GetReq` called `Author` of the `string` type. `1` is the field position in the proto. You cannot have repeated field numbers in a message, a field number should never change, and a field should not be removed (although it can be deprecated).

`service` defines a gRPC service with one RPC endpoint, `GetQOTD`. This call receives `GetReq` and returns `GetResp`.

Now that we have defined this protocol buffer file, we can use a proto compiler to generate packages for languages we are interested in. This will include all of our messages and the code needed to use the gRPC client and server.

Let's look at generating the Go packages from the protocol buffer file.

Stating the prerequisites

To use protocol buffers in this tutorial, you will need to install the following:

- The protocol buffer compiler: `https://grpc.io/docs/protoc-installation/`
- The Go plugins for the compiler: `https://grpc.io/docs/languages/go/quickstart/`
- The Buf tooling: `https://docs.buf.build/installation`

With these installed, you will be able to generate code for C++ and Go. Other languages require additional plugins.

Generating your packages

The first file we need to create is the `buf.yaml` file. We can generate the `buf.yaml` file inside the `proto` directory by entering it and issuing the following command:

```
buf config init
```

This should generate a file that has the following content:

```yaml
version: v1
lint:
  use:
    - DEFAULT
breaking:
  use:
    - FILE
```

Next, we need a file that tells us what output to generate. Create a file called `buf.gen.yaml` and give it the following contents:

```yaml
version: v1
plugins:
  - name: go
    out: ./
    opt:
      - paths=source_relative
  - name: go-grpc
    out: ./
    opt:
      - paths=source_relative
```

This indicates that we should generate our `go` and `go-grpc` files in the same directory as our `.proto` file.

Now, we should test that our proto will build. We can do this by issuing the following command:

```
buf build
```

If there is no output, then our proto file should compile. Otherwise, we will get a list of errors that we need to fix.

Finally, let's generate our proto files:

```
buf generate
```

If you named the proto file `qotd.proto`, this should generate the following:

- `qotd.pb.go`, which will contain all your messages
- `qotd_grpc.pb.go`, which will contain all the gRPC stubs

Now that we have our proto package, let's build a client.

Writing a gRPC client

In the root folder of your repository, let's create two directories:

- `client/`, which will hold our client code
- `internal/server/`, which will hold our server code

Now, let's create a `client/client.go` file with the following:

```
package client

import (
        "context"
        "time"
        "google.golang.org/grpc"
        pb "[repo]/grpc/proto"
)

type Client struct {
```

```go
                client pb.QOTDClient
                conn   *grpc.ClientConn
}
func New(addr string) (*Client, error) {
        conn, err := grpc.Dial(addr, grpc.WithInsecure())
        if err != nil {
                return nil, err
        }
        return &Client{
                client: pb.NewQOTDClient(conn),
                conn: conn,
        }, nil
}

func (c *Client) QOTD(ctx context.Context, wantAuthor string) (author, quote string, err error) {
        if _, ok := ctx.Deadline(); !ok {
                var cancel context.CancelFunc
                ctx, cancel = context.WithTimeout(ctx, 2 * time.Second)
                defer cancel()
        }

        resp, err := c.client.GetQOTD(ctx, &pb.GetReq{Author: wantAuthor})
        if err != nil {
                return "", "", err
        }
        return resp.Author, resp.Quote, nil
}
```

This is a simple wrapper around the generated client with our connection to the server established in our New() constructor:

- grpc.Dial() connects to the server's address:
  - grpc.WithInsecure() allows us to not use TLS. (In real services, you need to use TLS!)

- `pb.NewQOTDClient()` takes a gRPC connection and returns our generated client.
- `QOTD()` uses the client to make a call defined in our `GetQOTD()` proto:
  - This defines a timeout if one was not defined. The server receives this timeout.
  - This uses the generated client to call the server.

Creating a wrapper to use as a client isn't strictly required. Many developers prefer to have the user directly interact with the service using the generated client.

In our opinion, this is fine for simple clients. More complicated clients generally should ease the burden by either moving logic to the server or having custom client wrappers that are more language-friendly.

Now that we have defined a client, let's create our server package.

Writing a gRPC server

Let's create a server file at `internal/server/server.go`.

Now, let's add the following content:

```
package server

import (
        "context"
        "fmt"
        "math/rand"
        "net"
        "sync"

        "google.golang.org/grpc"
        "google.golang.org/grpc/codes"
        "google.golang.org/grpc/status"

        pb "[repo]/grpc/proto"
)

type API struct {
    pb.UnimplementedQOTDServer
    addr string
    quotes map[string][]string
```

```go
        mu sync.Mutex
        grpcServer *grpc.Server
}
func New(addr string) (*API, error) {
        var opts []grpc.ServerOption
        a := &API{
            addr: addr,
            quotes: map[string][]string{
                // Insert your quote mappings here
            },
            grpcServer: grpc.NewServer(opts...),
        }
        a.grpcServer.RegisterService(&pb.QOTD_ServiceDesc, a)
        return a, nil
}
```

This code does the following:

- Defines our API server:
  - `pb.UnimplementedQOTDServer` is a generated interface that contains all the methods that our server must implement. This is required.
  - `addr` is the address our server will run on.
  - `quotes` contains quotes the server is storing.
- Defines a `New()` constructor:
  - This creates an instance of our `API` server.
  - This registers the instance with our `grpcServer`.

Now, let's add methods to start and stop our `API` server:

```go
func (a *API) Start() error {
    a.mu.Lock()
    defer a.mu.Unlock()

    lis, err := net.Listen("tcp", a.addr)
    if err != nil {
        return err
```

```
        }
        return a.grpcServer.Serve(lis)
}

func (a *API) Stop() {
        a.mu.Lock()
        defer a.mu.Unlock()
        a.grpcServer.Stop()
}
```

This code does the following:

- Defines `Start()` to start our server, which does the following:
    - Uses `Mutex` to prevent stops and starts concurrently
    - Creates a TCP listener on the address passed in `New()`
    - Starts the gRPC server using our listener
- Defines `Stop()` to stop our server, which does the following:
    - Uses `Mutex` to prevent stops and starts concurrently
    - Tells the gRPC server to stop gracefully

Now, let's implement the `GetQOTD()` method:

```
func (a *API) GetQOTD(ctx context.Context, req *pb.GetReq)
(*pb.GetResp, error) {
        var (
                author string
                quotes []string
        )
        if req.Author == "" {
                for author, quotes = range s.quotes {
                        break
                }
        } else {
                author = req.Author
                var ok bool
```

```
                quotes, ok = s.quotes[req.Author]
                if !ok {
                    return nil, status.Error(
                        codes.NotFound,
                        fmt.Sprintf("author %q not found", req.
author),
                    )
                }
        }

        return &pb.GetResp{
            Author: author,
            Quote: quotes[rand.Intn(len(quotes))],
        }, nil
}
```

This code does the following:

- Defines the `GetQOTD()` method that the client will call
- Includes similar logic to our REST server
- Uses gRPC's error type defined in the `google.golang.org/grpc/status` package to return gRPC error codes

Now that we have our client and server packages, let's create a server binary to run our service.

Creating a server binary

Create a file called `qotd.go` that will hold our server's `main()` function:

```
package main

import (
    "flag"
    "log"
    "github.com/[repo]/internal/server"
    pb "[repo]/proto"
)
```

```
var addr = flag.String("addr", "127.0.0.1:80", "The address to
run on.")

func main() {
    flag.Parse()
    s, err := server.New(*addr)
    if err != nil {
        panic(err)
    }
    done := make(chan error, 1)

    log.Println("Starting server at: ", *addr)
    go func() {
        defer close(done)
        done <-s.Start()
    }()

    err <- done
    log.Println("Server exited with error: ", err)
}
```

This code does the following:

- Creates a flag, `addr`, that the caller passes to set the address that the server runs on.
- Creates an instance of our server.
- Writes that we are starting the server.
- Starts the server.
- If the server exists, the error is printed to the screen:
  - This might be something saying the port is already in use.

You can run this binary by using this command:

`go run qotd.go --addr="127.0.0.1:2562"`

If you do not pass the `--addr` flag, this will default to `127.0.0.1:80`.

You should see the following on your screen:

`Starting server at: 127.0.0.1:2562`

Now, let's create a binary that uses the client to fetch a QOTD.

Creating a client binary

Create a file called `client/bin/qotd.go`. Then, add the following:

```go
package main

import (
        "context"
        "flag"
        "fmt"
        "github.com/devopsforgo/book/book/code/1/4/grpc/client"
)

var (
        addr   = flag.String("addr", "127.0.0.1:80", "The address of the server.")
        author = flag.String("author", "", "The author whose quote to get")
)

func main() {
        flag.Parse()

        c, err := client.New(*addr)
        if err != nil {
                panic(err)
        }

        a, q, err := c.QOTD(context.Background(), *author)
        if err != nil {
                panic(err)
        }

        fmt.Println("Author: ", a)
        fmt.Printf("Quote of the Day: %q\n", q)
}
```

This code does the following:

- Sets up a flag for the address of the server
- Sets up a flag for the author of the quote you want
- Creates a new instance of `client.QOTD`
- Calls the server using the `QOTD()` client method
- Prints the results or an error to the terminal

You can run this binary by using this command:

```
go run qotd.go --addr="127.0.0.1:2562"
```

This will contact the server running at this address. If you are running the server at a different address, you will need to change this to match.

If you do not pass the `--author` flag, this randomly chooses an author.

You should see the following on your screen:

```
Author: [some author]

Quote: [some quote]
```

Now we've seen how to use gRPC to make a simple client and server application. But this is just the beginning of the features available to you in gRPC.

We are just scratching the surface

gRPC is a key piece of infrastructure for cloud technology such as Kubernetes. It was built after years of experience with Stubby, Google's internal predecessor. We have only scratched the surface of what gRPC can do. Here are some additional features:

- Running a gRPC gateway to export REST endpoints
- Providing interceptors that can deal with security and other needs
- Providing streaming data
- TLS support
- Metadata and trailers for extra information
- Client-side server load balancing

Here are just a few of the big companies that have made the switch:

- Square
- Netflix
- IBM
- CoreOS
- Docker
- CockroachDB
- Cisco
- Juniper Networks
- Spotify
- Zalando
- Dropbox

Let's talk a little about how best to provide REST or gRPC services inside your company.

Company-standard RPC clients and servers

One of the keys to Google's tech stack success has been a consolidation around technologies. While there is certainly a lot of duplication in technology, Google standardizes on certain software and infrastructure components. Inside Google, it is rare to see a client/server not using Stubby (Google's internal gRPC).

The libraries that engineers use for RPC are written to work the same in every language. In recent years, there have been pushes by **Site Reliability Engineering** (**SRE**) organizations to have wrappers around Stubby that offer a breadth of features and best practices to prevent every team from reinventing the wheel. This includes features such as the following:

- Authentication
- Compression handling
- Distributed service rate limiting
- Retries with backoff (or circuit breaking)

This removes a lot of threats to infrastructure by having clients retrying without any backoffs, removing the cost of teams figuring out a security model, and allowing fixes to these items to be done by experts. Changes to these libraries benefit everyone and lower the cost of discovering already-made services.

As a DevOps engineer or SRE who likely carries a pager, pushing for standardization in your RPC layer can provide innumerable benefits, such as not being paged!

While choice is often seen as a good thing, having limited choices can allow development teams and operators to continue to focus on their product and not infrastructure, which is key in having robust products.

If you decide on providing a REST framework, here are a few recommended practices:

- Only use `POST`.
- Do not use query variables.
- Use JSON only.
- Have all arguments inside your request.

This will greatly reduce the needed code within your framework.

In this section, we learned what RPC services are and how to write clients using two popular methods, REST and gRPC. You also learned how REST has a looser set of guidelines while gRPC prefers schema types and generates the components required to use the system.

Summary

This ends our chapter on interacting with remote data sources. We looked at how to connect to SQL databases with examples using Postgres. We looked at what RPCs are and talked about the two most popular types of RPC services, REST and gRPC. Finally, we have written servers and clients for both frameworks.

This chapter has given you the ability to connect to the most popular databases and cloud services to get and retrieve data. Now you can write your own RPC services to develop cloud applications.

In the next chapter, we will utilize this knowledge to build tooling that controls jobs on remote machines.

So, without further ado, let's jump into how to write command-line tools.

7
Writing Command-Line Tooling

Visit any DevOps engineer and you will find their screens filled with terminals executing **Command-Line Interface (CLI)** applications.

As a DevOps engineer, we don't want to only use applications that others have made for us; we want to be able to write our own CLI applications. These applications might communicate to various systems via REST or gRPC, as we discussed in our previous chapter. Or you might want to execute various applications and run their output through custom processing. An application might even set up a development environment and kick off a test cycle for a new release.

Whatever your use case, you will need to use some common packages to help you manage the application's input and output processing.

In this chapter, you will learn how to use the `flag` and `os` packages to write simple CLI applications. For more complex applications, you will learn how to use the Cobra package. These skills, combined with the skills gained from our previous chapter, will let you build a wide gamut of applications for your needs or those of your customers.

We will cover the following main topics in this chapter:

- Implementing application I/O
- Using Cobra for advanced CLI applications
- Handling OS signals

In this first section, we will jump into how to use the standard library's `flag` package to build basic command-line programs. Let's get started!

Technical requirements

The code files for this chapter can be downloaded from `https://github.com/PacktPublishing/Go-for-DevOps/tree/rev0/chapter/7`

Implementing application I/O

CLI applications require a way to understand how you want them to execute. This might include what files to read, what servers to contact, and what credentials to use.

There are a couple of ways to start an application with the parameters it requires:

- Using the `flag` package to define command-line flags
- Using `os.Args` to read arguments that are not defined

The `flag` package will help you when you have a command-line argument that has a strict definition. This might be an argument that defines the endpoint for a needed service. The program might want to have a default value for production, but allow an override when doing testing. This is perfect for a flag.

An example might be a program that queries our **Quote of the Day (QOTD)** server that we created earlier. We might want to have it automatically use our production endpoint unless we specify it to use another address. This might look like this:

```
qotd
```

This simply contacts our production server and gets our quote. The `--endpoint` flag, which defaulted to our production address, will use another address below:

```
qotd --endpoint="127.0.0.1:3850"
```

Sometimes, application arguments will suffice. Take an application that reformats JSON data for human readability. We might want to just read from STDIN if no files are provided. In this case, just reading the values from the command line will suffice, using the os package. This will give us executions that look like this:

```
reformat file1.json file2.json
```

Here, we are reading in `file1.json` and `file2.json` and outputting the reformatted text.

Here, we receive the output from the wget call and read that via STDIN to our reformat binary. This is similar to how cat and grep work. When our arguments are empty, they simply read from STDIN:

```
wget "http://some.server.com" | reformat
```

And sometimes, we may want a mix of flags and arguments. The flag package can help with that as well.

So, let's jump into using the flag package.

The flag package

To help take in command-line arguments, Go has the standard library flag package. With flag, you can set up default values for your flags, provide descriptions for flags, and allow users to override defaults at the command line.

Flags with the flag package are simply proceeded by --, similar to --endpoint. Values can simply be a contiguous string following the endpoint or a quoted string. While you can use a single - instead of --, there are some corner cases when dealing with Boolean flags. I would recommend using -- in all cases.

You can find the flag package documentation here: https://pkg.go.dev/flag.

Let's show a flag in action:

```
var endpoint = flag.String(
    "endpoint",
    "myserver.aws.com",
    "The server this app will contact",
)
```

This code does the following:

- Defines an `endpoint` variable that stores the flag
- Uses a `String` flag
- Defines the flag as `endpoint`
- Sets the flag's default value as `myserver.aws.com`
- Sets the flag's description

If we don't pass `--endpoint`, the code will use the default value. To have our program read the value, we simply do the following:

```
func main() {
    flag.Parse()

    fmt.Println("server endpoint is: ", *endpoint)
}
```

> **Important Note**
> `flag.String()` returns `*string`, hence `*endpoint` above.

`flag.Parse()` is crucial to making your flags available in your application. This should only be called inside your `main()` package.

> **Pro Tip**
> A best practice in Go is to never define flags outside your `main` package. Simply pass the values as function arguments or in object constructors.

`flag` also defines a few other flag functions other than `String()`:

- `Bool()` for capturing `bool`
- `Int()` for capturing `int`
- `Int64()` for capturing `int64`
- `Uint()` for capturing `uint`
- `Uint64()` for capturing `uint64`
- `Float64()` for capturing `float64`
- `Duration()` for capturing `time.Duration`, such as `3m10s`

Now that we have seen the basic types, let's talk about custom flag types.

Custom flags

Sometimes, we want to take values and put them in types that aren't defined in the `flag` package.

To use a custom flag, you must define a type that implements the `flag.Value` interface, defined as the following:

```
type Value interface {
    String() string
    Set(string) error
}
```

Next, we are going to borrow an example from Godoc that shows a custom value called `URLValue`, which handles flags that represent URLs, and store it in our standard `*url.URL` type:

```
type URLValue struct {
    URL *url.URL
}

func (v URLValue) String() string {
    if v.URL != nil {
        return v.URL.String()
    }
    return ""
}

func (v URLValue) Set(s string) error {
    if u, err := url.Parse(s); err != nil {
        return err
    } else {
        *v.URL = *u
    }
    return nil
}

var u = &url.URL{}
func init() {
    flag.Var(&URLValue{u}, "url", "URL to parse")
}
```

```go
func main() {
    flag.Parse()
    if reflect.ValueOf(*u).IsZero() {
        panic("did not pass an URL")
    }
    fmt.Printf(`{scheme: %q, host: %q, path: %q}`,
               u.Scheme, u.Host, u.Path)
}
```

This code does the following:

- Defines a `flag.Value` type called `URLValue`
- Creates a flag called `-url` that reads in a valid URL
- Uses the `URLValue` wrapper to store the URL in a `*url.URL` variable
- Uses the `reflect` package to determine whether `struct` is empty

By defining a `Set()` method on a type, as we did previously, you can read in any custom value.

Now that we have our flag types down, let's look at some basic error handling.

Basic flag error handling

When we enter flags that are not compatible or have a bad value, often we want the program to print out the bad flag and the flag values.

This can be accomplished with the `PrintDefaults()` option. Here's an example:

```go
var (
    useProd = flag.Bool("prod", true, "Use a production endpoint")
    useDev = flag.Bool("dev", false, "Use a development endpoint")
    help = flag.Bool("help", false, "Display help text")
)
func main() {
    flag.Parse()

    if *help {
        flag.PrintDefaults()
        return
```

```
        }
    switch {
    case *useProd && *useDev:
        log.Println("Error: --prod and --dev cannot both be
 set")
        flag.PrintDefaults()
        os.Exit(1)
    case !(*useProd || *useDev):
        log.Println("Error: either --prod or --dev must be
 set")
        flag.PrintDefaults()
        os.Exit(1)
    }
}
```

This code does the following:

- Defines a `--help` flag that just prints our defaults if set
- Defines two other flags, `--prod` and `--dev`
- If `--prod` and `--dev` are set, prints out an error message and the default flag values
- If neither are set, puts out an error message and the defaults

Here is an example of the output:

```
Error: --prod and --dev cannot both be set
  -dev
        Use a development endpoint (default false)
  -prod
        Use a production endpoint (default true)
```

This code illustrates how we can have flags with valid default values, but if the values are changed to cause an error, we can detect and handle the error. And in the spirit of good command-line tools, we provide `--help` to allow users to discover the flags they can use.

Shorthand flags

In the previous example, we had a `--help` flag. But often, you may want to offer a shorthand such as `-h` for the user to use. These need to have the same default values and both need to set the same variable, so they cannot have two separate values.

We can use the `flag.[Type]Var()` calls to help us accomplish this:

```
var (
    useProd = flag.Bool("prod", true,
                "Use a production endpoint")
    useDev = flag.Bool("dev", false,
                "Use a development endpoint")
    help = new(bool)
)
func init() {
    flag.BoolVar(help, "help", false, "Display help text")
    flag.BoolVar(help, "h", false,
                "Display help text (shorthand)")
}
```

Here, we store the results of `--help` and `--h` in our `help` variable. We use `init()` to do the setup, as `BoolVar()` does not return a variable; therefore, it cannot be used in a `var()` statement.

Now that we know how a shorthand flag works, let's have a look at non-flag arguments.

Accessing non-flag arguments

Arguments in Go are read in a few ways. You can read the raw arguments using `os.Args`, which will also include all the flags. This is great when no flags are used.

When using flags, `flag.Args()` can be used to retrieve only the non-flag arguments. If we want to send a list of authors to a development server and retrieve QOTDs for each author, the command might look like this:

```
qotd --dev "abraham lincoln" "martin king" "mark twain"
```

In this list, we use a --dev flag to indicate that we want to use the development server. Following our flag, we have a list of arguments. Let's retrieve those:

```
func main() {
    flag.Parse()

    authors := flag.Args
    if len(authors) == 0 {
        log.Println("did not pass any authors")
        os.Exit(1)
    }
    ...
```

In this code, we do the following:

- Retrieve the non-flag arguments using `flag.Args()`.
- Test that we received at least one author or exit with an error.

We have seen how to retrieve input that comes as arguments or flags. This can be used to define how to contact a server or what files to open. Let's look at receiving input from a stream.

Retrieving input from STDIN

Most applications that are written today in the DevOps community tend to revolve around flags and arguments, as seen previously. One of the less common methods of input that DevOps people use daily is piping input into a program.

Tools such as `cat`, `xargs`, `sed`, `awk`, and `grep` allow you to pipe the output of one tool into the input of the next to accomplish a task. A simple example might be just looking for lines in a file we retrieved from the web that contains the word `error`:

```
wget http://server/log | grep -i "error" > only_errors.txt
```

Programs such as `cat` read input from STDIN when no file has been specified. Let's duplicate that here for a program that looks for the word `error` on any input line and prints it out:

```
var errRE = regexp.MustCompile(`(?i)error`)
```

```
func main() {
    var s *bufio.Scanner
    switch len(os.Args) {
    case 1:
        log.Println("No file specified, using STDIN")
        s = bufio.NewScanner(os.Stdin)
    case 2:
        f, err := os.Open(os.Args[1])
        if err != nil {
            log.Println(err)
            os.Exit(1)
        }
        s = bufio.NewScanner(f)
    default:
        log.Println("too many arguments provided")
        os.Exit(1)
    }

    for s.Scan() {
        line := s.Bytes()
        if errRE.Match(line) {
            fmt.Printf("%s\n", line)
        }
    }
    if err := s.Err(); err != nil {
        log.Println("Error: ", err)
        os.Exit(1)
    }
}
```

This code does the following:

- Compiles a regex using the `regexp` package to look for a line containing `error` – the match is case-insensitive.
- Uses `os.Args()` to read our argument list. We use this instead of `flag.Args()`, as we haven't defined any flags.
- Uses `os.Stdin` if we have a single argument (the program name), which is an `io.Reader` that we wrap in a `bufio.Scanner`.

- Opens the file if we have a file argument and wraps the `io.Reader` in a `bufio.Scanner` object.
- Returns an error if we have more arguments.
- Reads input line by line and prints to `os.Stdout` every line containing the word `error`.
- Checks whether we had an input error – `io.EOF` is not considered an error and won't trip the `if` statement.

You can find this code in the repository `https://github.com/PacktPublishing/Go-for-DevOps/blob/rev0/chapter/7/filter_errors/main.go`.

Using this code compiled as `filter_errors`, we can use this to scan wget input (or any piped input) for lines containing the word `error` and then use `grep` to filter for a particular error code such as `401` (unauthorized):

```
wget http://server/log | filter_errors | grep 401
```

Or we can search a log file in the same way:

```
filter_errors log.txt | grep 401
```

This is a simplistic example that can easily be achieved with existing tools, but this gives a demonstration of how to build similar tooling.

In this section, we have looked at how to read different input from the command line in the form of flags and arguments. We looked at shorthand flags that share state with long-form flags. You saw how to create custom types to use as flags. And finally, we looked at how to successfully use STDIN to read input that is sent via a pipe.

Next, we will look at how to use Cobra, a third-party package, to create more sophisticated command-line applications.

Using Cobra for advanced CLI applications

Cobra is a set of packages that allows a developer to create more complex CLI applications. This becomes more useful than just the standard `flag` package when the complexity of an application causes a list of flags to become numerous.

In this section, we will talk about how to use Cobra to create structured CLI applications that are friendly to developers to add features and allow users to understand what is available in an application.

A few features that Cobra provides are as follows:

- Nested subcommands
- Command suggestions
- Aliases for commands so that you can make changes without breaking users
- Generation of help text from flags and commands
- Generation of autocompletion for various shells
- Man page creation

This section will borrow heavily from the Cobra documentation, which you can find here: https://github.com/spf13/cobra/blob/master/user_guide.md.

Code organization

To make effective use of Cobra and make it easy for developers to understand where to add and change commands, Cobra suggests the following structure:

```
appName/
    cmd/
        add.go
        your.go
        commands.go
        here.go
    main.go
```

This structure has your main `main.go` executable at the top-level directory and all of your commands under `cmd/`.

The main file for a Cobra application is primarily used to simply initialize Cobra and let it perform command executions. The file will look like this:

```
package main
import (
    "{pathToYourApp}/cmd"
)

func main() {
    cmd.Execute()
}
```

Next, we will look at using the Cobra generator application to generate boilerplate code.

The optional Cobra generator

Cobra provides an application that can generate boilerplate code for our application. To get started with the generator, we will create a configuration file for our application in our root directory called `~/.cobra.yaml`:

```
author: John Doak myemail@somedomain.com
year: 2021
license: MIT
```

This will handle printing our MIT license. You can use any of these values for the following built-in licenses:

- GPLv2
- GPLv3
- LGPL
- AGPL
- 2-Clause BSD
- 3-Clause BSD

If you need a license not found here, instructions on how to provide a custom license can be found here: `https://github.com/spf13/cobra-cli/blob/main/README.md#configuring-the-cobra-generator`.

By default, Cobra will use this configuration file from your home directory. If you need a different license, put the configuration in your repository and use `cobra --config="config/location.yaml` to use the alternate configuration file.

To download Cobra and build with the Cobra generator, type the following on your command line:

```
go get github.com/spf13/cobra/cobra
go install github.com/spf13/cobra/cobra
```

Now, to initialize the application, make sure that you are in the new application's root directory and do the following:

```
cobra init --pkg-name [repo path]
```

> **Important Note**
> [repo path] will be something such as `github.com/spf13/newApp`.

Let's create a few commands for our application:

```
cobra add serve
cobra add config
cobra add create -p 'configCmd'
```

This will deliver us the following:

```
app/
    cmd/
        serve.go
        config.go
        create.go
    main.go
```

> **Important Note**
> You are required to use camelCase for command names. Not doing this will cause you to encounter errors.

The `-p` option for `create` is used to make it a subcommand of `config`. The string that follows is the parent's name plus `Cmd`. All other `add` calls have `-p` set to `rootCmd`.

After you `go build` the application, we can run it like so:

- `app`
- `app serve`
- `app config`
- `app config create`
- `app help serve`

With the boilerplate now in place, we will only need to configure the commands to execute.

The command package

In the cmd package that has been generated, you will find a file for each command that can be executed. We will need to modify each file to give the correct help text, use flags, and execute the command.

We will look at a generated cmd/get.go file for an application created with the following commands:

```
cobra init --pkg-name [repo path]
cobra add get
```

This application will talk to the QOTD server that we created in *Chapter 6, Interacting with Remote Data Sources*.

The generated cmd/get.go file will look similar to this:

```go
var getCmd = &cobra.Command{
        Use:   "get",
        Short: "A brief description of your command",
        Long: `A longer description that spans multiple lines
and likely contains examples and usage of using your command.`,
        Run: func(cmd *cobra.Command, args []string) {
                fmt.Println("get called")
        },
}

func init() {
        rootCmd.AddCommand(getCmd)
}
```

This code does the following:

- Creates a variable called `serveCmd`:
  - Variable name is based on the command name plus `Cmd`.
  - `Use` is the argument name for the command line.
  - `Short` is the brief description.

- Long is a longer description with examples.
- Run is the entry point for the code you want to execute.

- Defines `init()`, which does the following:

  - Adds this command to the `rootCmd` object.

Let's use this to write our QOTD CLI:

```
...
Run: func(cmd *cobra.Command, args []string) {
    const devAddr = "127.0.0.1:3450"

    fs := cmd.Flags()

    addr := mustString(fs, "addr")

    if mustBool(fs, "dev") {
        addr = devAddr
    }

    c, err := client.New(addr)
    if err != nil {
        fmt.Println("error: ", err)
        os.Exit(1)
    }

    a, q, err := c.QOTD(cmd.Context(), mustString(fs,
"author"))) 
    if err != nil {
        fmt.Println("error: ", err)
        os.Exit(1)
    }

    switch {
    case mustBool(fs, "json"):
        b, err := json.Marshal(
            struct{
```

```
                        Author string
                        Quote string
                    }{a, q},
                )
                if err != nil {
                    panic(err)
                }
                fmt.Printf("%s\n", b)
            default:
                fmt.Println("Author: ", a)
                fmt.Println("Quote: ", q)
            }
        },
    }
```

This code does the following:

- Sets up an `addr` variable to hold our server address:
  - If `--dev` is passed, it sets `addr` to `devAddr`.
  - Otherwise, it uses the `--addr` flag's value.
  - `--addr` defaults to `127.0.0.1:80`.
- Creates a new client for our QOTD server
- Calls the QOTD server:
  - Uses `Context` passed to `*cobra.Command`
  - Uses the `--author` flag value, which defaults to an empty string
- Uses a `--json` flag to determine whether the output should be in JSON:
  - If JSON, it outputs an inline-defined struct as JSON.
  - Otherwise, it just pretty prints it to the screen.

> **Important Note**
>
> You will see the `mustBool()` and `mustString()` functions. These simply return the value from the flag name that is passed. If the flag isn't defined, it panics. This removes a lot of ugly code for something that must always work for the CLI application to be valid. These functions are in the repository version.
>
> The flags that you see are not from the standard library `flag` package. Instead, this package uses flag types from `https://github.com/spf13/pflag`. This package has more built-in types and methods than the standard `flag` package.

Now, we need to define the flags that we are using in our Run function:

```
func init() {
        rootCmd.AddCommand(getCmd)
        getCmd.Flags().BoolP("dev", "d", false,
            "Uses the dev server instead of prod")
        getCmd.Flags().String("addr", "127.0.0.1:80",
            "Set the QOTD server to use,
            defaults to production")
        getCmd.Flags().StringP("author", "a", "",
            "Specify the author to
            get a quote for")
        getCmd.Flags().Bool("json", false,
            "Output is in JSON format")
}
```

This code does the following:

- Adds a flag called `--dev` that can be shortened to `-d` and defaults to `false`
- Adds a flag called `--addr` that defaults to `"127.0.0.1:80"`
- Adds a flag called `--author` that can be shortened to `-a`
- Adds a flag called `--json` that defaults to `false`

> **Important Note**
>
> Methods followed by P, such as `BoolP()`, define shortened flags as well as the long flag names.

The flags we defined are only available when the `get` command is invoked. If we create subcommands on `get`, these will only be available on `get` with no sub-commands defined.

To add flags that work on all subcommands, use `.PersistentFlags()` instead of `.Flags()`.

The code for this client can be found in the repository here: https://github.com/PacktPublishing/Go-for-DevOps/tree/rev0/chapter/7/cobra/app/.

Now, we can run our app and call this command. In these examples, you will need to run the QOTD server from the gRPC chapter, like so:

```
$ go run qotd.go --addr=127.0.0.1:3560
$ go run main.go get --addr=127.0.0.1:3560 --author="Eleanor Roosevelt" -json
```

This runs our application using the server at the `127.0.0.1:3560` address and requests a quote from Eleanor Roosevelt, with output in JSON format:

```
{"Author":"Eleanor Roosevelt","Quote":"The future belongs to those who believe in the beauty of their dreams"}
```

This next example gets a random quote from the server at address `127.0.0.1:3560`:

```
$ go run main.go get --addr=127.0.0.1:3560
Author: Mark Twain
Quote: Golf is a good walk spoiled
```

In this section, we have learned what the Cobra package is, how to use the Cobra generator tool to bootstrap a CLI application, and finally, how to build commands for your application using this package.

Next, we are going to look at handling signals to do cleanup before exiting your applications.

Handling OS signals

When writing CLI applications, there are occasions when a developer wants to handle OS signals. The most common example is a user trying to exit a program, usually through a keyboard shortcut.

In these cases, you may want to do some file cleanup before exiting or cancel a call you made to a remote system.

In this section, we will talk about how you can capture and respond to these events to make your applications more robust.

Capturing an OS signal

Go deals with two types of OS signals:

- Synchronous
- Asynchronous

Synchronous signals generally revolve around program errors. Go treats these as runtime panics, and therefore, interception of these can be handled with a `defer` statement.

There are different asynchronous signals, depending on the platform, but for a Go programmer, the most relevant are as follows:

- `SIGHUP`: The connected terminal disconnected.
- `SIGTERM`: Please quit and do cleanup (generated from a program).
- `SIGINT`: The same as `SIGTERM` (sent from the terminal).
- `SIGQUIT`: The same as `SIGTERM` plus a core dump (sent from the terminal).
- `SIGKILL`: The program must quit; this signal cannot be captured.

In situations where these arise, it can be useful to intercept these signals so that you can cancel ongoing operations and do a cleanup before exiting. It should be noted that `SIGKILL` cannot be intercepted, and `SIGHUP` is simply an indication that a process has lost its terminal, not necessarily that it was canceled. This could be because it was moved to the background or another similar event.

To capture a signal, we can use the `os/signal` package. This package allows a program to receive notifications of a signal from an OS and respond. Here is a simple example:

```
signals := make(chan os.Signal, 1)
signal.Notify(
    signals,
    syscall.SIGINT,
    syscall.SIGTERM,
    syscall.SIGQUIT,
)

go func() {
    switch <-signals {
    case syscall.SIGINT, syscall.SIGTERM:
        cleanup()
```

```
                os.Exit(1)
        case syscall.SIGQUIT:
            cleanup()
            panic("SIGQUIT called")
        }
    }()
```

This code does the following:

- Creates a channel, `signals`, on which to receive signals
- Subscribes to signals of the `SIGINT`, `SIGTERM`, and `SIGQUIT` types
- Uses a goroutine to handle incoming signals, which does the following:
  - Calls the `cleanup()` function to handle program cleanup
  - Exits with the `1` code on `SIGINT` and `SIGTERM`
  - Panics, which gives a basic core dump on `SIGQUIT`

Signal-handling code should be done in your `main` package. The `cleanup()` function should contain function calls that handle outstanding items, such as remote call cancellations and file cleanup.

> **Important Note**
> You can control the amount of data and generation method of a core dump using an environmental variable, GOTRACEBACK. You can read about it here: `https://pkg.go.dev/runtime#hdr-Environment_Variables`.

Using Context to cancel

The key method in Go to cause operations to stop processing is to use the context cancellation feature of Go's `context.Context` object. This object was discussed in *Chapter 2, Go Language Essentials*, if you need a refresher.

By simply creating a `Context` object with cancellation in `main()` and passing it to all function calls, we can effectively cancel all ongoing work. This can be handy when we want to stop processing and do cleanup because a user hits *Ctrl + C*.

We are going to show an advanced signal handling method on a program that does the following:

- Creates a new temporary file every 1 second for 30 seconds
- Cleans up files if the program is canceled

Let's start by creating a function to handle our signals:

```go
func handleSignal(cancel context.CancelFunc) chan os.Signal {
    out := make(chan os.Signal, 1)

    notify := make(chan os.Signal, 10)
    signal.Notify(
        notify,
        syscall.SIGINT,
        syscall.SIGTERM,
        syscall.SIGQUIT,
    )

    go func() {
        defer close(out)
        for {
            sig := <-notify
            switch sig {
            case syscall.SIGINT, syscall.SIGTERM, syscall.SIGQUIT:
                cancel()
                out <- sig
                return
            default:
                log.Println("unhandled signal: ", sig)
            }
        }
    }()
    return out
}
```

This code does the following:

- Creates a new function called `handleSignal()`
- Has an argument called `cancel`, which is used to signal a function chain to stop processing
- Creates an `out` channel that we use to return with the signal received
- Creates a `notify` channel to receive signal notifications
- Creates a goroutine to receive signals:
  - If the signal is for exiting, call `cancel()`.
  - Return the signal that told us to exit.
  - If it is some other signal, just log it.

Now, let's create a function that creates our files:

```
func createFiles(ctx context.Context, tmpFiles string) error {
        for i := 0; i < 30; i++ {
                if err := ctx.Err(); err != nil {
                        return ctx.Err()
                }
                _, err := os.Create(filepath.Join(tmpFiles, strconv.Itoa(i)))
                if err != nil {
                        return err
                }
                fmt.Println("Created file: ", i)
                time.Sleep(1 * time.Second)
        }
        return nil
}
```

This code does the following:

- Loops 30 times, which does the following:
  - Checks whether our `ctx` is canceled
  - If so, returns the error

- Otherwise, creates a file in tmpFiles
- Sleeps for 1 second between file creations

This code will create files in tmpFiles named from 0 to 29 unless there is a problem writing the file or Context is canceled.

Now, we need some code to clean up the files if we receive a quit signal. If we don't, the files are left alone:

```
func cleanup(tmpFiles string) {
        if err := os.RemoveAll(tmpFiles); err != nil {
                fmt.Println("problem doing file cleanup: ", err)
                return
        }
        fmt.Println("cleanup done")
}
```

This code does the following:

- Uses os.RemoveAll() to remove the files:
  - Also removes the temporary directory
- Notifies the user that cleanup was done

Let's tie it all together with our main():

```
func main() {
        tmpFiles, err := os.MkdirTemp("", "myApp_*")
        if err != nil {
                log.Println("error creating temp file directory: ", err)
                os.Exit(1)
        }
        fmt.Println("temp files located at: ", tmpFiles)

        ctx, cancel := context.WithCancel(context.Background())
        recvSig := handleSignal(cancel)
```

```
            if err := createFiles(ctx, tmpFiles); err != nil {
                cleanup(tmpFiles)
                select {
                case sig := <-recvSig:
                        if sig == syscall.SIGQUIT {
                                panic("SIGQUIT called")
                        }
                default:
                // Prevents waiting on a
                // signal if none exists.
                }
                log.Println("error: ", err)
                os.Exit(1)
            }
            fmt.Println("Done")
}
```

This code does the following:

- Creates a temporary file directory
- Creates a root `Context` object, `ctx`:
  - `ctx` can be canceled with `cancel()`.
- Calls our `handleSignal()` to handle any signal to quit
- Executes our `createFiles()` function:
  - If we have an error, we call `cleanup()`.
  - After cleanup, we see whether we received a signal as opposed to just an error.
  - If it is a signal and it is `SIGQUIT`, we call `panic()`. This is because `SIGQUIT` should core-dump by definition.
  - If it was just an error, print the error and return an error code.

The full code for this can be found in the repository here: `https://github.com/PacktPublishing/Go-for-DevOps/tree/rev0/chapter/7/signals`.

> **Important Note**
>
> The code must be built with `go build` and run as a binary. It cannot be run with `go run`, as the go binary that forks our program will intercept the signal before our program can.
>
> Multiple types of core dumps can be created in Go, controlled by an environmental variable. This is controlled by GOTRACEBACK. You can read about it here: `https://pkg.go.dev/runtime#hdr-Environment_Variables`.

Cancellation with Cobra

When Cobra was initially created, the `context` package did not exist. In 2020, the program was patched to allow the passing of a `Context` object into `cobra.Command`. But unfortunately, the Cobra generator was not updated to generate the necessary boilerplate.

To add signal handling as we did previously, we simply need to make a couple of modifications – first, to the `main.go` file:

```go
func main() {
    ctx, cancel := context.WithCancel(context.Background())

    var sigCh chan os.Signal
    go func() {
            handleSignal(ctx, cancel)
    }()

    cmd.Execute(ctx)
    cancel()

    if sig := <-sigCh; sig == syscall.SIGQUIT {
            panic("SIGQUIT")
    }
}
```

We will also need to modify `handleSignal()`. You can see those changes here: https://go.dev/play/p/F4SdN-xC-V_L

Finally, you must change the `cmd/root.go` file like so:

```
func Execute(ctx context.Context) {
        cobra.CheckErr(rootCmd.ExecuteContext(ctx))
}
```

We now have signal handling. When writing our `Run` function, we can use `cmd.Context()` to retrieve the `Context` object and look for cancelation.

Case study – a lack of cancellation leads to a death spiral

One of the early Google systems to help automate the network was a system called Chipmunk. Chipmunk contained authoritative data on the network and would generate router configurations from that data.

Like most software, Chipmunk started off working fast and saving a lot of time. As the network continued its yearly tenfold growth, the limits of its design and language choice began to show.

Chipmunk was built on Django and Python and was not designed for horizontal scaling. As the system became busy, configuration requests would start to take 30 minutes or longer. Timers for these requests would have limits of no more than 30 minutes.

The design had a fatal flaw when generation approached these limits – if a request was canceled, the cancellation was not signaled to the running configuration generator.

This meant that if generation took 25 minutes but was canceled 1 minute in, the generator would spend the next 24 minutes working, with no one to receive the work.

When a call reached the time limit, the callers would time out and retry. But the generator was still working on the previous call. This would lead to a cascade failure, as multiple compute-heavy calculations were running, some of which no longer had a receiver. This would push the new call over the time limit, as the Python **Global Interpreter Lock (GIL** https://wiki.python.org/moin/GlobalInterpreterLock) prevents true multi-threading and each call was doubling CPU usage.

One of the keys to dealing with this type of failure scenario is being able to cancel jobs that are no longer needed. This is why it is so important to pipe a `context.Context` object throughout a function call chain and look for cancellation at logical points. This can greatly reduce the load on a system that reaches a threshold and reduce the damage of **Distributed Denial of Service (DDoS)** attacks.

This section has looked at how a program can intercept OS signals and respond to those signals. It has provided an example of using `Context` to handle canceling executions that can be used in any application. We have discussed how we can integrate that into programs generated with the Cobra generator.

Summary

This chapter has given you the skills to write basic and advanced command-line applications. We discussed how you can use the `flag` package and `os` package to receive signals from the user in the form of flags and arguments. We also discussed how to read data from `os.Stdin`, which allows you to string multiple executables into a chain for processing.

We have discussed more advanced applications, namely the Cobra package and its accompanying generator binary, to build advanced command-line tooling with help text, shortcuts, and sub-commands.

Finally, we have talked about dealing with signals and providing cleanup on cancellation from these signals. This included a case study on why cancellation can be critical.

The skills you have learned here will be critical in writing tooling in the future, from interacting with local files to interacting with services.

In the next chapter, we will talk about how to automate interactions with the command line on your local device or remote devices.

8
Automating Command-Line Tasks

Most jobs start out as some type of manual operation that an engineer performs. Over time, these should become documented procedures that have the best practice for doing some operation, and finally, that job should become the work of software that takes those best practices and runs them with the efficiency that only a machine can provide.

One of the core missions of a **development-operations** (**DevOps**) engineer is automating these tasks. This can be from the mundane, such as running a few commands, to changing the configuration on thousands of machines.

Automating systems often requires manipulating a system via its command line and calling other tools native to the **operating system** (**OS**). This can include using **RPM Package Manager** (**RPM**)/**Debian Package** (**dpkg**) for installing packages, grabbing stats for a system using common utilities, or configuring network routers.

A DevOps engineer may want to do this locally to automate a series of steps normally done manually (such as automating Kubernetes's `kubectl` tool) or remotely execute commands on hundreds of machines at the same time. This chapter will cover how these can be accomplished using Go.

In this chapter, you will learn how to execute command-line tools on the local machine to accomplish automation goals. To access a remote machine, we will learn about how to use **Secure Shell** (**SSH**) and Expect packages. But knowing how to call executables on machines is just one part of the skillset. We will also talk about the anatomy of a change and how to do concurrent changes safely.

We will cover the following topics in this chapter:

- Using `os/exec` to automate local changes
- Using SSH in Go to automate remote changes
- Designing safe, concurrent change automations
- Writing a system agent

Technical requirements

This chapter requires that you have the latest Go tooling installed and access to a Linux system for running any service binaries we create. All tooling in this chapter will be geared toward controlling a Linux system, as this is the most popular cloud computing platform.

For the remote machine access requirements, the remote Linux system will need to be running SSH to allow for remote connectivity.

To use the system agent in the final part of this chapter, you will also need to use a Linux distribution that has `systemd` installed. Most modern distributions use `systemd`.

Code written in this chapter can be found here:

```
https://github.com/PacktPublishing/Go-for-DevOps/tree/rev0/chapter/8
```

Using os/exec to automate local changes

Automating the execution of tools that are local to the machine can provide a series of benefits to end users. The first of these is that it can reduce the toil that your team experiences. One of the primary goals for DevOps and **Site Reliability Engineers** (**SRE**) is to remove repetitive, manual processes. That time can be put to better use by reading a good book (such as this one), organizing a sock drawer, or working on the next problem. The second benefit is to remove manual mistakes from a process. It is easy to type the wrong thing or copy and paste something incorrectly. And finally, it is the core underpinning of operating at scale. Automating locally can be combined with other techniques detailed in the book to make changes at a large scale.

The automation life cycle generally comes in three stages, moving from manually doing work to automation, as follows:

1. The first stage revolves around the manual execution of commands by an experienced engineer. While this is not automation itself, this starts a cycle that ends with some type of automation.
2. The second stage usually revolves around writing those stages down in order to document the procedure, to allow more than one person to share the workload. This might be a **method of procedure** (**MOP**) document, though more commonly, it is a bunch of notes that you spend an hour looking for. We highly recommend a central place to store these such as a wiki or markdown in a `git` repository.
3. The third stage is usually a script to make the task repeatable.

Once a company gets larger, these stages are usually condensed into developing a service to handle the task in a fully automated way when a need for it is identified.

A good example of this might be deploying pods on a Kubernetes cluster or adding a new pod configuration to your Kubernetes config. These are driven by calling command-line applications such as `kubectl` and `git`. These types of jobs start manually; eventually, they are documented and finally automated in some way. At some point, this might move into a **continuous integration/continuous deployment** (**CI/CD**) system that handles this for you.

The key to automating tooling locally is the `os/exec` package. This package allows for the execution of other tools and control of their `STDIN/STDOUT/STDERR` streams.

Let's take a closer look.

Determining the availability of essential tools

When writing an application that calls other applications on a system, it is critical to determine if the tools needed are available on the system before you start executing commands. Nothing is worse than being partway through a procedure to find that a critical tool is missing.

The `exec` package provides the `LookPath()` function to help determine if a binary exists. If only the name of the binary is provided, the `PATH` environmental variable is consulted and those paths will be searched for the binary. If a `/` is in the name, only that path will be consulted.

Let's say we are writing a tool that needs both `kubectl` and `git` to be installed in order to work. We can test if those tools are available in our PATH variable by executing the following code:

```go
const (
    kubectl = "kubectl"
    git = "git"
)
_, err := exec.LookPath(kubectl)
if err != nil {
    return fmt.Errorf("cannot find kubectl in our PATH")
}
_, err := exec.LookPath(git)
if err != nil {
    return fmt.Errorf("cannot find git in our PATH")
}
```

This code does the following:

- Defines constants for our binary names
- Uses `LookPath()` to determine if these binaries exist in our PATH variable

In this code, we simply return an error if we do not find the tool. There are other options, such as attempting to install these tools with the local package manager. Depending on the makeup of our fleet, we might want to test which version is deployed and only proceed if we are at a compatible version.

Let's look at using the `exec.CommandContext` type to call binaries.

Executing binaries with the exec package

The exec package allows us to execute a binary using the `exec.Cmd` type. To create one of these, we can use the `exec.CommandContext()` constructor. This takes in the name of the binary to execute and the arguments to the binary, as illustrated in the following code snippet:

```go
cmd := exec.CommandContext(ctx, kubectl, "apply", "-f", config)
```

This creates a command that will run the `kubectl` tool's `apply` function and tell it to apply the configuration at the path stored in the `config` variable.

Does this command seem to have a familiar syntax? It should! `kubectl` is written using Cobra from our last chapter!

We could execute this command using several different methods on `cmd`, as follows:

- `.CombinedOutput()`: Runs the command and returns the combined output of STDOUT/STDERR.
- `.Output()`: Runs the command and returns the output of STDOUT.
- `.Run()`: Runs the program and waits for it to exit. It returns an error on any issues.
- `.Start()`: Runs the command but doesn't block. Used when you want to interact with the command as it runs.

`.CombinedOuput()` and `.Output()` are the most common ways to start a program. The output that a user sees in the terminal can often be both from STDOUT and STDERR. Choosing which one of these to use depends on how you want to respond to the program's output.

`.Run()` is used when you only need to know the exit status and do not require any of the output.

There are two main reasons to use `.Start()`, as outlined here:

- There is a need to respond on STDIN to output on STDOUT.
- The program execution takes a while, and you want to output its content to your screen, instead of waiting for the program to complete.

If you need to respond on STDIN to a program's output, using Google's `goexpect` package (https://github.com/google/goexpect) or Netflix's `go-expect` package (https://github.com/Netflix/go-expect) is probably a better choice. These packages continue the proud tradition of porting the abilities of the **Tool Command Language** (**TCL**) Expect extension (https://en.wikipedia.org/wiki/Expect) to other languages.

Let's write a simple program that tests our ability to log in to hosts on a subnet. We will use the `ping` utility and the `ssh` client programs to test connectivity. We will be relying on your host to recognize your SSH key (we are not using password authentication here, as that is more complicated). Finally, we will use `uname` on the remote machine to determine the OS. The code is illustrated in the following snippet:

```
func hostAlive(ctx context.Context, host net.IP) bool {
    cmd := exec.CommandContext(ctx, ping, "-c", "1", "-t", "2", host.String())
```

```
            if err := cmd.Run(); err != nil {
                    return false
            }
            return true
}
```

> **Note**
> uname is a program found on Unix-like systems that will display information about the current OS and the hardware it runs on. Only Linux and Darwin machines are likely to have uname. As SSH is just a connection protocol, we may just get an error. Also, a given Linux distribution might not have uname installed. There can be subtle differences between versions of common utilities on similar platforms. Linux ping and OS X ping utilities share some flags, but also have different flags. Windows often has completely different utilities for accomplishing the same tasks. If you are trying to support all platforms with a tool that uses exec, you will need either build constraints (https://pkg.go.dev/cmd/go#hdr-Build_constraints) or to use the runtime package to run different utilities on different platforms.

This code does the following:

- Creates a *Cmd that pings a host
  - -c 1 sends a single **Internet Control Message Protocol (ICMP)** packet.
  - -t 2 causes a timeout after 2 seconds.
- Runs the command
  - If there is an error, the ping was unsuccessful.
  - Otherwise, the host responded to the ping.

Let's now use the ssh utility to send a command to be run on the remote machine, as follows:

```
func runUname(ctx context.Context, host net.IP, user string) (string, error) {
        if _, ok := ctx.Deadline(); !ok {
                var cancel context.CancelFunc
                ctx, cancel = context.WithTimeout(ctx, 5*time.Second)
                defer cancel()
        }
```

```go
        login := fmt.Sprintf("%s@%s", user, host)
        cmd := exec.CommandContext(
                ctx,
                ssh,
                "-o StrictHostKeyChecking=no",
                "-o BatchMode=yes",
                login,
                "uname -a",
        )
        out, err := cmd.CombinedOutput()
        if err != nil {
                return "", err
        }
        return string(out), nil
}
```

This code does the following:

- Sets a timeout of 5 seconds, if `ctx` has none
- Creates a `user@host` login line
- Creates a *CMD that issues the command: `ssh user@host "uname -a"`
  - The `StrictHostKeyChecking` option automatically adds host keys.
  - The `BatchMode` option prevents asking for passwords.
- Runs the command and captures the output from `STDOUT`
  - If successful, it runs `uname -a` and returns the output.
  - The host must have the user's SSH key for this to work.
    - Password authentication requires either the `sshpass` utility or an Expect package.

We need a type to store the data we gather. Let's create that, as follows:

```go
type record struct{
    Host net.IP
    Reachable bool
    LoginSSH bool
```

```
        Uname string
}
```

Now, we need some code to take a channel containing **Internet Protocol** (**IP**) addresses that need to be scanned. We want to do this in parallel, so we will be using goroutines, as illustrated in the following code snippet:

```
func scanPrefixes(ipCh chan net.IP) chan record {
        ch := make(chan record, 1)
        go func() {
                defer close(ch)

                limit := make(chan struct{}, 100)
                wg := sync.WaitGroup{}
                for ip := range ipCh {
                        limit <- struct{}{}
                        wg.Add(1)
                        go func(ip net.IP) {
                                defer func() { <-limit }()
                                defer wg.Done()
                                ctx, cancel := context.WithTimeout(context.Background(), 3*time.Second))
                                defer cancel()

                                rec := record{Host: ip}
                                if hostAlive(ctx, ip) {
                                        rec.Reachable = true
                                }
                                ch <- rec
                        }(ip)
                }
                wg.Wait()
        }()
        return ch
}
```

This code does the following:

- Takes in a channel of net.IP
- Creates a channel to put records on
- Spins off a goroutine to do all the scanning
    - Defers closure of our output channel
    - Loops through all IPs on the incoming channel
    - Uses the limit channel to limit 100 pings concurrently
    - Spins a goroutine for each ping
        - Decrements the limiter when we finish
        - Makes a timeout of 2 seconds for our ping
        - Calls our hostAlive() function
        - Outputs the result on our ch output channel
    - Waits for all pings to finish with WaitGroup
- Returns the channel

We now have a function that will asynchronously ping hosts in parallel and put the result on a channel.

Our ssh function has a similar function signature to scanPrefixes, as we can see here:

```
func unamePrefixes(user string, recs chan record) chan record
```

For brevity, we are not going to include the code here, but you can see it in the repository linked at the end of the exercise.

These are the big differences between scanPrefixes() and unamePrefixes():

- We receive a channel of record, the output of scanPrefixes().
- If rec.Reachable is false, we simply put rec on the output channel without adding OS information to the fields.
- Otherwise, we call runUname() instead of hostAlive().

Now, let's set up our `main()` function, as follows:

```
func main() {
    _, err := exec.LookPath(ping)
    if err != nil {
        log.Fatal("cannot find ping in our PATH")
    }
    _, err := exec.LookPath(ssh)
    if err != nil {
        log.Fatal("cannot find ssh in our PATH")
    }
    if len(os.Args) != 2 {
        log.Fatal("error: only one argument allowed, the
network CIDR to scan")
    }
    ipCh, err := hosts(os.Args[1])
    if err != nil {
            log.Fatalf("error: CIDR address did not parse: %s",
err)
    }
    u, err := user.Current()
    if err != nil {
        log.Fatal(err)
    }
```

This code does the following:

- Checks that our binaries exist in the path
- Checks we have the correct number of arguments, which is 1
  - We check that `len(os.Args) == 2` because the first argument is the binary name.
- Retrieves a channel of IPs in the network passed in the argument
  - The implementation of the `hosts()` function is not detailed here, but you will find it in the repository.
- Gets the current user's login name

Now, we need to scan our prefixes and concurrently process the results by doing a login and retrieving the `uname` output, as follows:

```
scanResults := scanPrefixes(ipCh)
unameResults := unamePrefixes(u.Username, scanResults)
for rec := range unameResults {
    b, _ := json.Marshal(rec)
    fmt.Printf("%s\n", b)
}
}
```

This code does the following:

- Sends `scanPrefixes()` a channel of IPs
- Receives the results on `scanResults`
- Sends the channel of results to `unamePrefixes()`
- Prints the **JavaScript Object Notation (JSON)** results to `STDOUT`

The key to this code is the channel read in the `for range` loops in `scanPrefixes()` and `unamePrefixes()`. When all IPs have been sent, `ipCh` will be closed. That will stop our `for range` loop in `scanPrefixes()`, which will cause its output channel to close. That causes `unamePrefixes` to see the closure and close its output channel. This will in turn close our `for rec := range unameResults` loop and stop printing.

Using this chaining concurrency model, we will be scanning up to 100 IPs while SSHing into a maximum of 100 hosts and printing the results to the screen, all at the same time.

We have stored the output of `uname -a` in our `record` variable but in an unparsed format. We could use a lexer/parser or **regular expression (regex)** to parse that into a `struct`. If you need to use the output of an executed binary, we recommend finding tools that can output in a structured format such as JSON instead of parsing it yourself.

You can see this code at the following link:

https://github.com/PacktPublishing/Go-for-DevOps/tree/rev0/chapter/8/scanner

Notes on using the exec package

There are some things you should look out for when using `exec`. One of the big ones is if the binary being invoked takes control of the terminal. `ssh` does this, for example, to get a password from the user. We suppressed this in our example, but when this happens, it bypasses the normal STDOUT you are reading.

This happens when someone uses terminal mode. In those cases, you will want to use `goexpect` or `go-expect` if you must deal with it. Generally, this is something where you want to find alternatives. However, some software and various routing equipment will implement menu-driven systems and use terminal modes that cannot be avoided.

In this section, we have talked about automating the command line with the `exec` package. You now have the skills to check for binaries on the system and execute those binaries. You can check the error condition and retrieve the output.

In the next section, we will talk about the basics of SSH in Go. While in this section, we showed how you could use the `ssh` binary, in the next, we will talk about using the `ssh` package to use SSH without the SSH library. This is faster and also provides benefits over calling the binary.

> **Note**
> In general, always use a package instead of a binary when available. This keeps system dependencies low and makes code more portable.

Using SSH in Go to automate remote changes

SSH is simply a network protocol that can be used to secure communication between two hosts.

While most people think that the `ssh` binary allows you to connect from a terminal on one host to a terminal on another host, that is only one use. SSH can be used to secure connections for services such as **Google Remote Procedure Call** (**gRPC**) or to tunnel graphical interfaces such as the **X Window System** (**X11**).

In this section, we will talk about how you can use the SSH package (https://pkg.go.dev/golang.org/x/crypto/ssh) for creating clients and servers.

Connecting to another system

The most basic use of SSH is to connect to another system and either send a single command or invoke a shell and issue commands. SSH is simply a transport mechanism, so there are many other uses of SSH such as connection tunneling or wrapping **remote procedure calls** (**RPCs**). We will not cover those here, as they are outside the use cases for general DevOps work.

As with most connection technologies, the hardest part of connecting to systems with an SSH client is resolving authentication. The most common forms of SSH authentication are outlined here:

- **Username/password**: Username/password is the most popular implementation. It's the default and therefore the one that people tend to use. With network equipment, sometimes this is the only way. With this method, the password database may be on the local system, or the system may pass the password hash to another system to validate.
- **Public key authentication**: Public key authentication is where a user creates a public/private key on their machine with an optional passphrase. The server has the public key installed for a user and your SSH client is set up to use the private key.
- **Challenge-response authentication**: There are varying types of challenge-response authentication for SSH. This is commonly used to allow **two-factor authentication** (**2FA**) through devices such as Yubikeys.

We will concentrate on using the first two methods and will assume that the remote end will be using OpenSSH. While installations should move to using 2FA, that setup is beyond what we can cover here.

We will be using Go's excellent SSH package: `http://golang.org/x/crypto/ssh`.

The first thing that will be required is to set up our authentication method. The initial method I will show here is username/password, as follows:

```
auth := ssh.Password("password")
```

That was simple enough.

> **Note**
>
> If you are writing a command-line application, it is not safe to retrieve a password using flags or arguments. You also do not want to echo a password to the screen. The password needs to come from a file only the current user has access to or by controlling the terminal. The SSH package has a terminal package (http://golang.org/x/crypto/ssh/terminal) that can help:
>
> ```
> fmt.Printf("SSH Passsword: ")
> password, err := terminal.ReadPassword(int(os.Stdin.Fd()))
> ```

For the public key, it is only slightly more complicated, as illustrated here:

```go
func publicKey(privateKeyFile string) (ssh.AuthMethod, error) {
    k, err := os.ReadFile(privateKeyFile)
    if err != nil {
            return nil, err
    }
    signer, err := ssh.ParsePrivateKey(k)
    if err != nil {
            return nil, err
    }
    return ssh.PublicKeys(signer), nil
}
```

This code does the following:

- Reads our private key file
- Parses our private key
- Returns a public key authorization implementation of `ssh.AuthMethod`

We can now authorize by simply providing our private key to our program. Many times your key is not stored locally but in a cloud service, such as Microsoft Azure's Key Vault. In that case, you simply need to change `os.ReadFile()` to use the cloud service.

Now that we have our authorization sorted out, let's create an SSH config, as follows:

```go
config := &ssh.ClientConfig{
    User: user,
    Auth: []ssh.AuthMethod{auth},
```

```
        HostKeyCallback: ssh.InsecureIgnoreHostKey(),
        Timeout: 5 * time.Second,
}
```

This code does the following:

- Creates a new *ssh.ClientConfig config
  - Uses the username is stored in the user variable
  - Supplies one AuthMethod, but you can use multiple AuthMethod(s)
  - Ignores the host key
    - Sets a dial timeout of 5 seconds

> **Important Note**
> Ignoring a host key with ssh.InsecureIgnoreHostKey() is not secure. This can lead to a typo where you are sending information to a system outside your control. That system could be masquerading as one of your systems in the hope of getting you to type something in the terminal, such as a password. When working in a production environment, it is critical not to ignore the host key and store a valid list of host keys that can be checked.

Let's make a connection to a host, as follows:

```
conn, err := ssh.Dial("tcp", host, config)
if err != nil {
    fmt.Println("Error: could not dial host: ", err)
    os.Exit(1)
}
defer conn.Close()
```

Now that we have established an SSH connection, let's build a function to run a simple command, as follows:

```
func combinedOutput(conn *ssh.Client, cmd string) (string, error) {
    sess, err := conn.NewSession()
    if err != nil {
            return "", err
    }
```

```
        defer sess.Close()

    b, err := sess.Output(cmd)
    if err != nil {
            return "", err
    }
    return string(b), nil
}
```

This code does the following:

- Creates an SSH session
  - One session per command is required
- Runs the command in the session and returns the output
  - This gets the STDOUT and STDERR in a single output

This code will let you issue commands against systems that are using OpenSSH or similar SSH implementations. It is best practice to hold the `conn` object open until you have issued all of the commands for a device.

You can see this code here:

https://github.com/PacktPublishing/Go-for-DevOps/blob/rev0/chapter/8/ssh/client/remotecmd/remotecmd.go

This is great for cases when you can simply issue a command to the far end and let it run. But what if the program requires some level of interaction? When interfacing with routing platforms over SSH, you often require more interaction.

When that need arises, Expect libraries are there to help. So, let's have a look at one of the more popular ones, up next.

Using Expect for complicated interactions

`expect` packages provide the ability to deal with output from a command, such as the following: `would you like to continue[y/n]`.

The most popular package for using `expect` comes from Google. You can find it here: https://github.com/google/goexpect.

Here's an example of an `expect` script to install the original TCL `expect` tools on an Ubuntu host using the **Advanced Packaging Tool** (**APT**) package manager. Note that this is not the best way to do this, but simply gives an uncomplicated example.

Let's start by configuring our `expect` client to use the SSH client, as follows:

```
config := &ssh.ClientConfig {
    User:              user,
    Auth:              []ssh.AuthMethod{auth},
    HostKeyCallback: ssh.InsecureIgnoreHostKey(),
}
conn, err := ssh.Dial("tcp", host, config)
if err != nil {
    return err
}
e, _, err := expect.SpawnSSH(conn, 5 * time.Second)
if err != nil {
    return err
}
defer e.Close()
```

This code does the following:

- Sets up an `*ssh.ClientConfig` config
- Uses it to make a connection
- Passes that connection to an `expect` client

Now we have an `expect` client logged in via SSH, let's make sure we have a prompt, as follows:

```
var (
    promptRE = regexp.MustCompile(`\$ `)
    aptCont = regexp.MustCompile(`Do you want to continue\? \
[Y/n\] `)
    aptAtNewest = regexp.MustCompile(`is already the newest`)
)
_, _, err = e.Expect(promptRE, 10*time.Second)
if err != nil {
        return fmt.Errorf("did not get shell prompt")
}
```

This code does the following:

- Compiles a $ regex to expect our prompt
- Calls `Expect()` to wait for the prompt for up to 10 seconds

Now, let's send our command to install `expect` via the `apt-get` tool. We will be using `sudo` to issue this command with root privileges. The code is illustrated in the following snippet:

```
if err := e.Send("sudo apt-get install expect\n"); err != nil {
        return fmt.Errorf("error on send command: %s", err)
}
```

`apt-get` will either prompt us if it is OK to install or tell us it is already installed. Let's handle those two cases, as follows:

```
f _, _, ecase, err := e.ExpectSwitchCase(
    []expect.Caser{
            &expect.Case{
                    R: aptCont,
                    T: expect.OK(),
            },
            &expect.Case{
                    R: aptAtNewest,
                    T: expect.OK(),
            },
    },
    10*time.Second,
)
if err != nil {
        return fmt.Errorf("apt-get install did not send what we expected")
}
```

This code does the following:

- Waits for either of these to be displayed:
  - `Do you want to continue\? [Y/n]`
  - `is already the newest`

- If neither happens, it gives an error
- `ecase` will contain the `case` type detailing which condition occurred

If we get the continue prompt, we need to send Y to the terminal by executing the following code:

```
switch ecase{
case 0:
        if err := e.Send("Y\n"); err != nil {
                return err
        }
}
```

Finally, we need to just make sure we received the prompt again by executing the following code:

```
_, _, err = e.Expect(promptRE, 10*time.Second)
if err != nil {
        return fmt.Errorf("did not get shell prompt")
}
return nil
```

You can see this code with a debug mode here:

https://github.com/PacktPublishing/Go-for-DevOps/blob/rev0/chapter/8/ssh/client/expect/expect.go

This section has shown how you can spawn an SSH session in pure Go, use it to send commands, and then retrieve the output. Finally, we looked at how you can interact with an application using `goexpect`.

Now, we will show how you can use this knowledge to write tooling that runs commands on multiple systems.

Designing safe, concurrent change automations

So far, we have shown how to execute commands locally or remotely.

In the modern day, we often need to run sets of commands across multiple systems to achieve some end state. Depending on your scale, you may want to run a system such as Ansible or Jenkins to attempt to automate these processes.

For some work, it is simpler to use Go directly to execute changes across a set of systems. This allows the DevOps group to simply understand the Go language and a small bit of code versus understanding the complexities of a workflow system such as Ansible, which requires its own skillset, system updates, and so on.

In this section, we are going to talk about the components of changing a set of systems, a framework for achieving this, and an example application to apply a set of changes.

Components of a change

When writing a system that makes a change, there are several types of actions that must be dealt with. In broad terms, I define these as the following:

- **Global preconditions**: Global preconditions are a set of conditions that need to be true to move forward. When doing network automation, this would be things such as the packet loss on the network being under a certain threshold. For devices, this might be that your services are in a green state before proceeding. No one wants to push changes during a problem.
- **Local preconditions**: Local preconditions are the state of the individual work unit (say, a server) that needs to be in a certain state to proceed.
- **Actions**: Actions are operations that will mutate the state of a work unit.
- **Action validations**: Checks that are done to validate an action was successful.
- **Local postconditions**: Local postconditions are checks that the work unit is both in the configuration state you want and meets some state. This might be that it is still reachable, possibly serving traffic or not serving traffic, whatever the end state should be.
- **Global postconditions**: Global postconditions are the state of conditions after execution, usually similar to global preconditions.

Not every set of changes on multiple systems requires all these, but they will at least need a subset of them.

Let's take a look at doing a rollout of jobs on a set of **virtual machines** (**VMs**) in a single data center. For small shops that have a limited number of machines, a setup such as this can be sufficient when you aren't large enough to use something such as Kubernetes but can't fit in the limitations of services such as Azure Functions or Amazon's **Elastic Container Service** (**ECS**). Or, it could be that you are running on your own machines and not in a cloud provider.

Writing a concurrent job

Let's tackle the actions we want to perform. We want to do the following:

- Remove our job from a load balancer
- Kill the job on the VM or server
- Copy our new software to the server
- Start our service
- Check the service is reachable
- Add the job back to the load balancer

In essence, this is what Kubernetes does for large-scale installations of microservices. We will be talking about this in an upcoming chapter. But at a small scale, it is seldom the best choice to take on the complexity of running a Kubernetes cluster, even when the infrastructure is managed by a cloud provider.

Let's define the overall structure of the code that executes our actions, as follows:

```
type stateFn func(ctx context.Context) (stateFn, error)

type actions struct {
    ... // Some set of attributes
}

func (s *actions) run(ctx context.Context) (err error) {
    fn := s.rmBackend
    if s.failedState != nil {
        fn = s.failedState
    }
    s.started = true
    for {
        if ctx.Err() != nil {
            s.err = ctx.Err()
```

```
                return ctx.Err()
            }
            fn, err = fn(ctx)
            if err != nil {
                s.failedState = fn
                s.err = err
                return err
            }
            if fn == nil {
                return nil
            }
        }
    }
}
func (a *actions) rmBackend(ctx context.Context) (stateFn, error) {...}
func (a *actions) jobKill(ctx context.Context) (stateFn, error) {...}
func (a *actions) cp(ctx context.Context) (stateFn, error) {...}
func (a *actions) jobStart(ctx context.Context) (stateFn, error) {...}
func (a *actions) reachable(ctx context.Context) (stateFn, error) {...}
func (a *actions) addBackend(ctx context.Context) (stateFn, error) {...}
```

> **Note**
> Much of this is just a skeleton—we will implement these methods in a moment.

This code does the following:

- Defines a `stateFn` type
  - If it returns an error, stop processing.
  - If it doesn't and returns a non-nil `stateFn` type, execute it.
  - If it returns a nil `stateFn` type and no error, we are done.

- Defines an `actions` type
  - This is a state machine for actions on a server
  - Calling `run()` does the following:
    - Executes one `stateFn` type at a time until an error or `stateFn == nil`
  - `rmBackend()`, `jobKill()`, `cp()`, and the rest are `stateFn` types we will define.
  - `.failedState` is there to allow retrying a failed state when using `.run()` more than once.

What we have is a simple state machine that will execute actions. This moves us through all the states that are required to do this type of action on a system.

Let's look at what a few of these `stateFn` types would look like when implemented, as follows:

```
func (a *actions) rmBackend(ctx context.Context) (stateFn, error) {
    err := a.lb.RemoveBackend(ctx, a.config.Pattern, a.backend)
    if err != nil {
        return nil, fmt.Errorf("problem removing backend from pool: %w", err)
    }
    return a.jobKill, nil
}
```

This code does the following:

- Calls a client to our network load balancer to remove our server endpoint
- If successful, sends back `jobKill` as the next state to execute
- If not successful, returns our error

`s.lb.RemoveBackend()` in the cloud might talk to a **REST** service that informs it to remove our service endpoint. Or, in your own data center, it might be a network load balancer that you log in to via an SSH client and issue commands.

Once this completes, it tells `run()` to execute `jobKill()`. Let's explore what that would look like, as follows:

```go
func (a *actions) jobKill(ctx context.Context) (stateFn, error) {
    pids, err := a.findPIDs(ctx)
    if err != nil {
        return nil, fmt.Errorf("problem finding existing PIDs: %w", err)
    }
    if len(pids) == 0 {
        return a.cp, nil
    }
    if err := a.killPIDs(ctx, pids, 15); err != nil {
        return nil, fmt.Errorf("failed to kill existing PIDs: %w", err)
    }
    if err := a.waitForDeath(ctx, pids, 30*time.Second); err != nil {
        if err := a.killPIDs(ctx, pids, 9); err != nil {
            return nil, fmt.Errorf("failed to kill existing PIDs: %w", err)
        }
        if err := a.waitForDeath(ctx, pids, 10*time.Second); err != nil {
            return nil, fmt.Errorf("failed to kill existing PIDs after -9: %w", err)
        }
        return a.cp, nil
    }
    return a.cp, nil
}
```

This code does the following:

- Executes `findPIDs()`
    - This logs on to a machine via SSH and runs the `pidof` binary

- Executes `killPIDs()`
    - This uses SSH to execute `kill` against our process
    - Uses signal 15 or `TERM` as a soft kill
- Executes `waitForDeath()`
    - This uses SSH to wait for the **process identifiers** (**PIDs**) to exit
    - Waits up to 30 seconds
    - If successful, we return our next state, `cp`
    - If not, execute `killPIDs()` with signal 9 or `KILL` and execute `waitForDeath()` again
    - If it fails, it returns an error
    - If successful, we return our next state, `cp`

This code is simply killing our jobs on the server before we copy our new binary and start it.

The rest of the code will be in our repository (link provided further on in this section). For now, assume we have written out the rest of these actions for our state machine.

We now need something to run all our actions. We will create a `workflow` struct with this basic structure:

```
type workflow struct {
    config *config
    lb     *client.Client
    failures int32
    endState endState
    actions []*actions
}
```

This code does the following:

- Has `*config` that will detail the settings for our rollout
- Creates a connection to our load balancer
- Tracks the number of failures we have had
- Outputs the final end state, which is an enumerator in the file
- Creates a list of all our actions

There are two phases to a typical rollout, as follows:

- **Canary**: The canary stage is where you test a few samples to make sure the rollout is working. You want to do this one sample at a time and wait some amount of time before continuing to the next canary. This allows administrators to have some time to stop potential problems that the rollout hasn't detected.
- **General**: The general rollout occurs after the canary stage. This usually sets some amount of concurrency and a maximum number of failures. Depending on the size of your environment, failures may be common due to an ever-changing environment. This may mean you tolerate a certain number of failures and continue to retry those failures until you have success, but if the failures reach some maximum level, you stop.

> **Note**
> Depending on the environment, you can have more sophisticated staging, but for smaller environments, this usually suffices. When doing concurrent rollouts, failures can exceed your maximum failure setting by large amounts, depending on the setting. If we have a maximum of failures and our concurrency is set to 5, it is possible to have between 5 and 9 failures happen. Keep this in mind when you deal with concurrent rollouts.

The main method on the workflow that handles the rollouts is called `run()`. Its job is to run our pre-checks, then run our canaries, and finally run the main jobs at some concurrency level. We should exit if we have too many problems. Let's have a look, as follows:

```go
func (w *workflow) run(ctx context.Context) error {
    preCtx, cancel := context.WithTimeout(ctx, 30*time.Second)
    if err := w.checkLBState(preCtx); err != nil {
        w.endState = esPreconditionFailure
        return fmt.Errorf("checkLBState precondition fail: %s", err)
    }
    cancel()
```

This part of the code does the following:

- Runs our `checkLBState()` precondition code
- If it fails, records an `esPreconditionFailure` end state

> **Note**
>
> You may notice a `cancel()` function that is created when we create a `Context` object with a timeout. This can be used to cancel our `Context` object at any time. It is best practice to cancel a `Context` object that has a timeout immediately after use to exit a Go routine that is running in the background, counting down to the timeout.

This is run before we make any changes to the system. We don't want to make changes when things are already unhealthy.

Next, we need to run our canaries, as follows:

```
for i := 0; i < len(w.actions) &&
int32(i) < w.config.CanaryNum; i++ {
    color.Green("Running canary on: %s", w.actions[i].endpoint)
    ctx, cancel := context.WithTimeout(ctx, 10*time.Minute)
    err := w.actions[i].run(ctx)
    cancel()
    if err != nil {
        w.endState = esCanaryFailure
        return fmt.Errorf("canary failure on endpoint(%s): %w\n", w.actions[i].endpoint, err)
    }
    color.Yellow("Sleeping after canary for 1 minutes")
    time.Sleep(1 * time.Minute)
}
```

This code does the following:

- Runs some defined number of canaries
- Runs them one at a time
- Sleeps for 1 minute in between

These settings would be configurable in the config file that will be defined. The sleep time could be made configurable to what makes sense for the service, to allow you to respond in case of problems that aren't detected in the workflow. You could even define a sleep time between all canaries and general rollout.

Now, we need to roll out at some concurrency level while checking for some maximum number of failures. Let's check that out, as follows:

```
limit := make(chan struct{}, w.config.Concurrency)
wg := sync.WaitGroup{}
for i := w.config.CanaryNum; int(i) < len(w.actions); i++ {
    i := i
    limit <- struct{}{}
    if atomic.LoadInt32(&w.failures) > w.config.MaxFailures {
        break
    }

    wg.Add(1)
    go func() {
        defer func(){<-limit}()
        defer wg.Done()

        ctx, cancel := context.WithTimeout(ctx, 10*time.Minute)
        color.Green("Upgrading endpoint: %s",
w.actions[i].endpoint)
        err := w.actions[i].run(ctx)
        cancel()
        if err != nil {
            color.Red("Endpoint(%s) had upgrade error: %s",
w.actions[i].endpoint, err)
            atomic.AddInt32(&w.failures, 1)
        }
    }()
}
wg.Wait()
```

This code does the following:

- Spins off goroutines running our actions.
- Concurrency is limited by our `limit` channel.
- Failures are limited by our `.failures` attribute check.

This is the first time we have shown the `atomic` package. `atomic` is a sub-package of `sync` that allows us to do thread-safe operations on numbers without using `sync.Mutex`. This is great for counters as it is **orders of magnitude (OOM)** faster than `sync.Mutex` for this particular type of operation.

We have now shown the basics of `.run()` for our `workflow` struct. You can find the complete code for this rollout application at https://github.com/PacktPublishing/Go-for-DevOps/tree/rev0/chapter/8/rollout.

The code for the application simply needs your SSH key, a file describing the rollout, and the binary to roll out to the server. That file would look like this:

```
{
    "Concurrency": 2,
    "CanaryNum": 1,
    "MaxFailures": 2,
    "Src": "/home/[user]/rollout/webserver",
    "Dst": "/home/[user]/webserver",
    "LB": "10.0.0.4:8081",
    "Pattern": "/",
    "Backends": [
            "10.0.0.5",
            "10.0.0.6",
            "10.0.0.7",
            "10.0.0.8",
            "10.0.0.9"
    ],
    "BackendUser": "azureuser",
    "BinaryPort": 8082
}
```

This describes everything the application needs to do a simple rollout.

Of course, we can make this application more general, have it record its running state and final states to storage, add flags to ignore beginning states so that we can do a rollback, put this behind a gRPC service, and so on...

In fewer than 1,000 lines of code, we have a simple alternative to systems such as Kubernetes when they aren't available or your scale doesn't justify them.

> **Note**
> This doesn't address the need for binary restarts if your program crashes, such as restarts achieved through software such as `systemd`. In those cases, it may be better to create an agent that runs on the device and provides RPCs to control local services, such as `systemd`.

Case study – Network rollouts

The principles laid out here have been the essence of rollouts of network device configuration on Google's B2 backbone for a decade.

Prior to this, we simply had scripts that took hand-crafted configuration or generated configurations and applied them to the network while an operator watched the progress and dealt with issues that might arise.

At scale, this became an issue. SRE service teams had been moving away from similar models as their complexity tended to grow faster than the networks.

Network engineering moved toward a more formalized system to centralize the execution of work on the backbone, giving us a single place to monitor and a central place to stop rollouts in case of emergencies.

In addition, there was a need to formalize any set of rollouts so that they were always executed the same way with the same automated checks, instead of relying on humans to do the right things.

The orchestration system I led the design and implementation on is simply a more complex and pluggable version of what is presented here. Teams built their actions into the system, and that system executed those actions based on arguments sent to perform some set of jobs.

At the time of my departure from Google, using this methodology had led to zero outages from automation (which is not the same as having zero rollout failures). My understanding is that as I am writing this, your cat videos are still in safe hands on this system.

In this section, we have learned about the components of change and what that might look like using Go, and we have written an example rollout application that uses these principles.

Next, we will talk about writing a system agent that can be deployed on systems to allow everything from system monitoring to controlling a local rollout.

Writing a system agent

So far, when we have automated operations on a device, we have either done it from an application that executes locally or through a command we run remotely with SSH.

But if we look toward managing a small fleet of machines, it can be more practical to write a service that runs on the device that we connect to via RPCs. Using knowledge of the gRPC services we discussed in previous chapters, we can combine these concepts to allow control of our machines in a more uniform way.

Here are a few things we can use system agents for:

- Installing and running services
- Gathering machine running stats
- Gathering machine inventory information

Some of these are the kinds of things Kubernetes does with its system agents. Others, such as inventory information, can be vital in running a healthy fleet of machines, often overlooked in smaller settings. Even in a Kubernetes environment, there may be advantages to running your own agent for certain tasks.

A system agent can provide several advantages. If we define one **application programming interface** (**API**) using gRPC, we can have multiple OSs with different agents implementing the same RPCs, allowing us to control our fleet in the same uniform way, regardless of the OS. And because Go will pretty much run on anything, you can write different agents using the same language.

Designing a system agent

For our example system agent, we are going to target Linux specifically, but we will make our API generic to allow implementation for other OSs to use the same API. Let's talk about a few things we might be interested in. We could consider the following:

- Installing/removing binaries using `systemd`
- Exporting both system and installed binary performance data

- Allowing the pulling of application logs
- Containerizing our application

For those of you not familiar with `systemd`, it is a Linux daemon that runs software services in the background. Taking advantage of `systemd` allows us to have automatic restarts of failed applications and automatic log rotation with `journald`.

Containerization, for those not familiar with the concept, executes an application within its own self-contained space with access to only the parts of the OS you want. This is a similar concept to what is called sandboxing. Containerization has been made popular by software such as Docker and has led to container formats that look like VMs with entire OS images within a container. However, these container formats and tooling are not required to containerize an application on Linux.

As we are going to use `systemd` to control our process execution, we will use the `Service` directives of `systemd` to provide containerization. These details can be seen in our repository in the file https://github.com/PacktPublishing/Go-for-DevOps/blob/rev0/chapter/8/agent/internal/service/unit_file.go

For exporting stats, we will use the `expvar` Go standard library package. This package allows us to publish stats on a **HTTP** page. `expvar` stats are a JSON object with string keys that map to values representing our stats or information. There are built-in stats automatically provided, along with ones we will define.

This allows you to quickly gather stat data using a collector or by simply querying it with a web browser or command-line tool such as `wget`.

An example `expvar` page that is output might return the following:

```
{
    "cmdline": ["/tmp/go-build7781/c0021/exe/main"],
    "cpu": "8",
    "goroutines": "16",
}
```

For the book portion of our example, we are going to concentrate on *installing and removing binaries* and *exporting system performance data* to show how we can use our RPC service for interactive calls and HTTP for read-only information. The version in our repository will implement more features than we can cover in the book.

Now that we've talked about what we want the system agent to do, let's design our proto for our service, as follows:

```proto
syntax = "proto3";
package system.agent;
option go_package = "github.com/[repo]/proto/agent";

message InstallReq {
    string name = 1;
    bytes package = 2;
    string binary = 3;
    repeated string args = 4;
}
message InstallResp {}
message CPUPerfs {
    int32 resolutionSecs = 1;
    int64 unix_time_nano = 2;
    repeated CPUPerf cpu = 3;
}
message CPUPerf {
    string id = 1;
    int32 user = 2;
    int32 system = 3;
    int32 idle = 4;
    int32 io_wait = 5;
    int32 irq = 6;
}
message MemPerf {
    int32 resolutionSecs = 1;
    int64 unix_time_nano = 2;
    int32 total = 3;
    int32 free = 4;
    int32 avail = 5;
}
service Agent {
   rpc Install(InstallReq) returns (InstallResp) {};
}
```

We now have a general framework for our RPCs, so let's look at implementing a method for our `Install` RPC.

Implementing Install

Implementing installations on Linux will require a multi-step process. First, we are going to install the package under `sa/packages/[InstallReq.Name]` in the agent's user home directory. `InstallReq.Name` will need to be a single name, containing only letters and numbers. If that name already exists, we will turn down the existing job and install this in its place. `InstallReq.Package` on Linux will be a ZIP file that will be unpacked in that directory.

`InstallReq.Binary` is the name of the binary in the root directory to execute. `InstallReq.Args` is a list of arguments to pass to the binary.

We will be using a third-party package to access `systemd`. You can find the package here: `https://github.com/coreos/go-systemd/tree/main/dbus`.

Let's look at the implementation here:

```
func (a *Agent) Install(ctx context.Context, req
*pb.InstallReq) (*pb.InstallResp, error) {
    if err := req.Validate(); err != nil {
        return nil, status.Error(codes.InvalidArgument,
err.Error())
    }
    a.lock(req.Name)
    defer a.unlock(req.Name, false)

    loc, err := a.unpack(req.Name, req.Package)
    if err != nil {
        return nil, err
    }
    if err := a.migrate(req, loc); err != nil {
        return nil, err
    }
    if err := a.startProgram(ctx, req.Name); err != nil {
        return nil, err
    }
    return &pb.InstallResp{}, nil
}
```

This code does the following:

- Validates our incoming request to ensure it is valid
  - Implementation is in the repository code
- Takes a lock for this specific install name
  - This prevents multiple installs with the same name at the same time
  - Implementation is in the repository code
- Unpacks our ZIP file into a temporary directory
  - Returns the location of the temporary directory
  - Validates that our `req.Binary` binary exists
  - Implementation is in the repository code
- Migrates our temporary directory to our `req.Name` location
  - If a `systemd` unit already exists, it is turned down
  - Creates a `systemd` unit file under `/home/[user]/.config/systemd/user/`
  - If the final path already exists, deletes it
  - Moves the temporary directory to the final location
  - Implementation is in the repository code
- Starts our binary
  - Makes sure it is up and running for 30 seconds

This is a simple example of the setup for our gRPC service to set up and run a service with `systemd`. We are skipping various implementation details, but you can find them inside the repository listed toward the end of the chapter.

Now that we have `Install` done, let's work on implementing `SystemPerf`.

Implementing SystemPerf

To gather our system information, we will be using the `goprocinfo` package, which you can find here: `https://github.com/c9s/goprocinfo/tree/master/linux`.

We want this to update us about every 10 seconds, so we will implement our gathering in a loop where all callers read from the same data.

Let's start by collecting our **central processing unit** (**CPU**) data for our system, as follows:

```
func (a *Agent) collectCPU(resolution int) error {
    stat, err := linuxproc.ReadStat("/proc/stat")
    if err != nil {
        return err
    }
    v := &pb.CPUPerfs{
        ResolutionSecs: resolution,
        UnixTimeNano:   time.Now().UnixNano(),
    }
    for _, p := range stat.CPUStats {
        c := &pb.CPUPerf{
            Id:     p.Id,
            User:   int32(p.User),
            System: int32(p.System),
            Idle:   int32(p.Idle),
            IoWait: int32(p.IOWait),
            Irq:    int32(p.IRQ),
        }
        v.Cpu = append(v.Cpu, c)
    }
    a.cpuData.Store(v)
    return nil
}
```

This code does the following:

- Reads our CPU state data
- Writes it to a protocol buffer
- Stores the data in `.cpuData`

`.cpuData` will be of the `atomic.Value` type. This type is useful when you wish to synchronize an entire value, not mutate the value. Every time we update `a.cpuData`, we put a new value into it. If you store a `struct`, `map`, or `slice` in an `atomic.Value`, you cannot change a key/field—you *MUST* make a new copy with all keys/indexes/fields and store it, instead of changing a single key/field.

This is much faster for reading than using a mutex when values are small, which is perfect when storing a small set of counters.

The `collectMem` memory collector is similar to `collectCPU` and is detailed in the repository code.

Let's have a look at the loop that will be started in our `New()` constructor for gathering perf data, as follows:

```go
func (a *Agent) perfLoop() error {
    const resolutionSecs = 10
    if err := a.collectCPU(resolutionSecs); err != nil {
        return err
    }
    expvar.Publish(
        "system-cpu",
        expvar.Func(
            func() interface{} {
                return a.cpuData.Load().(*pb.CPUPerfs)
            },
        ),
    )
    go func() {
        for {
            time.Sleep(resolutionSecs * time.Second)
            if err := a.collectCPU(resolutionSecs); err != nil {
                log.Println(err)
            }
        }
    }()
    return nil
}
```

This code does the following:

- Collects our initial CPU stats
- Publishes an `expvar.Var` type for `system-cpu`
  - Our variable type is `func() interface{}`, which implements `expvar.Func`
  - This simply reads our `atomic.Value` set by our `collectCPU()` function
    - A read occurs when someone queries our web page at `/debug/vars`
- Refreshes our collections every 10 seconds

`expvar` defines other simpler types such as `String`, `Float`, `Map`, and so on. However, I prefer using protocol buffers over `Map` for grouping content in a single, sharable message type that can be used in any language. Because a proto is JSON-serializable, it can be used as the return value for an `expvar.Func` with a little help from the `protojson` package. In the repository, that helper code is in `agent/proto/extra.go`.

This code only shares the latest data collection. It is important to not directly read from stat files on each call, as your system can be easily overloaded.

When you go to the `/debug/vars` web endpoint, you can now see the following:

```
"system-cpu":
{"resolutionSecs":10,"unixTimeNano":"1635015190106788056",
"cpu":[{"id":"cpu0","user":13637,"system":10706,
"idle":17557545,"ioWait":6663},{"id":"cpu1","user":12881,
"system":22465,"idle":17539705,"ioWait":2997}]},
"system-mem":  {"resolutionSecs":10,"unixTimeNano":"163501519010
6904757","total":8152984,"free":6594776,"avail":7576540}
```

There will be other stats there that are for the system agent itself, which can be useful in debugging the agent. These are automatically exported by `expvar`. By using a collector that connects and reads these stats, it is possible to see trends for these stats over time.

We now have an agent that is getting perf data every 10 seconds, giving us a functioning system agent. It is worth noting that we have shied away from talking about **authentication, authorization, and accounting** (**AAA**) when talking about RPC systems. gRPC has support for **Transport Layer Security** (**TLS**) to both secure the transport and allow for mutual TLS. You can also implement a user/password, **Open Authorization** (**OAuth**), or any other AAA system you are interested in.

Web services can implement their own security for things such as `expvar`. `expvar` publishes its stats on `/debug/vars`, and it is a good idea not to expose these to the outside world. Either prevent the export on all load balancers or implement some type of security on the endpoint.

You can find the complete code for our system agent here: https://github.com/PacktPublishing/Go-for-DevOps/tree/rev0/chapter/8/agent.

In our completed code, we have decided to implement our system agent over SSH. This allows us to use an authorization system we already have with strong transport security. In addition, the gRPC service is exporting services over a private Unix domain socket, so local services that are not `root` cannot access the service.

You will also find code that containerizes the applications we install via `systemd` directives. This provides native isolation to help protect the system.

In this section, we have learned the possible uses of a system agent, a basic design guide to building one, and finally walked through the implementation of a basic agent on Linux. We also discussed how our gRPC interface is designed to be generic, to allow for the implementation of the agent for other OSs.

As part of building the agent, we have given a brief introduction to exporting variables with `expvar`. In the next chapter, we will talk about the big brother of `expvar`—the Prometheus package.

Summary

This chapter has been an introduction to automating the command line. We have seen how to use the `exec` package to execute commands locally on a device. This can be useful when needing to string together a set of already made tools. We have shown how you can use the `ssh` package to run commands on remote systems or interact with complicated programs using `ssh` and `goexpect` packages. We tied this together with our Go knowledge from previous chapters to implement a basic workflow application that upgraded binaries on multiple systems concurrently and safely. Finally, in this chapter, we have learned how we can create a system agent that runs on a device to allow us to gather vital data and export it. We also have refined our ability to install programs by using the agent to control `systemd` on Linux devices.

This chapter has now given you new skills that will allow you to control local command-line applications, execute remote applications on any number of machines, and deal with interactive applications. You have also gained a basic understanding of building a workflow application, developing RPC services that can control a local machine, and how to export stats using Go's `expvar` package.

In our next chapter, we will be talking about how we can observe running software to detect issues before they become a problem and diagnose issues when an incident occurs.

Section 2: Instrumenting, Observing, and Responding

The nightmare of any DevOps engineer is the 3A.M. wake-up call that says the systems their paycheck relies on aren't working. To combat these types of problems, it is critical to have information at hand that gives you and your team insights that can be used to quickly diagnose and remediate the problem. Even better, can we avoid the situation altogether with automation?

This chapter will introduce the concepts of using OpenTelemetry to enable observability across distributed applications and reduce dependency on log analysis. We will continue the journey by demonstrating how application release workflows can be automated with Go and GitHub Actions, removing the need for human interactions that can lead to downtime. Finally, we will explore using ChatOps with Slack to enable insights across teams and remove toil from engineers tasked with deployments.

The following chapters will be covered in this section:

- *Chapter 9, Observability with OpenTelemetry*
- *Chapter 10, Automating Workflows with GitHub Actions*
- *Chapter 11, Using ChatOps to Increase Efficiency*

9
Observability with OpenTelemetry

In the early hours of the morning as you are sleeping in bed, your phone starts to ring. It's not the normal ring that you've set for friends and family but the red-alert ring you set for emergencies. As you are startled awake by the noise, you begin to come to your senses. You think of the recent release of your company's application. A sense of dread fills you as you pick up the call to be greeted by the automated voice on the other end, informing you that you've been requested to join a priority video conference with a team debugging a live site problem with the new release. You get out of bed quickly and join the call.

Once you are on the call, you are greeted by the on-call triage team. The triage team informs you that the application is experiencing a service outage affecting one of your largest customers, which represents a substantial portion of your company's revenue. This outage has been escalated by the customer to the highest levels of your company. Even your CEO is aware of the outage. The triage team is unable to determine the cause of the downtime and has called you in to help mitigate the issue and determine the root cause of the outage.

You go to work to determine the root cause. You open your administrative dashboard for the application but find no information about the application. There are no logs, no traces, and no metrics. The application is not emitting telemetry to help you to debug the outage. You are effectively blind to the runtime behavior of the application and what is causing the outage. A feeling of overwhelming terror fills you as you fear this could be the end of your company if you are unable to determine what is causing the outage.

Right about then is when I wake up. What I've just described is a reoccurring nightmare I have about waking up to an outage and not having the information I need to determine the runtime state of my application.

Without being able to introspect the runtime state of your application, you are effectively blind to what may be causing abnormal behaviors in the application. You are unable to diagnose and quickly mitigate issues. It is a profoundly helpless and terrifying position to be in during an outage.

Observability is the ability to measure the internal state of an application by measuring outputs from that application and infrastructure. We will focus on three outputs from an application: logs, traces, and metrics. In this chapter, you will learn how to instrument, generate, collect, and export telemetry data so that you will never find yourself in a situation where you do not have insight into the runtime behavior of your application. We will use OpenTelemetry SDKs to instrument a Go client and server so that the application will emit telemetry to the OpenTelemetry Collector service. The OpenTelemetry Collector service will transform and export that telemetry data to backend systems to enable visualization, analysis, and alerting.

We will cover the following topics in this chapter:

- An introduction to OpenTelemetry
- Logging with context
- Instrumenting for distributed tracing
- Instrumenting for metrics
- Alerting on metrics abnormalities

Technical requirements

This chapter will require Docker and Docker Compose.

Let's get started by learning about OpenTelemetry, its components, and how OpenTelemetry can enable a vendor-agnostic approach to observability. The code used in this chapter is derived from https://github.com/open-telemetry/opentelemetry-collector-contrib/tree/main/examples/demo with some changes made to provide additional clarity.

The code files for this chapter can be downloaded from https://github.com/PacktPublishing/Go-for-DevOps/tree/rev0/chapter/9

An introduction to OpenTelemetry

OpenTelemetry began as a project to merge the OpenTracing and OpenCensus projects to create a single project to achieve their shared mission of high-quality telemetry for all. OpenTelemetry is a vendor-agnostic set of specifications, APIs, SDKs, and tooling designed for the creation and management of telemetry data. OpenTelemetry empowers projects to collect, transform, and export telemetry data such as logs, traces, and metrics to the backend systems of choice.

OpenTelemetry features the following:

- Instrumentation libraries for the most popular programming languages with both automatic and manual instrumentation
- A single collector binary that can be deployed in a variety of ways
- Pipelines for collecting, transforming, and exporting telemetry data
- A set of open standards to protect against vendor lock-in

In this section, we will learn about the OpenTelemetry stack and the components we can use to make our complex systems observable.

Reference architecture for OpenTelemetry

Next, let's take a look at a conceptual reference architecture diagram for **OpenTelemetry (OTel)**:

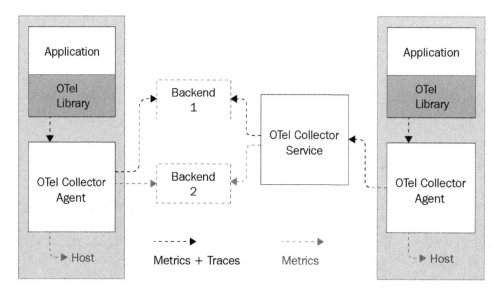

Figure 9.1 – OpenTelemetry reference architecture

The preceding reference architecture diagram shows two applications instrumented with the OTel libraries running on hosts, with the OTel Collector deployed as an agent on the hosts. The OTel Collector agents are collecting traces and metrics from the applications as well as logs from the host. The OTel Collector on the left host is exporting telemetry to Backend 1 and Backend 2. On the right side, the OTel Collector agent is receiving telemetry from the OTel instrumented application, collecting telemetry from the host, and then forwarding the telemetry to an OTel Collector running as a service. The OTel Collector running as a service is exporting telemetry to Backend 1 and Backend 2. This reference architecture illustrates how the OTel Collector can be deployed as both an agent on a host and a service for collecting, transforming, and exporting telemetry data.

The wire protocol the telemetry is being transmitted on is intentionally missing from the reference architecture diagram, since the OTel Collector is capable of accepting multiple telemetry input formats. For existing applications, accepting existing formats such as Prometheus, Jaeger, and Fluent Bit can make it easier to migrate to OpenTelemetry. For new applications, the OpenTelemetry wire protocol is preferred and simplifies collector configuration for ingesting telemetry data.

OpenTelemetry components

OpenTelemetry is composed of several components that form the telemetry stack.

OpenTelemetry specification

The OpenTelemetry specification describes the expectations and requirements for cross-language implementations using the following terms:

- **API**: Defines the data types and operations for generating and correlating tracing, metrics, and logging.
- **SDK**: Defines the implementation of the API in a specific languages. This includes configuration, processing, and exporting.
- **Data**: Defines the **OpenTelemetry Line Protocol** (**OTLP**), a vendor-agnostic protocol for communicating telemetry.

For more information about the specification, see `https://opentelemetry.io/docs/reference/specification/`.

OpenTelemetry Collector

The OTel Collector is a vendor-agnostic proxy that can receive telemetry data in multiple formats, transform and process it, and export it in multiple formats to be consumed by multiple backends (such as Jaeger, Prometheus, other open source backends, and many proprietary backends). The OTel Collector is composed of the following:

- **Receivers**: Push- or pull-based processors for collecting data
- **Processors**: Responsible for transforming and filtering data
- **Exporters**: Push- or pull-based processors for exporting data

Each of the preceding components is enabled through pipelines described in YAML configurations. To learn more about data collection, see `https://opentelemetry.io/docs/concepts/data-collection/`.

Language SDKs and automatic instrumentation

Each supported language in OpenTelemetry offers an SDK that enables application developers to instrument their applications to emit telemetry data. The SDKs also offer some common components that aid in instrumenting applications. For example, in the Go SDK, there are wrappers for HTTP handlers that will provide instrumentation out of the box. Additionally, some language implementations also offer automatic instrumentation that can take advantage of language-specific features to collect telemetry data, without the need of manually instrumenting application code.

For more information about instrumenting applications, see `https://opentelemetry.io/docs/concepts/instrumenting-library/`.

The correlation of telemetry

The correlation of telemetry is a killer feature for any telemetry stack. The correlation of telemetry data enables us to determine what events are related to each other across application boundaries and is the key to building insights into complex systems. For example, imagine we have a system composed of multiple interdependent microservices. Each of these services could be running on multiple different hosts and possibly authored using different languages. We need to be able to correlate a given HTTP request and all subsequent requests across our multiple services. This is what correlation in OpenTelemetry enables. We can rely on OpenTelemetry to establish a correlation ID across these disparate services and provide a holistic view of events taking place within a complex system:

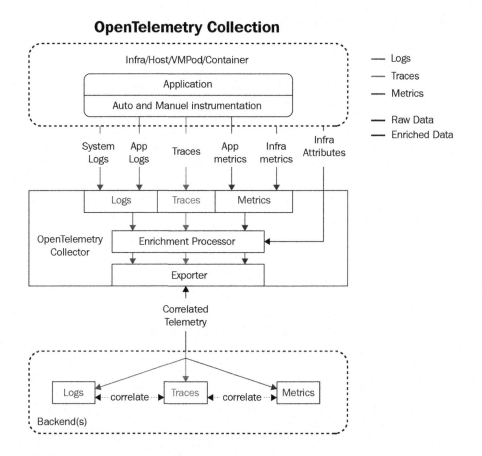

Figure 9.2 – Correlated telemetry

In this section, we have introduced the main concepts in the OpenTelemetry stack. In the next sections, we will learn more about logging, tracing, and metrics and how we can use OpenTelemetry to create an observable system.

Logging with context

Logging is probably the most familiar form of telemetry. You probably started logging in the first program you ever authored when you printed `Hello World!` to `STDOUT`. Logging is the most natural first step in providing some data about the internal state of an application to an observer. Think about how many times you have added a print statement to your application to determine the value of a variable. You were logging.

Printing simple log statements such as `Hello World!` can be helpful for beginners, but it does not provide the critical data we require to operate complex systems. Logs can be powerful sources of telemetry data when they are enriched with data to provide context for the events they are describing. For example, if our log statements include a correlation ID in the log entry, we can use that data to associate the log entry with other observability data.

Application or system logs often consist of timestamped text records. These records come in a variety of structures, ranging from completely unstructured text to highly structured schemas with attached metadata. Logs are output in a variety of ways – single files, rotated files, or even to `STDOUT`. We need to be able to gather logs from multiple sources, transform and extract log data in a consumable format, and then export that transformed data for consumption/indexing.

In this section, we will discuss how to improve our logging, moving from plain text to structured log formats, and how to consume and export various log formats using OpenTelemetry. We will learn using Go, but the concepts presented are applicable to any language.

Our first log statement

Let's start by using the standard Go log and write `Hello World!`:

```
package main

import "log"

func main() {
    log.Println("Hello World!")
}
// Outputs: 2009/11/10 23:00:00 Hello World!
```

The preceding `Println` statement outputs `2009/11/10 23:00:00 Hello World!` when run in `https://go.dev/play/p/XH5JstbL7U1`. Observe the plain text structure of the output and think about what you would need to do to parse the text to extract a structured output. It would be a relatively simple regular expression to parse, but with the addition of new data, the parse structure would change, breaking the parser. Additionally, there is very little context regarding the event or the context in which this event occurred.

The Go standard library logger has several other functions available, but we will not dive deeply into them here. If you are interested in learning more, I suggest you read `https://pkg.go.dev/log`. For the rest of this section, we will focus on structured and leveled loggers as well as the API described by `https://github.com/go-logr/logr`.

Structured and leveled logs with Zap

Structured loggers have several benefits over text loggers. Structured logs have a defined schema of keys and values that can be more easily parsed than plain text. You can take advantage of the keys and values to embed rich information such as a correlation ID or other useful contextual information. Additionally, you can filter out keys that might not be applicable given the log context.

V-levels are an easy way to control the amount of information in a log. For example, an application may output extremely verbose debug logs at the -1 log level but only critical errors at a log level of 4.

There has been a movement in the Go community to standardize the structured and leveled log interface via `https://github.com/go-logr/logr`. There are many libraries that implement the API described in the `logr` project. For our purposes, we'll focus on a single structured logging library, Zap, which also has a `logr` API implementation (`https://github.com/go-logr/zapr`).

Let's take a look at the key functions in the Zap logger interface:

```
// Debug will log a Debug level event
func (log *Logger) Debug(msg string, fields ...Field)
// Info will log an Info level event
func (log *Logger) Info(msg string, fields ...Field)
// Error will log an Error level event
func (log *Logger) Error(msg string, fields ...Field)
// With will return a logger that will log the keys and values
 specified for future log events
func (log *Logger) With(fields ...Field) *Logger
```

```
// Named will return a logger with a given name
func (log *Logger) Named(s string) *Logger
```

The preceding interface provides an easy-to-use strongly typed set of logging primitives. Let's see an example of structured logging with Zap:

```
package main

import (
    "time"
    "go.uber.org/zap"
)

func main() {
    logger, _ := zap.NewProduction()
    defer logger.Sync()

    logger = logger.Named("my-app")
    logger.Info
        ("failed to fetch URL",
        zap.String("url", "https://github.com"),
        zap.Int("attempt", 3),
        zap.Duration("backoff", time.Second),
    )
}
// Outputs: {"level":"info","ts":1257894000,"logger":"my
// app","caller":"sandbox4253963123/prog.go:15",
// "msg":"failed to fetch URL",
// "url":"https://github.com","attempt":3,"backoff":1}
```

The JSON structured output of the logger provides helpful, easy-to-parse, and contextual information through strongly typed keys and values. In the tracing section of this chapter, we will use these additional keys and values to embed correlation IDs to link our distributed traces with our logs. If you'd like to give it a go, see https://go.dev/play/p/EVQPjTdAwX_U.

We will not dive deeply into where to output logs (such as a filesystem, STDOUT, and STDERR) but instead assume that the application logs we wish to ingest will have a file representation.

Now that we are producing structured logs in our application, we can shift gears to ingesting, transforming, and exporting logs using OpenTelemetry.

Ingesting, transforming, and exporting logs using OpenTelemetry

In this example of using OpenTelemetry for ingesting, transforming, and exporting logs, we will use `docker-compose` to set up an environment that will simulate a Kubernetes host, with logs stored under `/var/logs/pods/*/*/*.log`. The OTel Collector will act as an agent running on the host. The logs will be ingested from the files in the log path, routed to appropriate operators in the `filelog` receiver, parsed per their particular format, have parsed attributes standardized, and then exported to `STDOUT` through the `logging` exporter.

For this demo we will using the code at: `https://github.com/PacktPublishing/Go-for-DevOps/tree/rev0/chapter/9/logging`. Now let's take a quick look at the layout of the demo directory:

```
.
├── README.md
├── docker-compose.yml
├── otel-collector-config.yml
└── varlogpods
    ├── containerd_logs 0_0000111122223333444455556666777788888
    │   └── logs
    │       └── 0.log
    ├── crio_logs-0_1111222233334444555566667777788889999
    │   └── logs
    │       └── 0.log
    ├── docker_logs-0_2222333344445555666677778888899990000
    │   └── logs
    │       └── 0.log
    └── otel_otel_8888777766665555444433332222211110000
        └── otel-collector
            └── 0.log
```

The `docker-compose.yml` file contains the service definition where we will run the OTel Collector and mount the collector configuration and log files directory, `varlogpods`, to simulate the collector running on a Kubernetes host. Let's take a look at `docker-compose.yml`:

```
version: "3"
services:
  opentelemetry-collector-contrib:
    image: otelcontribcol
```

```
        command: ["--config=/etc/otel-collector-config.yml"]
        volumes:
          - ./otel-collector-config.yml:/etc/otel-collector-config.
  yml
          - ./varlogpods:/var/log/pods
```

To run this demo, move to the chapter source code, cd into the logging directory, and run docker-compose up.

OTel Collector configuration

The OTel Collector configuration file contains the directives for how the agent is to ingest, process, and export the logs. Let's dive into the configuration and break it down:

```
receivers:
  filelog:
    include:
      - /var/log/pods/*/*/*.log
    exclude:
      # Exclude logs from all containers named otel-collector
      - /var/log/pods/*/otel-collector/*.log
    start_at: beginning
    include_file_path: true
    include_file_name: false
```

The receivers section contains a single filelog receiver that specifies the directories to include and exclude. The filelog receiver will start from the beginning of each log file and include the file path for metadata extraction in the operators. Next, let's continue to the operators:

```
    operators:
      # Find out which format is used by kubernetes
      - type: router
        id: get-format
        routes:
          - output: parser-docker
            expr: '$$body matches "^\\{"'
          - output: parser-crio
            expr: '$$body matches "^[^ Z]+ "'
          - output: parser-containerd
            expr: '$$body matches "^[^ Z]+Z"'
```

The filelog operators define a series of steps for processing the log files. The initial step is a router operation that will determine, based on the body of the log file, which parser will handle the log body entry specified in the output of the operator. Each parser operator will extract the timestamp from each record, according to the particular format of the log entry. Let's now continue to the parsers to see how the parser will extract information from each log entry once routed:

```yaml
      # Parse CRI-O format
      - type: regex_parser
        id: parser-crio
        regex: '^(?P<time>[^ Z]+) (?P<stream>stdout|stderr) (?P<logtag>[^ ]*) (?P<log>.*)$'
        output: extract_metadata_from_filepath
        timestamp:
          parse_from: time
          layout_type: gotime
          layout: '2006-01-02T15:04:05.000000000-07:00'
      # Parse CRI-Containerd format
      - type: regex_parser
        id: parser-containerd
        regex: '^(?P<time>[^ ^Z]+Z) (?P<stream>stdout|stderr) (?P<logtag>[^ ]*) (?P<log>.*)$'
        output: extract_metadata_from_filepath
        timestamp:
          parse_from: time
          layout: '%Y-%m-%dT%H:%M:%S.%LZ'
      # Parse Docker format
      - type: json_parser
        id: parser-docker
        output: extract_metadata_from_filepath
        timestamp:
          parse_from: time
          layout: '%Y-%m-%dT%H:%M:%S.%LZ'
      # Extract metadata from file path
      - type: regex_parser
        id: extract_metadata_from_filepath
        regex: '^.*\/(?P<namespace>[^_]+)_(?P<pod_name>[^_]+)_(?P<uid>[a-f0-9\-]{36})\/(?P<container_name>[^\._]+)\/(?P<restart_count>\d+)\.log$'
        parse_from: $$attributes["file.path"]
      # Move out attributes to Attributes
      - type: metadata
        attributes:
```

```
              stream: 'EXPR($.stream)'
              k8s.container.name: 'EXPR($.container_name)'
              k8s.namespace.name: 'EXPR($.namespace)'
              k8s.pod.name: 'EXPR($.pod_name)'
              k8s.container.restart_count: 'EXPR($.restart_count)'
              k8s.pod.uid: 'EXPR($.uid)'
         # Clean up log body
         - type: restructure
           id: clean-up-log-body
           ops:
             - move:
                 from: log
                 to: $
```

For example, the `parser-crio` operator will perform a regular expression on each log entry, parsing a time variable from the entry and specifying the time format for the extracted string. Contrast `parser-crio` with the `parser-docker` operator, which uses a JSON structured log format that has a JSON key of `time` in each log entry. The `parser-docker` operator only provides the key for the JSON entry and the layout of the string. No regex is needed with the structured log. Each of the parsers outputs to the `extract_metadata_from_filepath`, which extracts attributes from the file path using a regular expression. Following the parsing and extraction of file path information, the `metadata` operation executes adding attributes gathered from the parsing steps to enrich the context for future querying. Finally, the `restructure` operation moves the log key extracted from each parsed log entry to the `Body` attribute for the extracted structure.

Let's take a look at the CRI-O log format:

```
2021-02-16T08:59:31.252009327+00:00 stdout F example: 11 Tue
Feb 16 08:59:31 UTC 2021
```

Now, let's look at the Docker log format:

```
{"log":"example: 12 Tue Feb 16 09:15:12 UTC
2021\n","stream":"stdout","time":"2021-02-
16T09:15:12.50286486Z"}
```

When running the example, you should see output like the following:

```
opentelemetry-collector-contrib_1  | LogRecord #19
opentelemetry-collector-contrib_1  | Timestamp: 2021-02-16
09:15:17.511829776 +0000 UTC
opentelemetry-collector-contrib_1  | Severity:
opentelemetry-collector-contrib_1  | ShortName:
opentelemetry-collector-contrib_1  | Body: example: 17 Tue Feb
16 09:15:17 UTC 2021
opentelemetry-collector-contrib_1  |
opentelemetry-collector-contrib_1  | Attributes:
opentelemetry-collector-contrib_1  |      -> k8s.container.
name: STRING(logs)
opentelemetry-collector-contrib_1  |      -> k8s.container.
restart_count: STRING(0)
opentelemetry-collector-contrib_1  |      -> k8s.namespace.
name: STRING(docker)
opentelemetry-collector-contrib_1  |      -> k8s.pod.name:
STRING(logs-0)
opentelemetry-collector-contrib_1  |      -> k8s.pod.uid: STRIN
G(22223333444455556666777788889999 0000)
opentelemetry-collector-contrib_1  |      -> stream:
STRING(stdout)
opentelemetry-collector-contrib_1  | Trace ID:
opentelemetry-collector-contrib_1  | Span ID:
opentelemetry-collector-contrib_1  | Flags: 0
```

As you can see from the preceding output, the OTel Collector has extracted the timestamp, body, and specified attributes from the `metadata` operator, building a normalized structure for the exported logging data, and exported the normalized structure to `STDOUT`.

We have accomplished our goal of ingesting, transforming, and extracting log telemetry, but you should also be asking yourself how we can build a stronger correlation with this telemetry. As of now, the only correlations we have are time, pod, and container. We would have a difficult time determining the HTTP request or other specific information that led to this log entry. Note that `Trace ID` and `Span ID` are empty in the preceding output. In the next section, we will discuss tracing and see how we can build a stronger correlation between the logs and requests processed in our applications.

Instrumenting for distributed tracing

Traces track the progression of a single activity in an application. For example, an activity can be a user making a request in your application. If a trace only tracks the progression of that activity in a single process or a single component of a system composed of many components, its value is limited. However, if a trace can be propagated across multiple components in a system, it becomes much more useful. Traces that can propagate across components in a system are called **distributed traces**. Distributed tracing and correlation of activities is a powerful tool for determining causality within a complex system.

A trace is composed of spans that represent units of work within an application. Each trace and span can be uniquely identified, and each span contains a context consisting of `Request`, `Error`, and `Duration` metrics. A trace contains a tree of spans with a single root span. For example, imagine a user clicking on the checkout button on your company's commerce site. The root span would encompass the entire request/response cycle as perceived by the user clicking on the checkout button. There would likely be many child spans for that single root span, such as a query for product data, charging a credit card, and updating a database. Perhaps there would also be an error associated with one of the underlying spans within that root span. Each span has metadata associated with it, such as a name, start and end timestamps, events, and status. By creating a tree of spans with this metadata, we are able to deeply inspect the state of complex applications.

In this section, we will learn to instrument Go applications with OpenTelemetry to emit distributed tracing telemetry, which we will inspect using Jaeger, an open source tool for visualizing and querying distributed traces.

The life cycle of a distributed trace

Before we get into the code, let's first discuss how distributed tracing works. Let's imagine we have two services, A and B. Service A serves web pages and makes requests for data from service B. When service A receives a request for a page, the service starts a root span. Service A then requests some data from service B to fulfill the request. Service A encodes the trace and span context in request headers to service B. When service B receives the request, service B extracts the trace and span information from the request headers and creates a child span from the request. If service B received no trace/span headers, it will create a new root span. Service B continues processing the request, creating new child spans along the way as it requests data from a database. After service B has collected the requested information, it responds to service A and sends its spans to the trace aggregator. Service A then receives the response from service B, and service A responds to the user with the page. At the end of the activity, service A marks the root span as complete and sends its spans to the trace aggregator. The trace aggregator builds a tree with the shared correlation of the spans from both service A and service B, and we have a distributed trace.

For more details of the OpenTelemetry tracing specification, see https://
opentelemetry.io/docs/reference/specification/
overview/#tracing-signal.

Client/server-distributed tracing with OpenTelemetry

In this example, we will deploy and examine a client/server application that is instrumented with OpenTelemetry for distributed tracing, and view the distributed traces using Jaeger. The client application sends periodic requests to the server that will populate the traces in Jaeger. The https://github.com/PacktPublishing/Go-for-DevOps/tree/rev0/chapter/9/tracing directory contains the following:

```
.
├── readme.md
├── client
│   ├── Dockerfile
│   ├── go.mod
│   ├── go.sum
│   └── main.go
├── docker-compose.yaml
├── otel-collector-config.yaml
└── server
    ├── Dockerfile
    ├── go.mod
    ├── go.sum
    └── main.go
```

To run this demo, move to the chapter source code, `cd` into the `tracing` directory, run `docker-compose up -d`, and open `http://localhost:16686` to view the Jaeger-distributed traces.

Let's explore the `docker-compose.yaml` file first to see each of the services we are deploying:

```
version: "2"
services:
  # Jaeger
  jaeger-all-in-one:
    image: jaegertracing/all-in-one:latest
    ports:
      - "16686:16686"
      - "14268"
      - "14250"
```

```
  # Collector
  otel-collector:
    image: ${OTELCOL_IMG}
    command: ["--config=/etc/otel-collector-config.yaml",
"${OTELCOL_ARGS}"]
    volumes:
      - ./otel-collector-config.yaml:/etc/otel-collector-config.yaml
    ports:
      - "13133:13133" # health_check extension
    depends_on:
      - jaeger-all-in-one
  demo-client:
    build:
      dockerfile: Dockerfile
      context: ./client
    environment:
      - OTEL_EXPORTER_OTLP_ENDPOINT=otel-collector:4317
      - DEMO_SERVER_ENDPOINT=http://demo-server:7080/hello
    depends_on:
      - demo-server
  demo-server:
    build:
      dockerfile: Dockerfile
      context: ./server
    environment:
      - OTEL_EXPORTER_OTLP_ENDPOINT=otel-collector:4317
    ports:
      - "7080"
    depends_on:
      - otel-collector
```

The preceding `docker-compose.yaml` file deploys a Jaeger *all-in-one* instance, an OTel Collector, a client Go application, and a server Go application. These components are a slight derivation from the OpenTelemetry demo: `https://github.com/open-telemetry/opentelemetry-collector-contrib/tree/main/examples/demo`.

Next, let's take a look at the OTel Collector configuration to get a better understanding of its deployment model and configured behaviors:

```
receivers:
  otlp:
    protocols:
```

```yaml
      grpc:
exporters:
  jaeger:
    endpoint: jaeger-all-in-one:14250
    tls:
      insecure: true
processors:
  batch:
service:
  pipelines:
    traces:
      receivers: [otlp]
      processors: [batch]
      exporters: [jaeger]
```

The preceding OTel Collector configuration specifies that the collector will listen for **OpenTelemetry Line Protocol (OTLP)** over gRPC. It will batch the spans and export them to a Jaeger service running on port `14250`.

Next, let's break down the significant parts of the client `main.go`:

```go
func main() {
      shutdown := initTraceProvider()
      defer shutdown()

      continuouslySendRequests()
}
```

`func main()` initializes the tracing provider, which returns a shutdown function that is deferred until `func main()` exits. The `main()` func then calls `continuouslySendRequests` to send a continuous, periodic stream of requests to the server application. Next, let's look at the `initTraceProvider` function:

```go
func initTraceProvider() func() {
    ctx := context.Background()
    cancel = context.CancelFunc
    timeout := 1 * time.Second
    endPointEnv := "OTEL_EXPORTER_OTLP_ ENDPOINT"

    otelAgentAddr, ok := os.LookupEnv(endPointEnv)
    if !ok {
        otelAgentAddr = "0.0.0.0:4317"
    }
```

```
        closeTraces := initTracer(ctx, otelAgentAddr)

    return func() {
            ctx, cancel = context.WithTimeout(ctx, time.Second)
            defer cancel()

            // pushes any last exports to the receiver
            closeTraces(doneCtx)
    }
}
```

`initTraceProvider()` looks up the OTLP trace endpoint from an environment variable or defaults to `0.0.0.0:4317`. After setting up the trace endpoint address, the code calls `initTracer` to initialize the tracer, returning a function named `closeTraces`, which will be used to shut down the tracer. Finally, the `initTraceProvider()` returns a function that can be used to flush and close the tracer. Next, let's look at what is happening in `initTracer()`:

```
func initTracer(ctx context.Context, otelAgentAddr string)
func(context.Context) {
        traceClient := otlptracegrpc.NewClient(
            otlptracegrpc.WithInsecure(),
            otlptracegrpc.WithEndpoint(otelAgentAddr),
            otlptracegrpc.WithDialOption(grpc.WithBlock()))

        traceExp, err := otlptrace.New(ctx, traceClient)
        handleErr(err, "Failed to create the collector trace
exporter")

        res, err := resource.New(
            ctx,
            resource.WithFromEnv(),
            resource.WithProcess(),
            resource.WithTelemetrySDK(),
            resource.WithHost(),
            resource.WithAttributes(
                semconv.ServiceNameKey.String("demo-client"),
            ),
        )
        handleErr(err, "failed to create resource")

        bsp := sdktrace.NewBatchSpanProcessor(traceExp)
        tracerProvider := sdktrace.NewTracerProvider(
```

```
        sdktrace.WithSampler(sdktrace.AlwaysSample()),
        sdktrace.WithResource(res),
        sdktrace.WithSpanProcessor(bsp),
    )

    // set global propagator to tracecontext (the default is
no-op).
    otel.SetTextMapPropagator(propagation.TraceContext{})
    otel.SetTracerProvider(tracerProvider)

    return func(doneCtx context.Context) {
        if err := traceExp.Shutdown(doneCtx); err != nil {
            otel.Handle(err)
        }
    }
}
```

`initTracer()` builds a trace client that connects to the OTLP endpoint over gRPC. The trace client is then used to build a trace exporter, which is used to batch process and export spans. The batch span processor is then used to create a trace provider, configured to trace all spans, and is identified with the `"demo-client"` resource. Trace providers can be configured to sample stochastically or with custom sampling strategies. The trace provider is then added to the global OTel context. Finally, a function is returned that will shut down and flush the trace exporter.

Now that we have explored how to set up a tracer, let's move on to sending and tracing requests in the `continuouslySendRequests` func:

```
func continuouslySendRequests() {
    tracer := otel.Tracer("demo-client-tracer")

    for {
        ctx, span := tracer.Start(context.Background(),
"ExecuteRequest")
        makeRequest(ctx)
        span.End()
        time.Sleep(time.Duration(1) * time.Second)
    }
}
```

As the name suggests, the `continuouslySendRequests` func creates a named tracer from the global OTel context, which we initialized earlier in the chapter. The `otel.Tracer` interface only has one function, `Start(ctx context.Context, spanName string, opts ...SpanStartOption) (context.Context, Span)`, which is used to start a new span if one does not already exist in the `context.Context` values bag. The `for` loop in main will continue infinitely creating a new span, making a request to the server, doing a bit of work, and finally, sleeping for 1 second:

```go
func makeRequest(ctx context.Context) {
    demoServerAddr, ok := os.LookupEnv("DEMO_SERVER_ENDPOINT")
    if !ok {
        demoServerAddr = "http://0.0.0.0:7080/hello"
    }

    // Trace an HTTP client by wrapping the transport
    client := http.Client{
        Transport: otelhttp.NewTransport(http.DefaultTransport),
    }

    // Make sure we pass the context to the request to avoid broken traces.
    req, err := http.NewRequestWithContext(ctx, "GET", demoServerAddr, nil)
    if err != nil {
        handleErr(err, "failed to http request")
    }

    // All requests made with this client will create spans.
    res, err := client.Do(req)
    if err != nil {
        panic(err)
    }
    res.Body.Close()
}
```

`makeRequest()` should look pretty familiar to those of you who have used the Go `http` library. There is one significant difference from non-OTel instrumented HTTP requests: the transport for the `client` has been wrapped with `otelhttp.NewTransport()`. The `otelhttp` transport uses `request.Context()` in the Roundtrip implementation to extract the existing span from the context, and then the `otelhttp.Transport` adds the span information to the HTTP headers to enable the propagation of span data to the server application.

Now that we have covered the client, let's see the server `main.go`. The code for this section can be found here: https://github.com/PacktPublishing/Go-for-DevOps/blob/rev0/chapter/9/tracing/server/main.go:

```go
func main() {
    shutdown := initTraceProvider()
    defer shutdown()

    handler := handleRequestWithRandomSleep()
    wrappedHandler := otelhttp.NewHandler(handler, "/hello")

    http.Handle("/hello", wrappedHandler)
    http.ListenAndServe(":7080", nil)
}
```

func `main.go` calls `initTraceProvider` and `shutdown` in a similar manner to the client `main.go`. After initializing the trace provider, the server `main.go` code creates an HTTP server, handling requests to `"/hello"` on port `7080`. The significant bit is `wrappedHandler := otelhttp.NewHandler(handler, "/hello")`. `wrappedHandler()` extracts the span context from the HTTP headers and populates the request `context.Context` with a span derived from the client span. Within `handleRequestWithRandomSleep()`, the code uses the propagated span context to continue the distributed trace. Let's explore `handleRequestWithRandomSleep()`:

```go
func handleRequestWithRandomSleep() http.HandlerFunc {
    commonLabels := []attribute.KeyValue{
        attribute.String("server-attribute", "foo"),
    }

    return func(w http.ResponseWriter, req *http.Request) {
        //  random sleep to simulate latency
        var sleep int64
        switch modulus := time.Now().Unix() % 5; modulus {
        case 0:
            sleep = rng.Int63n(2000)
        case 1:
            sleep = rng.Int63n(15)
        case 2:
            sleep = rng.Int63n(917)
        case 3:
            sleep = rng.Int63n(87)
        case 4:
```

```
            sleep = rng.Int63n(1173)
        }
        time.Sleep(time.Duration(sleep) * time.Millisecond)
        ctx := req.Context()
        span := trace.SpanFromContext(ctx)
        span.SetAttributes(commonLabels...)
        w.Write([]byte("Hello World"))
    }
}
```

In `handleRequestWithRandomSleep()`, the request is handled, introducing a random sleep to simulate latency. `trace.SpanFromContext(ctx)` uses the span populated by `wrappedHandler` to then set attributes on the distributed span.

The viewable result in Jaeger at `http://localhost:16686` is the following:

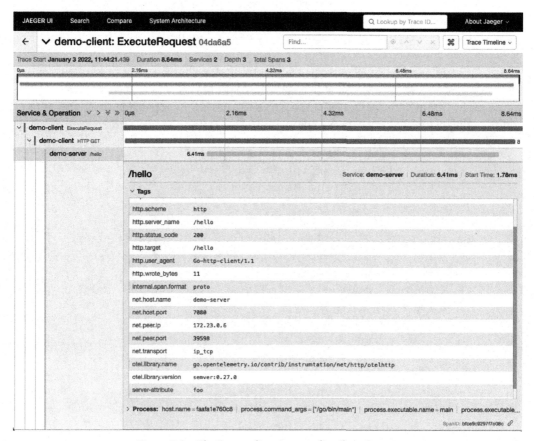

Figure 9.3 – The Jaeger client/server-distributed trace

In the preceding screenshot, you can see the distributed trace between the client and the server, including each span that was created in the request/response cycle. This is a simple example, but you can imagine how this simple example can be extrapolated into a more complex system to provide insight into the difficult-to-debug scenarios. The trace provides the information needed to gain insight into errors as well as more subtle performance issues.

Correlating traces and logs

In the *Logging with context* section, we discussed the correlation of log entries with activities. Without correlation to a given trace and span, you would not be able to determine which log events originated from a specific activity. Remember, log entries do not contain the trace and span data that enables us to build correlated trace views, as we see in Jaeger. However, we can extend our log entries to include this data and enable robust correlation with a specific activity:

```
func WithCorrelation(span trace.Span, log *zap.Logger) *zap.
Logger {
    return log.With(
        zap.String("span_id", convertTraceID(span.
SpanContext().SpanID().String())),
        zap.String("trace_id", convertTraceID(span.
SpanContext().TraceID().String())),
    )
}

func convertTraceID(id string) string {
    if len(id) < 16 {
        return ""
    }
    if len(id) > 16 {
        id = id[16:]
    }
    intValue, err := strconv.ParseUint(id, 16, 64)
    if err != nil {
        return ""
    }
    return strconv.FormatUint(intValue, 10)
}
```

In the preceding code, we use the `zap` structured logger to add the span and trace IDs to the logger, so each log entry written by a logger enhanced with `WithCorrelation()` will contain a strong correlation to a given activity.

Adding log entries to spans

Correlating logs with traces is effective for building correlations of logs with activities, but you can take it a step further. You can add your log events directly to the spans, instead of or in combination with correlating logs:

```
func SuccessfullyFinishedRequestEvent(span trace.Span, opts
...trace.EventOption) {
    opts = append(opts, trace.WithAttributes(attribute.
String("someKey", "someValue")))
    span.AddEvent("successfully finished request operation",
opts...)
}
```

`SuccessfullyFinishedRequestEvent()` will decorate the span with an event entry that shows as a log entry in Jaeger. If we were to call this function in the client's `main.go` after we complete the request, a log event would be added to the client request span:

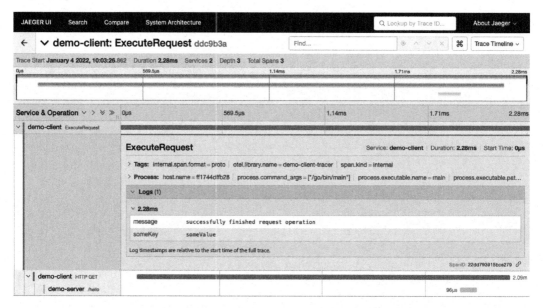

Figure 9.4 – The Jaeger client/server-distributed trace with the log entry

As you can see, the log entry is embedded within the span visualized in Jaeger. Adding log entries to spans adds even more context to your distributed traces, making it easier to understand what is happening with your application.

In the next section, we will instrument this example with metrics to provide an aggregated view of the application using Prometheus.

Instrumenting for metrics

Metrics are measurements at a given moment of a particular aspect of an application during runtime. An individual capture is called a **metric event** and consists of a timestamp, a measurement, and associated metadata. Metric events are used to provide an aggregated view of the behavior of an application at runtime. For example, a metric event can be a counter incremented by 1 when a request is handled by a service. The individual event is not especially useful. However, when aggregated into a sum of requests over a period of time, you can see how many requests are made to a service over that period of time.

The OpenTelemetry API does not allow for custom aggregations but does provide some common aggregations, such as sum, count, last value, and histograms, which are supported by backend visualization and analysis software such as Prometheus.

To give you a better idea of when metrics are useful, here are some example scenarios:

- Providing the aggregate total number of bits read or written in a process
- Providing CPU or memory utilization
- Providing the number of requests over a period of time
- Providing the number of errors over a period of time
- Providing the duration of requests to form a statistical distribution of the request processing time

OpenTelemetry offers three types of metrics:

- `counter`: To count a value over time, such as the number of requests
- `measure`: To sum or otherwise aggregate a value over a period of time, such as how many bytes are read per minute
- `observer`: To periodically capture a value, such as memory utilization every minute

In this section, we will learn to instrument Go applications with OpenTelemetry to emit metrics telemetry, which we will inspect using Prometheus, an open source tool for visualizing and analyzing metrics.

The life cycle of a metric

Before we get into the code, let's first discuss how metrics are defined and used. Before you can record or observe a metric, it must be defined. For example, a histogram of request latency would be defined as follows:

```
meter := global.Meter("demo-client-meter")
requestLatency := metric.Must(meter).NewFloat64Histogram(
    "demo_client/request_latency",
    metric.WithDescription(
        "The latency of requests processed"
    ),
)
requestCount := metric.Must(meter).NewInt64Counter(
    "demo_client/request_counts",
    metric.WithDescription("The number of requests processed"),
)
```

The preceding code fetches a global meter named `demo-client-meter` and then registers a new histogram instrument named `demo_client/reqeust_latency` and `demo_client/request_counts`, a counter instrument, both of which have a description of what is being collected. It's important to provide descriptive names and descriptions for your metrics, as it can become confusing later when analyzing your data.

Once the instrument has been defined, it can be used to record measurements, as follows:

```
meter.RecordBatch(
    ctx,
    commonLabels,
    requestLatency.Measurement(latencyMs),
    requestCount.Measurement(1),
)
```

The preceding code uses the global meter we defined previously to record two measurements, the request latency and an increment for the number of requests. Note that `ctx` was included, which will contain correlation information to correlate the activity to the measurement.

After events have been recorded, they will be exported based on the configuration of `MeterProvider`, which which we will explore next.

Client/server metrics with OpenTelemetry

We will extend the same client/server application described in the *Instrumenting for distributed tracing* section. Code for this section can be found here: https://github.com/PacktPublishing/Go-for-DevOps/tree/rev0/chapter/9/metrics. The directory has the following layout:

```
.
├── readme.md
├── client
│   ├── Dockerfile
│   ├── go.mod
│   ├── go.sum
│   └── main.go
├── .env
├── docker-compose.yaml
├── otel-collector-config.yaml
├── prometheus.yaml
└── server
    ├── Dockerfile
    ├── go.mod
    ├── go.sum
    └── main.go
```

The only addition to the preceding is the `prometheus.yaml` file, which contains the following:

```
scrape_configs:
  - job_name: 'otel-collector'
    scrape_interval: 10s
    static_configs:
      - targets: ['otel-collector:8889']
      - targets: ['otel-collector:8888']
```

The preceding configuration informs Prometheus of the endpoint to scrape to gather metrics data from the OTel Collector. Let's next look at the updates needed to add Prometheus to the `docker-compose.yaml` file:

```yaml
version: "2"
services:
  # omitted Jaeger config
  # Collector
  otel-collector:
    image: ${OTELCOL_IMG}
    command: ["--config=/etc/otel-collector-config.yaml", "${OTELCOL_ARGS}"]
    volumes:
      - ./otel-collector-config.yaml:/etc/otel-collector-config.yaml
    ports:
      - "8888:8888"   # Prometheus metrics exposed by the collector
      - "8889:8889"   # Prometheus exporter metrics
      - "4317"        # OTLP gRPC receiver
    depends_on:
      - jaeger-all-in-one
  # omitted demo-client and demo-server
  prometheus:
    container_name: prometheus
    image: prom/prometheus:latest
    volumes:
      - ./prometheus.yaml:/etc/prometheus/prometheus.yml
    ports:
      - "9090:9090"
```

As you can see from the preceding, we have added some additional ports for Prometheus to scrape on the OTel Collector, and the Prometheus service with `prometheus.yaml` mounted in the container. Next, let's take a look at the updated OTel Collector configuration:

```yaml
receivers:
  otlp:
    protocols:
      grpc:
exporters:
  prometheus:
    endpoint: "0.0.0.0:8889"
    const_labels:
```

```
      label1: value1
    logging:
    # omitted jaeger exporter
processors:
  batch:
service:
  pipelines:
    # omitted tracing pipeline
    metrics:
      receivers: [otlp]
      processors: [batch]
      exporters: [logging, prometheus]
```

The preceding configuration has omitted the Jaeger config used in the *Instrumenting for distributed tracing* section for brevity. The additions are the exporter for Prometheus as well as the metrics pipeline. The Prometheus exporter will expose port 8889 so that Prometheus can scrape metrics data collected by the OTel Collector.

Next, let's break down the significant parts of the client main.go:

```
func main() {
    shutdown := initTraceAndMetricsProvider()
    defer shutdown()

    continuouslySendRequests()
}
```

The only difference between the tracing version we explored earlier in the chapter is that instead of calling initTraceProvider, the code now calls initTraceAndMetricsProvdier to initialize both the trace and metrics providers. Next, let's explore initTraceAndMetricsProvider():

```
func initTraceAndMetricsProvider() func() {
    ctx := context.Background()
    var cancel context.CancelFunc
    timeout := 1 * time.Second
    endpoint := "OTEL_EXPORTER_OTLP_ ENDPOINT"

    otelAgentAddr, ok := os.LookupEnv(endpoint)
    if !ok {
        otelAgentAddr = "0.0.0.0:4317"
    }
```

```
    closeMetrics := initMetrics(ctx, otelAgentAddr)
    closeTraces  := initTracer(ctx, otelAgentAddr)

    return func() {
        ctx, cancel = context.WithTimeout(ctx, timeout)
        defer cancel()

        closeTraces(doneCtx)
        closeMetrics(doneCtx)
    }
}
```

The code in `initTraceAndMetricsProvider` establishes the OTel agent address and goes on to initialize the metrics and tracing providers. Finally, a function to close and flush both metrics and traces is returned. Next, let's explore `initMetrics()`:

```
func initMetrics(ctx context.Context, otelAgentAddr string)
func(context.Context) {
    metricClient := otlpmetricgrpc.NewClient(
        otlpmetricgrpc.WithInsecure(),
        otlpmetricgrpc.WithEndpoint(otelAgentAddr))

    metricExp, err := otlpmetric.New(ctx, metricClient)
    handleErr(err, "Failed to create the collector metric exporter")

    pusher := controller.New(
        processor.NewFactory(
            simple.NewWithHistogramDistribution(),
            metricExp,
        ),
        controller.WithExporter(metricExp),
        controller.WithCollectPeriod(2*time.Second),
    )
    global.SetMeterProvider(pusher)

    err = pusher.Start(ctx)
    handleErr(err, "Failed to start metric pusher")

    return func(doneCtx context.Context) {
        // pushes any last exports to the receiver
        if err := pusher.Stop(doneCtx); err != nil {
            otel.Handle(err)
```

```
                }
        }
}
```

In `initMetrics()`, we create a new `metricClient` to transmit metrics from the client to the OTel Collector in the OTLP format. After setting up the `metricClient`, we then create `pusher` to manage the export of the metrics to the OTel Collector, register `pusher` as the global `MeterProvider`, and start `pusher` to export metrics to the OTel Collector. Finally, we create a closure to shut down `pusher`. Now, let's move on to explore `continuouslySendRequests()` from client's `main.go`:

```
func continuouslySendRequests() {
        var (
                meter        = global.Meter("demo-client-meter")
                instruments  = NewClientInstruments(meter)
                commonLabels = []attribute.KeyValue{
                        attribute.String("method", "repl"),
                        attribute.String("client", "cli"),
                }
                rng = rand.New(rand.NewSource(time.Now().UnixNano()))
        )

        for {
                startTime := time.Now()
                ctx, span := tracer.Start(context.Background(), "ExecuteRequest")
                makeRequest(ctx)
                span.End()
                latencyMs := float64(time.Since(startTime)) / 1e6
                nr := int(rng.Int31n(7))
                for i := 0; i < nr; i++ {
                        randLineLength := rng.Int63n(999)
                        meter.RecordBatch(
                                ctx,
                                commonLabels,
                                instruments.LineCounts.Measurement(1),
                                instruments.LineLengths.Measurement(
   randLineLength
),
                        )
                        fmt.Printf("#%d: LineLength: %dBy\n", i,
   randLineLength)
                }
```

```
            meter.RecordBatch(
                ctx,
                commonLabels,
                instruments.RequestLatency.Measurement(
    latencyMs
),
                instruments.RequestCount.Measurement(1),
            )

            fmt.Printf("Latency: %.3fms\n", latencyMs)
            time.Sleep(time.Duration(1) * time.Second)
        }
    }
```

We first create a metrics meter with the name `demo-client-meter`, metric instruments to be used to measure metrics in this function, and a set of common labels to be added to the metrics collected. These labels enable scoped querying of metrics. After initializing the random number generator for artificial latency, the client enters the `for` loop, stores the start time of the request, makes a request to the server, and stores the duration of `makeRequest` as the latency in milliseconds. Following the execution of `makeRequest`, the client executes a random number of iterations between 0 and 7 to generate a random line length, recording a batch of metric events during each iteration, and measuring the count of executions and the random line length. Finally, the client records a batch of metric events, measuring the latency of `makeRequest` and a count for one request.

So, how did we define the instruments used in the preceding code? Let's explore `NewClientInstruments` and learn how to define counter and histogram instruments:

```
func NewClientInstruments(meter metric.Meter)
ClientInstruments {
    return ClientInstruments{
        RequestLatency: metric.Must(meter).
            NewFloat64Histogram(
                "demo_client/request_latency",
                metric.WithDescription("The latency of
requests processed"),
            ),
        RequestCount: metric.Must(meter).
            NewInt64Counter(
```

```
                    "demo_client/request_counts",
                    metric.WithDescription("The number of
requests processed"),
                ),
            LineLengths: metric.Must(meter).
                NewInt64Histogram(
                    "demo_client/line_lengths",
                    metric.WithDescription("The lengths of the
various lines in"),
                ),
            LineCounts: metric.Must(meter).
                NewInt64Counter(
                    "demo_client/line_counts",
                    metric.WithDescription("The counts of the
lines in"),
                ),
    }
}
```

`NewClientInstruments()` takes a meter and returns a struct of instruments used by the client. An instrument is used to record and aggregate measurements. This func sets up the two `Int64Counter` and `Int64Histogram` instruments. Each instrument is defined with a well-described name for easier analysis in the backend metric system. The `Int64Counter` instrument will monotonically increase and `Int64Histogram` will record `int64` the values and pre-aggregate values before pushing to the metrics backend.

Now that we have covered the client, let's look at the server's `main.go`:

```
func main() {
    shutdown := initProvider()
    defer shutdown()

    // create a handler wrapped in OpenTelemetry
instrumentation
    handler := handleRequestWithRandomSleep()
    wrappedHandler := otelhttp.NewHandler(handler, "/hello")

    http.Handle("/hello", wrappedHandler)
    http.ListenAndServe(":7080", nil)
}
```

The server's `main.go` calls `initProvider()` and `shutdown()` in a similar manner to the client's `main.go`. The interesting metric measures happen within `handleRequestWithRandomSleep()`. Next, let's export `handleRequestWithRandomSleep()`:

```go
func handleRequestWithRandomSleep() http.HandlerFunc {
    var (
        meter        = global.Meter("demo-server-meter")
        instruments  = NewServerInstruments(meter)
        commonLabels = []attribute.KeyValue{
            attribute.String("server-attribute", "foo"),
        }
    )

    return func(w http.ResponseWriter, req *http.Request) {
        var sleep int64
        switch modulus := time.Now().Unix() % 5; modulus {
        case 0:
            sleep = rng.Int63n(2000)
        case 1:
            sleep = rng.Int63n(15)
        case 2:
            sleep = rng.Int63n(917)
        case 3:
            sleep = rng.Int63n(87)
        case 4:
            sleep = rng.Int63n(1173)
        }
        time.Sleep(time.Duration(sleep) * time.Millisecond)
        ctx := req.Context()
        meter.RecordBatch(
            ctx,
            commonLabels,
            instruments.RequestCount.Measurement(1),
        )
        span := trace.SpanFromContext(ctx)
        span.SetAttributes(commonLabels...)
        w.Write([]byte("Hello World"))
    }
}
```

In the preceding code, `handleRequestWithRandomSleep()` creates a named meter from the global OTel context, initializes the server instruments in a similar way to the client example, and defines a slice of custom attributes. Finally, the function returns a handler function, which introduces a random sleep and records the request count.

The result is viewable in Prometheus at `http://localhost:9090/graph?g0.expr=rate(demo_server_request_counts%5B2m%5D)&g0.tab=0&g0.stacked=0&g0.show_exemplars=0&g0.range_input=1h`:

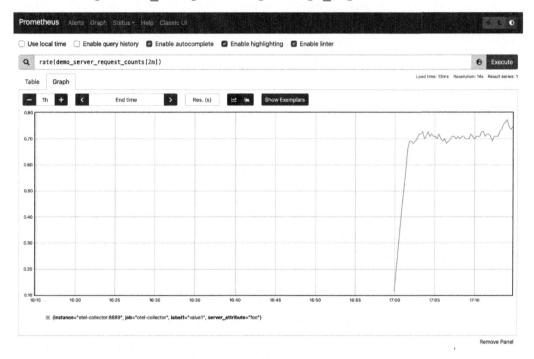

Figure 9.5 – The Prometheus server request rate

In the preceding screenshot, you can see the average requests per second for the server application in Prometheus. At the bottom of the screenshot, you will see the common labels and other associated metadata that was added in the server `main.go`. Prometheus provides a powerful query language to analyze and alert on metrics. Take some time and explore what you can do in the Prometheus UI. If you'd like to learn more about Prometheus, see `https://prometheus.io/docs/introduction/overview/`.

In this section, we learned how to instrument a Go application, export metrics to the OTel Collector, configure Prometheus to scrape metrics from the OTel Collector, and start to analyze metrics telemetry in Prometheus. With these newly gained skills, you will be able to understand more about the runtime characteristics of your applications.

Next up, let's look at how you can add alerting when your metrics are showing abnormalities that could indicate a problem.

Alerting on metrics abnormalities

Metrics provide time-series measurements of the behavior of our applications and infrastructure, but they provide no notification when those measurements deviate from the expected behavior of our applications. To be able to react to abnormal behaviors in our applications, we need to establish rules about what is normal behavior in our applications and how we can be notified when our applications deviate from that behavior.

Alerting on metrics enables us to define behavioral norms and specify how we should be notified when our applications exhibit abnormal behavior. For example, if we expect HTTP responses from our application to respond in under 100 milliseconds and we observe a time span of 5 minutes when our application is responding in greater than 100 milliseconds, we would want to be notified of the deviation from the expected behavior.

In this section, we will learn how to extend our current configuration of services to include an Alertmanager (https://prometheus.io/docs/alerting/latest/alertmanager/) service to provide alerts when observed behavior deviates from expected norms. We'll learn how to define alerting rules and specify where to send those notifications when our application experiences abnormal behaviors.

The code for this section is here: https://github.com/PacktPublishing/Go-for-DevOps/tree/rev0/chapter/9/alerting.

Adding and configuring Alertmanager

We will start by adding the Alertmanager service to the `docker-compose.yaml` file. Let's look at the updates needed to add Prometheus to the `docker-compose.yaml` file:

```
version: "2"
services:
  # omitted previous configurations
  prometheus:
    container_name: prometheus
    image: prom/prometheus:latest
    volumes:
      - ./prometheus.yaml:/etc/prometheus/prometheus.yml
      - ./rules:/etc/prometheus/rules
    ports:
      - "9090:9090"
```

```yaml
  alertmanager:
    container_name: alertmanager
    image: prom/alertmanager:latest
    restart: unless-stopped
    ports:
      - "9093:9093"
    volumes:
      - ./alertmanager.yml:/config/alertmanager.yaml
      - alertmanager-data:/data
    command: --config.file=/config/alertmanager.yaml -- log.
level=debug
volumes:
  alertmanager-data:
```

As you can see from the preceding, we have added a `rules` folder to the `prometheus` service, a new service called `alertmanager`, and a volume to store the `alertmanager` data called `alertmanager-data`. We will discuss the Prometheus `./rules` volume mount and contents later in this section, but for now, know that it contains our alerting rules for Prometheus. The new `alertmanager` service exposes an HTTP endpoint at `http://localhost:9093` and mounts an `alertmanager.yml` configuration as well as a data directory. Next, let's explore the contents of the `alertmanager.yml` file to see how Alertmanager is configured:

```yaml
route:
  receiver: default
  group_by: [ alertname ]
  routes:
    - match:
        exported_job: demo-server
      receiver: demo-server

receivers:
  - name: default
    pagerduty_configs:
      - service_key: "**Primary-Integration-Key**"

  - name: demo-server
    pagerduty_configs:
      - service_key: "**Server-Team-Integration-Key**"
```

Alertmanager configuration consists mainly of routes and receivers. A route describes where to send an alert based on it either being default or by some criteria. For example, we have a default route and a specialized route in the preceeding Alertmanager configuration. The default route will send alerts to the default receiver if they do not match `exported_job` attribute with the value `"demo-server"`. If alerts match the `exported_job` attribute with value `"demo-server"`, they are routed to the `demo-server` receiver, described in the receivers section.

In this example of Alertmanager receivers, we are using PagerDuty (`https://www.pagerduty.com`), but there are many other receivers that can be configured. For example, you can configure receivers for Slack, Teams, Webhooks, and so on. Note that the `service_key` values for each of the receivers requires a PagerDuty integration key, which can be set up by following the docs for integrating Prometheus with PagerDuty (`https://www.pagerduty.com/docs/guides/prometheus-integration-guide/`). If you wish to use another receiver such as email, feel free to mutate the receivers with email by following the Prometheus guide for email configuration (`https://prometheus.io/docs/alerting/latest/configuration/#email_config`).

Next, we will look at the changes that we need to make to the Prometheus configuration in `./prometheus.yaml` to make Prometheus aware of the Alertmanager service and the rules for sending alerts to the Alertmanager service:

```
scrape_configs:
  - job_name: 'otel-collector'
    scrape_interval: 10s
    static_configs:
        - targets: ['otel-collector:8889']
        - targets: ['otel-collector:8888']
alerting:
  alertmanagers:
    - scheme: http
      static_configs:
          - targets: [ 'alertmanager:9093' ]
rule_files:
  - /etc/prometheus/rules/*
```

In the preceding `./prometheus.yaml`, we see the original `scrape_config` and two new keys, `alerting` and `rule_files`. The `alerting` key describes the `alertmanager` services to send alerts and the connection details for connecting to those services. The `rules_files` key describes the glob rules for selecting files containing alerting rules. These rules can be set up in the Prometheus UI, but it is good practice to define these rules declaratively in code so that they are clear and visible to the rest of your team as source code.

Next, let's look at the `rules` file and see how we describe rules for alerting in `./rules/demo-server.yml`:

```
groups:
  - name: demo-server
    rules:
      - alert: HighRequestLatency
        expr: |
          histogram_quantile(0.5, rate(http_server_duration_bucket{exported_job="demo-server"}[5m])) > 200000
        labels:
          severity: page
        annotations:
          summary: High request latency
```

Rules in `rule_files` are categorized into groups. In the preceding example, we can see a single group named `demo-server` specifying a single rule named `HighRequestLatency`. The rule specifies an expression, which is a Prometheus query. The preceding query triggers when the mean request latency is exceeding 200,000 microseconds, or 0.2 seconds. The alert is triggered with a severity label of `page` and an annotation summary of `High request latency`.

Now, let's run the following to start the services:

```
$ docker-compose up -d
```

After the services start, we should see the following in Prometheus at `http://localhost:9090/alerts`:

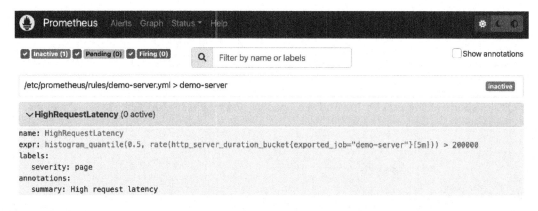

Figure 9.6 – The Prometheus alert for HighRequestLatency

The preceding screenshot shows the alert rules registered in Prometheus. As you can see, the `HighRequestLatency` alert is registered with the command we configured in the `./rules/demo-server` file.

After roughly 5 minutes of running the service, you should see the following:

Figure 9.7 – The Prometheus alert for HighRequestLatency triggered

In the preceding screenshot, you can see the triggered alert for `HighRequestLatency`. This is Prometheus triggering the alert for the mean request latency rising above 0.2 seconds. This will then trigger an alert that is sent to the Alertmanager which delegates to the appropriate receiver. The receiver will then send the alert on to the service configured to notify PagerDuty or, perhaps, another receiver you have configured. You have now established a flow for alerting yourself or others on your team that your application has entered into an aberrant state of behavior.

In this section, you learned to configure Prometheus alerting rules, deploy Alertmanager, and configure Alertmanager to send alerts to the notification service of your choice. With this knowledge, you should be able to establish rules for defining the normative behavior of your applications and alert you or your team when an application is behaving outside of those bounds.

Alerting is a key component of reacting to aberrant behaviors in applications. With proper metrics in place, you are now empowered to proactively respond when your applications are not meeting expectations, rather than responding to customer complaints.

Summary

In this chapter, we explored the basics of OpenTelemetry, how to instrument your applications and infrastructure, and how to export that telemetry into backend visualization and analysis tools such as Jaeger and Prometheus. We also extended the benefits of metrics by integrating alerting rules to proactively notify us when an application is operating outside of expected behavioral parameters. With the application of what you have learned, you will never be caught blind during a support call. You will have the data to diagnose and resolve issues in your complex system. Better yet, you will know about these problems before issues are raised by your customers.

We also established some relatively simple metrics, traces, and alerts. With this knowledge, you will be able to implement your own traces, metrics, and alerts to empower you and your team to react quickly and efficiently to failures in production.

In the next chapter, we will discuss how to automate workflows with GitHub Actions. We will learn about the basics of GitHub actions and build upon that to create our own Go-based GitHub actions to empower you to author any automation allowable by a Turing-complete language.

10
Automating Workflows with GitHub Actions

Have you ever been part of a project that required the completion of routine, monotonous tasks? Have you ever sat down to release software and read over the project wiki page, only to find 15 manual steps that you needed to cut, paste, and pray? What did it feel like when it was your turn to complete those tasks?

Tasks such as these are referred to as **toil** – *slow* and *difficult*. This kind of work reduces our teams' development velocity and, just as critically, grinds away the morale of the DevOps or **Site-Reliability Engineering** (**SRE**) team over time. Toilsome tasks are manual, and by their nature, manual tasks are error-prone. If we don't try to replace these tasks with appropriate automation, more will accumulate, worsening the situation.

As a DevOps engineer, you are the anti-entropy force driving automation and reducing toilsome work. In this chapter, we will learn how to use GitHub Actions to automate workflows to reduce toil and increase project velocity.

GitHub Actions provides a powerful platform for creating customizable automation workflows and is free for any open source project. GitHub Actions pairs a robust, customizable workflow engine with an equally powerful event model to trigger automation. The patterns and practices used in this chapter will leverage GitHub Actions but are transferable to many other developer workflow automation tools such as Jenkins and GitLab CI. The choice to use GitHub Actions is driven by the ubiquitous access for open source developers and the access to a wide community of contributed actions that amplify productivity.

In this chapter, you will start off by learning the basics of GitHub Actions. You will use these skills to build a continuous integration workflow to validate a pull request. Then, you will extend the workflow to add release automation to publish GitHub releases. Finally, you will build your own custom GitHub Action using Go and publish it to GitHub Marketplace.

We will cover the following topics in this chapter:

- Understanding the basics of GitHub Actions
- Building a continuous integration workflow
- Building a release workflow
- Creating a custom GitHub Action using Go
- Publishing a custom Go GitHub Action

Technical requirements

In this chapter, you need to have Docker, Git, and the Go tools installed on your machine. The code for this chapter is located at `https://github.com/PacktPublishing/B18275-09-Automating-Workflows-with-GitHub-Actions-Code-Files`.

The code files for this chapter can be downloaded from `https://github.com/PacktPublishing/Go-for-DevOps/tree/rev0/chapter/10`

Let's get started building our first GitHub Action.

Understanding the basics of GitHub Actions

GitHub Actions are event-driven automation tasks that live within a GitHub repository. An event like a pull request can trigger a set of tasks to be executed. An example is a pull request triggering a set of tasks to clone the Git repository and execute `go test` to run Go tests.

GitHub Actions is extremely flexible, enabling developers to author a wide variety of automations, even some that you might not normally associate with a traditional continuous integration/release pipeline. Actions are also composable, enabling groups of tasks to be packaged together as a published action and used in workflows together with other actions.

In this section, you will learn about the components of a GitHub Action: workflows, events, context and expressions, jobs, steps, and actions. After you have been introduced to these components, we'll build and trigger our first GitHub Action.

Exploring the components of a GitHub Action

Understanding the components of a GitHub Action, their relationships, and how they interact is the key to understanding how to compose your own automation. Let's get started with exploring the components of an action.

Workflows

A workflow is an automation file written in YAML that lives in a GitHub repository in the `./github/workflows/` folder. A workflow consists of one or more jobs and can be scheduled or triggered by an event. A workflow is the highest-level component of a GitHub Action.

Workflow syntax

Workflows require a developer to specify the events that will trigger automation via the `on` key and the jobs that automation will execute when it is triggered by the `jobs` key. Often, a name is also specified by the `name` keyword. Otherwise, the workflow will take the short name of the file that contains the workflow YAML. For example, the workflow defined in `./github/workflows/foo.yaml` will have the default name of `foo`.

An example of a workflow structure

The following is an example of a named workflow with the minimum set of keys defined. However, this is not a valid workflow, as we have not yet defined any events to trigger the workflow, nor any jobs to be executed once triggered:

```
name: my-workflow  # (optional) The name of your workflow;
                   # defaults to the file name.
 on:               # Events that will trigger the workflow
 jobs:             # Jobs to run when the event is triggered
```

Next, let's discuss how to trigger workflows.

Events

An event is a trigger that causes a workflow to start executing. Events come in a variety of flavors: webhook events, scheduled events, and manually dispatched events.

Webhook events can originate from an activity within the repository. Examples of triggering activities are pushing a commit, creating a pull request, or creating a new issue. Events raised from repository interactions are the most common triggers for workflows. Webhook events can also be created through external systems and relayed to GitHub through the repository dispatch Webhook.

Scheduled events are similar to cron jobs. These events trigger workflows on a defined schedule. Schedule events are a way to automate repetitive tasks, such as performing issue maintenance on older issues in GitHub or running a nightly reporting job.

Manual dispatch events are not triggered through repository activities but rather manually. For example, a project may have a Twitter account associated with it, and project maintainers may want to be able to send a tweet about a new feature but do not want to share the Twitter authentication secrets. An ad hoc event would enable automation to send out the tweet on behalf of the project.

Event syntax

Events require a developer to specify the type of events for the `on:` key in the workflow. Event types generally have child key-value pairs that define their behavior.

A single event example

A single event can be specified to trigger automation:

```
# the workflow will be triggered when a commit
# is pushed to any branch
on: push
on: push
```

A multiple events example

Multiple events can be specified to trigger automation:

```
# the workflow will execute when a commit is pushed
# to any branch or pull request is opened
on: [push, pull_request]
```

A scheduled event example

Scheduled event schedules are specified using **Portable Operating System Interface** (**POSIX**) cron syntax:

```
on:
  scheduled:
    - cron: '0,1,*,*,*'    # run every day at 01:00:00
```

A manual event example

Manual events are triggered through user interaction and can include input fields:

```
# a manually triggered event with a
# single "message" user input field
on:
  workflow_dispatch:
    inputs:
      message:
        description: 'message you want to tweet'
        required: true
```

Context and expressions

GitHub Actions exposes a rich set of context variables, expressions, functions, and conditionals to provide expressiveness in your workflows. This will not be an exhaustive study of all of these items, but we will highlight the most critical items.

Context variables

Context variables provide a way to access information about workflow runs, environment, steps, secrets, and so on. The most common context variables are `github`, `env`, `secrets`, and `matrix`. These variables are treated as maps and can be indexed using variable names and property names. For example, `env['foo']` resolves to the value of the `foo` environment key.

The `github` context variable provides information about the workflow run and contains information such as the `ref` that the workflow is executing on. This is useful if you would like to use that information to inject a version into an application at build time. You can access this information by indexing the `github` variable with `github['ref']` or `github.ref`.

The `env` context variable contains environment variables specified for the workflow run. The values can be accessed by using the index syntax.

The `secrets` context variable contains the secrets available for the workflow run. These values can also be accessed by the index syntax. Note that these values will be redacted in the logs, so the secret values will not be exposed.

The `matrix` context variable contains information about the matrix parameters you configure for the current job. For example, if you want to run a build on multiple operating systems with multiple versions of Go, the matrix variable allows you to specify the list of each one, which can be used to execute a set of concurrent job executions using each combination of operating system and Go version. We will go into more detail about this when we talk about jobs.

Expressions

The syntax used for an expression is `${{ expression }}`. Expressions consist of variables, literals, operators, and functions. Let's examine the following example:

```
jobs:
  job_with_secrets:
    if: contains(github.event.pull_request.labels.*.name, 'safe to test')
```

The preceding job will only execute if the pull request is labeled with `safe to test`. The `if` conditional will evaluate the `github.event.pull_request.labels.*.name` context variable and verify that one of the labels on the pull request is named `safe to test`. This is useful if you want to ensure that a workflow only executes after a repository maintainer has had an opportunity to verify that the pull request is safe.

Expressions can also be used as input. Let's examine the following example:

```
env:
  GIT_SHA: ${{ github.sha }}
```

The snippet of YAML shows how to set an environment variable called `GIT_SHA` to the value of the `github.sha` context variable. The `GIT_SHA` environment variable will now be available to all actions running within the job. Using context variables for input is useful for customizing the execution of scripts or actions executed in a workflow.

Jobs

A job is a collection of steps that run on an individual compute instance, or runner. You can think of a runner as a virtual machine for running your job. Jobs, by default, execute concurrently, so if a workflow defines multiple jobs, they will execute concurrently if enough runners are available. Jobs have the concept of dependency where a job can be dependent on another job, which will ensure the jobs execute sequentially rather than concurrently.

Job syntax

Jobs require a developer to specify an ID of the job, the type of runner the job will execute on using the `runs-on:` key, and a sequence of steps the job will execute using the `steps:` key. The `runs-on:` key is particularly interesting to us, as it is useful for executing a job on different **operating system** (**OS**) platforms such as multiple versions of Ubuntu, macOS, and Windows.

With the `runs-on:` key, a job is able to run on a specified platform, but that does not allow us to make a matrix of jobs to run on multiple platforms concurrently. To enable a job to execute in a matrix of configurations, one must use the `strategy:` key and expressions. By configuring the strategy, we can build a matrix of jobs executing the same job configuration. You will find an example of this configuration in the following example.

There are many other options to customize the execution of the job and the environment that the job executes within, but we will not dive deeply into them.

Executing jobs on multiple platforms

This example shows two jobs named `job_one` and `job_two`. Here, `job_one` is a matrix job that will run six concurrent templated jobs on the latest versions of Ubuntu, macOS, and Windows, which will each echo `1.17` and `1.16`. Running on Ubuntu 18.04, `job_two` will run concurrently with `job_one` and echo `"hello world!"`:

```
jobs:
  job_one:
    strategy:
      matrix:
        os: [ubuntu-latest, macos-latest, windows-latest]
        go_version: [1.17, 1.16]
    runs_on: ${{ matrix.os }}
      steps:
        - run: echo "${{ matrix.go_version }}"
  job_two:
    runs_on: ubuntu-18.04
```

```
steps:
  - run: echo "hello world!"
```

Steps

Steps are tasks that run in the context of a job and execute in the context of the job's associated runner. Steps can consist of a shell command or an action. Since steps execute in the same runner, they can share data between each of the steps. For example, if you create a file on the filesystem of the runner in a previous step, subsequent steps will be able to access that file. You can think of a step running within its own process and that any changes to environment variables will not carry over to the next step.

Steps syntax

Steps require a developer to specify an action with the `uses:` key or specify the shell commands to run with the `run:` key. Optional input allows you to customize the environment variables using the `env:` key and the working directory using the `working-directory:` key, and also to change the name that appears in the GitHub user interface for the step by using the `name` key. There are a wide variety of other options to customize the execution of steps, but we will not go into great depth about these.

Step for installing Go using an action

This example shows a step with no name that uses the v2 version of `actions/setup-go` to install version 1.17.0 or higher of Go. This action can be found at `https://github.com/actions/setup-go`. This is a great example of a publicly available action that you can use to add functionality to your automation. You can find actions for nearly any task at `https://github.com/marketplace?type=actions`. In a later section, we'll discuss how to build your own action and publish it to the GitHub Marketplace:

```
steps:
  - uses: actions/setup-go@v2
    with:
      go-version: '^1.17.0'
```

A step with a multiple line command

In this example, we've extended the previous one and added a `Run go mod download and test` step that runs the `go` tool, which was installed by `actions/setup-go@v2`. The run command uses | in the first line to indicate the start of a multiline string in YAML:

```
steps:
  - uses: actions/setup-go@v2
```

```
    with:
      go-version: '^1.17.0'
  - name: Run go mod download and test
    run: |
      go mod download
      go test
```

Actions

An action is a reusable combination of a set of steps formed into a single command, which can also have input and output. For example, the `actions/setup-go` action is used to execute a series of steps to install a version of Go on a runner. The Go toolchain can then be used within subsequent steps within the same job.

GitHub Actions is aptly named, as actions are the superpower of GitHub Actions. Actions are often published publicly and enable developers to leverage existing recipes to build complex automation quickly. Actions are similar to open source Go libraries, which enable developers to build Go applications quicker. As we build our own actions, you will quickly see the power of this feature.

If you are interested in seeing the source code for `actions/setup-go`, visit `https://github.com/actions/setup-go`. Later in this chapter, we will build our own Go action and publish it to the GitHub Marketplace.

How to build and trigger your first GitHub Action

Now that we have a general understanding of what the components of an action are, let's build one and explore how the components are structured and interact.

Creating and cloning a GitHub repository

If this is your first time creating and cloning a repository, you may find the following links useful:

- `https://docs.github.com/en/get-started/quickstart/create-a-repo`
- `https://docs.github.com/en/github/creating-cloning-and-archiving-repositories/cloning-a-repository-from-github/cloning-a-repository`

When creating the repository, I normally add `README.md`, `.gitignore`, and an **Massachusetts Institute of Technology (MIT)** license file. Once you have created and cloned your repository, you should have a local directory for your project, as shown in the following:

```
$ tree . -a -I '\.git'
.
├── .gitignore
├── LICENSE
└── README.md
```

Creating your first workflow

Remember that workflows live in the `.github/workflows` directory. The first step is to create that directory. The next step is to create the workflow file within the `.github/workflows` directory:

```
mkdir -p .github/workflows
touch .github/workflows/first.yaml
```

Open `.github/workflows/first.yaml` in your favorite editor and add the following workflow YAML:

```yaml
name: first-workflow
on: push
jobs:
  echo:
    runs-on: ubuntu-latest
    steps:
      - name: echo step
        run: echo 'hello world!'
```

The preceding workflow is named `first-workflow`. It will execute a single job called `echo` on the latest version of Ubuntu and execute a single step that will echo `hello world!` using the system's default shell. You can also specify the shell you would like with the `shell:` key.

Save `.github/workflows/first.yaml`. Commit and push the workflow to GitHub:

```
git add .
git commit -am 'my first action'
git push origin main
```

Normally, you'd create a branch first and then open a pull request before committing and pushing directly to the main branch, but for your first workflow, this will be the quickest way to see your results.

After you push your commit, you should be able to open your GitHub repository in your browser and click on the **Actions** tab. You should be greeted with a view of your first workflow having successfully executed. It should look like the following:

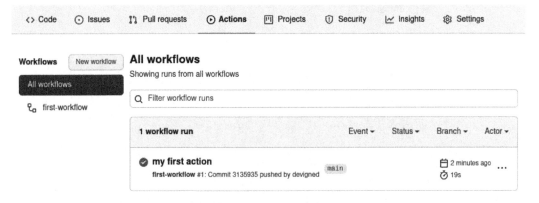

Figure 10.1 – The All workflows view

Note the list of workflows on the left and that there is one workflow named **first-workflow**. We can see that the first run of the workflow was for our commit with the **my first action** message.

If you click on the workflow run for **my first action**, you should see the following:

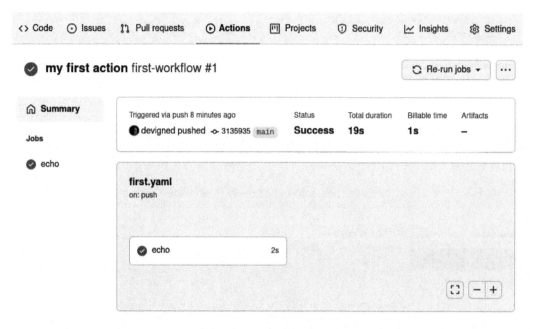

Figure 10.2 – The workflow job view

Note the **Jobs** list on the left with the **echo** job marked with a green check, signifying the successful execution of the job. On the right, you can see the details of the execution.

You can click on the **echo** job to see output from it and the steps that were executed:

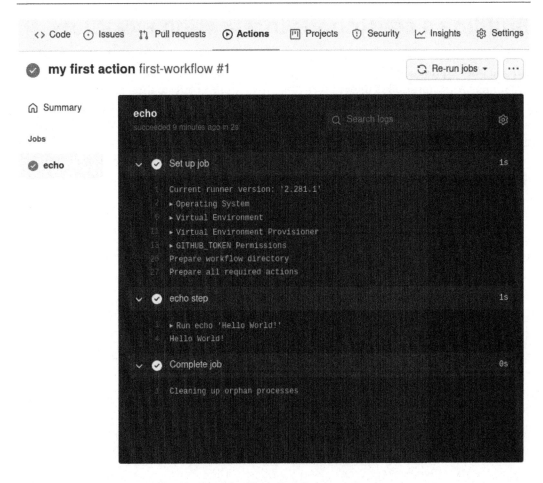

Figure 10.3 – The echo job output view

Note the job setup, which provides details about the runner and the environment the job executed within. Also, note the **echo step** single step executed a `echo 'Hello World!'` single shell command and echoed the "`Hello World!`" string to the console log. Finally, the job completed successfully due to `echo step` returning a 0 error code upon completion.

In this section, you have learned the basics of GitHub Actions and created your first simple automation. You now have the tools needed to start building more complex automation that will eliminate the toilsome tasks we discussed earlier in the chapter. In the upcoming sections, you will learn how to use these skills to build continuous integration and release workflows and, later, your own custom action written in Go.

Building a continuous integration workflow

In this section, we will use GitHub Actions to execute continuous integration automation when a pull request is opened or when code is pushed to a repository. If you are unfamiliar with continuous integration, it is the practice of automating the integration of code changes from multiple contributors into a code repository. Continuous integration automation tasks include cloning the repository at a specific commit, linting, building, and testing code, and evaluating changes to test coverage. The goal of continuous integration automation is to provide a guard against code changes that will lower the quality of a project or violate the rules codified in automation.

In this section, you will learn how to create a continuous integration workflow. In your continuous integration workflow, you will learn to execute jobs across multiple operating systems concurrently. You will install build tools onto the job executors, which you will use to build the software project. You will clone the source code for the project using an action. Finally, you will enforce passing tests and code quality by running a code linter and executing unit tests.

Introducing the tweeter command-line tool

You cannot have a continuous integration workflow without a software project to run the workflow upon. We will be using a simple Go command-line tool called **tweeter**. The source code for the project can be found at `https://github.com/PacktPublishing/B18275-08-Automating-Workflows-with-GitHub-Actions-Code-Files`.

Tweeter is a simple Go command-line tool that will send tweets to Twitter. The source code consists of two packages, `main` and `tweeter`. The `tweeter` package contains Go tests that will be executed by our continuous integration workflow.

Cloning and testing tweeter

Create a new repository from the template at `https://github.com/PacktPublishing/B18275-08-Automating-Workflows-with-GitHub-Actions-Code-Files` by clicking the **Use this template** button in the repository. This will create a copy of the repository in your account. Run the following commands to clone and test tweeter (replace `{your-account}` with your account name):

```
git clone https://github.com/{your-account}/B18275-08-
Automating-Workflows-with-GitHub-Actions-Code-Files
cd B18275-08-Automating-Workflows-with-GitHub-Actions-Code-
Files
go test ./...
```

Executing `tweeter` with the `-h` argument will provide usage documentation:

```
$ go run . -h
Usage of /tmp/go-build3731631588/b001/exe/github-actions:
      --accessToken string          twitter access token
      --accessTokenSecret string    twitter access token secret
      --apiKey string               twitter api key
      --apiKeySecret string         twitter api key secret
      --dryRun                      if true or if env var DRY_
RUN=true, then a tweet will not be sent
      --message string              message you'd like to send
to twitter
      --version                     output the version of
tweeter
pflag: help requested
exit status 2
```

Twitter usage is not required

If you are not inclined to use social media, tweeter also allows users to simulate sending a tweet. When `--dryRun` is specified, the message value will be output to `STDOUT`, rather than being sent to Twitter as a tweet.

Next, we will build a continuous integration workflow to test tweeter.

Goals of the tweeter continuous integration workflow

Before building a continuous integration workflow, you should consider what you want to accomplish with the workflow. For the tweeter workflow, our goals are the following:

- Trigger on pushes to `main` and tags formatted as a semantic version – for example, `v1.2.3` must build and validate.
- Pull requests against the `main` branch must build and validate.
- Tweeter must build and validate on Ubuntu, macOS, and Windows concurrently.
- Tweeter must build and validate using Go 1.16 and 1.17 concurrently.
- Tweeter source code must pass a code-linting quality check.

Continuous integration workflow for tweeter

With our goals for the tweeter continuous integration workflow specified, we can construct a workflow to achieve those goals. The following is a continuous integration workflow that achieves each goal:

```yaml
name: tweeter-automation
on:
  push:
    tags:
      - 'v[0-9]+.[0-9]+.*'
    branches:
      - main
  pull_request:
    branches:
      - main
jobs:
  test:
    strategy:
      matrix:
        go-version: [ 1.16.x, 1.17.x ]
        os: [ ubuntu-latest, macos-latest, windows-latest ]
    runs-on: ${{ matrix.os }}
    steps:
      - name: install go
        uses: actions/setup-go@v2
        with:
          go-version: ${{ matrix.go-version }}
      - uses: actions/checkout@v2
      - name: lint with golangci-lint
        uses: golangci/golangci-lint-action@v2
      - name: run go test
        run: go test ./...
```

The preceding workflow is a lot to absorb initially. However, if we break down the workflow, the behavior will become clear.

Triggering the workflow

The first two goals for the tweeter continuous integration workflow are as follows:

- Pushes to `main` and tags matching `v[0-9]+.[0-9]+.*` must build and validate.
- Pull requests against the `main` branch must build and validate.

These goals are accomplished by specifying the following event triggers:

```
on:
  push:
    tags:
      - 'v[0-9]+.[0-9]+.*'
    branches:
      - main
  pull_request:
    branches:
      - main
```

The `push:` trigger will execute the workflow if a tag is pushed matching `v[0-9]+.[0-9]+.*` – for example, `v1.2.3` would match the pattern. The `push:` trigger will also execute the workflow if a commit is pushed to `main`. The `pull_request` trigger will execute the workflow on any changes to a pull request targeting the `main` branch.

Note that using the `pull_request` trigger will allow us to update the workflow and see the changes to the workflow each time the changes are pushed in a pull request. This is the desired behavior when developing a workflow, but it does open automation to malicious actors. For example, a malicious actor can open a new pull request, mutating the workflow to exfiltrate secrets exposed in it. There are multiple mitigations to prevent this, which can be applied independently or together, depending on the security preferences of a given project:

- Only allow maintainers to trigger workflows.
- Use the `pull_request_target` event to trigger, which will use workflows defined in the base of the pull request without regard to workflow changes in the pull request.
- Add a label guard for executing a workflow so that it will only execute if a maintainer adds the label to the pull request. For example, a pull request can be reviewed by a maintainer, and then if the user and code changes are safe, the maintainer will apply a `safe-to-test` label, allowing the job to proceed.

Next, we'll extend automation to include multiple platforms and Go versions.

Entering the matrix

The next two goals for the tweeter continuous integration workflow are as follows:

- Tweeter must build and validate on Ubuntu, macOS, and Windows concurrently.
- Tweeter must build and validate using Go 1.16 and 1.17 concurrently.

These goals are accomplished by specifying the following `matrix` configuration:

```
jobs:
  test:
    strategy:
      matrix:
        go-version: [ 1.16.x, 1.17.x ]
        os: [ ubuntu-latest, macos-latest, windows-latest ]
    runs-on: ${{ matrix.os }}
    steps:
      - name: install go
        uses: actions/setup-go@v2
        with:
          go-version: ${{ matrix.go-version }}
```

The `test` job specifies a matrix strategy with two dimensions, `go-version` and `os`. There are two Go versions and three OSs specified. This variable combinations will create six concurrent jobs, [(`ubuntu-latest`, `1.16.x`), (`ubuntu-latest`, `1.17.x`), (`macos-latest`, `1.16.x`), (`macos-latest`, `1.17.x`), (`windows-latest`, `1.16.x`), and (`windows-latest`, `1.17.x`)]. The values of the matrix will be substituted in `runs-on:` and `go-version:` to execute a concurrent job, satisfying the goals of running on each combination of platform and Go version:

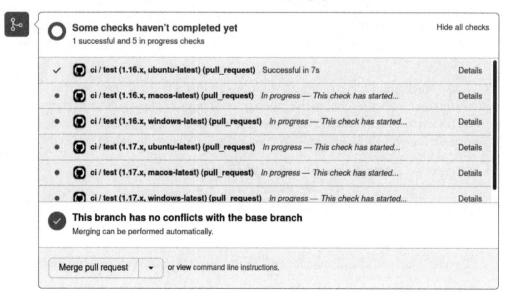

Figure 10.4 – A pull request showing matrix builds

In the preceding figure, you can see each matrix job executing concurrently. Note that each job specifies the name of the job, `test`, and the matrix variables for the job.

Building, testing, and linting

There is an overlap of build, testing, and linting in the last three goals:

- Tweeter must build and validate on Ubuntu, macOS, and Windows concurrently.
- Tweeter must build and validate using Go 1.16 and 1.17 concurrently.
- The Tweeter source code must pass a code-linting quality check.

The following steps will satisfy these requirements:

```
steps:
  - name: install go
    uses: actions/setup-go@v2
    with:
      go-version: ${{ matrix.go-version }}
  - uses: actions/checkout@v2
  - name: lint with golangci-lint
    uses: golangci/golangci-lint-action@v2
  - name: run go test
    run: go test ./...
```

In the preceding steps, the following occurs:

1. Go is installed with the `actions/setup-go@v2` action using the matrix-specified Go version. This action is available to all GitHub users and is published through the GitHub Marketplace. There are numerous actions available in the Marketplace that can simplify workflow authoring.

2. The source code for the current `ref` is cloned with the `actions/checkout@v2` action in the current working directory. Note that the action is not named. For commonly used actions, it is idiomatic to not provide a name.

3. Linting is run with the `golangci/golangci-lint-action@v2`, which installs and executes the `golangci-lint` tool on the source of the repository, satisfying the goal of ensuring that the code passes a lint quality check. This particular action includes several sub-linters that run a rigorous check of common Go performance and stylistic errors.

4. The code is functionally validated by running an ad hoc `go test ./...` script, which tests the packages recursively in the repository. Note that in a previous step, the Go tools have been installed and are available for use in subsequent steps.

With the preceding steps, we have satisfied the goals of our continuous integration workflow. With the preceding workflow, we executed a matrix of concurrent jobs, installed build tools, cloned source code, linted, and tested the change set. In this example, we learned to build a continuous integration workflow for a Go project, but any language and set of tools can be used to create a continuous integration workflow.

In the next section, we will build a release workflow that will automate the process of building and releasing new versions of the tweeter project.

Building a release workflow

In this section, we will take the manual, toilsome process of publishing a new release and transform it into GitHub workflow automation, triggered by pushing a tag to the repository. This automation will result in a GitHub release containing build notes and release artifacts for a tagged, semantic version of the tweeter command-line tool. Automating manual processes such as releases reduces the possibility of manual errors and increases the productivity of project maintainers.

In this section, you will learn how to create a release automation workflow. You will learn how to trigger automation to run after the successful completion of dependent automation. You will learn how to build binaries targeting multiple platforms. Finally, you will automate the creation of a GitHub release, including automatically generated release notes.

GitHub releases

GitHub releases are deployable software iterations for a repository that are based on Git tags. A release declares to the world that a new version of the software is available. A release is composed of a title, an optional description, and an optional set of artifacts. The title provides a name for the release. The description is used to provide insight into what is contained in the release – for example, what new features or pull requests were included in the release, and which GitHub contributors contributed to the release. The description is formatted in GitHub Markdown. Release artifacts are files associated with the release that users can download – for example, a command-line application might publish compiled binaries ready for download and use.

Git tags

A Git tag is a named pointer to a specific reference in the Git repository and are often formatted as semantic versions, such as `v1.2.3`. Semantic versioning is a convention for naming tags that provides some insight into the significance of a new release. A semantic version tag is formatted as `Major.Minor.Patch`. The following behavior is expressed by incrementing the individual field:

- `Major`: Increment when incompatible API changes occur, such as breaking changes.
- `Minor`: Increment when functionality is added in a backward-compatible manner, such as new features.
- `Patch`: Increment when making backward-compatible bug fixes.

Release automation for tweeter

In the *Continuous integration workflow for tweeter* section, we created a CI automation for the tweeter command-line tool. We will build upon the CI automation and add release automation for tweeter.

Goals for automation

In our release automation, we are going to accomplish the following goals:

- Trigger automation when the repository is tagged with a semantic version
- Run unit tests and validation prior to creating the release
- Inject the semantic version of the release into the tweeter application
- Build cross-platform versions of the tweeter application
- Generate release notes from the pull requests in the release
- Tag the contributors in the release
- Create a GitHub release containing the following:
  - A title containing the semantic version of the release
  - A description containing the generated release notes
  - Artifacts consisting of the cross-platform binaries

Next, we will create release automation to satisfy these requirements.

Creating the release automation

With our goals for the tweeter release automation specified, we are ready to extend the existing continuous integration workflow that we built in the previous section and add a release job to achieve those goals. The release job is longer than the continuous integration workflow, so we'll approach it one piece at a time.

Triggering the automation

The first goal for the tweeter release workflow is triggering the automation when the repository is tagged with a semantic version:

```yaml
name: tweeter-automation
on:
  push:
    tags:
      - 'v[0-9]+.[0-9]+.*'
    branches:
      - main
  pull_request:
    branches:
      - main
```

The preceding snippet of YAML is unchanged from the continuous integration workflow. It will trigger the workflow with any tag matching the semantic version in the form of `v1.2.3`. However, the workflow will also trigger on pull requests and pushes. We want the continuous integration workflow to execute on pull requests and pushes, but we do not want to execute a release each time. We will need to restrict execution of the release job to only when executing on a `tag` push.

Restricting release execution

The first and second goal for the tweeter release workflow is as follows:

- Triggering the automation when the repository is tagged with a semantic version
- Running unit tests and validation prior to creating the release

Let's make sure the release job only executes when the repository is tagged:

```yaml
jobs:
  test:
    # continuous integration job omitted for brevity
  release:
    needs: test
```

```
    if: startsWith(github.ref, 'refs/tags/v')
    runs-on: ubuntu-latest
    steps:
```

The preceding job definition completes the first goal of only running the release when a tag starting with `v` is pushed by specifying an `if` statement to verify that the `github.ref` context variable starts with `refs/tags/v`. The second goal of ensuring the `test` job executes successfully before attempting to execute the `release` job is achieved by specifying `needs: test`. If `needs: test` was not specified on the `release` job, both jobs will execute concurrently, which can cause a release to be created without passing validation.

Workspace and environmental setup

To achieve the rest of the automation goals, we will need to set up the workspace:

```
# Previous config of the release job omitted for brevity
steps:
  - uses: actions/checkout@v2
  - name: Set RELEASE_VERSION ENV var
    run: echo "RELEASE_VERSION=${GITHUB_REF:10}" >> $GITHUB_ENV
  - name: install go
    uses: actions/setup-go@v2
    with:
      go-version: 1.17.x
```

The preceding code does the following:

- Checks out the source at the Git ref associated with the tag
- Creates a `RELEASE_VERSION` environment variable with the tag, such as `v1.2.3`
- Installs Go 1.17 tools

Building cross-platform binaries and version injection

The third and fourth goals of the tweeter release flow are as follows:

- Inject the semantic version of the release into the tweeter application.
- Build cross-platform versions of the tweeter application.

Let's get started by injecting the semantic version of the release into the compiled binary:

```
steps:
  # Previous steps of the release job omitted for brevity
```

```yaml
      - name: install gox
        run: go install github.com/mitchellh/gox@v1.0.1
      - name: build cross-platform binaries
        env:
          PLATFORMS: darwin/amd64 darwin/arm64 windows/amd64 linux/amd64 linux/arm64
          VERSION_INJECT: github.com/devopsforgo/github-actions/pkg/tweeter.Version
          OUTPUT_PATH_FORMAT: ./bin/${{ env.RELEASE_VERSION }}/{{.OS}}/{{.Arch}}/tweeter
        run: |
          gox -osarch="${PLATFORMS}" -ldflags "-X ${VERSION_INJECT}=${RELEASE_VERSION}" -output "${OUTPUT_PATH_FORMAT}"
```

The preceding steps do the following:

1. Install the `gox` command-line tool for simplifying Go cross-compilation.
2. Build cross-platform binaries for each specified platform/architecture while injecting the `RELEASE_VERSION` environment variable into a Go `ldflag`. The `ldflag` `-X` replaces the default value of the `Version` variable in the `github.com/devopsforgo/github-actions/pkg/tweeter` package with the semantic version tag of the build. The output of `gox` is structured by `OUTPUT_PATH_FORMAT` – for example, the output directory looks like the following:

```
$ tree ./bin/
./bin/
└── v1.0.0
    ├── darwin
    │   ├── amd64
    │   │   └── tweeter
    │   └── arm64
    │       └── tweeter
    └── linux
        └── amd64
            └── tweeter
```

One of the most compelling reasons to use Golang for building applications is the relative ease of building cross-platform, statically linked binaries. With a couple of steps, we can build versions of tweeter for Linux, Windows, macOS targeting AMD64 and ARM64, as well as many other platforms and architectures. These small, statically linked binaries are simple to distribute and execute across platforms and architectures.

With the preceding steps, the release job has compiled the semantic version of the release into the platform and architecture-specific, statically linked binaries. In the next step, we will use the semantic version to generate release notes.

Generating release notes

We have the following goals associated with generating release notes:

- Generate release notes from the pull requests in the release.
- Tag the contributors in the release.
- Create a GitHub release containing the following:
  - A description containing the generated release notes

Here's some great news! With a bit of configuration and tagging, release note generation is automatically handled by GitHub. We'll start by adding a new file to the repository, `./.github/release.yml`, with the following content:

```yaml
changelog:
  exclude:
    labels:
      - ignore-for-release
  categories:
    - title: Breaking Changes
      labels:
        - breaking-change
    - title: New Features
      labels:
        - enhancement
    - title: Bug Fixes
      labels:
        - bug-fix
    - title: Other Changes
      labels:
        - "*"
```

The preceding release configuration will tell GitHub to filter and categorize pull requests based on the applied labels. For example, pull requests labeled with `ignore-for-release` will be excluded from the release notes, but a pull request labeled with `enhancement` will be grouped under the `New Features` header in the release notes:

```yaml
steps:
  # Previous steps of the release job omitted for brevity
```

```yaml
    - name: generate release notes
      env:
        GITHUB_TOKEN: ${{ secrets.GITHUB_TOKEN }}
      run: |
        gh api -X POST 'repos/{owner}/{repo}/releases/generate-notes' \
          -F commitish=${{ env.RELEASE_VERSION }} \
          -F tag_name=${{ env.RELEASE_VERSION }} \
          > tmp-release-notes.json
```

The preceding step generates release notes. The step executes an API call to the GitHub API to generate the release notes for the given tag. The command captures the JSON body of the response in a `tmp-release-notes.json` filename. Note that gh requires a GitHub token to interact with the GitHub APIs. The GitHub secret is passed into the `GITHUB_TOKEN` environment variable and is used by gh to authenticate.

The following is an example of JSON returned from the `generate-notes` API call:

```
{
  "name": "name of the release",
  "body": "markdown body containing the release notes"
}
```

We will use `tmp-release-notes.json` to create the release in the next step.

Creating the GitHub release

The final goal of creating the release automation is as follows:

- A title containing the semantic version of the release
- A description containing the generated release notes
- Artifacts consisting of the cross-platform binaries

Let's get started creating our release automation:

```yaml
steps:
  # Previous steps of the release job omitted for brevity
  - name: gzip the bins
    env:
      DARWIN_BASE: ./bin/${{ env.RELEASE_VERSION }}/darwin
      WIN_BASE: ./bin/${{ env.RELEASE_VERSION }}/windows
      LINUX_BASE: ./bin/${{ env.RELEASE_VERSION }}/linux
    run: |
```

```yaml
        tar -czvf "${DARWIN_BASE}/amd64/tweeter_darwin_amd64.tar.gz" -C "${DARWIN_BASE}/amd64" tweeter
        tar -czvf "${DARWIN_BASE}/arm64/tweeter_darwin_arm64.tar.gz" -C "${DARWIN_BASE}/arm64" tweeter
        tar -czvf "${WIN_BASE}/amd64/tweeter_windows_amd64.tar.gz" -C "${WIN_BASE}/amd64" tweeter.exe
        tar -czvf "${LINUX_BASE}/amd64/tweeter_linux_amd64.tar.gz" -C "${LINUX_BASE}/amd64" tweeter
        tar -czvf "${LINUX_BASE}/arm64/tweeter_linux_arm64.tar.gz" -C "${LINUX_BASE}/arm64" tweeter
    - name: create release
      env:
        OUT_BASE: ./bin/${{ env.RELEASE_VERSION }}
        GITHUB_TOKEN: ${{ secrets.GITHUB_TOKEN }}
      run: |
        jq -r .body tmp-release-notes.json > tmp-release-notes.md
        gh release create ${{ env.RELEASE_VERSION }} \
          -t "$(jq -r .name tmp-release-notes.json)" \
          -F tmp-release-notes.md \
"${OUT_BASE}/darwin/amd64/tweeter_darwin_amd64.tar.gz#tweeter_osx_amd64" \
"${OUT_BASE}/darwin/arm64/tweeter_darwin_arm64.tar.gz#tweeter_osx_arm64" \
"${OUT_BASE}/windows/amd64/tweeter_windows_amd64.tar.gz#tweeter_windows_amd64" \
"${OUT_BASE}/linux/amd64/tweeter_linux_amd64.tar.gz#tweeter_linux_amd64" \
"${OUT_BASE}/linux/arm64/tweeter_linux_arm64.tar.gz#tweeter_linux_arm64"
```

The preceding steps do the following:

- Execute `tar` and `gzip` on the binaries. With Go 1.17, tweeter bins are roughly 6.5 MB. After `gzip`, each artifact is less than 4 MB.
- Create a GitHub release using the `gh` command-line tool, which is available on all GitHub job executors. `gh` requires a GitHub token to interact with the GitHub APIs. The GitHub secret is passed into the `GITHUB_TOKEN` environment variable and is used by `gh` to authenticate. `gh release create` creates a release and uploads each of the files specified after the arguments. Each file uploaded becomes an artifact on the release. Note # after each artifact file path. The text after # is the name that the artifact will display, as in the GitHub UI. We also specify the title and the release notes using the captured `tmp-release-notes.json` and `jq` to parse and select the JSON content.

At this point, we have a created release targeting multiple platforms and architectures, satisfying all our goals for automation. Let's kick off a release and see the results.

Creating a release of tweeter

Now that we have built a release job that will automate the releases of tweeter, we can now tag the repository and release a version of the application. To start the release automation, we are going to create and push the v0.0.1 tag to the repository by executing the following:

```
git tag v0.0.1
git push origin v0.0.1
```

After the tag is pushed, you should be able to go to the **Actions** tab on your GitHub repository and see the tag workflow executing. If you navigate to the workflow, you should see something like the following:

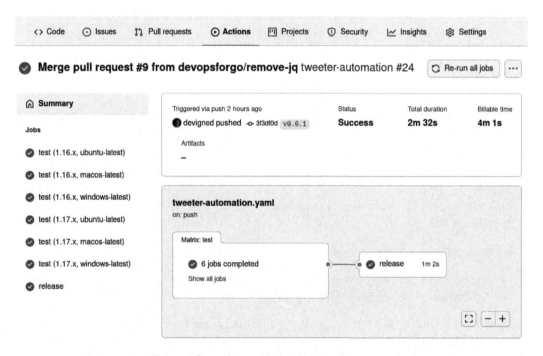

Figure 10.5 – The workflow job view showing dependent test and release jobs

As you can see in the preceding figure, the tests have been executed and, subsequently, the release job has been too. If you navigate to the **release** job, you should see something like the following:

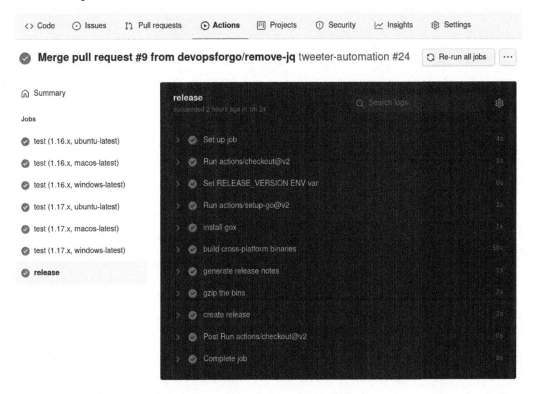

Figure 10.6 – The release job output view

As you can see in the preceding figure, the release job has successfully executed each of the steps and the release was created. If you go to the landing page of the repository, you should see that a new release has been created. If you click on that release, you should see something like the following:

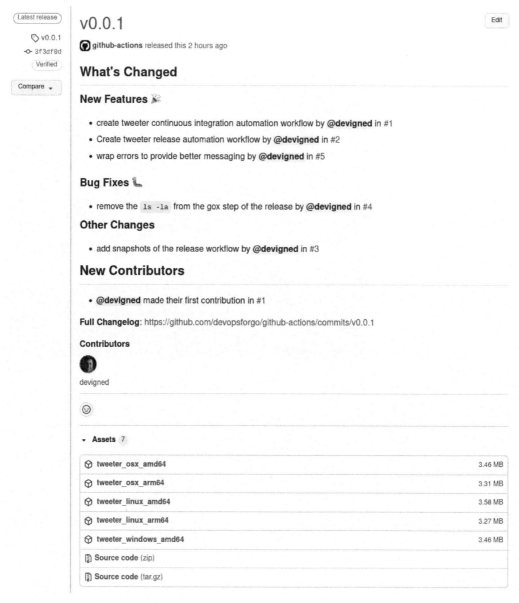

Figure 10.7 – The release view, containing assets, the release note, and the semantic version title

In the preceding figure, you can see that the release named `v0.0.1` has been autogenerated with categorized release notes that link to the pull requests, the contributor, and artifacts for each platform/architecture combination.

With the preceding steps, we have satisfied the goals of our release automation job. We triggered the release job after the tests executed to ensure a release will always pass our validations before being published. We built statically linked binaries for each of the specified platform/architecture combinations using `gox`. We leveraged GitHub release notes autogeneration to create beautifully formatted release notes. And finally, we created a release with the generated notes and artifacts from the build.

In this example, we learned to build a release automation job for a Go project, but any language and set of tools can be used in a similar manner to create release automation for any language.

We have no more manual toil to release the tweeter project. All that needs to be done is to push a tag to the repository. Our use of open source actions has enhanced our ability to author these automations. In the next section, we will learn to create our own packaged action that will allow others to use an action we author.

Creating a custom GitHub Action using Go

In this section, we will extend upon our work by turning the tweeter command line into a GitHub Action. This will allow anyone on GitHub building automation to use tweeter to tweet from their own pipeline. Furthermore, we'll use our tweeter action to tweet when we release new versions of tweeter by extending the release job to use our new action.

In this section, you will learn the basics of authoring GitHub Actions. You will create a custom GitHub Action using Go. You will then optimize the start up time of your custom action by creating a container image.

Basics of custom actions

Custom actions are individual tasks that wrap a collection of related tasks. Custom actions can be executed as individual tasks in workflows and can be shared with the GitHub community.

Types of actions

There are three types of actions: container, JavaScript, and composite actions. Container-based actions use a Dockerfile or a container image reference as the entry point, the starting point of execution for the action, and are useful if you want to author an action in anything but JavaScript or existing actions. Container-based actions offer flexibility in customizing the execution environment of an action, but it comes at the cost of start up time. If a container-based action depends on a large container image or a slow-building Dockerfile, then the action start up time will be adversely affected. JavaScript actions can run directly on the runner machine and are the native expression of an action. JavaScript actions start up quickly and can leverage the GitHub Actions Toolkit, a set of JavaScript packages to make creating actions easier. Composite actions are a collection of steps within a wrapper action. They enable an author to combine a set of disparate steps into a higher-order behavior.

Action metadata

To define an action, you must create an `action.yaml` file in a GitHub repository. If the action is to be shared publicly, the `action.yaml` file should be created in the root of the repository. If the action is not to be shared publicly, it is recommended to create the `action.yaml` file in `./.github/{name-of-action}/action.yaml` where `{name-of-action}` should be substituted with the name of the action. For example, if the tweeter action was only to be used internally, the path of the action metadata would be `./.github/tweeter/action.yaml`:

```yaml
name: Name of the Action
author: @author
description: Description of your action
branding:
  icon: message-circle
  color: blue
inputs:
  sample:
    description: sample description
    required: true
outputs:
  sampleOutput:
    description: some sample output
runs:
  using: docker
  image: Dockerfile
  args:
```

```
        - --sample
        - "${{ inputs.sample }}"
```

The preceding `action.yaml` defines the following:

- The name of the action that will be shown in the GitHub UI
- The author of the action
- The description of the action
- Branding that will be used for the action in the GitHub UI
- Input the action will accept
- Output the action will return
- The `runs` section, which describes how the action will be executed

In this example, we are using a Dockerfile, which will build a container from the Dockerfile and execute the container entry point with the specified arguments. Note how the `inputs.sample` context variable is used to map input to command-line arguments.

The preceding action can be executed with the following step:

```
jobs:
  sample-job:
    runs-on: ubuntu-latest
    steps:
      - name: Sample action step
        id: sample
        uses: devopsforgo/sample-action@v1
        with:
          sample: 'Hello from the sample!'
      # Use the output from the `sample` step
      - name: Get the sample message
        run: echo "The message is ${{
            steps.sample.outputs.sampleOutput }}"
```

The preceding sample execution does the following:

- Executes a step using the sample action with the assumption that the action is tagged with `v1` in the `devopsforgo/sample-action` repository, with `action.yaml` at the root of that repository, and specifies the required input variable `sample`.
- Echoes the `sampleOutput` variable.

Next, we will discuss how to tag action releases.

Action release management

In all of our examples of using actions in our workflows, the `uses:` value for the action has always included the version of the action. For example, in the preceding sample, we used `devopsforgo/sample-action@v1` to specify that we wanted to use the action at the Git tag of `v1`. By specifying that version, we are telling the workflow to use the action at the Git reference pointed to by that tag. By convention, the `v1` tag of an action can point to any Git reference that is tagged in the semantic version range of `v1.x.x`. That means that the `v1` tag is a floating tag and not static, and will advance as new releases in the `v1.x.x` range are released. Recall from the description of semantic versions earlier in this chapter that increments of the major version indicate breaking changes. The author of the action is making a promise to users that anything tagged with `v1` will not include breaking changes.

The conventions used for versioning actions can cause friction when an action is included in the same repository as another versioned software project. It is advised to consider the implications of action versioning, and consider creating a repository dedicated to an action rather than creating it within a repository containing other versioned projects.

Goals for the tweeter custom GitHub Action

In our custom GitHub Action for tweeter, we are going to accomplish the following:

- Build a Dockerfile for building and running the tweeter command-line tool.
- Create an action metadata file for the custom action.
- Extend the continuous integration job to test the action.
- Create an image release workflow for publishing the tweeter container image.
- Optimize the tweeter custom action by using the published container image.

Next, we will create a custom Go action using a Dockerfile.

Creating the tweeter action

With our goals for the tweeter custom action specified, we are ready to create the Dockerfile required to run tweeter, define the metadata for the action to map input and output from the tweeter command-line tool, extend our continuous integration job to test the action, and finally, optimize the start time for the action by using a pre-built container image in the custom action. We will break down each step and create our custom Go action.

Defining a Dockerfile

The first goal for the tweeter custom GitHub Action is building a Dockerfile for building and running the tweeter command-line tool.

Let's get started by building a Dockerfile in the root of the tweeter repository that we will use to build a container image:

```
FROM golang:1.17 as builder
WORKDIR /workspace
# Copy the Go Modules manifests
COPY go.mod go.mod
COPY go.sum go.sum
# Cache deps before building and copying source
# so that we don't need to re-download as much
# and so that source changes don't invalidate
# our downloaded layer
RUN go mod download
# Copy the sources
COPY ./ ./
RUN CGO_ENABLED=0 GOOS=linux GOARCH=amd64 \
    go build -a -ldflags '-extldflags "-static"' \
    -o tweeter .
# Copy the action into a thin image
FROM gcr.io/distroless/static:latest
WORKDIR /
COPY --from=builder /workspace/tweeter .
ENTRYPOINT ["/tweeter"]
```

The preceding Dockerfile does the following:

1. Uses the `golang:1.17` image as an intermediate builder container, which contains the Go build tools needed to compile the tweeter command-line tool. Using the builder pattern creates an intermediate container, containing build tools and source code that will not be needed in the end product. It allows us a scratch area to build a statically linked Go application that can be added to a slimmed-down container at the end of the build process. This enables the final container to only contain the Go application and nothing more.
2. The build then copies in `go.mod` and `go.sum`, and then downloads the Go dependencies for the tweeter application.
3. The source for the tweeter application is copied into the builder container and then compiled as a statically linked binary.
4. The production image is created from the `gcr.io/distroless/static:latest` base image, and the tweeter application is copied from the intermediate builder container.
5. Finally, the default entry point is set to the tweeter binary, which will enable us to run the container and directly execute the tweeter application.

To build and then execute the preceding Dockerfile, you can run the following:

```
$ docker build . -t tweeter
# output from the docker build

$ docker run tweeter -h
pflag: help requested
Usage of /tweeter:
      --accessToken string        twitter access token
      # More help text removed for brevity.
```

The preceding script does the following:

- Builds the Dockerfile and tags it with the name `tweeter`
- Runs the tagged tweeter container image, passing the tweeter application the `-h` argument, causing the tweeter application to print the help text

Now that we have a working Dockerfile, we can use that to define a custom container action defined in `action.yaml`.

Creating action metadata

The second goal for the tweeter custom GitHub Action is creating an action metadata file for the custom action.

Now that we have defined the Dockerfile, we can author a Docker action with the following action metadata in an `action.yaml` file in the root of the repository:

```
name: Tweeter Action
author: DevOps for Go
description: Action to send a tweet via a GitHub Action.
inputs:
  message:
    description: 'message you want to tweet'
    required: true
  apiKey:
    description: 'api key for Twitter api'
    required: true
  apiKeySecret:
    description: 'api key secret for Twitter api'
    required: true
  accessToken:
    description: 'access token for Twitter api'
    required: true
  accessTokenSecret:
    description: 'access token secret for Twitter api'
    required: true
outputs:
  errorMessage:
    description: 'if something went wrong, the error message'
  sentMessage:
    description: 'the message sent to Twitter'
runs:
  using: docker
  image: Dockerfile
  args:
    - --message
    - "${{ inputs.message }}"
    - --apiKey
    - ${{ inputs.apiKey }}
    - --apiKeySecret
```

```
      - ${{ inputs.apiKeySecret }}
      - --accessToken
      - ${{ inputs.accessToken }}
      - --accessTokenSecret
      - ${{ inputs.accessTokenSecret }}
```

The preceding action metadata does the following:

- Defines the action name, author, and description metadata
- Defines the expected input to the action
- Defines the output variable for the action
- Executes the Dockerfile, mapping the input of the action to the `args` of the tweeter application

How the input variables map to the tweeter `args` command line is apparent due to the mapping of the input to the arguments, but it is not clear how the output variables are mapped. The output variables are mapped by specially encoding the variables in STDOUT in the Go application:

```
func printOutput(key, message string) {
    fmt.Printf("::set-output name=%s::%s\n", key, message)
}
```

The preceding function prints to STDOUT the key and the message for an output variable. To return the `sentMessage` output variable, the Go application calls `printOutput("sendMessage", message)`. The action runtime will read STDOUT, recognize the encoding, and then populate the context variable for `steps.{action.id}.outputs.sentMessage`.

With our action metadata defined, we are now ready to test our action by extending the tweeter continuous integration workflow to execute the action in the local repository.

Testing the action

The third goal of the tweeter custom GitHub Action is to extend the continuous integration job to test the action.

With the `action.yaml` file authored, we can add a workflow job to test the action:

```
test-action:
  runs-on: ubuntu-latest
  steps:
    - uses: actions/checkout@v2
    - name: test the tweeter action in DRY_RUN
      id: tweeterAction
      env:
        DRY_RUN: true
      uses: ./
      with:
        message: hello world!
        accessToken: fake
        accessTokenSecret: fake
        apiKey: fake
        apiKeySecret: fake
    - run: echo ${{ steps.tweeterAction.outputs.sentMessage }} from dry run test
```

The preceding `test-action` job does the following:

- Checks out the code to the local workspace
- Executes the local action, specifying all required input and setting the `DRY_RUN` environment variable to `true` so that the action will not try to send the message to Twitter
- Runs an `echo` command, fetching the echoed output from the action

Let's see what happens when we trigger this workflow:

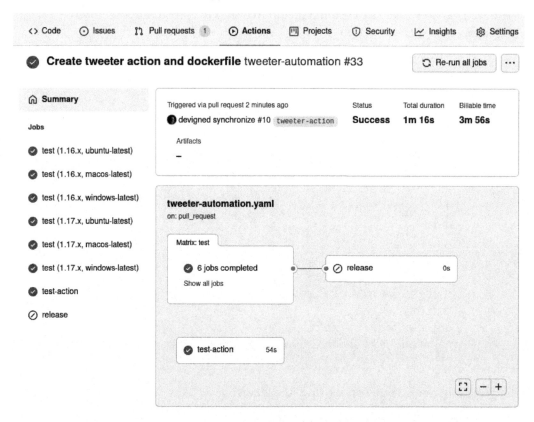

Figure 10.8 – The workflow run with the new test-action job

In the preceding screenshot, you can see that the `test-action` job is now part of the tweeter automation that will validate the action. Note the runtime of 54 seconds for executing the job. It seems like a long time to call a command-line application:

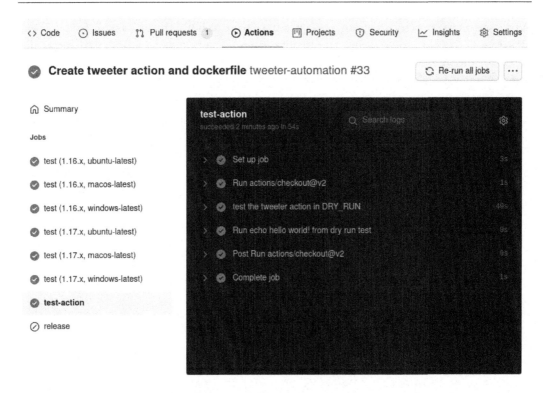

Figure 10.9 – The test-action job output

In the preceding screenshot, you can see that the test for the tweeter action took 49 seconds out of the total job runtime of 54 seconds. That is the vast majority of the time it took to execute the job. Most of that time was spent compiling tweeter and building the `docker` image prior to executing the action. In the next part, we'll optimize the action execution time by referencing a pre-built version of the tweeter container image.

Creating a container image release workflow

The fourth goal of the tweeter custom GitHub Action is creating an image release workflow for publishing the tweeter container image.

As we saw in the previous section, the amount of time to build the Dockerfile was significant. There is little reason to do that for every execution of an action, which can be avoided by publishing the container image to a container registry and then using the registry image in place of the Dockerfile:

```yaml
name: release image
on:
  # push events for tags matching image-v for version (image-v1.0, etc)
  push:
    tags:
      - 'image-v*'
permissions:
  contents: read
  packages: write
jobs:
  image:
    runs-on: ubuntu-latest
    steps:
      - uses: actions/checkout@v2
      - name: set env
        # refs/tags/image-v1.0.0 substring starting at 1.0.0
        run: echo "RELEASE_VERSION=${GITHUB_REF:17}" >> $GITHUB_ENV
      - name: setup buildx
        uses: docker/setup-buildx-action@v1
      - name: login to GitHub container registry
        uses: docker/login-action@v1
        with:
          registry: ghcr.io
          username: ${{ github.repository_owner }}
          password: ${{ secrets.GITHUB_TOKEN }}
      - name: build and push
        uses: docker/build-push-action@v2
        with:
          push: true
          tags: |
            ghcr.io/devopsforgo/tweeter:${{ env.RELEASE_VERSION }}
            ghcr.io/devopsforgo/tweeter:latest
```

The preceding workflow definition does the following:

- Triggers only when tags starting with `image-v` are pushed
- Requests permissions to write to the `ghcr.io` image repository and read the Git repository
- Contains a single container image build and steps to publish the image.
- Checks out the repository
- Builds the `RELEASE_VERSION` environment variable based on the tag format
- Sets up `buildx` for building the container image
- Logs in to `ghcr.io`, the GitHub container registry
- Builds and pushes the container image tagged with both the release version and the latest version

With the preceding workflow in place, we can tag the repository with the following commands and have the container image published to the GitHub container registry for use in the tweeter action:

```
git tag image-v1.0.0
git push origin image-v1.0.0
```

Let's see the result of our image release workflow:

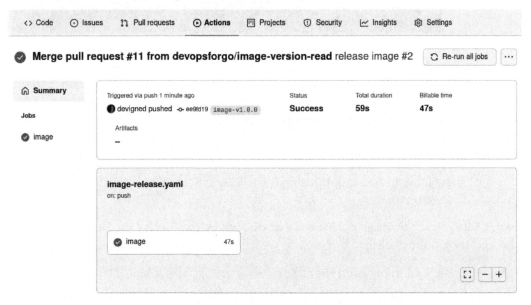

Figure 10.10 – The workflow job view for the image-release job

The preceding screenshot shows the `release image` workflow that was triggered by pushing the `image-v1.0.0` tag. The following screenshot details the results of each step of the `release image` workflow:

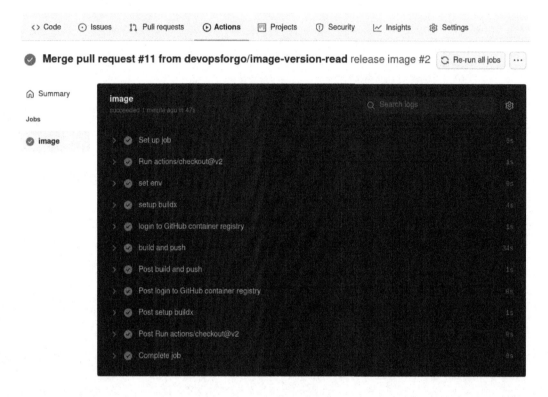

Figure 10.11 – The image release job output

The result of the preceding workflow is that we now have a container image pushed to `ghcr.io/devopsforgo/tweeter`, tagged with `v1.0.0` and `latest`. We can now update the action metadata to use the tagged image version.

Optimizing the custom Go action

The final goal of this section is optimizing the tweeter custom action by using the published container image.

Now that we have the image published to `ghcr.io`, we can replace the Dockerfile with the reference to the published image:

```
# omitted the previous portion of the action.yaml
runs:
```

```
using: docker
image: docker://ghcr.io/devopsforgo/tweeter:1.0.0
# omitted the subsequent portion of the action.yaml
```

The preceding portion of the `action.yaml` file illustrates replacing the Dockerfile with the published tweeter container image. Now that the Dockerfile has been replaced, let's run the workflow and see the performance optimization in action:

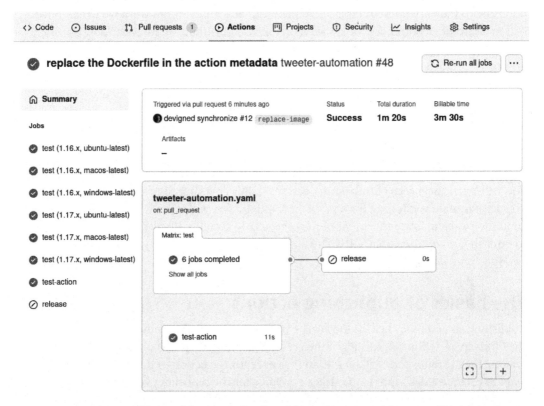

Figure 10.12 – The workflow view showing the speed increase of the test-action job

The preceding screenshot illustrates the gains from using a pre-built container image. Recall, when using a Dockerfile, that the workflow execution was 54 seconds. Now, using the tweeter container image from the registry, the workflow executes in 11 seconds. This is a significant optimization and should be used when possible.

In this section, we learned to build custom actions using Go, which enables a DevOps engineer to build complex actions and package them in easily accessible units of automation. We also learned how to test and optimize these actions locally, ensuring that when custom actions are published, they function as intended.

In the next section, we will build upon the ability to author custom actions and publish an action to the entire GitHub community. By publishing an action to the GitHub marketplace, an action can become a key tool for other DevOps engineers authoring automation.

Publishing a custom Go GitHub Action

The superpower of GitHub Actions is the community and the actions that the community publishes to the GitHub Marketplace. Think about how much more work we would have had to do in the previous sections if we didn't have community actions available for use. Our workflows would have had to start from first principles, involving authoring long, tedious scripts to complete tasks that we were able to express in a handful of YAML instead.

Open source software is not only about having access to free software but also about giving back to the community. We are going to learn how to give back to the GitHub Actions community through publishing an action to GitHub Marketplace. This will enable the entire user community of GitHub to benefit from it.

In this section, you will learn how to publish a custom action to the GitHub Marketplace. You will learn the basics of publishing actions. After covering the basics, you will learn how to automate versioning for a published action. You will learn how to use the tweeter action to tweet an announcement of new releases to tweeter. Finally, you will learn how to publish your action to the GitHub Marketplace so that it can be used by the rest of the GitHub community across the world.

The basics of publishing actions

Publishing an action to the GitHub Marketplace adds some requirements and best practices that, for a local action, as we built in the previous section, do not apply. For example, the readme for the repository will be the landing page for the action in the marketplace, so you'd want to provide a description and usage guidance for the repository readme.

The following are the requirements for publishing an action to the GitHub Marketplace:

- The action must be in a public GitHub repository.
- In the root of the repository must be a single action named `action.yaml` or `action.yml`.
- The name of the action in `action.yaml` must be unique to the marketplace. The name may not overlap with any GitHub features or products, or any other names that GitHub reserves.

- A public action should follow v1 and v1.2.3 semantic version guidance so that users of the action can specify a full semantic version, or simply v1 to denote the latest in the v1 major semantic version series.

Goals for publishing the tweeter custom action

The following are goals for publishing the tweeter custom action:

- Set up a release-triggered workflow that will handle semantic version management.
- Publish the tweeter action to the GitHub Marketplace.

Managing action semantic versioning

The first and second goals of publishing the tweeter custom action to the marketplace are as follows:

- Set up a release-triggered workflow that will handle semantic version management.
- Use the action to tweet an announcement of the new release of the action.

We are going to build a workflow to update the major version tag – for example, v1 – to point to the latest release in the v1.x.x series of semantic versions. The workflow will also be responsible for creating new major version tags as new major semantic versions are released:

```
name: Release new tweeter version
on:
  release:
    types: [released]
  workflow_dispatch:
    inputs:
      TAG_NAME:
        description: 'Tag name that the major tag will point to'
        required: true

permissions:
  contents: write

env:
  TAG_NAME: ${{ github.event.inputs.TAG_NAME || github.event.release.tag_name }}
jobs:
```

```
  update_tag:
    name: Update the major tag to include the ${{ env.TAG_NAME
}} changes
    runs-on: ubuntu-latest
    steps:
      - name: Update the ${{ env.TAG_NAME }} tag
        uses: actions/publish-action@v0.1.0
        with:
          source-tag: ${{ env.TAG_NAME }}
      - uses: actions/checkout@v2
      - name: Tweet about the release
        uses: ./
        with:
          message: Hey folks, we just released the ${{ env.TAG_
NAME }} for the tweeter GitHub Action!!
          accessToken: ${{ secrets.ACCESS_TOKEN }}
          accessTokenSecret: ${{ secrets.ACCESS_TOKEN_SECRET }}
          apiKey: ${{ secrets.API_KEY }}
          apiKeySecret: ${{ secrets.API_KEY_SECRET }}
```

The preceding workflow does the following:

- Triggers on a release being published or on a manual UI submission. This means that a project maintainer can trigger the workflow via the GitHub UI if ad hoc execution was required.

- Declares that the workflow requires rights to write to the repository. This is used to write tags.

- Declares the `TAG_NAME` environment variable, which is either the ad hoc job input or the tag of the release.

- The `update_tag` takes the tag in `v1.2.3` format and updates the tag's major semantic version tag to the latest version within that major semantic version. For example, if the new release tag is `v1.2.3`, then the `v1` tag will point to the same Git ref as `v1.2.3`.

- Clones the source code using `actions/checkout@v2`.

- Tweets about the new release using Twitter developer credentials embedded in GitHub repository secrets. To set up Twitter developer credentials, see `https://developer.twitter.com/en/portal/dashboard` and set up an account and application. After you gather the secrets, you can add them to the repository secrets under the **Settings** tab, as shown in the following screenshot:

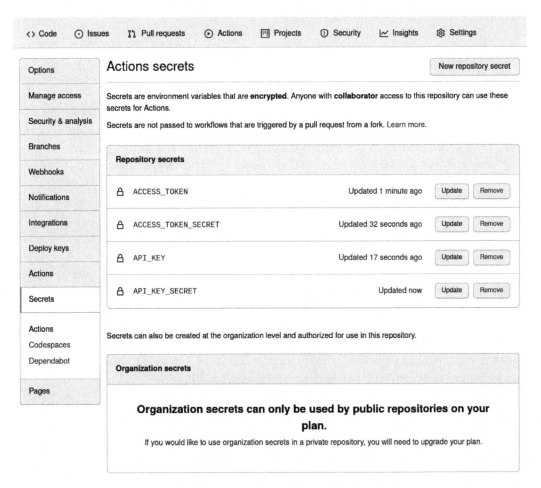

Figure 10.13 – Repository secrets

With the preceding workflow, when we apply a tag – for example, `v1.2.3` – the repository will also be tagged at the same Git `ref` with `v1`. After the tags are set, the tweeter action will execute, announcing the release to the world.

Recall from the previous section that when we tag the tweeter repository with a semantic version, the release workflow will trigger, causing a new release to be created. This workflow will then trigger the action version update release workflow, which will tag the action with the major version and announce through Twitter that the action release is available.

All that is left to do is to release the action to the GitHub Marketplace. This only needs to be done the first time the action is released.

Publishing the tweeter action to the GitHub Marketplace

The final goal of publishing the tweeter custom action is to publish the tweeter action to the GitHub Marketplace. The first publication of your GitHub Action is a manual process and can be accomplished by following the guide here: `https://docs.github.com/en/actions/creating-actions/publishing-actions-in-github-marketplace`. After taking this first set of manual steps, they will not need to be repeated for future releases.

Summary

GitHub Actions is a powerful system for project maintainers to automate toilsome processes, enabling greater developer satisfaction and increased project velocity. We targeted Go in this chapter as the language of choice for GitHub Actions due to its type safety, low memory overhead, and speed. We believe that it is the best choice for writing GitHub Actions. However, many of the skills taught here are transferable to other languages. Each of the patterns, continuous integration, release pipelines, semantic versioning, and action creation can be applied to any project that you come into contact with.

The key to the chapter is to understand the impact of community contributions in the GitHub Marketplace. By using, building, and contributing to the marketplace, an engineer can make their automation more composable and empower community members to solve more complex problems through the contributions of the community.

We learned the basics of GitHub Actions with a focus on its features, which enable us to be functional quickly. With these basic skills, we were able to build a continuous integration automation workflow to clone, build, lint, and test the tweeter project. We extended the continuous integration automation to create a release pipeline trigger from Git tags. The release pipeline transformed manual tasks such as authoring release notes and made them an automated part of the release workflow. Finally, we created and published a custom Go GitHub Action that can be used by the entire community.

I hope that at the end of this chapter you feel confident in your ability to create automation to eliminate toilsome tasks that burdened your team's day. Remember that if you can automate a task that happens once a week and takes an hour, you are saving a full week of work from one of your team members! That is time that is likely better spent adding value to your business.

In the next chapter, we are going to learn about ChatOps. You will learn how to use chat applications such as Slack to trigger automation and alerts when events occur, providing you and your team an interactive robotic DevOps partner.

11
Using ChatOps to Increase Efficiency

As DevOps engineers, we often work as part of a team of engineers that help manage a network, service infrastructure, and public-facing services. This means there are a lot of moving parts and communication that needs to occur, especially in an emergency.

ChatOps provides teams with a central interface to tooling to ask questions about current states and to interact with other DevOps tools while recording those interactions for posterity. This can improve feedback loops and real-time communication between teams and help manage incidents effectively.

One of our colleagues, Sarah Murphy, has a saying – *Don't talk to the bus driver*. As a release engineer for Facebook in the early days, she was responsible for releasing Facebook across their data centers. This was a high-stress and detail-oriented job that required her complete attention. Many of the engineers wanted to know if their feature or patch was being included in the current release and, of course, asked the release engineer.

As any engineer who does high-impact rollouts will tell you, you need to focus. Having hundreds of engineers ping you about the status of their particular patch is not ideal. This is where ChatOps comes into play. Instrumenting ChatOps can allow a central place where questions about rollout status and what revision is in a release can stave off those hundreds of questions. It certainly did for Sarah.

In this chapter, we will dive into how to build a ChatOps bot for Slack. We will show how we can use that bot to ask the status of a service. We will show how we can use a bot to get deployment information. And finally, we will show how we can use the bot to deploy our software.

We will cover the following topics in this chapter:

- Environment architecture
- Using an Ops service
- Building a basic chatbot
- Creating event handlers
- Creating our Slack application

Technical requirements

The following are the prerequisites for this chapter:

- A Slack user account: Create a Slack user if you do not have one by following the instructions here: `https://slack.com/get-started#/createnew`.
- A Slack workspace to experiment: Instructions for creating a Slack workspace can be found here: `https://slack.com/help/articles/206845317-Create-a-Slack-workspace`.
- Creation of a Slack application.

It is highly suggested that you use a workspace you control instead of using a corporate one. That process requires approval by admins for your corporate Slack.

You will also need to create a Slack application, but this is covered in a later section.

The code files for this chapter can be downloaded from `https://github.com/PacktPublishing/Go-for-DevOps/tree/rev0/chapter/11`

Environment architecture

Our example ChatOps program will need to interact with several services to provide information to users.

To enable this, we have built a more robust version of the `Petstore` application that we built in our previous chapters. This version does the following:

- Implements **create, read, update and delete** (**CRUD**).

- Is gRPC based.
- Has deeper Open Telemetry tracing that flows through RPC calls and records events.
- Deeper metrics that can be used to inform Prometheus alarms.
- Replaces logging with tracing events.
- All errors are automatically added to traces.
- Traces can be turned on by a client.
- Traces are sampled by default but can be changed via an RPC.

You can find this new Petstore here: `https://github.com/PacktPublishing/Go-for-DevOps/tree/rev0/chapter/11/petstore`. There is a `README` file that details the architecture if you want to dive into the details, but you do not need to for this chapter.

Our new Petstore is more capable and will allow us to show some of the power ChatOps can provide by combining our other lessons from this chapter.

The following is what our service architecture would look like:

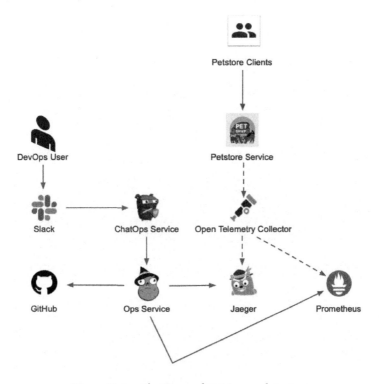

Figure 11.1 – ChatOps and Petstore architecture

> **Attribution**
>
> Poodle dog vector created by `gstudioimagen-www.freepik.com`
>
> Gophers by Egon Elbe: `github.com/egonelbre/gophers`

There are two services we will concentrate on creating here:

- **Ops service**: The Ops service does the real work, such as talking to Jaeger, Prometheus, running jobs, or anything else that is needed. This allows us to have multiple ChatOps services running in parallel (which might be needed if your company migrates from Slack to Microsoft Teams, for example).

  This architecture has the benefit of allowing other teams to write tools using these functions in any language they choose.

- **ChatOps service**: The ChatOps service acts as the glue between Slack and the Ops service. It interprets messages sent to the Slack bot, which are forwarded to our ChatOps service, and makes requests to the Ops service. It uses the open source `slack-go` package, which can be found at `https://github.com/slack-go/slack`.

Let's jump into the basic details of the Ops service.

Using an Ops service

We are not going to go into complete detail about this service, as we have covered how gRPC works in previous chapters. As this service just makes gRPC or REST calls to other services, let's talk about the calls that need to be implemented.

The protocol buffer service definition is as follows:

```
service Ops {
    rpc ListTraces(ListTracesReq) returns (ListTracesResp) {};
    rpc ShowTrace(ShowTraceReq) returns (ShowTraceResp) {};
    rpc ChangeSampling(ChangeSamplingReq) returns (ChangeSamplingResp) {};
    rpc DeployedVersion(DeployedVersionReq) returns (DeployedVersionResp) {};
    rpc Alerts(AlertsReq) returns (AlertsResp) {};
}
```

For our example service, these RPCs are targeted at a single deployed instance, but in a production environment, this would work on multiple entities that exist on a site.

This allows users to get some information quickly, such as the following:

- See the traces we have in a certain time period, and the ability to filter by tags (such as `error`).
- Retrieve basic trace data and the Jaeger URL of a trace given a trace ID.
- Change the sampling type and rate for traces in the service.
- Tell us what version has been deployed according to Prometheus.
- Display any alerts that Prometheus shows are firing.

You can read the code on how this is implemented here: `https://github.com/PacktPublishing/Go-for-DevOps/tree/rev0/chapter/11/ops`.

We include a `README` file that goes over the basic architecture, but it is your standard gRPC service that makes calls using gRPC to the Petstore service/Jaeger and REST calls to Prometheus.

Now, let's jump into something new, writing the basic Slack bot.

Building a basic chatbot

Go has a few clients that can interact with popular chat services such as Slack, either as a general Slack client or as a ChatOps-focused bot.

We have found that it is best to have an architecture that separates the bot from the operations that you want to perform. This allows other tooling in other languages to access the capabilities.

By keeping the chatbot separate, you can focus on a single type of chat service and use all its features, instead of only features shared by each chat service client.

For this reason, we will use the `slack-go` package to interact with Slack.

Our bot will be basic, simply listening to when someone mentions our bot in a message. This is called an `AppMention` event. Slack supports other events and has events specifically for commands that you can install. In our case, we just want to answer whenever we are mentioned, but `slack-go` has many other capabilities we will not explore.

Let's create a package called `bot` and add some imports:

```
package bot

import (
        "log"
        "context"
        "regexp"
        "encoding/json"

        "github.com/slack-go/slack"
        "github.com/slack-go/slack/slackevents"
        "github.com/slack-go/slack/socketmode"
)
```

Details on our third-party package are as follows:

- `slack` is what is used to build a basic client.
- `slackevents` details the various events we can receive.
- `socketmode` provides a method of connecting to Slack from a bot that is behind a firewall.

Let's create a type that can handle an event we receive:

```
type HandleFunc func(ctx context.Context, m Message)

type register struct{
        r *regexp.Regexp
        h HandleFunc
}
```

`HandleFunc` receives a message that can be used to write to channels and get information about the message that was received.

We have also defined a register type that is used to register a `HandleFunc` with a **regular expression (regex)**. The regex will be used to determine whether the message should be handled by that specific `HandleFunc`.

Let's define the `Message` type:

```
type Message struct {
        User *slack.User
        AppMention *slackevents.AppMentionEvent
```

```
        Text string
}
```

This contains information about the Slack user who sent the message, information about the `AppMention` event, and the cleaned-up text that the user sent (removes the `@User` text and leading/trailing spaces).

Now, let's define our `Bot` type and its constructor:

```
type Bot struct {
    api *slack.Client
    client *socketmode.Client
    ctx context.Context
    cancel context.CancelFunc

    defaultHandler HandleFunc
    reg []register
}

func New(api *slack.Client, client *socketmode.Client) (*Bot, error) {
    b := &Bot{
            api: api,
            client: client,
            ctx: ctx,
            cancel: cancel,
    }
    return b, nil
}
```

This code contains our clients that will be used to interact with Slack, a context for canceling our bot's goroutines, `defaultHandler` for handling the case where no regex matches happen, and a list of registrations that we check on any message receipt.

We now need some methods to start and stop our bot:

```
func (b *Bot) Start() {
    b.ctx, b.cancel = context.WithCancel(context.Background())
    go b.loop()

    b.client.RunContext(b.ctx)
}

func (b *Bot) Stop() {
```

```
        b.cancel()
        b.ctx = nil
        b.cancel = nil
}
```

This simply starts our event loop and calls `RunContext` to listen to our event stream. We cancel our bot using the supplied `context`. `Bot.Start()` blocks until `Stop()` is called.

Our next method will allow us to register our regexes and their handlers:

```
func (b *Bot) Register(r *regexp.Regexp, h HandleFunc) {
    if h == nil {
        panic("HandleFunc cannot be nil")
    }
    if r == nil {
        if b.defaultHandle != nil {
            panic("cannot add two default handles")
        }
        b.defaultHandle = h
        return
    }
    b.reg = append(b.reg, register{r, h})
}
```

In this code, if we don't supply a regex, then `HandleFunc` is used as the default handler when no regexes match. You can only have one default handler. When the bot checks a message, it matches regexes in the order they are added; the first match wins.

Now, let's look at our event loop:

```
func (b *Bot) loop() {
    for {
        select {
        case <-b.ctx.Done():
            return
        case evt := <-b.client.Events:
            switch evt.Type {
            case socketmode.EventTypeConnectionError:
                log.Println("connection failed. Retrying later...")
```

```
                case socketmode.EventTypeEventsAPI:
                        data, ok := evt.Data.(slackevents.
EventsAPIEvent)
                        if !ok {
                                log.Println("bug: got type(%v) 
which should be a slackevents.EventsAPIEvent, was %T", evt.
Data)
                                continue
                        }
                        b.client.Ack(*evt.Request)
                        go b.appMentioned(data)
                }
            }
        }
}
```

Here, we pull events off the `socketmode` client. We switch on the type of event. For our purposes, we are only interested in two types of events:

- Error connecting to the WebSocket
- An `EventTypeEventsAPI` event

An `EventTypeEventsAPI` type is an interface that we turn into its concrete type, `slackevents.EventsAPIEvent`. We acknowledge receipt of the event and send the event to be handled by a method called `appMentioned()`.

There are other events you might be interested in. You can find a list of the official events supported by Slack here: https://api.slack.com/events.

The Go package event support may be slightly different and can be found here: https://pkg.go.dev/github.com/slack-go/slack/slackevents#pkg-constants.

Now, let's build `appMentioned()`:

```
func (b *Bot) appMentioned(ctx context.Context, data 
slackevents.EventsAPIEvent) {
    switch data.Type {
    case slackevents.CallbackEvent:
            callback := data.Data.(*slackevents.
EventsAPICallbackEvent)
```

```
            switch ev := data.InnerEvent.Data.(type) {
            case *slackevents.AppMentionEvent:
                msg, err := b.makeMsg(ev)
                if err != nil {
                    log.Println(err)
                    return
                }
                for _, reg := range b.reg {
                    if reg.r.MatchString(m.Text) {
                        reg.h(ctx, b.api, b.client, m)
                        return
                    }
                }
                if b.defaultHandler != nil {
                    b.defaultHandler(ctx, m)
                }
            }
    default:
        b.client.Debugf("unsupported Events API event received")
    }
```

Slack events are events wrapped inside events, so it takes a little decoding to get to the information you need. This code looks at the event data type and uses that information to know what type to decode.

For appMentioned(), this should always be slackevents.CallbackEvent, which decodes its .Data field into a *slackevents.EventsAPICallbackEvent type.

That has .InnerEvent, which can decode into a few other event types. We are only interested if it decodes to *slackevents.AppMentionEvent.

If it does, we call another internal method called makeMsg() that returns the message type we defined earlier. We are going to skip the makeMsg() implementation, as it has some deep JSON data conversions that, due to the nature of JSON, are a little convoluted and uninteresting. You can just lift it from the linked code.

We then loop through our regexes looking for a match. If we find one, we call `HandleFunc` on that message and stop processing. If we don't find a match, we call `defaultHandler`, if it exists.

Now, we have a bot that can listen for when it is mentioned in a message and dispatch the message to a handler. Let's tie that into making some calls to our Ops service.

Creating event handlers

The `HandleFunc` type we defined in the last sections handles the core of our functionality. This is also where we decide on how we want to turn a bunch of text into a command to run.

There are a few ways to interpret raw text:

- Regexes via the `regexp` package
- String manipulation via the `strings` package
- Designing or using a lexer and parser

Regexes and string manipulation are the fastest ways for an application of this type where we have single lines of text.

Lexers and parsers are great when you need to deal with complex inputs or multi-line text and cannot afford mistakes. This is the method that compilers use to read your textual code into instructions that eventually lead to a compiled binary. Rob Pike has a great talk on writing one in Go that you can view here: `https://www.youtube.com/watch?v=HxaD_trXwRE`. The downside is that they are tedious to build and hard to train new people on. If you need to watch that video a few times to get the concept, you are not alone.

Case Study – Regexes versus Lexer and Parser

One of the biggest jobs for network automation is getting information out of different devices made by different vendors. Some vendors provide information via the **Simple Network Management Protocol** (**SNMP**), but for many types of information or debugging, you have to go to the CLI to get information.

On newer platforms, this can come in the form of JSON or XML. Many platforms don't have structured output, and sometimes, the XML is so badly formed that it is easier to use unstructured data.

At Google, we started with writing tools that used regexes. Regexes were buried in every individual tool, which lead to multiple implementations of data wrangling for the same data. This was a huge waste of effort and introduced different bugs to different tools.

Router output can be complex, so eventually, a special regex engine was made to deal with these complex multi-line regexes and a central repository was created where command output regexes could be found.

Unfortunately, we were trying to use a tool that wasn't suited for the job. That package was so complex that it required its own debugger for development. More importantly, it would fail silently, inputting zero values in fields when a vendor would change the output slightly on new OS releases. This caused a few not-so-minor issues in production.

We eventually moved to a lexer and parser that would always detect when the output was not as expected. We didn't want it to be quite as complex as a full lexer and parser, so we wrote a package that allowed very limited regex usage and validation of many of the data fields.

There is a certain amount of love/hate for that package when you have to interpret new data with it. The great thing is it doesn't fail silently on changes, it is lightning fast, requires minimal effort to update, and uses minimal memory.

But it does take a while to get your brain around the concepts and it takes a lot longer to write the matches. There is a public version I recreated after I left Google called the Half-Pike that you can find here: `https://github.com/johnsiilver/halfpike`.

For our first handler, we want to return a list of traces to the user. The main command is `list traces` followed by optional arguments. For options, we want the following:

- `operation=<operation name>`
- `start=<mm/dd/yyyy-hh:mm>`
- `end=<mm/dd/yyyy-hh:mm, now>`

- `limit=<number of items>`
- `tags=<[tag1,tag2]>`

These options allow us to limit what traces we see. Maybe we only want to see traces for some certain period and only want the ones we tagged with `error`. This allows us to do filtered diagnostics.

A quick example of using this command would be as follows:

```
list traces operation=AddPets() limit=25
```

All of our handlers will be talking to the Ops service via gRPC. We will create a type that can hold all the `HandlFunc` types we define and the clients they will need to access our Ops service and Slack:

```go
type Ops struct {
    OpsClient *client.Ops
    API       *slack.Client
    SMClient  *socketmode.Client
}

func (o Ops) write(m bot.Message, s string, i ...interface{}) error {
    _, _, err := o.API.PostMessage(
        m.AppMention.Channel,
        slack.MsgOptionText(fmt.Sprintf(s, i...), false),
    )
    return err
}
```

This defines our basic type that will hold a single client to our Ops service. We will attach methods that implement the `HandleFunc` type. It also defines a `write()` method for writing text back to the user in Slack.

Now, we need to define a package level variable for the regex we need to tease apart our options. We define it at the package level so that we only need to compile it once:

```go
var listTracesRE = regexp.MustCompile(`(\S+)=(?:(\S+))`)

type opt struct {
    key string
    val string
}
```

You can see how our regex matches a key/value pair separated by =. The opt type is meant to hold our option key and value once we tease it apart with the regex.

Now for the handler that lists the traces we specify with our filters:

```go
func (o Ops) ListTraces(ctx context.Context, m bot.Message) {
    sp := strings.Split(m.Text, "list traces")

    if len(sp) != 2 {
        o.write(m, "The 'list traces' command is malformed")
        return
    }

    t := strings.TrimSpace(sp[1])

    kvOpts := []opt{}
    matches := listTracesRE.FindAllStringSubmatch(t, -1)
    for _, match := range matches {
        kvOpts = append(
            kvOpts,
            opt{
                strings.TrimSpace(match[1]),
                strings.TrimSpace(match[2]),
            },
        )
    }
}
```

`ListTraces` implements the `HandleFunc` type we created earlier. We split the list traces text from `Message.Text` that the user sent and remove any excess space at the beginning or end using `strings.TrimSpace()`. We then use our regex to create all our options.

Now, we need to process those options so we can send them to the Ops server:

```go
    options := []client.CallOption{}

    for _, opt := range kvOpts {
        switch opt.key {
        case "operation":
            options = append(
                options,
                client.WithOperation(opt.val),
            )
```

```go
            case "start":
                t, err := time.Parse(
                    `01/02/2006-15:04:05`, opt.val,
                )
                if err != nil {
                    o.write(m, "The start option must be in the form `01/02/2006-15:04:05` for UTC")
                    return
                }
                options = append(options, client.WithStart(t))
            case "end":
                if opt.val == "now" {
                    continue
                }
                t, err := time.Parse(
                    `01/02/2006-15:04:05`, opt.val,
                )
                if err != nil {
                    o.write(m, "The end option must be in the form `01/02/2006-15:04:05` for UTC")
                    return
                }
                options = append(options, client.WithEnd(t))

            case "limit":
                i, err := strconv.Atoi(opt.val)
                if err != nil {
                    o.write(m, "The limit option must be an integer")
                    return
                }
                if i > 100 {
                    o.write(m, "Cannot request more than 100 traces")
                    return
                }
                options = append(options, client.WithLimit(int32(i)))
            case "tags":
                tags, err := convertList(opt.val)
                if err != nil {
                    o.write(m, "tags: must enclosed in [], like tags=[tag,tag2]")
```

```
                        return
                }
                options = append(options, client.
WithLabels(tags))
        default:
                o.write(m, "don't understand an option 
type(%s)", opt.key)
                return
        }
    }
}
```

This code loops through the options we teased from the command and appends call options for sending to the Ops service. If there are any errors, we write to Slack to let them know there was a problem.

Finally, let's make our gRPC call to the Ops service:

```
        traces, err := o.OpsClient.ListTraces(ctx, options...)
        if err != nil {
                o.write(m, "Ops server had an error: %s", err)
                return
        }

        b := strings.Builder{}
        b.WriteString("Here are the traces you requested:\n")
        table := tablewriter.NewWriter(&b)
        table.SetHeader([]string{"Start Time(UTC)", "Trace ID"})

        for _, item := range traces {
                table.Append(
                        []string{
                                item.Start.Format("01/02/2006 04:05"),
                                "http://127.0.0.1:16686/trace/" + item.ID,
                        },
                )
        }
        table.Render()
        o.write(m, b.String())
}
```

This code uses our Ops service client to get a list of traces with the options that we passed. We use an ASCII table writing package (github.com/olekukonko/tablewriter) to write out our traces table.

But how do users know what commands they can send? This is handled by providing a help handler for the bot. We will create a map that will hold our various help messages and another variable that will hold a list of all commands in alphabetical order:

```go
var help = map[string]string{
    "list traces": `
list traces <opt1=val1 op2=val2>
Ex: list traces operation=AddPets() limit=5
...
`,
}

var cmdList string

func init() {
    cmds := []string{}
    for k := range help {
        cmds = append(cmds, k)
    }
    sort.Strings(cmds)

    b := strings.Builder{}
    for _, cmd := range cmds {
        b.WriteString(cmd + "\n")
    }
    b.WriteString("You can get more help by saying `help <cmd>` with a command from above.\n")
    cmdList = b.String()
}
```

Our help text is indexed in our `help` map. `init()` sets up a complete list of commands in `cmdList` during program initialization.

Now, let's use those commands in a handler that provides help text if a user passed `help` to our bot:

```go
func (o Ops) Help(ctx context.Context, m bot.Message) {
	sp := strings.Split(m.Text, "help")
	if len(sp) < 2 {
		o.write(m, "%s,\nYou have to give me a command you want help with", m.User.Name)
		return
	}
	cmd := strings.TrimSpace(strings.Join(sp[1:], ""))
	if cmd == "" {
		o.write(m, "Here are all the commands that I can help you with:\n%s", cmdList)
		return
	}

	if v, ok := help[cmd]; ok {
		o.write(m, "I can help you with that:\n%s", v)
		return
	}

	o.write(m, "%s,\nI don't know what %q is to give you help", m.User.Name, cmd)
}
```

This code receives as input the command they want help with and outputs the help text if it exists. If they don't pass a command, it simply prints the list of commands we support.

If we don't have a handler to handle a particular command (maybe they misspelled the command), we need a handler as the last resort:

```go
func (o Ops) lastResort(ctx context.Context, m bot.Message) {
	o.write(m, "%s,\nI don't have anything that handles what you sent. Try the 'help' command", m.User.Name)
}
```

This simply informs the user that we don't know what they want, as it is not something we support.

We have a minimum set of handlers, but we still need to have a way to register it with the bot:

```
func (o Ops) Register(b *bot.Bot) {
    b.Register(regexp.MustCompile(`^\s*help`), o.Help)
    b.Register(regexp.MustCompile(`^\s*list traces`), o.ListTraces)
    b.Register(nil, o.lastResort)
}
```

This takes in a bot and registers our three handlers with regexes that will are used to determine which handler to use.

Now, it's time for our `main()` function:

```
func main() {
    ... // Other setup like slack client init

    b, err := bot.New(api, client)
    if err != nil {
        panic(err)
    }
    h := handlers.Ops{
        OpsClient: opsClient,
        API: api,
        SMClient: smClient,
    }
    h.Register(b)
    b.Start()
}
```

This creates our Ops object and registers any `HandleFunc` types we created with our bot. You can find the full code for the ChatOps bot here: https://github.com/PacktPublishing/Go-for-DevOps/tree/rev0/chapter/11/chatbot/.

Now that we've seen the foundation of writing our bot, let's setup our Slack application and run our example code.

Creating our Slack application

For the bot to interact with Slack, we need to set up a Slack application:

1. Navigate to `https://api.slack.com/apps` on your browser.

    Here, you will need to click on the following button:

    Figure 11.2 – Create New App button

    You will then be presented with the following dialog box:

    Create an app   ×

    Choose how you'd like to configure your app's scopes and settings.

    From scratch
    Use our configuration UI to manually add basic info, scopes,   >
    settings, & features to your app.

    From an app manifest BETA
    Use a manifest file to add your app's basic info, scopes,   >
    settings & features to your app.

    Need help? Check our documentation, or see an example

    Figure 11.3 – Create an app options

2. Choose the **From an app manifest** option. This will present the following:

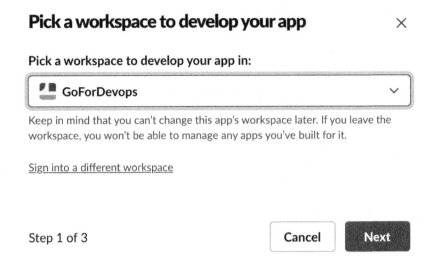

Figure 11.4 – Choosing a workspace

3. Choose the workspace you created at the beginning of this section and then press **Create App**. Click the **Next** button.

4. Copy the text from the file present at `https://github.com/PacktPublishing/Go-for-DevOps/tree/rev0/chapter/11/chatbot/slack.manifest` and paste it onto the screen that is shown as follows as YAML:

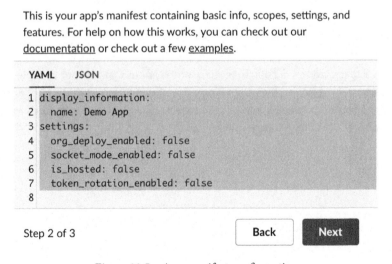

Figure 11.5 – App manifest configuration

5. The text you see in the preceding figure should be replaced with the text from the file. Click the **Next** button.

    You will be presented with a summary of the bots permissions, shown as follows:

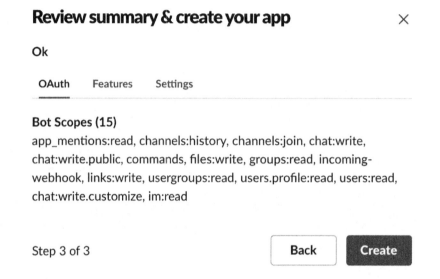

Figure 11.6 – Bot creation summary

6. Click the **Create** button.
7. This will move you to a page that is called **Basic Information**. Scroll down the page until you get to **App-Level Tokens**, as can be seen in the following figure:

Figure 11.7 – App-level token list

8. Click the **Generate Token and Scopes** button. This will lead you to the following dialog box:

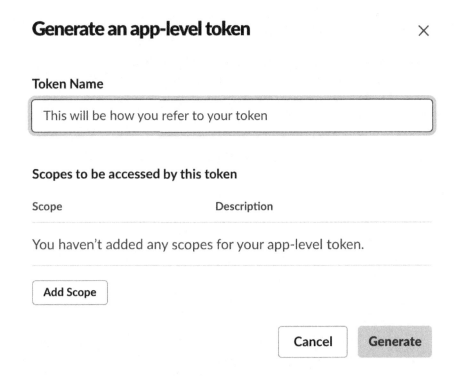

Figure 11.8 – App token creation

9. Set the token name to `petstore-bot`.
10. Provide these scopes in the **Scope** field – `connections:write` and `authorizations:read`. Now, click **Generate**.

11. On the next screen, you will receive an app-level token. You will need to hit the **Copy** button and put the token somewhere for the time being.

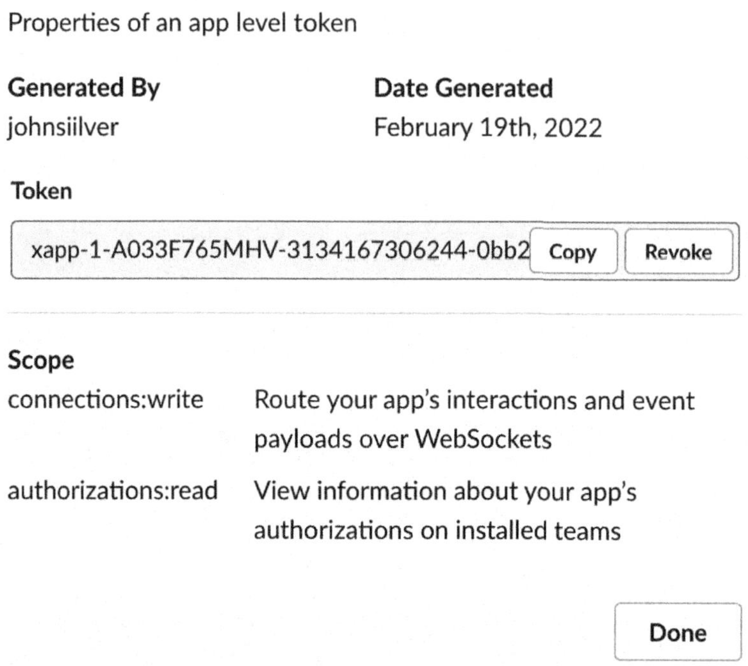

Properties of an app level token

Generated By
johnsiilver

Date Generated
February 19th, 2022

Token

| xapp-1-A033F765MHV-3134167306244-0bb2 | Copy | Revoke |

Scope

connections:write — Route your app's interactions and event payloads over WebSockets

authorizations:read — View information about your app's authorizations on installed teams

Done

Figure 11.9 – App token information

In a production environment, you want to put this in some type of secure key store, such as Azure Key Vault or AWS Key Management Service. You will need to put it in a file called the `.env` file that you should never check into a repository. We will cover making this file in the *Running the applications* section.

> **Note**
> The key here is for a bot that was deleted right after this screenshot.

12. Click the **Done** button.
13. In the left menu pane, choose **OAuth and Permissions**. On the screen that looks like the following, click **Install to Workspace**:

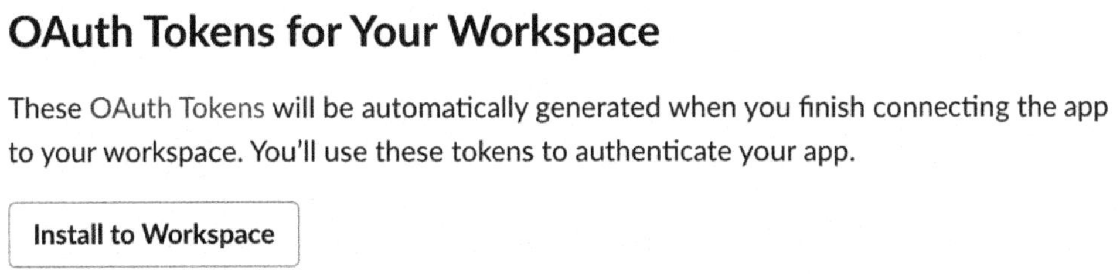

OAuth Tokens for Your Workspace

These OAuth Tokens will be automatically generated when you finish connecting the app to your workspace. You'll use these tokens to authenticate your app.

`Install to Workspace`

Figure 11.10 – Install tokens in your workspace

14. There is a dialog box that asks for a channel to post as an app. Choose any channel you like and hit **Allow**.

You are now back to **OAuth and Permissions**, but you will see your bot's **auth token** listed. Hit the **Copy** button and store this where you stored the app token from earlier.

Running the applications

Here, we are going to use Docker Compose to turn up our Open Telemetry services, Jaeger, Prometheus, and our Petstore application. Once those are running we will use Go to compile and run our ChatOps service that implements the chatbot connected to Slack:

1. In the `Go-for-DevOps` repository (https://github.com/PacktPublishing/Go-for-DevOps/), go to the `chapter/11` directory.
2. Turn up the Docker containers:

    ```
    docker-compose up -d
    ```

3. Once the environment is running, change to the `chapter/11/chatops` directory.
4. You will need to create a `.env` file in this directory that contains the following:

    ```
    AUTH_TOKEN=xoxb-[the rest of the token]
    APP_TOKEN=xapp-[the rest of the token]
    ```

    These were generated when we set up the Slack app.

5. Run the ChatOps server with the following command:

    ```
    go run chatbot.go
    ```

6. You should be able to see the following message printed to standard output:

    ```
    Bot started
    ```

In the background, there is a demonstration client that is adding pets to the pet store and doing searches for pets (some searches will cause errors). The service is set to Float sampling, so not every call will generate a trace.

In another terminal, you can interact with the pet store by using the CLI application. This will let you add your own pets, delete pets, and search for pets with a filter. That client can be found here: `chapter/11/petstore/client/cli/petstore`. You can find instructions on its use by running the following:

```
go run go run petstore.go --help
```

Traces can be observed at `http://127.0.0.1:16686/search`.

Prometheus metrics can be queried at `http://127.0.0.1:9090/graph`.

To interact with our ChatOps bot, you need to open Slack and add the bot to a channel. You can do this simply by doing a `@PetStore` mention in a channel. Slack will ask if you would like to add the bot to the channel.

Once that happens, you can try out various operations. Start by asking the bot for help, as follows:

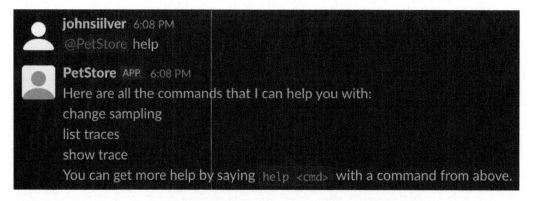

Figure 11.11 – Basic help command output

Let's ask for some help on how we can list some traces:

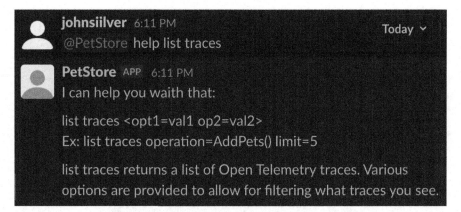

Figure 11.12 – Help output for the list traces command

How about we ask the system to give us five recent traces:

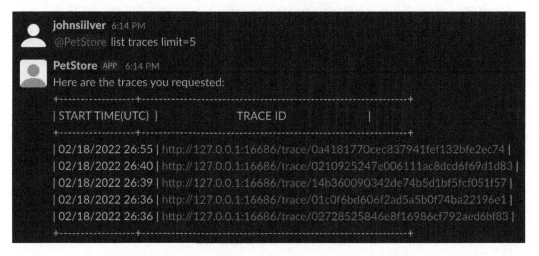

Figure 11.13 – Output from a command to list the last five traces

We can also ask about a particular trace:

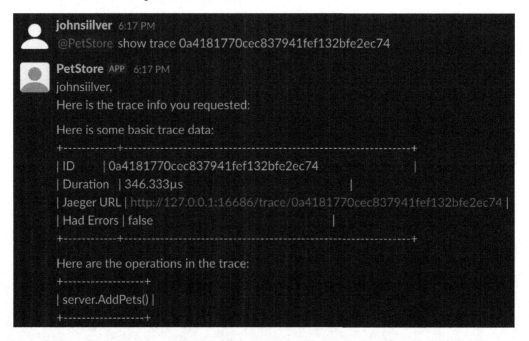

Figure 11.14 – Output showing a specific trace's data

> **Note**
> You cannot directly paste a trace ID copied from list traces. This is because those are hyperlinks; you need to remove the rich text from an ID if you want to directly paste it for `show trace`.

There are more options for you to play with in the bot. Give them a try.

This ChatOps application is just the tip of the iceberg. You can make the ChatOps application more powerful than the one we have here. You can have it display graphs, grab profile information from a `pprof` dump from the service and give you a link to view it, have it deploy new versions of your application, or roll a version back. Push files to the service by simply dragging them into the Slack window (such as a configuration change). Important events such as alerts can be broadcast to people who are on call by having the Ops service send messages to the ChatOps service, and the use of ChatOps increases observability of what your service is doing and what operations are being done against the service.

And as a side effect, unlike tools that must be run on a laptop or desktop, Slack and many other chat applications have mobile versions, so you can interact or do emergency operations with your cell phone with no extra cost in development.

Summary

In *Chapter 9, Observability with OpenTelemetry*, we explored how using Open Telemetry can provide observability into your application and the applications it depends on. We discussed how to set up telemetry for your application using the two most popular backends: Jaeger and Prometheus, which are both written in Go. In *Chapter 10, Automating Workflows with GitHub Actions*, we showed how you can use GitHub actions to automate your code deployments and how to add custom actions using Go. Finally, in this chapter, we looked at the architecture for interacting with a service. We built an interaction layer using Slack to do operations such as filtering traces, getting the currently deployed version, and showing alerts.

In the next set of chapters, we will talk about how to use Go, and tools written in Go, to ease the burden of working in the cloud. This will cover building standard images that can be deployed to VMs or other node infrastructure. We will show how you can extend Kubernetes, the most popular container orchestration system on the market today. Finally, we will guide you on how you can design DevOps workflows and systems to protect yourself from the chaos that is inherent in running operations against infrastructure.

Section 3: Cloud ready Go

This section is a discussion of the practice of release engineering, using common tools for creating service builds ready for deployment and leading tools for deploying distributed applications.

Unless you have been living under a rock, you might have noticed that the vast majority of new system deployments have moved out of corporate data centers and into cloud providers such as Amazon Web Services (AWS), Azure, and Google Cloud. The process of moving existing in-house applications is well underway, from the finance industry to telecommunication providers. DevOps engineers need to be well versed in building managed distributed platforms that enable their companies to operate in cloud, multi-cloud, and hybrid-cloud environments.

In this section, we will show you how to automate the process of creating system images using Packer on the AWS platform, use Go with Terraform to create your own custom Terraform provider, program the Kubernetes API to extend its capabilities for your needs, provision resources using Azure's cloud SDK, and design resilient DevOps software that can avoid the mistakes that large cloud providers have already made.

The following chapters will be covered in this section:

- Chapter 12, *Creating Immutable Infrastructure Using Packer*
- Chapter 13, *Infrastructure as Code with Terraform*
- Chapter 14, *Deploying and Building Applications in Kubernetes*
- Chapter 15, *Programming the Cloud*
- Chapter 16, *Designing for Chaos*

12
Creating Immutable Infrastructure Using Packer

Managing compute infrastructure, even in the era of the cloud, is still a challenge. With the innovations in containerization, **virtual machines** (**VMs**), and serverless computing, developers might believe that compute infrastructure is a solved problem.

Nothing could be farther from the truth. For cloud providers or others running their own data centers, bare metal machines (the machine's OS not running in virtualization) must be managed. This has become more complicated in the era of cloud computing. Not only does your provider need to manage their OS rollouts and patches, but so do cloud customers who want to run fleets of VMs and containers. Container orchestration systems such as Kubernetes must still provide container images that contain an OS image.

In the cloud, just like a physical data center, it is important to force OS compliance for all containers and VMs. Allowing anyone to run whatever OS they want is the gateway to a security breach. To provide a secure platform for developers, you must provide a minimal OS standardized across all deployments.

Standardization of an OS across a fleet comes with nothing but upsides and very few downsides. Standardizing on an OS image is easiest when your company is small. Large companies, including cloud providers that have not done this in the early days, have suffered through massive projects to standardize OS images at later stages.

In this section, we are going to talk about how we can use Packer, a software package written in Go by HashiCorp, to manage the creation and patching of VM and container images. HashiCorp is the leader in the trend of **Infrastructure as Code (IaC)** that is moving through the industry.

Packer lets us use YAML and Go to provide a consistent way to build images across a multitude of platforms. Be it in VM images, Docker images, or bare metal images, Packer can create consistent environments for your workloads to run on.

As we write Packer configuration files and use the Packer binary, you will begin to see how Packer was written. Many of the interactions Packer defines were written using libraries such as `os/exec` that we have talked about earlier. Maybe you will be writing the next Packer that will sweep through the DevOps community!

We will cover the following topics in this chapter:

- Building an Amazon Machine Image
- Validating images with Goss
- Customizing Packer with plugins

Technical requirements

The prerequisites for this chapter are as follows:

- An AWS account
- An AWS Linux VM running on the AMD64 platform
- An AWS user account with administrator access and access to its secret
- Installation of Packer on the AWS Linux VM
- Installation of Goss on the AWS Linux VM
- Access to the book's GitHub repository

To do the exercises in this chapter requires an AWS account. This will use compute time and storage on AWS, which will cost money, though you may be able to use an AWS Free Tier account (https://aws.amazon.com/free/). None of the authors at the time of writing are currently affiliated with Amazon. There is no financial incentive for us. If anything, it costs us money to develop this chapter on AWS.

When running Packer, we recommend running on Linux, both for cloud images and Docker images. Windows is a special niche for cloud computing and Microsoft provides its own sets of tools for handling Windows images. We don't recommend using a Mac for running these, as the move to Apple silicon and the interaction with multiple tools with varying support can lead to a long debug time. While macOS is POSIX-compliant, it still isn't Linux, the main target of these tools.

Getting an AWS account set up with a Linux VM and setting up user accounts is beyond what we can cover in the book. See the AWS documentation for help with that. For this exercise, please choose either an Amazon Linux or Ubuntu distribution.

User setup is done using AWS IAM tools, and the user name can be whatever you choose. You will also need to obtain an access key and secret for this user. Do not store these in a repository or any place that is publicly accessible, as they are equivalent to username/password. The user will need to do the following:

- Belong to a group with `AdministratorAccess` permissions set.
- Attach the existing policy, `AmazonSSMAutomationRole`.

We recommend a personal account for this exercise, as this access is quite extensive. You can also set up a specific set of permissions or use another method that isn't as permissible. Instructions on those methods can be found here: https://www.packer.io/docs/builders/amazon.

Once you have logged into your VM, you need to install Packer. This is going to depend on what Linux version you have.

The following is for Amazon Linux:

```
sudo yum install -y yum-utils
sudo yum-config-manager --add-repo https://rpm.releases.hashicorp.com/AmazonLinux/hashicorp.repo
sudo yum -y install packer
```

The following is for Ubuntu:

```
curl -fsSL https://apt.releases.hashicorp.com/gpg | sudo apt-key add -
sudo apt-add-repository "deb [arch=amd64] https://apt.releases.hashicorp.com $(lsb_release -cs) main"
sudo apt-get update && sudo apt-get install packer
```

For other Linux versions, see the following:

https://learn.hashicorp.com/tutorials/packer/get-started-install-cli.

To test Packer is installed, run the following:

```
packer version
```

This should output the version of Packer you have.

Once Packer is installed, issue the following commands:

```
mkdir packer
cd packer
touch amazon.pkr.hcl
mkdir files
cd files
ssh-keygen -t rsa -N "" -C "agent.pem" -f agent
mv agent ~/.ssh/agent.pem
wget https://raw.githubusercontent.com/PacktPublishing/Go-for-DevOps/rev0/chapter/8/agent/bin/linux_amd64/agent
wget https://raw.githubusercontent.com/PacktPublishing/Go-for-DevOps/rev0/chapter/12/agent.service
cd ..
```

These commands do the following:

- Set up a directory called `packer` in your user's home directory
- Create an `amazon.pkr.hcl` file to store our Packer configuration
- Create a `packer/files` directory
- Generate an SSH key pair for a user, `agent`, which we will add to the image

- Move the `agent.pem` private key into our `.ssh` directory
- Copy our system agent from the Git repository
- Copy a `systemd` service configuration for the system agent from the Git repository

Now that we have the prerequisites out of the way, let's have a look at building custom **Ubuntu** images for AWS.

The code files for this chapter can be downloaded from `https://github.com/PacktPublishing/Go-for-DevOps/tree/rev0/chapter/12`

Building an Amazon Machine Image

Packer supports a wide variety of plugins that are used by the program to target a specific image format. For our example, we are going to target the **Amazon Machine Image** (**AMI**) format.

There are other build targets for Docker, Azure, Google Cloud, and others. You may find a list of other build targets here: `https://www.packer.io/docs/builders/`.

For images that are used in cloud environments, Packer plugins generally take an existing image that lives on the cloud provider and lets you repackage and upload the image to the service.

And, if you need to build multiple images for multiple cloud providers, containers, Packer can do simultaneous builds.

For Amazon, there are currently four methods for building an AMI:

- Amazon **Elastic Block Store** (**EBS**) launches a source AMI, provisions it, and then repackages it.
- Amazon instance virtual server, which launches an instance VM, rebundles it, and then uploads it to S3 (an Amazon object storage service).

The two other methods are for advanced use cases. As this is an introduction to Packer using AWS, we are going to avoid these. However, you can read about all these methods here: `https://www.packer.io/docs/builders/amazon`.

There are two configuration file formats used by Packer:

- **JavaScript Object Notation (JSON)**
- **HashiCorp Configuration Language 2 (HCL 2)**

As JSON is deprecated, we will be using HCL2. This format was created by HashiCorp and you can find their Go parser here: `https://github.com/hashicorp/hcl2`. The parser can be useful if you wish to write your own tools around Packer or want to support your own configurations in HCL2.

Now, let's create a Packer configuration file that we can use to access the Amazon plugin.

Open the file called `amazon.pkr.hcl` in the `packer/` directory we created.

Add the following:

```
packer {
  required_plugins {
    amazon = {
      version = ">= 0.0.1"
      source = "github.com/hashicorp/amazon"
    }
  }
}
```

This tells Packer the following:

- We require the `amazon` plugin.
- The version of the plugin we want, which is the latest plugin that must be newer than version `0.0.1`.
- The `source` location in which to retrieve the plugin.

As we are using a cloud provider, we need to set up the AWS source information.

Setting up an AWS source

We are going to use the **Amazon EBS** build method, as this is the easiest method to deploy on AWS. Add the following to the file:

```
source "amazon-ebs" "ubuntu" {
  access_key = "your key"
  secret_key = "your secret"
  ami_name      = "ubuntu-amd64"
  instance_type = "t2.micro"
  region        = "us-east-2"
  source_ami_filter {
    filters = {
```

```
    name                      = "ubuntu/images/*ubuntu-xenial-
16.04-amd64-server-*"
    root-device-type          = "ebs"
    virtualization-type       = "hvm"
  }
  most_recent = true
  owners      = ["099720109477"]
 }
 ssh_username = "ubuntu"
}
```

There is some key information here, so we are going to take it one step at a time:

```
source "amazon-ebs" "ubuntu" {
```

This sets up the source for our base image. As we are using the amazon plugin, the source will have fields related to that plugin. You can find a complete list of fields here: https://www.packer.io/docs/builders/amazon/ebs.

This line names our source as having two parts, amazon-ebs and ubuntu. When we refer to this source in our build stanza, it will be referred to as source.amazon-ebs.ubuntu.

Now, we have a few field values:

- access_key is the IAM user key to use.
- secret_key is the IAM user's secret to use.
- ami_name is the name of the resulting AMI in the AWS console.
- instance_type is the AWS instance type to use to build the AMI.
- region is the AWS region for the build instance to spawn in.
- source_ami_filter filters the AMI image to find the image to apply.
- filters contain a way to filter our base AMI image.
- name gives the name of the AMI image. This can be any matching name returned by this API: https://docs.aws.amazon.com/AWSEC2/latest/APIReference/API_DescribeImages.html.
- root-device-type specifies we are using ebs as our source.

- `virtualization-type` indicates which of two AMI virtualization technologies to use, hvm or pv. Due to enhancements to hvm, is it now the choice to use.
- `most_recent` indicates to use the most recent image found.
- `owners` must list an ID of an owner of the base image AMI we are using. `"099720109477"` is a reference to Canonical, the maker of Ubuntu.
- `ssh_username` is the user name to SSH into the image with. `ubuntu` is the default user.

As alternates to the authentication method here, you can use IAM roles, shared credentials, or other methods. However, each of the others is too complicated for this book to cover. See the link in the *Technical requirements* section if you wish to use another method.

`secret_key` needs to be secured like any password. In production, you will want to use IAM roles to avoid using `secret_key` or fetch this from a secure password service (AWS Secrets Manager, Azure Key Vault, or GCP Secret Manager) and use the environmental variable method to allow Packer to use the key.

Next, we need to define a `build` block to allow us to change the image from the base to one customized for us.

Defining a build block and adding some provisioners

Packer defines a `build` block that references the source we defined in the previous section and makes the changes we want to that image.

To do this, Packer uses `provisioner` configurations inside `build`. Provisioners let you make changes to an image by using the shell, Ansible, Chef, Puppet, files, or other methods.

A full list of provisioners can be found here:

https://www.packer.io/docs/provisioners.

For long-term maintenance of your running infrastructure, Chef or Puppet have been the choice for many installations. This allows you to update the fleet without having to wait for an instance to be rebooted with the latest image.

By integrating it with Packer, you can make sure to apply the latest patches to your image during the build process.

While this is certainly helpful, we cannot explore these during this chapter. Setting up Chef or Puppet is simply beyond what we can do here. But for long-term maintenance, it is worth exploring these provisioners.

For our example, we are going to do the following:

- Install the Go 1.17.5 environment.
- Add a user, `agent`, to the system.
- Copy SSH keys to the system for that user.
- Add our system agent from a previous chapter.
- Set systemd to run the agent from the `agent` user.

Let's start by using the `shell` provisioner to install Go's 1.17.5 version using `wget`.

Let's add the following:

```
build {
  name    = "goBook"
  sources = [
    "source.amazon-ebs.ubuntu"
  ]
  provisioner "shell" {
    inline = [
      "cd ~",
      "mkdir tmp",
      "cd tmp",
      "wget https://golang.org/dl/go1.17.5.linux-amd64.tar.gz",
      "sudo tar -C /usr/local -xzf go1.17.5.linux-amd64.tar.gz",
      "echo 'export PATH=$PATH:/usr/local/go/bin' >> ~/.profile",
      ". ~/.profile",
      "go version",
      "cd ~/",
      "rm -rf tmp/*",
      "rmdir tmp",
    ]
  }
}
```

Our `build` block contains the following:

- `name`, which names this block.
- `sources`, which is a list of source blocks to include. This includes the source we just defined.
- `provisioner "shell"` says we are going to use the `shell` provisioner, which logs in via the shell to do work. You may have multiple provisioner blocks of this type or of other types.
- `inline` sets up commands to be run, one after another, in a shell script. This set of shell commands downloads Go version 1.17.5, installs it, tests it, and removes the install files.

It should be noted that you could also use `file provisioner`, which we will show later, to take a local copy of the file instead of retrieving it with `wget`. But, we wanted to show how you can also just use standard Linux tools to pull from a trusted repository.

Next, we will add another provision *inside* the `build` that adds a user to the system:

```
// Setup user "agent" with SSH key file
provisioner "shell" {
  inline = [
    "sudo adduser --disabled-password --gecos '' agent",
  ]
}
provisioner "file" {
  source = "./files/agent.pub"
  destination = "/tmp/agent.pub"
}
provisioner "shell" {
  inline = [
    "sudo mkdir /home/agent/.ssh",
    "sudo mv /tmp/agent.pub /home/agent/.ssh/authorized_keys",
    "sudo chown agent:agent /home/agent/.ssh",
    "sudo chown agent:agent /home/agent/.ssh/authorized_keys",
    "sudo chmod 400 .ssh/authorized_keys",
  ]
}
```

The preceding code block is structured as follows:

- The first `shell` block: Adds a user, `agent`, with a disabled password.
- The second `file` block: Copies a local file, `./files/agent.pub`, to `/tmp`, as we can't copy directly to a user other than `ubuntu` using `file provisioner`.
- The third shell block:
  - Makes our new user's `.ssh` directory.
  - Moves the `agent.pub` file out of `/tmp` to `.ssh/authorized_keys`.
  - Modifies all directories and files to have the right owners and permissions.

Now, let's add provisioners that install our system agent and sets up `systemd` to manage it. The following section uses the shell provisioner to install `dbus`, which is used to communicate with `systemd`. We set an environmental variable that prevents some pesky Debian interactive questions when we install using `apt-get`:

```
// Setup agent binary running with systemd file.
provisioner "shell" { // This installs dbus-launch
    environment_vars = [
      "DEBIAN_FRONTEND=noninteractive",
    ]
    inline = [
      "sudo apt-get install -y dbus",
      "sudo apt-get install -y dbus-x11",
    ]
}
```

This uses the file provisioner to copy the agent we want to run from our source files onto the image at the `/tmp/agent` location:

```
provisioner "file" {
  source = "./files/agent"
  destination = "/tmp/agent"
}
```

The following section creates a directory in the user agent's home directory called `bin` and moves the agent we copied over in the previous section into it. The rest is some necessary permissions and ownership changes:

```
provisioner "shell" {
  inline = [
    "sudo mkdir /home/agent/bin",
    "sudo chown agent:agent /home/agent/bin",
    "sudo chmod ug+rwx /home/agent/bin",
    "sudo mv /tmp/agent /home/agent/bin/agent",
    "sudo chown agent:agent /home/agent/bin/agent",
    "sudo chmod 0770 /home/agent/bin/agent",
  ]
}
```

This copies over the `systemd` file from our source directory to our image:

```
provisioner "file" {
  source = "./files/agent.service"
  destination = "/tmp/agent.service"
}
```

This last section moves the `agent.service` file to its final location, tells `systemd` to enable the service described in `agent.service`, and validates that it is active. The `sleep` parameter is used to simply allow the daemon to start before it is checked:

```
provisioner "shell" {
  inline = [
    "sudo mv /tmp/agent.service /etc/systemd/system/agent.service",
    "sudo systemctl enable agent.service",
    "sudo systemctl daemon-reload",
    "sudo systemctl start agent.service",
    "sleep 10",
    "sudo systemctl is-enabled agent.service",
    "sudo systemctl is-active agent.service",
  ]
}
```

Finally, let's add the Goss tool, which we will be using in the next section:

```
provisioner "shell" {
    inline = [
        "cd ~",
        "sudo curl -L https://github.com/aelsabbahy/goss/releases/latest/download/goss-linux-amd64 -o /usr/local/bin/goss",
        "sudo chmod +rx /usr/local/bin/goss",
        "goss -v",
    ]
}
```

This downloads the latest Goss tool, sets it to be executable, and tests that it works.

Now, let's look at how we could execute a Packer build to create an image.

Executing a Packer build

There are four stages to doing a Packer build:

- Initializing Packer to download the plugins
- Validating the build
- Formatting the Packer configuration file
- Building the image

The first thing to do is initialize our plugins. To do this, simply type the following:

```
packer init .
```

> **Note**
>
> If you see a message such as `Error: Unsupported block type`, it is likely you put the `provisioner` blocks outside the `build` block.

Once the plugins are installed, we need to validate our build:

```
packer validate .
```

This should yield `The configuration is valid`. If it doesn't, you will need to edit the file to fix the errors.

At this time, let's format the Packer template files. This is a concept I'm sure HashiCorp borrowed from Go's `go fmt` command and works in the same way. Let's give it a try with the following:

```
packer fmt .
```

Finally, it's time to do our build:

```
packer build .
```

There will be quite a bit of output here. But if everything is successful, you will see something like the following:

```
Build 'goBook.amazon-ebs.ubuntu' finished after 5 minutes 11
seconds.

==> Wait completed after 5 minutes 11 seconds

==> Builds finished. The artifacts of successful builds are:
--> goBook.amazon-ebs.ubuntu: AMIs were created:
us-east-2: ami-0f481c1107e74d987
```

> **Note**
> If you see errors about permissions, this will be related to your user account setup. See the necessary permissions listed in the earlier part of the chapter.

You now have an AMI image available on AWS. You can launch AWS VMs that use this image and they will be running our system agent. Feel free to launch a VM set to your new AMI and play with the agent. You can access the agent from your Linux device using `ssh agent@[host]`, where `[host]` is the IP or DNS entry of the host on AWS.

Now that we can use Packer to package our images, let's look at Goss for validating our image.

Validating images with Goss

Goss is a tool for checking server configurations using a spec file written in YAML. This way you can test that the server is working as expected. This can be from testing access to the server over SSH using expected keys to validating that various processes are running.

Not only can Goss test your server for compliance, but it can be integrated with Packer. That way, we can test that our server is running as expected during the provisioning step and before deployment.

Let's have a look at making a Goss spec file.

Creating a spec file

A spec file is a set of instructions that tells Goss what to test for.

There are a couple of ways to make a spec file for Goss. The spec file is used by Goss to understand what it needs to test.

While you could write it by hand, the most efficient way is to use one of two Goss commands:

- `goss add`
- `goss autoadd`

The most efficient way to use Goss is to launch a machine with your custom AMI, log in using the `ubuntu` user, and use `autoadd` to generate the YAML file.

Once logged onto your AMI instance, let's run the following:

```
goss -g process.yaml autoadd sshd
```

This will generate a `process.yaml` file with the following content:

```
service:
  sshd:
    enabled: true
    running: true
user:
  sshd:
    exists: true
    uid: 110
    gid: 65534
    groups:
```

```
        - nogroup
      home: /var/run/sshd
      shell: /usr/sbin/nologin
process:
  sshd:
    running: true
```

This states that we expect the following:

- A system service called `sshd` should be enabled and running via systemd.
- The service should be running with user `sshd`:
  - With user ID `110`.
  - With group ID `65534`.
  - Belonging to no other groups.
  - The user's home directory should be `/var/run/sshd`.
  - The user should have no login shell.
- A process called `sshd` should be running.

Let's add the agent service we deployed:

```
goss -g process.yaml autoadd agent
```

This will add similar lines inside the YAML file.

Now, let's validate the agent location:

```
goss -g files.yaml autoadd /home/agent/bin/agent
```

This will add a section such as the following:

```
file:
  /home/agent/bin/agent:
    exists: true
    mode: "0700"
    size: 14429561
    owner: agent
    group: agent
    filetype: file
    contains: []
```

This states the following:

- The /home/agent/bin/agent file must exist.
- Must be in mode 0700.
- Must have a size of 14429561 bytes.
- Must be owned by agent:agent.
- Is a file, versus a directory or symlink.

Let's add another, but being more specific, using goss add:

```
goss -g files.yaml add file /home/agent/.ssh/authorized_keys
```

Instead of making a guess at what an argument is as autoadd does, we had to specify it was a file. This renders us the same entry as autoadd would. For this file, let's validate the contents of the authorized_keys file. To do this, we will use a SHA256 hash. First, we can get the hash by running the following:

```
sha256sum /home/agent/.ssh/authorized_keys
```

This will return the hash of the file. In the file entry for authorized_keys in our YAML file, add the following:

```
sha256: theFileHashJustGenerated
```

Unfortunately, Goss does not have a way to simply add entire directories of files or automatically add SHA256 to the entry. An example of that might be to validate that all of Go's 1.17.5 files were present as expected on our image.

You might be tempted to do something like the following:

```
find /usr/local/go -print0 | xargs -0 -I{} goss -g golang.yaml
add file {}
```

However, this is quite slow because goss reads in the YAML file on each run. You might be tempted to try to use xargs -P 0 to speed things up, but it will cause other problems.

If you have a need to include lots of files and SHA256 hashes, you will need to write a custom script/program to handle this. Fortunately, we have Go, so it's easy to write something that can do this. And, because Goss is written in Go, we can reuse the data structures from the program. You can see an example of a tool to do this here: https://github.com/PacktPublishing/Go-for-DevOps/tree/rev0/chapter/12/goss/allfiles.

You simply can run it against a directory structure (after compiling it) like so:

```
allfiles /usr/local/go > goinstall_files.yaml
```

This would output a `goinstall_files.yaml` file that provides a Goss configuration to check these files and their SHA256 hashes.

Remember when we installed `dbus`? Let's validate that our `dbus` packages are installed:

```
goss -g dbus.yaml add package dbus
goss -g dbus.yaml add package dbus-x11
```

This now makes sure that our `dbus` and `dbus-x11` packages are installed. The `-g dbus.yaml` file writes this to another file called `dbus.yaml` instead of the default `goss.yaml`.

We now need to create our `goss.yaml` file that references the other files we created. We could have run `goss` without the `-g` option, but this keeps things a little more organized. Let's create our root file:

```
goss add goss process.yaml
goss add goss files.yaml
goss add goss dbus.yaml
```

This creates a `goss.yaml` file that references all our other files.

Let's use it to validate everything:

```
goss validate
```

This will output text similar to the following:

```
..........................

Total Duration: 0.031s
Count: 26, Failed: 0, Skipped: 0
```

Note, yes, it did run in less than a second!

Adding a Packer provisioner

It's great that we can verify what we already had, but what we really want is to validate every image build. To do this, we can use a custom Packer provisioner that Yale University developed.

To do that, we need to get the YAML files off the image and onto our build machine.

From the build machine, issue the following commands (replacing things in `[]`):

```
cd /home/[user]/packer/files
mkdir goss
cd goss
scp ubuntu@[ip of AMI machine]:/home/ubuntu/*.yaml ./
```

You need to replace `[user]` with the username on the build machine and `[ip of AMI machine]` with the IP address or DNS entry for the AMI machine you launched. You may also need to supply a `-i [location of pem file]` after `scp`.

As the Goss provisioner is not built in, we need to download the release from Yale's GitHub repository and install it:

```
mkdir ~/tmp
cd ~/tmp
wget https://github.com/YaleUniversity/packer-provisioner-goss/releases/download/v3.1.2/packer-provisioner-goss-v3.1.2-linux-amd64.tar.gz
sudo tar -xzf packer-provisioner-goss-v3.1.2-linux-amd64.tar.gz
cp sudo packer-provisioner-goss /usr/bin/packer-provisioner-goss
rm -rf ~/tmp
```

With the provisioner installed, we can add the configuration to the `amazon.pkr.hcl` file:

```
// Setup Goss for validating an image.
provisioner "file" {
  source = "./files/goss/*"
  destination = "/home/ubuntu/"
}

provisioner "goss" {
    retry_timeout = "30s"
    tests = [
      "files/goss/goss.yaml",
      "files/goss/files.yaml",
      "files/goss/dbus.yaml",
      "files/goss/process.yaml",
    ]
}
```

You can find other `provisioner` settings for Goss at https://github.com/YaleUniversity/packer-provisioner-goss.

Let's reformat our Packer file:

```
packer fmt .
```

We cannot build the `packer` image yet, because it would have the same name as the image we already have uploaded to AWS. We have two choices: remove the AMI image we built earlier from AWS or change the name held in our Packer file to the following:

```
ami_name        = "ubuntu-amd64"
```

Either choice is fine.

Now, let's build our AMI image:

```
packer build .
```

When you run it this time, you should see something similar to the following in the output:

```
==> goBook.amazon-ebs.ubuntu: Running goss tests...
==> goBook.amazon-ebs.ubuntu: Running GOSS render command: cd /
tmp/goss &&   /tmp/goss-0.3.9-linux-amd64    render > /tmp/goss-
spec.yaml
==> goBook.amazon-ebs.ubuntu: Goss render ran successfully
==> goBook.amazon-ebs.ubuntu: Running GOSS render debug
command: cd /tmp/goss &&   /tmp/goss-0.3.9-linux-amd64    render
-d > /tmp/debug-goss-spec.yaml
==> goBook.amazon-ebs.ubuntu: Goss render debug ran
successfully
==> goBook.amazon-ebs.ubuntu: Running GOSS validate command: cd
/tmp/goss &&   /tmp/goss-0.3.9-linux-amd64    validate --retry-
timeout 30s --sleep 1s
    goBook.amazon-ebs.ubuntu: ........................
    goBook.amazon-ebs.ubuntu:
    goBook.amazon-ebs.ubuntu: Total Duration: 0.029s
    goBook.amazon-ebs.ubuntu: Count: 26, Failed: 0, Skipped: 0
==> goBook.amazon-ebs.ubuntu: Goss validate ran successfully
```

This indicates that the Goss tests ran successfully. If Goss fails, a debug output will be downloaded to the local directory.

You can find the final version of the Packer file here:

https://github.com/PacktPublishing/Go-for-DevOps/blob/rev0/chapter/12/packer/amazon.final.pkr.hcl

You have now seen how to use the Goss tool to build validations for your images and integrate them into Packer. There are more features to explore and you can read about them here: https://github.com/aelsabbahy/goss.

Now that we have used Goss as a provisioner, what about writing our own?

Customizing Packer with plugins

The built-in provisioners that we used are pretty powerful. By providing shell access and file uploads, it is possible to do almost everything inside a Packer provisioner.

For large builds, this can be quite tedious. And, if the case is something common, you might want to simply have your own Go application do the work for you.

Packer allows for building plugins that can be used as the following:

- A Packer builder
- A Packer provisioner
- A Packer post-processor

Builders are used when you need to interact with the system that will use your image: Docker, AWS, GCP, Azure, or others. As this isn't a common use outside cloud providers or companies such as VMware adding support, we will not cover this.

Post-processors are normally used to push an image to upload the artifacts generated earlier. As this isn't common, we will not cover this.

Provisioners are the most common, as they are part of the build process to output an image.

Packer has two ways of writing these plugins:

- Single-plugins
- Multi-plugins

Single plugins are an older style of writing plugins. The Goss provisioner is written in the older style, which is why we installed it manually.

With the newer style, `packer init` can be used to download the plugin. In addition, a plugin can register multiple builders, provisioners, or post-processors in a single plugin. This is the recommended way of writing a plugin.

Unfortunately, the official documentation for multi-plugins and doing releases that support `packer init` is incomplete at the time of this writing. Following the directions will not yield a plugin that can be released using their suggested process.

The instructions included here will fill in the gaps to allow building a multi-plugin that users can install using `packer init`.

Let's get into how we can write a custom plugin.

Writing your own plugin

Provisioners are powerful extensions to the Packer application. They allow us to customize the application to do whatever we need.

We have already seen how a provisioner can execute Goss to validate our builds. This allowed us to make sure future builds follow a specification for the image.

To write a custom `provisioner`, we must implement the following interface:

```
type Provisioner interface {
    ConfigSpec() hcldec.ObjectSpec
    Prepare(...interface{}) error
    Provision(context.Context, Ui, Communicator,
        map[string] interface{}) error
}
```

The preceding code is described as follows:

- `ConfigSpec()` returns an object that represents your provisioner's HCL2 spec. This will be used by Packer to translate a user's config to a structured object in Go.

- `Prepare()` prepares your plugin to run and receives a slice of `interface{}` that represents the configuration. Generally, the configuration is passed as a single `map[string]interface{}`. `Prepare()` should do preparation operations such as pulling information from sources or validating the configuration, things that should cause a failure before even attempting to run. This should have no side effects, that is, it should not change any state by creating files, instantiating VMs, or any other changes to the system.

- `Provision()` does the bulk of the work. It receives a `Ui` object that is used to communicate to the user and `Communicator` that is used to communicate with the running machine. There is a provided `map` that holds values set by the builder. However, relying on values there can tie you to a `builder` type.

For our example provisioner, we are going to pack the Go environment and install it on the machine. While Linux distributions will often package the Go environment, they are often several releases behind. Earlier, we were able to do this by using `file` and `shell` (which can honestly do almost anything), but if you are an application provider and you want to make something repeatable for other Packer users across multiple platforms, a custom provisioner is the way to go.

Adding our provisioner configuration

To allow the user to configure our plugin, we need to define a configuration. Here is the config option we want to support: `Version (string) [optional]`, the specific version to download defaults to `latest`.

We will define this in a subpackage: `internal/config/config.go`.

In that file, we will add the following:

```go
package config

//go:generate packer-sdc mapstructure-to-hcl2 -type Provisioner

// Provisioner is our provisioner configuration.
type Provisioner struct {
    Version string
}

// Default inputs default values.
func (p *Provisioner) Defaults() {
    if p.Version == "" {
        p.Version = "latest"
    }
}
```

Unfortunately, we now need to be able to read this from an `hcldec.ObjectSpec` file. This is complicated, so HashiCorp has created a code generator to do this for us. To use this, you must install their `packer-sdc` tool:

```
go install github.com/hashicorp/packer-plugin-sdk/cmd/packer-sdc@latest
```

To generate the file, we can execute the following from inside `internal/config`:

```
go generate ./
```

This will output a `config.hcl2spec.go` file that has the code we require. This uses the `//go:generate` line defined in the file.

Defining the plugin's configuration specification

At the root of our plugin location, let's create a file called `goenv.go`.

So, let's start by defining the configuration the user will input:

```
package main

import (
    ...
    "[repo location]/packer/goenv/internal/config"
    "github.com/hashicorp/packer-plugin-sdk/packer"
    "github.com/hashicorp/packer-plugin-sdk/plugin"
    "github.com/hashicorp/packer-plugin-sdk/version"
    packerConfig "github.com/hashicorp/packer-plugin-sdk/template/config"
    ...
)
```

This imports the following:

- The `config` package we just defined
- Three packages required to build our plugin:
  - `packer`
  - `plugin`
  - `version`
- A `packerConfig` package for dealing with HCL2 configs

> **Note**
> The `...` is a stand-in for standard library packages and a few others for brevity. You can see them all in the repository version.

Now, we need to define our provisioner:

```go
// Provisioner implements packer.Provisioner.
type Provisioner struct{
    packer.Provisioner // Embed the interface.
    conf *config.Provisioner
    content []byte
    fileName string
}
```

This is going to hold our configuration, some file content, and the Go tarball filename. We will implement our `Provisioner` interface on this struct.

Now, it's time to add the required methods.

Defining the ConfigSpec() function

`ConfigSpec()` is defined for internal use by Packer. We simply need to provide the spec so that Packer can read in the configuration.

Let's use `config.hcl2spec.go` we generated a second ago to implement `ConfigSpec()`:

```go
func (p *Provisioner) ConfigSpec() hcldec.ObjectSpec {
    return new(config.FlatProvisioner).HCL2Spec()
}
```

This returns `ObjectSpec` that handles reading in our HCL2 config.

Now that we have that out of the way, we need to prepare our plugin to be used.

Defining Prepare()

Remember that `Prepare()` simply needs to interpret the intermediate representation of the HCL2 config and validate the entries. It should not change the state of anything.

Here's what that would look like:

```go
func (p *Provisioner) Prepare(raws ...interface{}) error {
    c := config.Provisioner{}
    if err := packerConfig.Decode(&c, nil, raws...); err != nil {
        return err
    }
    c.Defaults()
    p.conf = &c
```

```
        return nil
}
```

This code does the following:

- Creates our empty config
- Decodes the raw config entries into our internal representation
- Puts defaults into our config if values weren't set
- Validates our config

We could also use this time to connect to services or any other preparation items that are needed. The main thing is not to change any state.

With all the preparation out of the way, it's time for the big finale.

Defining Provision()

`Provision()` is where all the magic happens. Let's divide this into some logical sections:

- Fetch our version
- Push a tarball to the image
- Unpack the tarball
- Test our Go tools installation

The following code wraps other methods that execute the logical sections in the same order:

```
func (p *Provisioner) Provision(ctx context.Context, u packer.
Ui, c packer.Communicator, m map[string]interface{}) error {
    u.Message("Begin Go environment install")
    if err := p.fetch(ctx, u, c); err != nil {
            u.Error(fmt.Sprintf("Error: %s", err))
            return err
    }
    if err := p.push(ctx, u, c); err != nil {
            u.Error(fmt.Sprintf("Error: %s", err))
            return err
    }
    if err := p.unpack(ctx, u, c); err != nil {
            u.Error(fmt.Sprintf("Error: %s", err))
            return err
```

```
        }
        if err := p.test(ctx, u, c); err != nil {
                u.Error(fmt.Sprintf("Error: %s", err))
                return err
        }
        u.Message("Go environment install finished")
        return nil
}
```

This code calls all our stages (which we will define momentarily) and outputs some messages to the UI. The `Ui` interface is defined as follows:

```
type Ui interface {
    Ask(string) (string, error)
    Say(string)
    Message(string)
    Error(string)
    Machine(string, ...string)
    getter.ProgressTracker
}
```

Unfortunately, the UI is not well documented in the code or in the documentation. Here is a breakdown:

- You can use `Ask()` to ask a question of the user and get a response. As a general rule, you should avoid this, as it removes automation. Better to make them put it in the configuration.
- `Say()` and `Message()` both print a string to the screen.
- `Error()` outputs an error message.
- `Machine()` simply outputs a statement into the log generated on the machine using `fmt.Printf()` that is prepended by `machine readable:`.
- `getter.ProgressTracker()` is used by `Communicator` to track download progress. You don't need to worry about it.

Now that we have covered the UI, let's cover `Communicator`:

```
type Communicator interface {
  Start(context.Context, *RemoteCmd) error
  Upload(string, io.Reader, *os.FileInfo) error
  UploadDir(dst string, src string, exclude []string) error
  Download(string, io.Writer) error
```

```
    DownloadDir(src string, dst string, exclude []string) error
}
```

Methods in the preceding code block are described as follows:

- `Start()` runs a command on the image. You pass `*RemoteCmd`, which is similar to the `Cmd` type we used from `os/exec` in previous chapters.
- `Upload()` uploads a file to the machine image.
- `UploadDir()` uploads a local directory recursively to the machine image.
- `Download()` downloads a file from the machine image. This allows you to capture debugs logs, for example.
- `DownloadDir()` downloads a directory recursively from the machine to a local destination. You can exclude files.

You can see the full interface comments here: https://pkg.go.dev/github.com/hashicorp/packer-plugin-sdk/packer?utm_source=godoc#Communicator.

Let's look at building our first helper, `p.fetch()`. The following code determines what URL to use to download the Go tools. Our tool is targeted at Linux, but we support installing versions for multiple platforms. We use Go's runtime package to determine the architecture (386, ARM, or AMD 64) we are currently running on to determine which package to download. The users can specify a particular version or `latest`. In the case of `latest`, we query a URL provided by Google that returns the latest version of Go. We then use that to construct the URL for download:

```
func (p *Provisioner) fetch(ctx context.Context, u Ui,
c Communicator) error {
    const (
        goURL = `https://golang.org/dl/go%s.linux-%s.tar.gz`
        name  = `go%s.linux-%s.tar.gz`
    )
    platform := runtime.GOARCH
    if p.conf.Version == "latest" {
        u.Message("Determining latest Go version")
        resp, err := http.Get("https://golang.org/VERSION?m=text")
        if err != nil {
            u.Error("http get problem: " + err.Error())
            return fmt.Errorf("problem asking Google for latest Go version: %s", err)
```

```
            }
            ver, err := io.ReadAll(resp.Body)
            if err != nil {
                    u.Error("io read problem: " + err.Error())
                    return fmt.Errorf("problem reading latest Go
version: %s", err)
            }
            p.conf.Version = strings.TrimPrefix(string(ver),
"go")
            u.Message("Latest Go version: " + p.conf.Version)
    } else {
            u.Message("Go version to use is: " + p.conf.Version)
    }
```

This code makes the HTTP request for the Go tarball and then stores that in .content:

```
    url := fmt.Sprintf(goURL, p.conf.Version, platform)

    u.Message("Downloading Go version: " + url)
    resp, err := http.Get(url)
    if err != nil {
        return fmt.Errorf("problem reaching golang.org for
version(%s): %s", p.conf.Version, err)
    }
    defer resp.Body.Close()

    p.content, err = io.ReadAll(resp.Body)
    if err != nil {
        return fmt.Errorf("problem downloading file: %s", err)
    }

    p.fileName = fmt.Sprintf(name, p.conf.Version, platform)
    u.Message("Downloading complete")
    return nil
}
```

Now that we have fetched our Go `tarball` content, let's push it to the machine:

```
func (p *Provisioner) push(ctx context.Context, u Ui,
c Communicator) error {
    u.Message("Pushing Go tarball")
    fs := simple.New()
    fs.WriteFile("/tarball", p.content, 0700)
```

```
        fi, _ := fs.Stat("/tarball")
        err := c.Upload(
                "/tmp/"+p.fileName,
                bytes.NewReader(p.content),
                &fi,
        )
        if err != nil {
                return err
        }
        u.Message("Go tarball delivered to: /tmp/" + p.fileName)
        return nil
}
```

The preceding code uploads our content to the image. `Upload()` requires that we provide `*os.FileInfo`, but we don't have one because our file does not exist on disk. So, we use a trick where we write the content to a file in an in-memory filesystem and then retrieve `*os.FileInfo`. This prevents us from writing unnecessary files to disk.

> **Note**
>
> One of the odd things about `Communicator.Upload()` is that it takes a pointer to an interface (`*os.FileInfo`). This is almost always a mistake by an author. Don't do this in your code.

The next thing needed is to unpack this on the image:

```
func (p *Provisioner) unpack(ctx context.Context, u Ui,
c Communicator) error {
        const cmd = `sudo tar -C /usr/local -xzf /tmp/%s`
        u.Message("Unpacking Go tarball to /usr/local")
        b := bytes.Buffer{}
        rc := &packer.RemoteCmd{
                Command: fmt.Sprintf(cmd, p.fileName),
                Stdout: &b,
                Stderr: &b,
        }
        if err := c.Start(rc); err != nil {
                return fmt.Errorf("problem unpacking tarball(%s):\
n%s", err, b.String())
        }
        u.Message("Unpacked Go tarball")
```

```
        return nil
}
```

This code does the following:

- Defines a command that unwraps our tarball and installs to /usr/local
- Wraps that command in *packerRemoteCmd and captures STDOUT and STDERR
- Runs the command with Communicator: If it fails, returns the error and STDOUT/STDERR for debug

The last step for Provisioner is to test that it installed:

```
func (p *Provisioner) test(ctx context.Context, u Ui,
c Communicator) error {
    u.Message("Testing Go install")
    b := bytes.Buffer{}
    rc := &packer.RemoteCmd{
        Command: `/usr/local/go/bin/go version`,
        Stdout: &b,
        Stderr: &b,
    }
    if err := c.Start(rc); err != nil {
        return fmt.Errorf("problem testing Go install(%s):\
n%s", err, b.String())
    }
    u.Message("Go installed successfully")
    return nil
}
```

This code does the following:

- Runs /usr/local/go/bin/go version to get the output
- If it fails, returns the error and STDOUT/STDERR for debug

Now, the final part of the plugin to write is main():

```
const (
        ver     = "0.0.1"
        release = "dev"
)

var pv *version.PluginVersion
```

```
func init() {
    pv = version.InitializePluginVersion(ver, release)
}

func main() {
    set := plugin.NewSet()
    set.SetVersion(pv)
    set.RegisterProvisioner("goenv", &Provisioner{})
    err := set.Run()
    if err != nil {
        fmt.Fprintln(os.Stderr, err.Error())
        os.Exit(1)
    }
}
```

This code does the following:

- Defines our release version as `"0.0.1"`.
- Defines the release as a `"dev"` version, but you can use anything here. The production version should use `""`.
- Initializes `pv`, which holds the plugin version information. This is done in `init()` simply because the package comments indicate it should be done this way instead of in `main()` to cause a panic at the earliest time if a problem exists.
- Makes a new Packer `plugin.Set`:
  - Sets the version information. If not set, all GitHub releases will fail.
  - Registers our provisioner with the `"goenv"` plugin name:
    - Can be used to register other provisioners
    - Can be used to register a builder, `set.RegisterBuilder()`, and a post processor, `set.RegisterPostProcessor()`
- Runs `Set` we created and exits on any error.

We can register with a regular name, which would get appended to the name of the plugin. If using `plugin.DEFAULT_NAME`, our provisioner can be referred to simply by the plugin's name.

So, if our plugin is named `packer-plugin-goenv`, our plugin can be referred to as `goenv`. If we use something other than `plugin.DEFAULT_NAME`, such as `example`, our plugin would be referred to as `goenv-example`.

We now have a plugin, but to make it useful we must allow people to initialize it. Let's look at how we can release our plugins using GitHub.

> **Testing Plugins**
>
> In this exercise, we don't go into testing Packer plugins. As of the time of publishing, there is no documentation on testing. However, Packer's GoDoc page has public types that can mock various types in Packer to help test your plugin.
>
> This includes mocking the `Provisioner`, `Ui`, and `Communicator` types to allow you to test. You can find these here: `https://pkg.go.dev/github.com/hashicorp/packer-plugin-sdk/packer`.

Releasing a plugin

Packer has strict release requirements for allowing the `packer` binary to find and use a plugin. To have the plugin downloadable, the following requirements must be met:

- Must be released on GitHub; no other source is allowed.
- Have a repository named `packer-plugin-*`, where `*` is the name of your plugin.
- Only use dashes not underscores.
- Must have a plugin release that includes certain assets we will describe.

The official release document can be found here: `https://www.packer.io/docs/plugins/creation#creating-a-github-release`.

HashiCorp also has a 30-minute video showing how to publish release documents to Packer's website here: `https://www.hashicorp.com/resources/publishing-packer-plugins-to-the-masses`.

The first step for generating a release is to create a **GNU Privacy Guard** (**GPG**) key to sign releases. The GitHub instructions can be found here (but see notes directly underneath first): `https://docs.github.com/en/authentication/managing-commit-signature-verification/generating-a-new-gpg-key`.

Before you follow that document, remember these things while following the instructions:

- Make sure you add the public key to your GitHub profile.
- Do not use $ or any other symbol in your passphrase, as it will cause issues.

Once that is completed, you need to add the private key to your repository so that the GitHub actions we define will be able to sign the releases. You will need to go to your GitHub repository's **Settings** | **Secrets**. Click the provided **New Repository Secret** button.

Choose the name `GPG_PRIVATE_KEY`.

In the value section, you will need to paste in your GPG private key that you can export with:

```
gpg --armor --export-secret-keys [key ID or email]
```

`[key ID or email]` is the identity you gave for the key, typically your email address.

Now, we need to add the passphrase for your GPG key. You can add this as a secret with the name `GPG_PASSPHRASE`. The value should be the passphrase for the GPG key.

Once that is completed, you will need to download the GoReleaser scaffolding HashiCorp provides. You can do that with the following:

```
curl -L -o ".goreleaser.yml" \
  https://raw.githubusercontent.com/hashicorp/packer-plugin-scaffolding/main/.goreleaser.yml
```

Now, we need the GitHub Actions workflow provided by HashiCorp set up in your repository. This can be done with the following:

```
mkdir -p .github/workflows &&
  curl -L -o ".github/workflows/release.yml" \
  https://raw.githubusercontent.com/hashicorp/packer-plugin-scaffolding/main/.github/workflows/release.yml
```

Finally, we need to download `GNUmakefile`, which is used by the scaffolding. Let's grab it:

```
curl -L -o "GNUmakefile" \
  https://raw.githubusercontent.com/hashicorp/packer-plugin-scaffolding/main/GNUmakefile
```

Our plugin only works for Linux systems. The `.goreleaser.yml` file defines releases for multiple platforms. You can restrict this by modifying the `builds` section of `.goreleaser.yml` to be more restrictive. You can see an example of that here: https://github.com/johnsiilver/packer-plugin-goenv/blob/main/.goreleaser.yml.

With your code buildable and these files included, you need to commit these files to your repository.

The next step will be to create a release. This needs to be tagged with a semantic version, similar to what you set the `ver` variable to in your plugin's `main` file. The slight difference is that while it will be strictly numbers and dots in `ver string`, it is prepended with v when tagging on GitHub. So `ver = "0.0.1` will be a GitHub release with `v0.0.1`. The GitHub documentation on releases can be found here: `https://docs.github.com/en/repositories/releasing-projects-on-github/managing-releases-in-a-repository`.

Once you have created a release, you can view the actions being run by viewing the **Actions** tab. This will show the results and detail any problems encountered by the actions.

Using our plugin in a build

To use our plugin in the build, we need to modify the HCL2 configuration. First, we need to modify `packer.required_plugins` to require our plugin:

```
packer {
  required_plugins {
    amazon = {
      version = ">= 0.0.1"
      source = "github.com/hashicorp/amazon"
    }
    installGo = {
      version = ">= 0.0.1"
      source = "github.com/johnsiilver/goenv"
    }
  }
}
```

This does a few things:

- Creates a new variable, `installGo`, that gives access to all plugins defined in our multi-plugin. There is only one: `goenv`.
- Sets the version to use to be greater or equal to version `0.0.1`.
- Gives the source of the plugin. You will notice that the path is missing `packer-plugin-`. As that is standard for every plugin, they remove the need to type it.

> **Note**
> You will see that the source is different than our location for the code. This is because we wanted to have a copy of the code in our normal location, but Packer requires a plugin to have its own repository. The code is located at both locations. You may view this copy of the code at: `https://github.com/johnsiilver/packer-plugin-goenv`.

Now, we need to remove the `shell` section under `build.provisioner` that installs Go. Replace it with the following:

```
provisioner "goenv-goenv" {
  version = "1.17.5"
}
```

Finally, you will need to update the AMI name to something new to store this under.

As an alternative, you may also download the modified HCL2 file here: `https://github.com/PacktPublishing/Go-for-DevOps/blob/rev0/chapter/12/packer/amazon.goenv.pkr.hcl`.

In the terminal, format the file and download our plugin with the following:

```
packer fmt .
packer init .
```

This should cause our plugin to download with output text similar to this:

```
Installed plugin github.com/johnsiilver/goenv v0.0.1 in "/home/ec2-user/.config/packer/plugins/github.com/johnsiilver/goenv/packer-plugin-goenv_v0.0.1_x5.0_linux_amd64"
```

We can finally build our image with the following:

```
packer build .
```

If successful, you should see the following in the Packer output:

```
goBook.amazon-ebs.ubuntu: Begin Go environment install
goBook.amazon-ebs.ubuntu: Go version to use is: 1.17.5
goBook.amazon-ebs.ubuntu: Downloading Go version: https://golang.org/dl/go1.17.5.linux-amd64.tar.gz
goBook.amazon-ebs.ubuntu: Downloading complete
goBook.amazon-ebs.ubuntu: Pushing Go tarball
goBook.amazon-ebs.ubuntu: Go tarball delivered to: /tmp/go1.17.5.linux-amd64.tar.gz
```

```
goBook.amazon-ebs.ubuntu: Unpacking Go tarball to /usr/local
goBook.amazon-ebs.ubuntu: Unpacked Go tarball
goBook.amazon-ebs.ubuntu: Testing Go install
goBook.amazon-ebs.ubuntu: Go installed successfully
goBook.amazon-ebs.ubuntu: Go environment install finished
```

This plugin has been pre-tested. Let's have a look at what you can do if the plugin fails.

Debugging a Packer plugin

When `packer build .` fails, you may or may not receive relevant information in the UI output. This will depend on whether the problem was a panic or an error.

Panics return an `Unexpected EOF` message because the plugin crashed and the Packer application only knows that it didn't receive an RPC message on the Unix socket.

We can get Packer to help us out by providing this option when we run:

```
packer build -debug
```

This will output a `crash.log` file if the build crashes. It also uses `press enter` between each step before continuing and allows only a single `packer` build to run at a time.

You may see other files show up, as some plugins (such as Goss) detect the `debug` option and output debug configuration files and logs.

You may also want to turn on logging for any log messages you or other plugins write. This can be done by setting a few environmental variables:

```
PACKER_LOG=1 PACKER_LOG_PATH="./packerlog.txt" packer build .
```

This takes care of most debugging needs. However, sometimes the debug information required is part of the system logs and not the plugin itself. In those cases, you may want to use the communicator's `Download()` or `DownloadDir()` methods to retrieve files when you detect an error.

For more debugging information, the official debugging documentation is here: https://www.packer.io/docs/debugging.

In this section, we have detailed the building of a Packer multi-plugin, shown how to set up the plugin in GitHub to be used with `packer init`, and updated our Packer configuration to use the plugin. In addition, we have discussed the basics of debugging Packer plugins.

Summary

This chapter has taught you the basics of using Packer to build a machine image, using Amazon AWS as the target. We have covered the most important plugins Packer offers to customize an AMI. We then built a custom image that installed multiple packages with the `apt` tool, downloaded and installed other tools, set up directories and users, and finally, set up a system agent to run with systemd.

We have covered how to use the Goss tool to validate your images and how to integrate Goss into Packer using a plugin developed at Yale.

Finally, we have shown you how to create your own plugins to extend the capabilities of Packer.

Now, it is time to talk about IaC and how another of HashiCorp's tools has taken the DevOps world by storm. Let's talk about Terraform.

13
Infrastructure as Code with Terraform

Infrastructure as Code (**IaC**) is the practice of provisioning computing infrastructure using machine-readable, declarative specifications or imperative code, rather than using an interactive configuration tool. IaC became increasingly popular with the rise of cloud computing. Infrastructure administrators who were previously maintaining long-lived infrastructure found themselves needing to scale in both agility and capacity as companies adopted cloud infrastructure.

Remember that at this time, software teams and infrastructure teams were unlikely to work closely together until a software project needed to be deployed. IaC created a bridge between infrastructure administrators and software developers by establishing a shared set of documents that described the desired infrastructure for the software project. The IaC specifications or code often live within or alongside the project. By establishing this shared context between software developers and infrastructure administrators, these two teams were able to work together earlier in the software development life cycle and establish a shared vision for infrastructure.

In this chapter, we'll start off by learning about how Terraform approaches IaC and the basics of its usage. After we have a handle on how Terraform works, we'll discuss Terraform providers and see how the vast ecosystem of providers can empower us to describe and provision a wide variety of resources, not just compute infrastructure such as virtual machines. Finally, we'll learn how to extend Terraform by building our own pet store Terraform provider.

We will cover the following topics in this chapter:

- An introduction to IaC
- Understanding the basics of Terraform
- Understanding the basics of Terraform providers
- Building a pet store Terraform provider

Technical requirements

In this chapter, you will need to have the following:

- Docker
- Git
- Go
- The Terraform CLI: `https://learn.hashicorp.com/tutorials/terraform/install-cli`
- The Azure CLI: `https://docs.microsoft.com/en-us/cli/azure/install-azure-cli`
- The code for this chapter: `https://github.com/PacktPublishing/Go-for-DevOps/tree/main/chapter/13/petstore-provider`

Let's get started by learning some Terraform basics.

The code files for this chapter can be downloaded from `https://github.com/PacktPublishing/Go-for-DevOps/tree/rev0/chapter/13/petstore-provider`

An introduction to IaC

IaC had a significant impact beyond bringing infrastructure and software development teams together; the practice also made it much easier and safer to deploy infrastructure for projects. By defining the infrastructure and storing the specifications in a software project, the infrastructure code could be tested in the same way that the software project was tested. As with testing code, consistently testing infrastructure code reduces bugs, surfaces inefficiencies, and increases confidence in the infrastructure deployment process.

We take it for granted today, but in many organizations, working with infrastructure administrators to build a cluster for a non-trivial application could take weeks. Taking that same experience, condensing it into a handful of files, and then being able to deploy a cluster in minutes was a game changer.

There are many IaC tools available. Each has its own flavor for how the tool approaches the problem of describing and provisioning infrastructure. Though they are all a bit different, each tool can be categorized using a couple of facets, by how the code is specified by the author, and by how it deals with changes to code. The foremost category is how the infrastructure code is specified. Specifically, the code is a declarative specification describing the desired state (what to provision), or the code is a set of imperative steps described in a programming language (how to provision). The second category is how the tool applies the infrastructure, push or pull. Pull IaC tools watch for changes to code in a centralized repository. Push IaC tools apply their changes to the destination system.

IaC is a critical practice in bridging the gap between writing, delivering, and operating software. It is one of the key areas where development overlaps with operations. Mastering the practice will better enable your team to deliver software faster with greater agility and reliability.

Understanding the basics of Terraform

Terraform (https://www.terraform.io/) is an open source IaC tool written in Go and created by HashiCorp that provides a consistent command-line experience for managing a wide variety of resources. With Terraform, infrastructure engineers define the desired state of a set of hierarchical resources using declarative Terraform configuration files or with imperative code (https://www.terraform.io/cdktf), which results in Terraform configurations files. These configuration files are the code in IaC. They can be used to manage the full life cycle of creating, mutating, and destroying resources, plan and predict changes to resources, provide a graph of dependencies in complex resource topologies, and store the last observed state of a system.

Terraform is simple to get started and has a fairly linear learning curve. There are many features of Terraform we will not cover in this chapter that will be useful as you deepen your adoption of the tool. The goal of this chapter is not to become an expert with Terraform but rather to show you how to get started and be effective quickly.

In this section, you will learn the basics of how Terraform operates, and how to use the Terraform CLI. We'll start off with a simple example and discuss what happens at execution time. By the end of the section, you should feel comfortable defining resources, initializing, and applying using the Terraform CLI.

Initializing and applying infrastructure specs using Terraform

In the first part of this section, we will discuss resources rather than infrastructure components. Discussing resources and components is rather abstract. Let's use a concrete example to explain the normal flow of actions with Terraform.

For our first example, we will use a directory structured like the following:

```
.
├── main.tf
```

In the preceding block, we have a directory with a single `main.tf` file. In that file, we will add the following content:

```
resource "local_file" "foo" {

    content  = "foo!"

    filename = "${path.module}/foo.txt"

}
```

In the preceding Terraform `main.tf` configuration file, we define a `local_file` resource named `foo` with the `foo!` content located at `${path.module}/foo.txt`. `${path.module}` is the filesystem path of the module, in this case, `./foo.txt`.

We can simply run the following to initialize Terraform in the directory and apply the desired state:

```
$ terraform init && terraform apply
```

The preceding `terraform init` command will check the validity of `main.tf`, pull down the providers needed, and initialize the local state of the project. After the `init` command is executed, the `apply` command will be executed. We'll break these down into two parts, `init` and then `apply`. The `init` command should output the following:

```
$ terraform init && terraform apply

Initializing the backend...

Initializing provider plugins...
- Finding latest version of hashicorp/local...
- Installing hashicorp/local v2.2.2...
- Installed hashicorp/local v2.2.2 (signed by HashiCorp)

Terraform has created a lock file .terraform.lock.hcl to record the provider
selections it made preceding. Include this file in your version control repository
so that Terraform can guarantee to make the same selections by default when
you run "terraform init" in the future.

Terraform has been successfully initialized!

You may now begin working with Terraform. Try running "terraform plan" to see
any changes that are required for your infrastructure. All Terraform commands
should now work.

If you ever set or change modules or backend configuration for Terraform,
rerun this command to reinitialize your working directory. If you forget, other
commands will detect it and remind you to do so if necessary.
```

As you can see from the preceding output, Terraform installed the `hashicorp/local` provider at a specific version. Terraform then saved the version to a local lock file, `.terraform.lock.hcl`, to ensure that the same version is used in the future, establishing the information needed to have a reproducible build. Finally, Terraform provides instructions for using `terraform plan` to see what Terraform will do to reach the desired state described in `main.tf`.

After initialization, running `terraform apply` will trigger Terraform to determine the current desired state and compare it to the known state of the resources in `main.tf`. `terraform apply` presents the operator with a plan of the operations that will be executed. Upon operator approval of the plan, Terraform executes the plan and stores the updated state of the resources. Let's see the output from `terraform apply`:

```
Terraform used the selected providers to generate the following
execution plan. Resource actions are indicated with the
following symbols:
  + create

Terraform will perform the following actions:

  # local_file.foo will be created
  + resource "local_file" "foo" {
      + content              = "foo!"
      + directory_permission = "0777"
      + file_permission      = "0777"
      + filename             = "./foo.txt"
      + id                   = (known after apply)
    }

Plan: 1 to add, 0 to change, 0 to destroy.

Do you want to perform these actions?
  Terraform will perform the actions described preceding.
  Only 'yes' will be accepted to approve.

  Enter a value: yes

local_file.foo: Creating...
local_file.foo: Creation complete after 0s
[id=4bf3e335199107182c6f7638efaad377acc7f452]

Apply complete! Resources: 1 added, 0 changed, 0 destroyed.
```

After confirming the plan by entering `yes`, Terraform has applied the desired state and created the resource, a local file. The directory should look like the following:

```
.
├── .terraform
│   └── providers
│       └── registry.terraform.io
│           └── hashicorp
│               └── local
│                   └── 2.2.2
│                       └── darwin_arm64
│                           └── terraform-provider-local_v2.2.2_x5
├── .terraform.lock.hcl
├── foo.txt
├── main.tf
└── terraform.tfstate
```

In the preceding directory structure, we can see the local provider that Terraform used to provision the file, the Terraform lock file, the `foo.txt` file, and a `terraform.tfstate` file. Let's explore `foo.txt` and the `terraform.tfstate` files:

```
$ cat foo.txt
foo!
```

As we described in `main.tf`, Terraform has created `foo.txt` with the `foo!` content. Next, let's look at `terraform.tfstate`:

```
$ cat terraform.tfstate
{
  "version": 4,
  "terraform_version": "1.1.7",
  "serial": 1,
  "lineage": "384e96a1-5878-ed22-5368-9795a3231a00",
  "outputs": {},
  "resources": [
    {
      "mode": "managed",
      "type": "local_file",
      "name": "foo",
      "provider": "provider[\"registry.terraform.io/hashicorp/local\"]",
      "instances": [
```

```
{
  "schema_version": 0,
  "attributes": {
    "content": "foo!",
    "content_base64": null,
    "directory_permission": "0777",
    "file_permission": "0777",
    "filename": "./foo.txt",
    "id": "4bf3e335199107182c6f7638efaad377acc7f452",
    "sensitive_content": null,
    "source": null
  },
  "sensitive_attributes": [],
  "private": "bnVsbA=="
}
          ]
        }
      ]
    }
```

The `terraform.tfstate` file is a bit more interesting than `foo.txt`. The `tfstate` file is where Terraform stores its last known state for the resources applied in the plan. This enables Terraform to inspect the differences with the last known state and build a plan for updating the resource if the desired state changes in the future.

Next, let's change the desired state in `main.tf` and see what happens when we apply the configuration again. Let's update `main.tf` to the following:

```
resource "local_file" "foo" {
    content  = "foo changed!"
    filename = "${path.module}/foo.txt"
    file_permissions = "0644"
}
```

Note that we've changed the content of `foo.txt` and added file permissions to the resource. Now, let's apply the desired state and see what happens:

```
$ terraform apply -auto-approve
local_file.foo: Refreshing state...
[id=4bf3e335199107182c6f7638efaad377acc7f452]

Terraform used the selected providers to generate the following
execution plan. Resource actions are indicated with the
following symbols:
```

```
-/+ destroy and then create replacement

Terraform will perform the following actions:

  # local_file.foo must be replaced
-/+ resource "local_file" "foo" {
    ~ content           = "foo!" -> "foo changed!" # forces replacement
    ~ file_permission   = "0777" -> "0644" # forces replacement
    ~ id                = "4bf3e335199107182c6f7638efaad377acc7f452" -> (known after apply)
      # (2 unchanged attributes hidden)
  }

Plan: 1 to add, 0 to change, 1 to destroy.
local_file.foo: Destroying... [id=4bf3e335199107182c6f7638efaad377acc7f452]
local_file.foo: Destruction complete after 0s
local_file.foo: Creating...
local_file.foo: Creation complete after 0s [id=5d6b2d23a15b5391d798c9c6a6b69f9a57c41aa5]

Apply complete! Resources: 1 added, 0 changed, 1 destroyed.
```

Terraform was able to determine the attributes of the resource that have changed and create a plan for reaching the desired state. As the plan output states with 1 to add, 0 to change, 1 to destroy, the local `foo.txt` file will be deleted and then recreated, since a change to the file permissions forces the replacement of the file. This example illustrates that a single attribute change can, but does not always, cause the deletion and recreation of a resource. Note that we added the `-auto-approve` flag to the `apply` command. As the name implies, this will not prompt approval of the plan before it is applied. You may want to use caution when using that flag, as it's good practice to check the plan to ensure that the actions you expect are the actions described in the plan.

Let's see the new contents of `foo.txt`:

```
$ cat foo.txt
foo changed!
```

As you can see, the content of foo.txt has been updated to reflect the desired state. Now, let's examine the directory:

```
.
├── foo.txt
├── main.tf
├── terraform.tfstate
└── terraform.tfstate.backup
```

Note that a new file was created, terraform.tfstate.backup. This is a copy of the previous tfstate file in case the new tfstate file is corrupted or lost.

By default, the tfstate files are stored locally. When working individually, this is perfectly fine; however, when working with a team, it would become difficult to share the most recent state with others. This is where remote state (https://www.terraform.io/language/state/remote) becomes extremely useful. We will not cover this feature here, but you should be aware of it.

Finally, we will destroy the resource we have created:

```
$ terraform destroy
local_file.foo: Refreshing state...
[id=5d6b2d23a15b5391d798c9c6a6b69f9a57c41aa5]

Terraform used the selected providers to generate the following
execution plan. Resource actions are indicated with the
following symbols:
  - destroy

Terraform will perform the following actions:

  # local_file.foo will be destroyed
  - resource "local_file" "foo" {
      - content              = "foo changed!" -> null
      - directory_permission = "0777" -> null
      - file_permission      = "0644" -> null
      - filename             = "./foo.txt" -> null
      - id                   =
"5d6b2d23a15b5391d798c9c6a6b69f9a57c41aa5" -> null
    }

Plan: 0 to add, 0 to change, 1 to destroy.

Do you really want to destroy all resources?
```

```
        Terraform will destroy all your managed infrastructure, as
    shown above.
        There is no undo. Only 'yes' will be accepted to confirm.

        Enter a value: yes

    local_file.foo: Destroying...
    [id=5d6b2d23a15b5391d798c9c6a6b69f9a57c41aa5]
    local_file.foo: Destruction complete after 0s

    Destroy complete! Resources: 1 destroyed.
```

Running `terraform destroy` will clean up all of the resources described in the desired state. If you examine your directory, you will see that the `foo.txt` file has been deleted.

Congratulations! You have covered the absolute basics of Terraform. We have learned at a high level how Terraform operates and how to use the Terraform CLI. We created a simple local file resource, mutated it, and destroyed it. In the next section, we'll discuss Terraform providers and explore the world that opens up when we take advantage of the vast ecosystem of them.

Understanding the basics of Terraform providers

At its heart, Terraform is a platform for reconciling an expressed desired state with an external system. The way Terraform interacts with external APIs is through plugins called **providers**. A provider is responsible for describing the schema for its exposed resources, and implementing **Create, Read, Update, and Delete** (**CRUD**) interactions with external APIs. Providers enable Terraform to express nearly any external API's resources as Terraform resources.

Through its thousands of community and verified providers, Terraform is able to manage resources including databases such as Redis, Cassandra, and MongoDB, cloud infrastructure for all major cloud service providers, communication and messaging services such as Discord and SendGrid, and a vast number of other providers. If you are interested, you can explore a listing of them in the Terraform Registry (https://registry.terraform.io/). You can simply write, plan, and apply your way to your desired infrastructure.

In this section, we will build on our experience of using a local provider and extend what we learned to use a provider that interacts with an external API. We will define the desired state for a set of cloud resources and provision them.

Defining and provisioning cloud resources

Imagine that we want to deploy infrastructure to our cloud service provider. In this case, we're going to use Microsoft Azure via the `hashicorp/azurerm` provider. In an empty directory, let's start by authoring a simple `main.tf` file like the following:

```
# Configure the Azure provider
terraform {
  required_providers {
    azurerm = {
      source  = "hashicorp/azurerm"
      version = "~> 3.0"
    }
  }
}

provider "azurerm" {
  features {}
}

resource "azurerm_resource_group" "mygroup" {
  name     = "mygroup"
  location = "southcentralus"
}
```

The preceding Terraform configuration file requires the `hashicorp/azurerm` provider and defines a resource group named `mygroup` in the `southcentralus` region (a resource group is an Azure concept that groups infrastructure resources together).

To run the rest of the examples in this section, you will need an Azure account. If you do not have an Azure account, you can sign up for a free account with $200 of Azure credits: https://azure.microsoft.com/en-us/free/.

Once you have an account, log in with the Azure CLI:

```
$ az login
```

The preceding command will log you into your Azure account and set the default context to your primary Azure subscription. To see what subscription is active, run the following:

```
$ az account show
{
  "environmentName": "AzureCloud",
  "isDefault": true,
  "managedByTenants": [],
  "name": "mysubscription",
  "state": "Enabled",
  "tenantId": "888bf....db93",
  "user": {
      ...
  }
}
```

The preceding command output shows the name of the subscription and other details about the current context of the Azure CLI. The `azurerm` provider will use the authentication context of the Azure CLI to interact with the Azure APIs.

Now that we have an authenticated Azure session on the Azure CLI, let's use `init` and `apply` to create our desired state. Within the directory containing the `main.tf` file, run the following:

```
$ terraform init && terraform apply
```

`terraform init` will initialize the directory, pulling down the latest `azurerm` provider. By specifying the `~> 3.0` version constraint, Terraform is directed to install the latest version of the provider in the `3.0.x` series. You should see something like the following output from `init`:

```
Initializing the backend...

Initializing provider plugins...
- Finding hashicorp/azurerm versions matching "~> 3.0"...
- Installing hashicorp/azurerm v3.0.2...
- Installed hashicorp/azurerm v3.0.2 (signed by HashiCorp)

Terraform has created a lock file .terraform.lock.hcl to record the provider
selections it made above. Include this file in your version control repository
so that Terraform can guarantee to make the same selections by default when
you run "terraform init" in the future.

Terraform has been successfully initialized!

You may now begin working with Terraform. Try running "terraform plan" to see
any changes that are required for your infrastructure. All Terraform commands
should now work.

If you ever set or change modules or backend configuration for Terraform,
rerun this command to reinitialize your working directory. If you forget, other
commands will detect it and remind you to do so if necessary.
```

This output should look familiar from the *Initializing and applying infrastructure specs using Terraform* section. After initialization, you will again be greeted with the plan for creating the desired resources. Once the plan is approved, the desired resources are created. The output should look like the following:

```
Terraform used the selected providers to generate the following
execution plan. Resource actions are indicated with the
following symbols:
  + create

Terraform will perform the following actions:

  # azurerm_resource_group.rg will be created
  + resource "azurerm_resource_group" "mygroup" {
      + id       = (known after apply)
      + location = "southcentralus"
      + name     = "mygroup"
    }

Plan: 1 to add, 0 to change, 0 to destroy.

Do you want to perform these actions?
  Terraform will perform the actions described above.
  Only 'yes' will be accepted to approve.

  Enter a value: yes

azurerm_resource_group.mygroup: Creating...
azurerm_resource_group.mygroup: Creation complete after 2s
[id=/subscriptions/8ec-...-24a/resourceGroups/mygroup]
```

As you can see from the preceding output, the resource group is created.

> **Note**
>
> If you are using a free Azure account, you may not have regional capacity in the `southcentralus` location. You may need to use a different region such as `centralus` or `northeurope`. To find out more information on what region would be best for you, view the Azure geography guidance here: `https://azure.microsoft.com/en-us/global-infrastructure/geographies/#geographies`.

Opening the Azure portal and navigating to the **Resource groups** view, you should see the following:

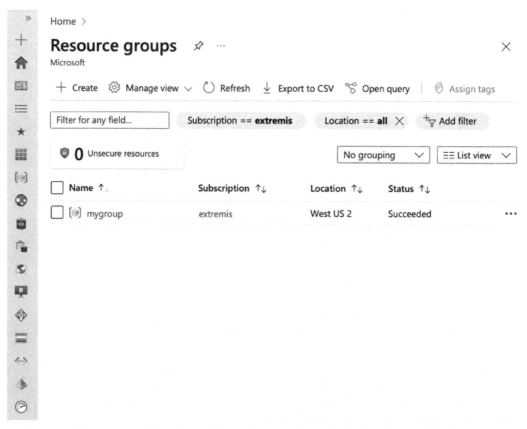

Figure 13.1 – The created resource group in Azure

In the preceding screenshot, we can see our newly created Azure resource group, `mygroup`.

Let's see what new files have been added to our local directory after running `init` and `apply`:

```
.
├── .terraform
│   └── providers
│       └── registry.terraform.io
│           └── hashicorp
│               └── azurerm
│                   └── 3.0.2
│                       └── darwin_arm64
```

```
|                                          └── terraform-provider-azurerm_
v3.0.2_x5
├── .terraform.lock.hcl
├── main.tf
└── terraform.tfstate
```

Similar to the previous section, we can see the Terraform lock and state files. However, in the `providers` directory, we now see that the `azurerm` provider was installed.

Let's add some more resources and apply them. You can find a listing of all of the supported resources in the Azure provider documentation (https://registry.terraform.io/providers/hashicorp/azurerm/latest/docs). We'll update the `main.tf` file to contain the following resources:

```
resource "azurerm_resource_group" "mygroup" {
  name     = "mygroup"
  location = "southcentralus"
}

resource "azurerm_service_plan" "myplan" {
  name                = "myplan"
  resource_group_name = azurerm_resource_group.mygroup.name
  location            = azurerm_resource_group.mygroup.location
  os_type             = "Linux"
  sku_name            = "S1"
}

resource "random_integer" "ri" {
  min = 10000
  max = 99999
}

resource "azurerm_linux_web_app" "myapp" {
  name                = "myapp-${random_integer.ri.result}"
  resource_group_name = azurerm_resource_group.mygroup.name
  location            = azurerm_service_plan.myplan.location
  service_plan_id     = azurerm_service_plan.myplan.id
  site_config {
    application_stack {
      docker_image     = "nginxdemos/hello"
      docker_image_tag = "latest"
    }
  }
}
```

```
}

output "host_name" {
    value = azurerm_linux_web_app.myapp.default_hostname
}
```

The resources added to the preceding `main.tf` file include two Azure resources, an App Service plan, a Linux web app, and one `random_integer` resource. The Azure App Service plan defines a regional deployment of compute infrastructure for running a Linux-based web application. The Azure Linux web app is associated with the Azure App Service plan and is configured to run a hello world NGINX demo container image. The `random_integer` resource is needed to provide some random input for the **Fully Qualified Domain Name** (**FQDN**) for the Linux web app.

Note the use of variables. For example, we use `azurerm_resource_group.mygroup.name` to provide the value for `resource_group_name` in the `azure_service_plan` resource. Variable usage helps to minimize the number of string literals in the configuration files. This is helpful when making a change because you can make it in one place, rather than each occurrence of the string.

Also, note the use of an output variable, `host_name`. This instructs Terraform to output the `host_name` key with the value of `azurerm_linux_web_app.myapp.default_hostname` after the completion of `terraform apply`. We'll use this output to make it easier to open the website after it is provisioned.

Let's run `terraform apply` again and see what happens:

```
$ terraform apply
|
| Error: Inconsistent dependency lock file
|
| The following dependency selections recorded in the lock file
are inconsistent with the current configuration:
|    - provider registry.terraform.io/hashicorp/random: required
by this configuration but no version is selected
|
| To update the locked dependency selections to match a changed
configuration, run:
|    terraform init -upgrade
|
```

Oh no! `terraform apply` responds with an error, informing us that we have a new provider added to the configuration that we didn't have last time. Run `terraform init -upgrade`, and the `random` module will be added:

```
$ terraform init -upgrade

Initializing the backend...

Initializing provider plugins...
- Finding latest version of hashicorp/random...
- Finding hashicorp/azurerm versions matching "~> 3.0"...
- Installing hashicorp/random v3.1.2...
- Installed hashicorp/random v3.1.2 (signed by HashiCorp)
- Using previously-installed hashicorp/azurerm v3.0.2
```

You should see some output like the preceding that shows Terraform installing the latest version of the `hashicorp/random` provider. Let's see what our directory looks like now that we've added the provider:

```
.
├── .terraform
│   └── providers
│       └── registry.terraform.io
│           └── hashicorp
│               ├── azurerm
│               │   └── 3.0.2
│               │       └── darwin_arm64
│               │           └── terraform-provider-azurerm_v3.0.2_x5
│               └── random
│                   └── 3.1.2
│                       └── darwin_arm64
│                           └── terraform-provider-random_v3.1.2_x5
```

As you can see, the `random` provider is now installed. We should be ready to use `apply` again:

```
$ terraform apply -auto-approve
azurerm_resource_group.mygroup: Refreshing state...
...
Plan: 3 to add, 0 to change, 0 to destroy.

Changes to Outputs:
  + host_name = (known after apply)
random_integer.ri: Creating...
random_integer.ri: Creation complete after 0s [id=18515]
azurerm_service_plan.myplan: Creating...
azurerm_service_plan.myplan: Still creating... [10s elapsed]
azurerm_service_plan.myplan: Creation complete after 12s [id=/
subscriptions/8ec-...-24a/resourceGroups/mygroup/providers/
Microsoft.Web/serverfarms/myplan]
azurerm_linux_web_app.myapp: Creating...
azurerm_linux_web_app.myapp: Still creating... [10s elapsed]
azurerm_linux_web_app.myapp: Still creating... [20s elapsed]
azurerm_linux_web_app.myapp: Creation complete after 28s [id=/
subscriptions/8ec-...-24a/resourceGroups/mygroup/providers/
Microsoft.Web/sites/myapp-18515]

Apply complete! Resources: 3 added, 0 changed, 0 destroyed.

Outputs:

host_name = "myapp-18515.azurewebsites.net"
```

We've omitted some of the output of `terraform apply`. The things to note here are that we are creating each of the resources we described in `main.tf`, they have provisioned successfully, and `host_name` contains a **Universal Resource Identifier (URI)** for accessing the newly deployed web application.

Take the `host_name` URI and open it in a browser. You should see the following:

Figure 13.2 – NGINX running in Azure App Service

If you go back to the Azure portal, you will also see the resources created within your resource group.

I hope you will take some time to experiment by defining and applying other resources. Once you get the hang of using providers and some basic syntax, Terraform is a joy to work with. When you are done with your resources, just run `terraform destroy`, and they will be deleted.

In this section, we learned some basics about using providers to manipulate cloud resources. We only need to use a couple of providers, but as discussed in the opening of the section, there are thousands of providers out there. It's very likely that you will be able to find a provider to solve your problem. However, there may be APIs and resources you would like to manage with Terraform without an existing provider. In the next section, we will build a Terraform provider for a fictional pet store.

Building a pet store Terraform provider

Even though the Terraform provider registry (https://registry.terraform.io/) has almost every provider you can think of, there is a chance that a provider you need does not yet exist. Perhaps you want to use Terraform to interact with resources of a proprietary API internal to your company. If you want to manage resources that don't yet exist in the Terraform provider ecosystem, you will need to write a provider for that API. The good news is that writing a Terraform provider is relatively simple. The thoughtful folks at HashiCorp provide great documentation, SDKs, and tools to make building a provider a breeze.

In the previous sections, we learned the basics of Terraform and how to use providers to interact with resources in both local and external systems. We were able to build cloud resources to deploy a Linux web application running in a container.

In this section, we will build upon the previous sections and learn how to build our own provider. The Terraform provider we are building in this section will expose pet resources and will interact with a local `docker-compose`-hosted pet store service to simulate an external API.

You will learn how to define custom resources with a strong schema and validations, create data sources, and implement CRUD interactions for our pet resources. Finally, we'll discuss publishing a module for the world to use via the Terraform provider registry.

Resources for building custom providers

HashiCorp provides an extensive set of tutorials for building custom providers (https://learn.hashicorp.com/collections/terraform/providers). I highly recommend reviewing the content if you intend on building your own custom provider.

The code for this section is located in https://github.com/PacktPublishing/Go-for-DevOps/tree/main/chapter/13/petstore-provider. We will not cover all of the code, but we will dive into the most interesting parts. I've done my best to keep to only the most simple implementation; however, simple is not always elegant.

Additionally, our pet store custom provider uses the Terraform plugin SDK v2 (https://www.terraform.io/plugin/sdkv2/sdkv2-intro) rather than the new (at the time of writing) Terraform plugin framework. I chose this path as the majority of existing providers use the SDK v2, and *the Terraform plugin framework* (https://www.terraform.io/plugin/framework) has not reached stability yet. If you are interested in weighing the benefits, read the *Which SDK Should I Use?* article from HashiCorp (https://www.terraform.io/plugin/which-sdk).

Now that we have established a foundation of content and learning, let's proceed to the code.

The pet store provider

Our pet store Terraform provider is just another Go application. Most of the interactions between Terraform and the provider are handled at the Terraform SDK level, and very little gets in the way of the provider developer. Let's start off by taking a look at the directory structure of the provider:

```
.
├── Makefile
├── docker-compose.yml
├── examples
│   └── main.tf
├── go.mod
├── go.sum
├── internal
│   ├── client # contains the grpc pet store API client
│   │   └── ...
│   ├── data_source_pet.go
│   ├── provider.go
│   ├── resource_pets.go
│   └── schema.go
└── main.go
```

As I said, it's a standard Go application with an entry point in `main.go`. Let's start at the top and work our way down the files. The first on the list is the Makefile:

```
HOSTNAME=example.com
NAMESPACE=gofordevops
NAME=petstore
BINARY=terraform-provider-${NAME}
VERSION=0.1.0
GOARCH   := $(shell go env GOARCH)
GOOS   := $(shell go env GOOS)

default: install

build:
    go build -o ${BINARY}

install: build
    mkdir -p ~/.terraform.d/plugins/${HOSTNAME}/${NAMESPACE}/${NAME}/${VERSION}/${GOOS}_${GOARCH}
    mv ${BINARY} ~/.terraform.d/plugins/${HOSTNAME}/${NAMESPACE}/${NAME}/${VERSION}/${GOOS}_${GOARCH}

test:
    go test ./... -v

testacc:
    TF_ACC=1 go test ./... -v $(TESTARGS) -timeout 120m
```

The preceding Makefile offers some helpful build tasks and environmental configuration. For example, `make` or `make install` will build the provider for the current architecture and place it in the `~/.terraform.d/plugins` directory tree, which will enable us to use the provider locally without publishing it to the registry.

Next, we have the `docker-compose.yml` file. Let's take a look:

```
version: '3.7'
services:
  petstore:
    build:
      context: ../../10/petstore/.
    command:
      - /go/bin/petstore
```

```
    - --localDebug
  ports:
    - "6742:6742"
```

The docker-compose.yml file runs the pet store service from *Chapter 10, Automating Workflows with GitHub Actions*, and exposes the gRPC service on port 6742. The pet store service stores pets in an in-memory store, so to wipe out the pets currently stored, just restart the service. We'll talk more about starting and stopping the service later in the section.

Next up, we have examples/main.tf. Let's see what an example of defining our pet resources will look like:

```
terraform {
  required_providers {
    petstore = {
      version = "0.1.0"
      source  = "example.com/gofordevops/petstore"
    }
  }
}
...


resource "petstore_pet" "thor" {
  name     = "Thor"
  type     = "dog"
  birthday = "2021-04-01T00:00:00Z"
}
resource "petstore_pet" "tron" {
  name     = "Tron"
  type     = "cat"
  birthday = "2020-06-25T00:00:00Z"
}


data "petstore_pet" "all" {
  depends_on = [petstore_pet.thor, petstore_pet.tron]
}
```

In the preceding `main.tf` file, we can see the provider registered and configured to use the local pet store service. We can also see the definition for two `petstore_pet` resources, `Thor` and `Tron`. After the resources, we define a `petstore_pet` data source. We will walk through bits of this file in more detail later in the section.

The main reason I'd like you to see `main.tf` before we get into the code is that it will give you an idea of the interface we want to achieve in the provider implementation. I believe seeing the usage of the provider will help you to better understand the provider implementation.

The rest of the source code is all in Go, so rather than going from top to bottom, I'm going to move to the entry point in `main.go` and dive into the actual implementation:

```
package main

import (
    "github.com/hashicorp/terraform-plugin-sdk/v2/helper/schema"
    "github.com/hashicorp/terraform-plugin-sdk/v2/plugin"

    petstore "github.com/PacktPublishing/Go-for-DevOps/chapter/13/petstore-provider/internal"
)

func main() {
    plugin.Serve(&plugin.ServeOpts{
        ProviderFunc: func() *schema.Provider {
            return petstore.Provider()
        },
    })
}
```

Well, `main.go` is simple enough. All we are doing in `main` is starting a plugin server via the Terraform plugin SDK v2 and providing it with an implementation of our pet store provider. Let's next look at the `petstore.Provider` implementation in `internal/provider.go`:

```
// Provider is the entry point for defining the Terraform
provider, and will create a new Pet Store provider.
func Provider() *schema.Provider {
    return &schema.Provider{
        Schema: map[string]*schema.Schema{
            "host": {
```

```
                Type:        schema.TypeString,
                Optional:    true,
                DefaultFunc: schema.
EnvDefaultFunc("PETSTORE_HOST", nil),
            },
        },
        ResourcesMap: map[string]*schema.Resource{
            "petstore_pet": resourcePet(),
        },
        DataSourcesMap: map[string]*schema.Resource{
            "petstore_pet": dataSourcePet(),
        },
        ConfigureContextFunc: configure,
    }
}
```

There are only two funcs in `provider.go`. The `Provider` func creates an `*schema.Provider` that describes the schema for configuring the provider, the resources of the provider, the data sources of the provider, and the configure func for initializing the provider. The resource map for the provider contains resources by a string name and their schemas. The schemas for each of the structures describe the domain-specific language to Terraform for interacting with their fields and resource hierarchies. We will examine the schemas for these structures in more detail soon.

Next, let's look at the `configure` func in `provider.go`:

```
// configure builds a new Pet Store client the provider will
use to interact with the Pet Store service
func configure(_ context.Context, data *schema.ResourceData)
(interface{}, diag.Diagnostics) {
    // Warning or errors can be collected in a slice type
    var diags diag.Diagnostics

    host, ok := data.Get("host").(string)
    if !ok {
        return nil, diag.Errorf("the host (127.0.0.1:443)
must be provided explicitly or via env var PETSTORE_HOST")
    }

    c, err := client.New(host)
    if err != nil {
        return nil, append(diags, diag.Diagnostic{
            Severity: diag.Error,
```

```
                Summary:  "Unable to create Pet Store client",
                Detail:   "Unable to connect to the Pet Store
service",
        })
    }

    return c, diags
}
```

The `configure` func is responsible for handling provider configuration. Note how the `host` data described in the preceding `Provider` schema is available via the `data` argument. This is a common pattern you will see throughout the provider. We use the `host` configuration data to construct the client for the pet store service. If we are unable to construct a pet store client, we append a `diag.Diagnostic` structure to the slice of `diag.Diagnostics`. These diagnostic structures inform Terraform of an event of varying severity occurring in the provider. In this case, it is an error if we are unable to build the client, which should be communicated back to the user. If all goes well, we return the `client` instance and an empty slice of `diag.Diagnostics`.

Next, let's examine the pet store data source.

Implementing the pet store data source

The pet store data source is a bit simpler than the resource implementation, given that a data source is intended as a way for Terraform to pull in data from an external API and is read-only in this case. The pet store data source is defined in `internal/data_source_pet.go`.

There are three functions of primary interest in the pet store data source. We will approach them one at a time. Let's start with the `dataSourcePet` func:

```
func dataSourcePet() *schema.Resource {
    return &schema.Resource{
        ReadContext: dataSourcePetRead,
        Schema:      getPetDataSchema(),
    }
}
```

The preceding function creates the `*schema.Resource` data source by providing a schema for the data being provided via `getPetDataSchema`. `ReadContext` expects a function that is responsible for translating the input schema, querying the external API, and returning data to Terraform that matches the structure defined in the schema.

The definition of `getPetDataSchema` is located in `internal/schema.go`, and it is helpful to review it prior to examining the code in `dataSourcePetRead`. We will break down the function into two parts, the input and the computed output:

```
func getPetDataSchema() map[string]*schema.Schema {
    return map[string]*schema.Schema{
        "pet_id": {
            Type:     schema.TypeString,
            Optional: true,
        },
        "name": {
            Type:             schema.TypeString,
            Optional:         true,
            ValidateDiagFunc: validateName(),
        },
        "type": {
            Type:             schema.TypeString,
            Optional:         true,
            ValidateDiagFunc: validateType(),
        },
        "birthday": {
            Type:             schema.TypeString,
            Optional:         true,
            ValidateDiagFunc: validateBirthday(),
        },
```

The preceding schema describes the data structure for the pet store pet data source. Each of the top-level keys is marked as optional and will be used to filter the data source. For example, the name key specifies that it is optional, is of type string, and should be validated with the `validateName` func. We will examine validations in more detail later in the section.

The following is the schema for the output of the data source:

```
        "pets": {
            Type:     schema.TypeList,
            Computed: true,
            Elem: &schema.Resource{
                Schema: map[string]*schema.Schema{
                    "id": {
                        Type:     schema.TypeString,
```

```
                            Computed: true,
                    },
                    "name": {
                        Type:     schema.TypeString,
                        Computed: true,
                    },
                    "type": {
                        Type:     schema.TypeString,
                        Computed: true,
                    },
                    "birthday": {
                        Type:     schema.TypeString,
                        Computed: true,
                    },
                },
            },
        },
    }
}
```

The `pets` key contains all the `Computed` values, which means each of the values is read-only. These represent the list result of the query.

Now that we have a better understanding of the data schema we are working with, let's continue with the implementation of `dataSourcePetRead`:

```
// dataSourcePetRead finds pets in the pet store given an ID
func dataSourcePetRead(ctx context.Context, data *schema.
ResourceData, meta interface{}) diag.Diagnostics {
    psClient, err := clientFromMeta(meta)
    if err != nil {
        return diag.FromErr(err)
    }

    pets, err := findPetsInStore(ctx, psClient,
findPetsRequest{
        Name:     data.Get("name").(string),
        Birthday: data.Get("birthday").(string),
        Type:     PetType(data.Get("type").(string)),
        ID:       data.Get("pet_id").(string),
    })
    if err != nil {
        return diag.FromErr(err)
```

```
        }

        // always run
        data.SetId(strconv.FormatInt(time.Now().Unix(), 10))

        if err := data.Set("pets", flattenPets(pets)); err != nil
{
                return diag.FromErr(err)
        }

        return nil
}
```

In `dataSourcePetRead`, we instantiate a client for the pet store service, populate the filter criteria from the data schema supplied, and then set the `pets` key in the `data` argument with the pets returned from the pet store service in the key value format specified by the schema. The `flattenPets` function is responsible for transforming the protobuf structures we receive from the pet store service into the format expected by the schema. If you are interested in the implementation, it is not terribly elegant, but it is simple.

I purposely didn't mention the `data.SetId` function. We are setting the value of that to a value that will cause the data to be fetched from the pet store service each time. Terraform identifies that data has changed if the ID for that data has changed. This ensures that the ID changes each time the function is executed.

In the `configure` func, we created the pet store client, so how did we gain access to that client in the data source? We can find the answer to that in the `clientFromMeta` func:

```
// clientFromMeta casts meta into a Pet Store client or returns
an error
func clientFromMeta(meta interface{}) (*client.Client, error) {
    psClient, ok := meta.(*client.Client)
    if !ok {
            return nil, errors.New("meta does not contain a Pet
Store client")
    }

    return psClient, nil
}
```

The `clientFromMeta` func takes the `meta interface{}` argument passed into the `ReadContext` func and casts it as the pet store client. The `meta` variable contains the variable returned in the `configure` func. This is not as intuitive as we would like, but it is effective.

With the code described previously and some helpers from `internal/data_source_pet.go`, we have implemented a filtered data source to the pet store API that we can use in Terraform configuration files.

Next, let's take a look at how we handle CRUD interactions for pet resources.

Implementing the Pet resource

The implementation for the Pet resource follows many of the same patterns as the pet store data source, but with the pet resources, we also need to implement create, update, and delete interactions in addition to read. Unless otherwise stated, the code we cover for the pet resource implementation is in `internal/resource_pet.go`.

Let's start by examining the `resourcePet` func, which is the func called when we created the provider schema:

```go
func resourcePet() *schema.Resource {
    return &schema.Resource{
        CreateContext: resourcePetCreate,
        ReadContext:   resourcePetRead,
        UpdateContext: resourcePetUpdate,
        DeleteContext: resourcePetDelete,
        Schema:        getPetResourceSchema(),
        Importer: &schema.ResourceImporter{
            StateContext: schema.ImportStatePassthroughContext,
        },
    }
}
```

Just like the pet store data source, the pet resource defines handlers for each CRUD operation as well as a schema. Before we get into the CRUD operations, let's first look at the schema, which is in `internal/schema.go`:

```go
func getPetResourceSchema() map[string]*schema.Schema {
    return map[string]*schema.Schema{
        "id": {
            Type:     schema.TypeString,
            Optional: true,
            Computed: true,
        },
        "name": {
            Type:     schema.TypeString,
            Required: true,
```

```
                ValidateDiagFunc: validateName(),
        },
        "type": {
                Type:             schema.TypeString,
                Required:         true,
                ValidateDiagFunc: validateType(),
        },
        "birthday": {
                Type:             schema.TypeString,
                Required:         true,
                ValidateDiagFunc: validateBirthday(),
        },
    }
}
```

The schema defined here is simpler than the data source schema, since we are not defining query filters. Note that the `id` key is computed, but all the others are not. The `id` value is generated by the pet store service and is not to be specified by the user.

Since these values are specified by the user as a string, validation becomes more significant. For a better user experience, we want to provide feedback to a user when a value is invalid. Let's take a look at how we validate the `type` field with the `validateType` func:

```
func validateType() schema.SchemaValidateDiagFunc {
    return validateDiagFunc(validation.StringInSlice([]string{
        string(DogPetType),
        string(CatPetType),
        string(ReptilePetType),
        string(BirdPetType),
    }, true))
}
```

The `validateType` func returns a validation constructed with each valid value of the enumeration. This prevents a user from entering a string value for a pet type that is not supported in the pet store. The rest of the validations take a similar approach to validating the range of input values.

Now that we have explored the schema, we are prepared to explore the CRUD operations. Let's start with the `read` operation:

```go
// resourcePetRead finds a pet in the pet store by ID and
populate the resource data
func resourcePetRead(ctx context.Context, data *schema.
ResourceData, meta interface{}) diag.Diagnostics {
    psClient, err := clientFromMeta(meta)
    if err != nil {
        return diag.FromErr(err)
    }

    pets, err := findPetsInStore(ctx, psClient,
findPetsRequest{ID: data.Id()})
    if err != nil {
        return diag.FromErr(err)
    }

    if len(pets) == 0 {
        return nil
    }

    return setDataFromPet(pets[0], data)
}
```

The `resourcePetRead` func fetches the pet store client from the `meta` argument and then finds the pet by ID in the store. If the pet is found, the `data` argument is updated with data from the pet.

That's simple enough. Next, let's look at create:

```go
// resourcePetCreate creates a pet in the pet store
func resourcePetCreate(ctx context.Context, data *schema.
ResourceData, meta interface{}) diag.Diagnostics {
    psClient, err := clientFromMeta(meta)
    if err != nil {
        return diag.FromErr(err)
    }

    pet := &client.Pet{Pet: &pb.Pet{}}
    diags := fillPetFromData(pet, data)
    ids, err := psClient.AddPets(ctx, []*pb.Pet{pet.Pet})
    if err != nil {
        return append(diags, diag.FromErr(err)...)
```

```
        data.SetId(ids[0])
        return diags
}
```

The `resourcePetCreate` func follows a similar pattern. The difference is that the pet is constructed from fields in the `data` argument, and then the pet store API is called to add the pet to the store. In the end, the ID for the new pet is set.

Next, let's look at update:

```
// resourcePetUpdate updates a pet in the pet store by ID
func resourcePetUpdate(ctx context.Context, data *schema.ResourceData, meta interface{}) diag.Diagnostics {
    psClient, err := clientFromMeta(meta)
    if err != nil {
        return diag.FromErr(err)
    }

    pets, err := findPetsInStore(ctx, psClient, findPetsRequest{ID: data.Id()})
    if err != nil {
        return diag.FromErr(err)
    }

    if len(pets) == 0 {
        return diag.Diagnostics{
            {
                Severity: diag.Error,
                Summary:  "no pet was found",
                Detail:   "no pet was found when trying to update the pet by ID",
            },
        }
    }

    pet := pets[0]
    diags := fillPetFromData(pet, data)
    if diags.HasError() {
        return diags
    }
```

```
        if err := psClient.UpdatePets(ctx, []*pb.Pet{pet.Pet});
err != nil {
                return append(diags, diag.FromErr(err)...)
        }

        return diags
}
```

The `resourcePetUpdate` func combines parts of read and create. Initially, we need to check to see whether the pet is in the store and fetch the pet data. If we don't find the pet, we return an error. If we do find the pet, we update the fields of the pet and call `UpdatePets` on the pet store client.

The delete operation is relatively trivial, so I will not dive into it here. If you want, you can take a look at `resourcePetDelete` to see for yourself.

At this point, we have now implemented the pet resource and are ready to see our Terraform provider in action.

Running the pet store provider

Now that we have a fully implemented pet store provider, the fun part is running it. From the root of the pet store provider, run the following commands. Be sure to have Docker running:

```
$ docker-compose up -d
$ make
$ cd examples
$ terraform init && terraform apply
```

The preceding commands will start the pet store service using `docker-compose`, build and install the provider, move it into the example directory, and finally, use `init` and `apply` to create our desired state containing our pets.

When `init` executes, you should see something like the following:

```
Initializing the backend...

Initializing provider plugins...
- Finding example.com/gofordevops/petstore versions matching "0.1.0"...
- Installing example.com/gofordevops/petstore v0.1.0...
- Installed example.com/gofordevops/petstore v0.1.0 (unauthenticated)
```

Yay! The provider is installed and Terraform is ready to apply our resources.

After Terraform has applied the resources, you should see the following output:

```
Apply complete! Resources: 2 added, 0 changed, 0 destroyed.

Outputs:

all_pets = {
  "birthday" = tostring(null)
  "id" = "1648955761"
  "name" = tostring(null)
  "pet_id" = tostring(null)
  "pets" = tolist([
    {
      "birthday" = "2020-06-25T00:00:00Z"
      "id" = "495b1c94-6f67-46f2-9d4d-e84cc182d523"
      "name" = "Tron"
      "type" = "cat"
    },
    {
      "birthday" = "2021-04-01T00:00:00Z"
      "id" = "36e65cb2-18ea-4aec-a410-7bad64d7b00d"
      "name" = "Thor"
      "type" = "dog"
    },
  ])
  "type" = tostring(null)
}
thor = {
  "36e65cb2-18ea-4aec-a410-7bad64d7b00d" = {
    "birthday" = "2021-04-01T00:00:00Z"
    "id" = "36e65cb2-18ea-4aec-a410-7bad64d7b00d"
    "name" = "Thor"
    "type" = "dog"
  }
}
```

We can see from the preceding output that both of our resources, Tron and Thor, have been added, and our data source when queried with no filters returned each of the pets. Lastly, we can see the thor output was returned, containing the data for Thor.

Let's review examples/main.tf again and see where the thor output came from:

```
variable "pet_name" {
  type    = string
  default = "Thor"
}

data "petstore_pet" "all" {
  depends_on = [petstore_pet.thor, petstore_pet.tron]
}

# Only returns Thor by name
output "thor" {
  value = {
    for pet in data.petstore_pet.all.pets :
    pet.id => pet
    if pet.name == var.pet_name
  }
}
```

In the preceding main.tf file, we defined a pet_name variable with the value of Thor. We then queried the pet store data source, providing no filters but depending on the completion of both of the resources in the file. Lastly, we output a key of thor, with the value being a query that matches only when pet.name equals var.pet_name. This filtered the data source for only pets named Thor.

You can now use any of the Terraform skills you've learned thus far to manipulate pet store resources. There really wasn't all that much code to implement.

Publishing custom providers

Anyone can publish a provider to the Terraform Registry by logging into it using a GitHub account. Again, HashiCorp has excellent documentation on how to publish a provider. We will not walk through the process in this book, as the documentation for *Release and Publish a Provider to the Terraform Registry* (https://learn.hashicorp.com/tutorials/terraform/provider-release-publish) is likely sufficient if you have reached this far in your journey building your own Terraform provider.

Summary

In this chapter, we learned about the history of IaC and the advantages of leveraging the practice to bring software development and operations together by setting a shared context for expressing and continuously testing infrastructure. We learned where Terraform lies in the ecosystem of IaC tooling and how to use it to describe desired infrastructure states, mutate existing infrastructure, deploy a cloud infrastructure, and finally, create our own resources for automating external APIs. You should now be prepared with the tools needed to improve your own software projects.

In the next chapter, we will learn how to use Go to deploy applications to Kubernetes and build upon that knowledge to understand how to extend it with Go. We'll enable our Kubernetes users to reconcile pets as custom Kubernetes resources.

14
Deploying and Building Applications in Kubernetes

It's difficult to overstate the impact Kubernetes has had on the world of DevOps. Over the years since it was open sourced by Google in 2014, Kubernetes has experienced a meteoric rise in popularity. In that period, Kubernetes has become the preeminent solution for orchestrating cloud-native container workloads, differentiating itself from a field of orchestrators such as Apache Mesos and Docker Swarm. By providing a common API over heterogeneous environments, Kubernetes has become the common tool for deploying applications across cloud and hybrid environments.

So, what is Kubernetes? According to its documentation, *"Kubernetes is a portable, extensible, open source platform for managing containerized workloads and services, that facilitates both declarative configuration and automation"* (`https://kubernetes.io/docs/concepts/overview/what-is-kubernetes/`). That is a lot to unpack. I'll sum up that statement a little differently. Kubernetes is a set of APIs and abstractions that makes running containerize applications easier. It provides services such as service discovery, load balancing, storage abstraction and orchestration, automated rollouts and rollbacks, self-healing, and secret, certificate, and configuration management. Furthermore, if Kubernetes doesn't offer a specific bit of functionality you need directly, there is likely a solution available in the vibrant open source ecosystem built around the core of Kubernetes. The Kubernetes ecosystem is a vast set of tools for you to achieve your operational objectives without needing to reinvent the wheel.

All of the aforementioned functionality is exposed through the Kubernetes API and is infinitely programmable.

This chapter will not be a deep dive into all aspects of Kubernetes. To properly explore Kubernetes in depth would require multiple books. The good news is there are many great books on the topic: `https://www.packtpub.com/catalogsearch/result?q=kubernetes`. Also, the fantastic community-driven documentation (`https://kubernetes.io/docs/home/`) for Kubernetes is an invaluable resource for getting a deeper understanding of it.

The goal of this chapter is to provide a starting point for your journey in programming Kubernetes using Go. We will start by creating a simple Go program to deploy a Kubernetes resource to a local Kubernetes cluster to run a load-balanced HTTP service. We will then learn how to extend the Kubernetes API with custom resources to show how Kubernetes can be used to orchestrate and manage any external resource. We will build custom pet resources that will be stored in our pet store service running within the cluster to illustrate the concept of managing external resources. By the end of this chapter, you will be equipped with the knowledge to work effectively with the Kubernetes API and understand some of the core design principles of Kubernetes.

We will cover the following topics in this chapter:

- Interacting with the Kubernetes API
- Deploying a load-balanced HTTP application using Go
- Extending Kubernetes with custom resources and operators
- Building a pet store operator

Technical requirements

This chapter will require the following tools:

- Docker: `https://docs.docker.com/get-docker/`
- KinD: `https://kind.sigs.k8s.io/#installation-and-usage`
- operator-sdk: `https://sdk.operatorframework.io/docs/installation/`
- Tilt.dev: `https://docs.tilt.dev/install.html`
- ctlptl: `https://github.com/tilt-dev/ctlptl#how-do-i-install-it`

The code files for this chapter can be downloaded from `https://github.com/PacktPublishing/Go-for-DevOps/tree/rev0/chapter/14`

Interacting with the Kubernetes API

In the introduction, we talked about the Kubernetes API as if it is just one thing, although in a sense it can be thought of in that way. However, the Kubernetes API we have been talking about is an aggregation of multiple APIs served by the core of Kubernetes, the control plane API server. The API server exposes an HTTP API that exposes the aggregated API and allows for the query and manipulation of API objects such as Pods, Deployments, Services, and Namespaces.

In this section, we will learn how to use KinD to create a local cluster. We will use the local cluster to manipulate a namespace resource using `kubectl`. We will examine the basic structure of a Kubernetes resource and see how we can address individual resources by their Group, Version, Kind, Name, and usually, Namespace. Lastly, we'll discuss authentication and the `kubeconfig` file. This section will prepare us for interacting with the Kubernetes API at a lower level using Go.

Creating a KinD cluster

Prior to getting started interacting with the Kubernetes API, let's build a local Kubernetes cluster using **KinD**. This is a tool that enables us to create a Kubernetes cluster locally using Docker rather than running as services on the host. To create the cluster, run the following:

```
$ kind create cluster
```

The preceding command will create a cluster named `kind`. It will build a Kubernetes control plane and set the current context of `kubectl` to point to the newly created cluster.

You can list the clusters created by `kind` by running the following:

```
$ kind get clusters
kind
```

You can see from the output of `get clusters` that there is a new cluster named `kind` created.

Using kubectl to interact with the API

Kubernetes offers a command-line tool for interacting with the API, `kubectl`. There are some nice developer experience features in `kubectl`, but its main use is to perform **Create, Read, Update, Delete** (**CRUD**) operations targeting the API server. For example, let's look at two ways to create a namespace using `kubectl`:

```
$ kubectl create namespace petstore
```

The preceding command creates a namespace named `petstore`:

```
$ cat <<EOF | kubectl create -f -
apiVersion: v1
kind: Namespace
metadata:
  name: petstore
EOF
```

The preceding command creates the same namespace with an inline YAML document. Next, let's use `kubectl` to fetch the namespace as YAML:

```
$ kubectl get namespace petstore -o yaml
apiVersion: v1
kind: Namespace
metadata:
  creationTimestamp: "2022-03-06T15:55:09Z"
  labels:
    kubernetes.io/metadata.name: petstore
  name: petstore
  resourceVersion: "2162"
  uid: cddb2eb8-9c46-4089-9c99-e31259dfcd1c
spec:
  finalizers:
  - kubernetes
```

```
status:
  phase: Active
```

The preceding command fetched the `petstore` namespace and output the entire resource in the `.yaml` format. Pay special attention to the top-level keys, `apiVersion`, `kind`, `metadata`, `spec`, and `status`. The values and structures in these keys will be common to all resources in Kubernetes.

The Group Version Kind (GVK) namespace name

In the Kubernetes API, you can identify any resource by the combination of its group, kind, version, name, and usually, namespace. I say usually namespace since not all resources belong to a namespace. A namespace is an example of a resource that exists outside a namespace (as well as other low-level resources such as Nodes and PersistentVolumes). However, most other resources such as Pods, Services, and Deployments exist within a namespace. For the namespace example from the previous section, the group is omitted, since it is in the Kubernetes core API and is assumed by the API server. Effectively, the identifier for the `petstore` namespace is `apiVersion: v1`, `kind: Namespace`, and `metadata.name: petstore`.

Internalize the idea of a group, version, kind, namespace, and name. It will be critical to understand how to interact with the Kubernetes API.

The spec and status sections

Each resource in Kubernetes has a `spec` and a `status` section. The `spec` section of the resource is a structure that describes the desired state of the resource. It is Kubernetes' job to reconcile the state of the system to achieve that desired state. In some cases, `spec` will describe the desired state of an external system. For example, `spec` can be a description of a load balancer, including the desired external IP. The reconciler for that resource would be responsible for creating a network interface and setting up routing to ensure that the IP routes to that specific network interface.

The `status` section of the resource is a structure that describes the current state of the resource. It is intended to be mutated by Kubernetes, not the user. For example, `status` for a Deployment includes the number of ready replicas of a given Deployment. `spec` for the Deployment will contain the desired number of replicas. It is Kubernetes' job to drive toward that desired state and update the `status` with the current state of the resource.

We will learn more about `spec` and `status` as we progress in this chapter.

Authentication

So far, we have just assumed access to the Kubernetes cluster, but that was actually handled for us by `kind` and its ability to set the default context for `kubectl`. The default context for `kubectl` is stored in your home directory. You can see what was set by running the following command:

```
$ cat ~/.kube/config
apiVersion: v1
clusters:
- cluster:
    certificate-authority-data:
    server: https://127.0.0.1:55451
  name: kind-kind
contexts:
- context:
    cluster: kind-kind
    user: kind-kind
  name: kind-kind
current-context: kind-kind
kind: Config
preferences: {}
users:
- name: kind-kind
  user:
    client-certificate-data:
    client-key-data:
```

In the preceding output, I've omitted the certificate data to provide a more concise view of the config. It contains all the information we need to create a secure connection to the local cluster instance. Note the address of the service and the names of the cluster and the user.

By running the following command, we can get the `kubeconfig` for the `kind` cluster:

```
$ kind get kubeconfig --name kind > .tmp-kubeconfig
```

If you cat the contents of the file, you will see a very similar structure in ~/.kube/config. The kubeconfig file is a convenient way to encapsulate the information needed to authenticate to the API server and is used with many of the tools in the Kubernetes ecosystem. For example, you can override the context of kubectl to use a different kubeconfig with the following command:

```
$ KUBECONFIG=./.tmp-kubeconfig kubectl get namespaces
```

The preceding command will list all the namespaces in the kind cluster, but it will use the local kubeconfig file we just created.

There are a variety of tools for managing whichever cluster you are using. One great example is kubectx (https://ahmet.im/blog/kubectx/) from Ahmet Alp Balkan, which can be used to work fluently with multiple clusters. As I mentioned previously, the vibrant open source ecosystem provides a wide variety of tools to make your experience using Kubernetes delightful.

Finally, let's clean up the petstore namespace and delete our kind cluster:

```
$ kubectl delete namespace petstore
$ kind delete cluster --name kind
```

In this section, we learned the basics of interacting with the Kubernetes API and the basic structure of Kubernetes resources. We are able to create a local Kubernetes experience, and we are ready to approach building an application to interact with Kubernetes using Go.

In the next section, we are going to leverage what we have learned about the Kubernetes API and use that to build a Go application to deploy a load-balanced HTTP application.

Deploying a load-balanced HTTP application using Go

Now that we understand a bit more about the Kubernetes API and the resources exposed by the API, we can move away from kubectl toward using Go.

In this section, we will use Go to do many of the same things we did in the previous section using kubectl. We will authenticate using our default context and create a namespace. However, we will not stop there. We will deploy a load-balanced HTTP application to our cluster and watch the logs stream to STDOUT as we make requests to the service.

The code for this section can be found at https://github.com/PacktPublishing/Go-for-DevOps/tree/rev0/chapter/14/workloads. The demo we are about to walk through can be executed with the following commands:

```
$ kind create cluster --name workloads --config kind-config.yaml
$ kubectl apply -f https://raw.githubusercontent.com/kubernetes/ingress-nginx/main/deploy/static/provider/kind/deploy.yaml
$ kubectl wait --namespace ingress-nginx \
  --for=condition=ready pod \
  --selector=app.kubernetes.io/component=controller \
  --timeout=90s
$ go run .
```

The preceding command will create a KinD cluster named `workloads` and use a config file that will enable host network ingress for the cluster. We will use ingress to expose the service running in the cluster on `localhost:port`. The command then deploys the NGINX ingress controller and waits for it to be ready. Finally, we run our Go program to deploy our application. After the service has been deployed and is running, open a browser at `http://localhost:8080/hello`. You should see the following when you browse there:

Figure 14.1 – The deployed NGINX hello world

You should see the request logs stream to STDOUT. They should look like the following:

```
10.244.0.7 - - [07/Mar/2022:02:34:59 +0000] "GET /hello
HTTP/1.1" 200 7252 "-" "Mozilla/5.0 (Macintosh; Intel Mac OS X
10_15_7) AppleWebKit/605.1.15 (KHTML, like Gecko) Version/15.3
Safari/605.1.15" "172.22.0.1"
```

If you refresh the page, you should see the server name change, indicating that the requests are load balancing across the two pod replicas in the deployment. Press *Ctrl + C* to terminate the Go program.

To tear down the cluster, run the following command:

```
$ kind delete cluster --name workloads
```

The preceding command will delete the `kind` cluster named `workloads`. Next, let's explore this Go application to understand what just happened.

It all starts with main

Let's dive right into the code and see what is happening in this Go program:

```go
func main() {
    ctx, cancel := context.WithCancel(context.Background())
    defer cancel()

    clientSet := getClientSet()

    nsFoo := createNamespace(ctx, clientSet, "foo")
    defer func() {
        deleteNamespace(ctx, clientSet, nsFoo)
    }()

    deployNginx(ctx, clientSet, nsFoo, "hello-world")
    fmt.Printf("You can now see your running service: http://localhost:8080/hello\n\n")

    listenToPodLogs(ctx, clientSet, nsFoo, "hello-world")

    // wait for ctrl-c to exit the program
    waitForExitSignal()
}
```

In the preceding code, we establish a context derived from the background context. This is largely ineffectual in this scenario but would be a powerful tool in the future if you needed to cancel a request that is taking too long. Next, we create `clientSet`, which is a strongly typed client for interacting with the Kubernetes API. We then use `clientSet` in `createNamespace`, `deployNginx`, and `listenToPodLogs`. Finally, we wait for a signal to terminate the program. That's it!

Next, let's delve into each function, starting with `getClientSet`.

Creating a ClientSet

Let's take a look at `getClientSet`:

```go
func getClientSet() *kubernetes.Clientset {
    var kubeconfig *string
    if home := homedir.HomeDir(); home != "" {
        kubeconfig = flag.String(
            "kubeconfig",
            filepath.Join(home, ".kube", "config"),
            "(optional) absolute path to the kubeconfig file",
        )
    } else {
        kubeconfig = flag.String(
            "kubeconfig",
            "",
            "absolute path to the kubeconfig file",
        )
    }
    flag.Parse()
    // use the current context in kubeconfig
    config, err := clientcmd.BuildConfigFromFlags(
        "",
        *kubeconfig,
    )
    panicIfError(err)

    // create the clientSet
    cs, err := kubernetes.NewForConfig(config)
    panicIfError(err)
    return cs
}
```

In the preceding code, you can see that we build flag bindings to either use the existing `~/.kube/config` context or accept a `kubeconfig` file via an absolute file path. We then build a config using this flag or default. The config is then used to create `*kubernetes.ClientSet`. As we learned in the kubectl section, `kubeconfig` contains all the information we need to connect and authenticate to the server. We now have a client ready to interact with the Kubernetes cluster.

Next, let's see the `ClientSet` in action.

Creating a namespace

Now that we have a `ClientSet`, we can use it to create the resource we need to deploy our load-balanced HTTP application. Let's take a look at `createNamespace`:

```go
func createNamespace(
    ctx context.Context,
    clientSet *kubernetes.Clientset,
    name string,
) *corev1.Namespace {
    fmt.Printf("Creating namespace %q.\n\n", name)
    ns := &corev1.Namespace{
        ObjectMeta: metav1.ObjectMeta{
            Name: name,
        },
    }
    ns, err := clientSet.CoreV1().
        Namespaces().
        Create(ctx, ns, metav1.CreateOptions{})
    panicIfError(err)
    return ns
}
```

In the preceding code, we build a `corev1.Namespace` structure, supplying the name in the `ObjectMeta` field. If you recall from our YAML example that created a namespace using `kubectl`, this field maps to `metadata.name`. The Go structures of the Kubernetes resource map closely to their YAML representations. Finally, we use `clientSet` to create the namespace via the Kubernetes API server and return the namespace. The `metav1.CreateOptions` contains some options for changing the behavior of the `create` operation, but we will not explore this structure in this book.

We have now created the namespace where we will deploy our application. Let's see how we will deploy the application.

Deploying the application into the namespace

Now that we have `clientSet` and namespace created, we are ready to deploy the resources that will represent our application. Let's have a look at the `deployNginx` func:

```
func deployNginx(
    ctx context.Context,
    clientSet *kubernetes.Clientset,
    ns *corev1.Namespace,
    name string,
) {
    deployment := createNginxDeployment(
        ctx,
        clientSet,
        ns,
        name,
    )
    waitForReadyReplicas(ctx, clientSet, deployment)
    createNginxService(ctx, clientSet, ns, name)
    createNginxIngress(ctx, clientSet, ns, name)
}
```

In the preceding code, we create the NGINX deployment resource and wait for the replicas of the deployment to be ready. After the deployment is ready, the code creates the service resource to load-balance across the pods in the deployment. Finally, we create the ingress resource to expose the service on a local host port.

Next, let's review each of these functions to understand what they are doing.

Creating the NGINX deployment

The first function in deploying our application is `createNginxDeployment`:

```
func createNginxDeployment(
    ctx context.Context,
    clientSet *kubernetes.Clientset,
    ns *corev1.Namespace,
    name string,
) *appv1.Deployment {
    var (
        matchLabel = map[string]string{"app": "nginx"}
        objMeta    = metav1.ObjectMeta{
            Name:       name,
```

```go
                Namespace: ns.Name,
                Labels:    matchLabel,
        }
            [...]
    )
    deployment := &appv1.Deployment{
            ObjectMeta: objMeta,
            Spec: appv1.DeploymentSpec{
                    Replicas: to.Int32Ptr(2),

                    Selector: &metav1.LabelSelector{
                            MatchLabels: matchLabel,
                    },
                    Template: template,
            },
    }
    deployment, err := clientSet.
            AppsV1().
            Deployments(ns.Name).
            Create(ctx, deployment, metav1.CreateOptions{})
    panicIfError(err)
    return deployment
}
```

The preceding code initializes `matchLabel` with a key/value pair that will be used to connect the Deployment with the Service. We also initialize `ObjectMeta` for the Deployment resource using the namespace and `matchLabel`. Next, we build a Deployment structure containing a spec with two desired replicas, a `LabelSelector` using the `matchLabel` we built earlier, and a pod template that will run a single container with the `nginxdemos/hello:latest` image exposing port `80` on the container. Finally, we create the deployment specifying the namespace and the Deployment structure we've built.

Now that we have created our Deployment, let's see how we wait for the pods in the Deployment to become ready.

Waiting for ready replicas to match desired replicas

When a Deployment is created, pods for each replica need to be created and start running before they will be able to service requests. There is nothing about Kubernetes or the API requests we are authoring that requires us to wait for these pods. This is here just to provide some user feedback and illustrate a use for the status portion of the resource. Let's take a look at how we wait for the Deployment state to match the desired state:

```
func waitForReadyReplicas(
    ctx context.Context,
    clientSet *kubernetes.Clientset,
    deployment *appv1.Deployment,
) {
    fmt.Printf("Waiting for ready replicas in: %q\n", deployment.Name)
    for {
        expectedReplicas := *deployment.Spec.Replicas
        readyReplicas := getReadyReplicasForDeployment(
            ctx,
            clientSet,
            deployment,
        )
        if readyReplicas == expectedReplicas {
            fmt.Printf("replicas are ready!\n\n")
            return
        }
        fmt.Printf("replicas are not ready yet. %d/%d\n",
            readyReplicas, expectedReplicas)
        time.Sleep(1 * time.Second)
    }
}

func getReadyReplicasForDeployment(
    ctx context.Context,
    clientSet *kubernetes.Clientset,
    deployment *appv1.Deployment,
) int32 {
    dep, err := clientSet.
        AppsV1().
        Deployments(deployment.Namespace).
        Get(ctx, deployment.Name, metav1.GetOptions{})
    panicIfError(err)
```

```
        return dep.Status.ReadyReplicas
}
```

In the preceding code, we loop to check for the desired number of replicas to match the number of ready replicas and return if they do. If they do not match, then we sleep for a second and try again. This code is not very resilient, but it illustrates the goal-seeking nature of Kubernetes operations.

Now that we have a running deployment, we can build the Service to load-balance across the pods in the deployment.

Creating a Service to load-balance

The two pod replicas in the deployment are now running the NGINX demo on port 80, but each has its own interface. We can address traffic to each one individually, but it would be more convenient to address a single address and load-balance the requests. Let's create a Service resource to do that:

```
func createNginxService(
    ctx context.Context,
    clientSet *kubernetes.Clientset,
    ns *corev1.Namespace,
    name string,
) {
    var (
        matchLabel = map[string]string{"app": "nginx"}
        objMeta    = metav1.ObjectMeta{
            Name:      name,
            Namespace: ns.Name,
            Labels:    matchLabel,
        }
    )
    service := &corev1.Service{
        ObjectMeta: objMeta,
        Spec: corev1.ServiceSpec{
            Selector: matchLabel,
            Ports: []corev1.ServicePort{
                {
                    Port:     80,
                    Protocol: corev1.ProtocolTCP,
                    Name:     "http",
                },
```

```
            },
        },
    }
    service, err := clientSet.
        CoreV1().
        Services(ns.Name).
        Create(ctx, service, metav1.CreateOptions{})
    panicIfError(err)
}
```

In the preceding code, we initialize the same `matchLabel` and `ObjectMeta` as we did in the deployment. However, instead of creating a Deployment resource, we create a Service resource structure, specifying the Selector to match on and the port to expose over **Transmission Control Protocol** (**TCP**). The Selector label is the key to ensuring that the correct pods are in the backend pool for the load balancer. Finally, we create the Service as we have with the other Kubernetes resources.

We only have one step left. We need to expose our service via an ingress so that we can send traffic into the cluster via a port on the local machine.

Creating an ingress to expose our application on a local host port

At this point, we are unable to reach our service via `localhost:port`. We can forward traffic into the cluster via `kubectl`, but I'll leave that for you to explore. We are going to create an ingress and open a port on our local host network. Let's see how we create the ingress resource:

```
func createNginxIngress(
    ctx context.Context,
    clientSet *kubernetes.Clientset,
    ns *corev1.Namespace,
    name string,
) {
    var (
        prefix  = netv1.PathTypePrefix
        objMeta = metav1.ObjectMeta{
            Name:      name,
            Namespace: ns.Name,
        }
```

```
            ingressPath = netv1.HTTPIngressPath{
                PathType: &prefix,
                Path:     "/hello",
                Backend: netv1.IngressBackend{
                    Service: &netv1.IngressServiceBackend{
                        Name: name,
                        Port: netv1.ServiceBackendPort{
                            Name: "http",
                        },
                    },
                },
            }

    ingress := &netv1.Ingress{
        ObjectMeta: objMeta,
        Spec: netv1.IngressSpec{
            Rules: rules,
        },
    }

    ingress, err := clientSet.
            NetworkingV1().
            Ingresses(ns.Name).
            Create(ctx, ingress, metav1.CreateOptions{})
    panicIfError(err)
}
```

In the preceding code, we initialize a prefix, the same `objMeta` as previously, and `ingressPath`, which will map the path prefix of `/hello` to the service name and port name we created. Yes, Kubernetes does the magic of tying the networking together for us! Next, we build the Ingress structure as we saw with the previous structures and create the ingress using `clientSet`. With this last bit, we deploy our entire application stack using Go and the Kubernetes API.

Next, let's return to `main.go` and look at how we can use Kubernetes to stream the logs of the pods to show the incoming HTTP requests while the program is running.

Streaming pod logs for the NGINX application

The Kubernetes API exposes a bunch of great features for running workloads. One of the most basic and useful is the ability to access logs for running pods. Let's see how we can stream logs from multiple running pods to STDOUT:

```
func listenToPodLogs(
    ctx context.Context,
    clientSet *kubernetes.Clientset,
    ns *corev1.Namespace,
    containerName string,
) {
    // list all the pods in namespace foo
    podList := listPods(ctx, clientSet, ns)
    for _, pod := range podList.Items {
        podName := pod.Name
        go func() {
            opts := &corev1.PodLogOptions{
                Container: containerName,
                Follow:    true,
            }
            podLogs, err := clientSet.
                CoreV1().
                Pods(ns.Name).
                GetLogs(podName, opts).
                Stream(ctx)
            panicIfError(err)
            _, _ = os.Stdout.ReadFrom(podLogs)
        }()
    }
}

func listPods(
    ctx context.Context,
    clientSet *kubernetes.Clientset,
    ns *corev1.Namespace,
) *corev1.PodList {
    podList, err := clientSet.
        CoreV1().
        Pods(ns.Name).
        List(ctx, metav1.ListOptions{})
    panicIfError(err)
```

```
        /* omitted some logging for brevity */
        return podList
}
```

In the preceding code, `listenToPodLogs` lists the pods in the given namespace and then starts `go func` for each one. In `go func`, we use the Kubernetes API to request a stream of `podLogs`, which returns `io.ReadCloser` to deliver logs from the pod as they are created. We then tell STDOUT to read from that pipe, and the logs land in our STDOUT.

If you thought that getting logs from your running workloads was going to be a lot tougher than this, I don't think you would be alone. Kubernetes is quite complex, but the concept that everything is exposed as an API makes the platform incredibly flexible and programmable.

We have explored every function except `waitForExitSignal`, which is relatively trivial and doesn't add anything to the Kubernetes story told here. If you'd like to take a look at it, refer to the source repository.

Having explored this example of using the Kubernetes API to programmatically deploy an application using Go, I hope you will take away from the experience a feeling of empowerment to go and learn, build, and feel relatively comfortable interacting with the Kubernetes API. There is so much more to the Kubernetes API, and it's ever-growing. In fact, in the next section, we are going to start talking about how we can extend the Kubernetes API with our own custom resources.

Extending Kubernetes with custom resources and operators

In the previous sections, we've learned that the Kubernetes API is not just a single API but also an aggregation of APIs backed by cooperative services called **operators** and **controllers**. Operators are extensions to Kubernetes that make use of custom resources to manage systems and applications via controllers. Controllers are components of operators that execute control loops for a kind of resource. A control loop for a custom resource is an iterative process that observes a desired state of the resource and works, possibly over several loops, to drive the state of a system to that desired state.

Those previous sentences are rather abstract. I like to sum it up differently. Kubernetes is a platform for automation. An automation is a series of steps and decision trees that drives to reach an end goal. I like to think of operators in a similar way. I think of writing operators as taking a runbook, the human steps for completing an operational activity, and making the computer execute the automation. Operators and controllers are like crystallizing operational knowledge into code to be run in Kubernetes.

Custom resources can represent anything. They can be things related to Kubernetes resources, or they can be something completely external to Kubernetes. For an example of a custom resource related to cluster workloads, in *Chapter 9, Observability with OpenTelemetry*, we discussed the OTel collector and deployed it via its container image in `docker-compose`, but we could have used the Kubernetes operator for OTel to do the same thing in a Kubernetes cluster. The OTel operator exposes a custom resource, like the following:

```
apiVersion: opentelemetry.io/v1alpha1
kind: OpenTelemetryCollector
metadata:
  name: simplest
spec:
  config: |
    receivers:
      otlp:
        protocols:
          grpc:
          http:
    processors:

    exporters:
      logging:

    service:
      pipelines:
        traces:
          receivers: [otlp]
          processors: []
          exporters: [logging]
```

In the preceding code block, we see a custom resource describing the OTel collector from `https://github.com/open-telemetry/opentelemetry-operator`. This custom resource describes in a domain-specific language how the OpenTelemetry operator should configure and run an OpenTelemetry collector. However, a custom resource can as easily be a custom `Pet` resource that represents a pet in a pet store, as we will see in the next section.

Do you remember how to identify the group, version, kind, namespace, and name for the preceding resource? The answer is `group: opentelemetry.io`, `version: v1alpha1`, `kind: OpenTelemetryCollector`, `namespace: default`, and `name: simplest`.

In this section, I want to impress upon you that if someone were to strip away pods, nodes, storage, networks, and much of the rest of the Kubernetes container workload scheduling and all that was left was the Kubernetes API server, it would still be an incredibly useful piece of software. In this section, we are going to cover a bit of background about operators, **custom resource definitions** (**CRDs**), controllers, and powerful features of the Kubernetes API server. We will not be able to cover all of it in depth, but this survey will help to implement our first operator and hopefully encourage you to learn more about extending the Kubernetes API.

Custom Resource Definitions

CRDs are resources that can be applied to a Kubernetes cluster to create a new RESTful resource path for a custom resource. Let's take a look at the example of a CronJob from the Kubernetes docs: `https://kubernetes.io/docs/tasks/extend-kubernetes/custom-resources/custom-resource-definitions/#create-a-customresourcedefinition`.

```
apiVersion: apiextensions.k8s.io/v1
kind: CustomResourceDefinition
metadata:
  # name must be in the form: <plural>.<group>
  name: crontabs.stable.example.com
spec:
  # group name to use for REST API: /apis/<group>/<version>
  group: stable.example.com
  # list of versions supported by this CustomResourceDefinition
  versions:
    - name: v1
      # Each version can be enabled/disabled by Served flag.
      served: true
```

```yaml
      # only one version must be marked as the storage version.
      storage: true
      schema:
        openAPIV3Schema:
          type: object
          properties:
            spec:
              type: object
              properties:
                cronSpec:
                  type: string
                image:
                  type: string
                replicas:
                  type: integer
  # either Namespaced or Cluster
  scope: Namespaced
  names:
    plural: crontabs
    singular: crontab
    kind: CronTab
    shortNames:
    - ct
```

As you can see from the preceding YAML, a CRD is specified as any other resource in Kubernetes. The CRD resource has `group`, `version`, `kind`, and `name`, but within the `spec`, you can see metadata describing a new resource type with a strongly typed schema, using OpenAPI V3 to describe the schema. Also, note that the spec contains the group, version, and kind of the custom resource. As implied by the YAML structure, there can be multiple versions of the custom resource served at any given time, but only one version can be marked as the storage version.

In the next section, we'll discuss how Kubernetes is able to store only one version but serve multiple versions.

Custom resource versioning and conversion

As mentioned in the previous section, Kubernetes will store only one version of a resource. A new version of a resource is usually introduced when there is a change to the schema of that resource – for example, a new field was added or some other mutation of the schema. In this case, Kubernetes would need some way to translate between resource versions. The Kubernetes approach to this is to use conversion Webhooks. That means that you can register a Webhook to convert from the storage version of a resource to the requested version. This forms a hub and spoke model for versioning where the hub is the storage version and the spokes are the other supported versions. You can see an example of this in the Kubernetes docs here: `https://kubernetes.io/docs/tasks/extend-kubernetes/custom-resources/custom-resource-definition-versioning/#configure-customresourcedefinition-to-use-conversion-webhooks`.

Take that in for a moment. This is a powerful feature for any API platform to offer. Having a standardized way of translating one API version to another allows for a more graceful adoption of components in a microservice environment.

Structured schema, validation, and defaulting

As we saw in the previous example of the CronJob CRD spec, we are able to use OpenAPI to describe a strongly typed schema for resources. This is highly beneficial for generating API clients for programming languages that may need to interact with the API. Furthermore, we have the ability to describe a variety of validations to ensure different aspects of structure and values for resources. For example, we are able to describe what fields are required, valid ranges of values, valid patterns of strings, and many other aspects of the structures and values. Additionally, we can provide default values for fields and specify them in the schema.

Beyond just the schema, the API server exposes validating and mutating Webhooks that can fill the void where the schema fails – for example, if you want to validate or mutate a resource based on some logic that is beyond the scope of schema. These Webhooks can be employed to make the developer experience when using your customer resources much better than accepting a possibly invalid resource, or defaulting some difficult-to-calculate value so that the user doesn't need to provide it.

Controllers

The heart of reconciliation is a controller, which executes a control loop for a specific resource kind. The controller watches a resource kind in the Kubernetes API and observes that there has been a change. The controller receives the new version of the resource, observes the desired state, observes the state of the system it controls, and attempts to make progress toward changing the state of the system into the desired state expressed in the resource. A controller does not act on the difference between the version of a resource but rather on the current desired state. I've noticed there is an initial drive for people who are new to controller development to try to think about acting only on things that have changed between two resource versions, but that is not recommended.

Usually, a controller has the ability to reconcile many resources concurrently but will never reconcile the same resource concurrently. This simplifies the model for reconciliation quite a bit.

Furthermore, most controllers will run with only one leader at a time. For example, if there are two instances of your operator running, only one will be a leader at a time. The other will be idle, waiting to become the leader if the other process crashes.

Standing on the shoulders of giants

I'm sure this sounds quite complex, and it truly is. However, we can thankfully rely on some projects that have paved the way to make building operators, controllers, and CRDs so much easier. There is a vibrant, growing ecosystem for Kubernetes operators.

The projects that most come to mind and which we will depend on in the next section are `controller-runtime` (https://github.com/kubernetes-sigs/controller-runtime), `kubebuilder` (https://github.com/kubernetes-sigs/kubebuilder), and `operator-sdk` (https://github.com/operator-framework/operator-sdk). `controller-runtime` provides a set of Go libraries that makes it easier to build controllers and is used in both `kubebuilder` and `operator-sdk`. `kubebuilder` is a framework for building Kubernetes APIs and offers a set of tools that makes it easy to generate API structure, controllers, and related manifests for Kubernetes APIs. `operator-sdk` is a component in the Operator Framework (https://github.com/operator-framework), which extends from `kubebuilder` and attempts to solve life cycle, publication, and other higher-level problems faced by operator developers.

If you are interested in a highly ambitious project that extends the Kubernetes API to create declarative cluster infrastructure and enables Kubernetes to build new Kubernetes clusters, I encourage you to check out the Cluster API (https://github.com/kubernetes-sigs/cluster-api).

I hope this section has left you in awe of how powerful the Kubernetes API is and spurred you on to want to learn more. I believe we have covered enough of the basics of extending the Kubernetes API that we can approach building our own reconciler without too much trouble. In the upcoming section, we will use `operator-sdk` to build a `Pet` resource and operator to reconcile pets in a pet store service.

Building a pet store operator

In this section, we will build on the background information we learned in the previous section about CRDs, operators, and controllers to implement our own operator. This operator will have only one CRD, `Pet`, and only one controller to reconcile those `Pet` resources. The desired state of `Pet` will be reconciled to our pet store service, which we used in previous chapters.

As we discussed in the previous section, this will be an example of using Kubernetes control loops to reconcile the state of a resource that has no dependency on other resources within Kubernetes. Remember, you can model anything in CRDs and use Kubernetes as a tool for building robust APIs for any type of resource.

In this section, you will learn to build an operator from scratch. You will define a new CRD and controller. You will examine the build tools and the different code generation tools used to eliminate the majority of boilerplate code. You will deploy your controller and the pet store service to a local `kind` cluster and learn how to use `Tilt.dev` for faster inner-loop development cycles. The code for this repository is located at https://github.com/PacktPublishing/Go-for-DevOps/tree/rev0/chapter/14/petstore-operator.

Initializing the new operator

In this section, we will initialize the new operator using the `operator-sdk` command-line tool. This will be used to scaffold out a project structure for our operator:

```
$ operator-sdk init --domain example.com --repo github.com/Go-for-DevOps/chapter/14/petstore-operator
Writing kustomize manifests for you to edit...
Writing scaffold for you to edit...
Get controller runtime:
$ go get sigs.k8s.io/controller-runtime@v0.11.0
Update dependencies:
$ go mod tidy
Next: define a resource with:
$ operator-sdk create api
```

By executing the preceding command, `operator-sdk` will scaffold a new operator project using an example domain, which will form the suffix of the group name for our future CRDs. The `-repo` flag is based on the repo for the book's code, but you would want that to reflect the repo path for your project or omit it and allow it to default. Let's see what is in the repo after scaffolding:

```
$ ls -al
total 368
-rw-------  1 david  staff     776 Feb 27 10:15 Dockerfile
-rw-------  1 david  staff    9884 Feb 27 10:16 Makefile
-rw-------  1 david  staff     261 Feb 27 10:16 PROJECT
drwx------  8 david  staff     256 Feb 27 10:16 config/
-rw-------  1 david  staff    3258 Feb 27 10:16 go.mod
-rw-r--r--  1 david  staff   94793 Feb 27 10:16 go.sum
drwx------  3 david  staff      96 Feb 27 10:15 hack/
-rw-------  1 david  staff    2791 Feb 27 10:15 main.go
```

The preceding listing shows the top-level structure of the project. The Dockerfile contains commands to build the controller image. The Makefile contains a variety of helpful tasks; however, we will not use it much in this walk-through. The `PROJECT` file contains metadata about the operator. The `config` directory contains the manifests needed to describe and deploy the operator and CRDs to Kubernetes. The `hack` directory contains a boilerplate license header that will be added to generated files and is a good place to put helpful development or build scripts. The rest of the files are just regular Go application code.

Now that we have a general idea of what was scaffolded for us, we can move on to generating our `Pet` resources and controller:

```
$ operator-sdk create api --group petstore --version v1alpha1
--kind Pet --resource --controller
Writing kustomize manifests for you to edit...
Writing scaffold for you to edit...
api/v1alpha1/pet_types.go
controllers/pet_controller.go
Update dependencies:

$ go mod tidy
Running make:

$ make generate
go: creating new go.mod: module tmp
# ... lots of go mod output ...
```

Next: implement your new API and generate the manifests (e.g.
CRDs,CRs) with:

```
$ make manifests
```

By executing the preceding commands, I've instructed `operator-sdk` to create a new API in the `petstore` group with the `v1alpha1` version of the `Pet` kind and generate both the CRD and the controller for the type. Note that the command created `api/v1alpha1/pet_types.go` and `controllers/pet_controller.go`, and then ran `make generate` and `make manifests`. Shortly, we will see that code comments in both of the Go files cause `make generate` and `make manifests` to generate CRD manifests as well as Kubernetes' **Role-Based Authorization Controls** (**RBAC**) for the controller. The RBAC entries for the operator will give rights to the controller to perform CRUD operations on the newly generated resource. The CRD manifest will contain the schema for our newly created resource.

Next, let's take a quick look at the files that have changed:

```
$ git status
M   PROJECT
A   api/v1alpha1/groupversion_info.go
A   api/v1alpha1/pet_types.go
A   api/v1alpha1/zz_generated.deepcopy.go
A   config/crd/bases/petstore.example.com_pets.yaml
A   config/crd/kustomization.yaml
A   config/crd/kustomizeconfig.yaml
A   config/crd/patches/cainjection_in_pets.yaml
A   config/crd/patches/webhook_in_pets.yaml
A   config/rbac/pet_editor_role.yaml
A   config/rbac/pet_viewer_role.yaml
A   config/samples/kustomization.yaml
A   config/samples/petstore_v1alpha1_pet.yaml
A   controllers/pet_controller.go
A   controllers/suite_test.go
M   go.mod
M   main.go
```

As we can see, there are quite a few changes to files. I will not go into depth on each of the changes. The most notable is the generation of `config/crd/bases/petstore.example.com_pets.yaml`, which contains the CRD for our `Pet` resource. In operator projects, it is common to describe the resources in the API in the `api/` directory, the Kubernetes manifests under `config/`, and the controllers under `controllers/`.

Next, let's see what has been generated in `api/v1alpha1/pet_types.go`:

```
// EDIT THIS FILE!  THIS IS SCAFFOLDING FOR YOU TO OWN!
// NOTE: json tags are required.  Any new fields you add must
have json tags for the fields to be serialized.

// PetSpec defines the desired state of Pet
type PetSpec struct {
	// INSERT ADDITIONAL SPEC FIELDS - desired state of cluster
	// Important: Run "make" to regenerate code after modifying this file

	// Foo is an example field of Pet. Edit pet_types.go to remove/update
	Foo string `json:"foo,omitempty"`
}

// PetStatus defines the observed state of Pet
type PetStatus struct {
	// INSERT ADDITIONAL STATUS FIELD - define observed state of cluster
	// Important: Run "make" to regenerate code after modifying this file
}
```

The preceding code shows a snippet from the `pet_types.go` file. The `create api` command has generated a `Pet` resource with `spec` and `status`. The `PetSpec` contains one field named `Foo`, which will serialize with the key `foo` and is optional to provide when creating or updating the resource. `status` contains nothing.

Note the comments in the file. They instruct us that this is the place to add new fields to the type and to run `make` after we do to ensure that the CRD manifests are updated in the `config/` directory.

Now, let's look at the rest of the file:

```
//+kubebuilder:object:root=true
//+kubebuilder:subresource:status

// Pet is the Schema for the pets API
type Pet struct {
	metav1.TypeMeta   `json:",inline"`
	metav1.ObjectMeta `json:"metadata,omitempty"`
```

```
        Spec     PetSpec    `json:"spec,omitempty"`
        Status   PetStatus  `json:"status,omitempty"`
}

//+kubebuilder:object:root=true

// PetList contains a list of Pet
type PetList struct {
        metav1.TypeMeta  `json:",inline"`
        metav1.ListMeta  `json:"metadata,omitempty"`
        Items            []Pet `json:"items"`
}

func init() {
        SchemeBuilder.Register(&Pet{}, &PetList{})
}
```

Here, we can see the definition of Pet and PetList, which both get registered in the following schema builder. Note the //+kubebuilder build comments. These build comments instruct kubebuilder on how to generate the CRD manifests.

Note that Pet has the spec and status defined with the json tags that we have seen in the other Kubernetes resources we have worked with. Pet also includes both TypeMeta, which informs Kubernetes of the group version kind information, and ObjectMeta, which contains the name, namespace, and other metadata about the resource.

With these structures, we already have a fully functional custom resource. However, the resource doesn't represent the fields we want to represent our pet resource and will need to be updated to better represent our pet structure.

Next, let's look at what was generated for PetReconciler in controllers/pet_controller.go, the controller that will run the control loop for reconciling pets:

```
type PetReconciler struct {
        client.Client
        Scheme *runtime.Scheme
}

//+kubebuilder:rbac:groups=petstore.example.com,resources=pets,verbs=get;list;watch;create;update;patch;delete
//+kubebuilder:rbac:groups=petstore.example.com,resources=pets/status,verbs=get;update;patch
//+kubebuilder:rbac:groups=petstore.example.com,resources=pets/
```

```
finalizers,verbs=update

func (r *PetReconciler) Reconcile(ctx context.Context, req
ctrl.Request) (ctrl.Result, error) {
    _ = log.FromContext(ctx)

    return ctrl.Result{}, nil
}

func (r *PetReconciler) SetupWithManager(mgr ctrl.Manager)
error {
    return ctrl.NewControllerManagedBy(mgr).
        For(&petstorev1alpha1.Pet{}).
        Complete(r)
}
```

In the preceding code, we can see a `PetReconciler` type that embeds a `client.Client`, which is a generic Kubernetes API client, and `*runtime.Scheme`, which contains the known types and the schemas registered. If we continue downward, we can see a collection of `//+kubebuilder:rbac build` comments that instruct the code generator to create RBAC rights for the controller to be able to manipulate the `Pet` resource. Next, we can see the `Reconcile func`, which will be called each time a resource has been changed and needs to be reconciled with the pet store. Finally, we can see the `SetupWithManager` function, which is called from `main.go` to start the controller and inform it and the manager what kind of resource the controller will reconcile.

We have covered the impactful changes from the scaffolding process. We can proceed to implement our `Pet` resource to reflect the domain model we have in the pet store. The pet entity in our pet store has three mutable, required properties, `Name`, `Type`, and `Birthday`, and one read-only property, `ID`. We need to add these to our `Pet` resource to expose them to the API:

```
// PetType is the type of the pet. For example, a dog.
// +kubebuilder:validation:Enum=dog;cat;bird;reptile
type PetType string

const (
    DogPetType      PetType = "dog"
    CatPetType      PetType = "cat"
    BirdPetType     PetType = "bird"
    ReptilePetType  PetType = "reptile"
)
```

```go
// PetSpec defines the desired state of Pet
type PetSpec struct {
    // Name is the name of the pet
    Name string `json:"name"`
    // Type is the type of pet Type PetType `json:"type"`
    // Birthday is the date the pet was born
    Birthday metav1.Time `json:"birthday"`
}

// PetStatus defines the observed state of Pet
type PetStatus struct {
    // ID is the unique ID for the pet
    ID string `json:"id,omitempty"`
}
```

The preceding are the code changes I've made to `Pet` to reflect the domain model of the pet store service. Note `// +kubebuilder:validation:Enum` preceding the `PetType` type. That indicates to the CRD manifest generator that the schema should add validation to ensure only those strings can be supplied for the `Type` field of `PetSpec`. Also, note that each of the fields in `spec` does not have the `omitempty` JSON tag. That will inform the CRD manifest generator that those fields are required.

The status of `Pet` has only an `ID` field, which is allowed to be empty. This will store the unique identifier returned from the pet store service.

Now that we have defined our `Pet`, let's reconcile `pet` with the pet store in the controller loop:

```go
// Reconcile moves the current state of the pet to be the
desired state described in the pet.spec.
func (r *PetReconciler) Reconcile(ctx context.Context, req
ctrl.Request) (result ctrl.Result, errResult error) {
    logger := log.FromContext(ctx)

    pet := &petstorev1.Pet{}
    if err := r.Get(ctx, req.NamespacedName, pet); err != nil
{
        if apierrors.IsNotFound(err) {
            logger.Info("object was not found")
            return reconcile.Result{}, nil
        }

        logger.Error(err, "failed to fetch pet from API
server")
```

```
                // this will cause this pet resource to be requeued
                return ctrl.Result{}, err
        }

        helper, err := patch.NewHelper(pet, r.Client)
        if err != nil {
                return ctrl.Result{}, errors.Wrap(err, "failed to create patch helper")
        }
        defer func() {
                // patch the resource
                if err := helper.Patch(ctx, pet); err != nil {
                        errResult = err
                }
        }()

        if pet.DeletionTimestamp.IsZero() {
                // the pet is not marked for delete
                return r.ReconcileNormal(ctx, pet)
        }

        // pet has been marked for delete
        return r.ReconcileDelete(ctx, pet)
}
```

The preceding code has been added to reconcile the `pet` resource. When we receive a change from the API server, we are not given much information. We are only provided with `NamespacedName` of the pet. `NamespacedName` contains both the namespace and the name of the pet that has changed. Remember that `PetReconciler` has a `client.Client` embedded on it. It provides us with access to the Kubernetes API server. We use the `Get` method to request the pet we need to reconcile. If the pet is not found, we return an empty reconcile result and a nil error. This informs the controller to wait for another change to occur. If there is an error making the request, we return an empty reconcile result and an error. If the error is not nil, the reconciler will try again and back off exponentially.

If we are able to fetch the pet, we then create a patch helper, which will allow us to track changes to the `Pet` resource during the reconciliation loop and patch the resource change back to the Kubernetes API server at the end of the reconcile loop. The defer ensures that we patch at the end of the `Reconcile` func.

If the pet has no deletion timestamp set, then we know that Kubernetes has not marked the resource for deletion, so we call `ReconcileNormal`, where we will attempt to persist the desired state to the pet store. Otherwise, we call `ReconcileDelete` to delete the pet from the pet store.

Let's next look at `ReconcileNormal` and understand what we do when we have a state change to a non-deleted pet resource:

```go
func (r *PetReconciler) ReconcileNormal(ctx context.Context,
pet *petstorev1.Pet) (ctrl.Result, error) {
    controllerutil.AddFinalizer(pet, PetFinalizer)

    psc, err := getPetstoreClient()
    if err != nil {
        return ctrl.Result{}, errors.Wrap(err, "unable to construct petstore client")
    }

    psPet, err := findPetInStore(ctx, psc, pet)
    if err != nil {
        return ctrl.Result{}, errors.Wrap(err, "failed trying to find pet in pet store")
    }

    if psPet == nil {
        // no pet was found, create a pet in the store
        err := createPetInStore(ctx, pet, psc)
        return ctrl.Result{}, err
    }

    // pet was found, update the pet in the store
    if err := updatePetInStore(ctx, psc, pet, psPet.Pet); err != nil {
        return ctrl.Result{}, err
    }
    return ctrl.Result{}, nil
}
```

In `ReconcileNormal`, we always make sure that `PetFinalizer` has been added to the resource. Finalizers are the way that Kubernetes knows when it can garbage-collect a resource. If a resource still has a finalizer on it, then Kubernetes will not delete the resource. Finalizers are useful in controllers when a resource has some external resource that needs to be cleaned up prior to deletion. In this case, we need to remove `Pet` from the pet store prior to the Kubernetes `Pet` resource being deleted. If we didn't, we may have pets in the pet store that don't ever get deleted.

After we set the finalizer, we build a pet store client. We won't go into more detail here, but suffice it to say that it builds a gRPC client for the pet store service. With the pet store client, we query for the pet in the store. If we can't find the pet, then we create one in the store; otherwise, we update the pet in the store to reflect the desired state specified in the Kubernetes `Pet` resource.

Let's take a quick look at the `createPetInStore` func:

```
func createPetInStore(ctx context.Context, pet *petstorev1.Pet,
psc *psclient.Client) error {
    pbPet := &pb.Pet{
        Name:     pet.Spec.Name,
        Type:     petTypeToProtoPetType(pet.Spec.Type),
        Birthday: timeToPbDate(pet.Spec.Birthday),
    }
    ids, err := psc.AddPets(ctx, []*pb.Pet{pbPet})

    if err != nil {
        return errors.Wrap(err, "failed to create new pet")
    }
    pet.Status.ID = ids[0]
    return nil
}
```

When we create the pet in the pet store, we call `AddPets` on the gRPC client with the Kubernetes `Pet` resource desired state and record `ID` in the Kubernetes `Pet` resource status.

Let's move on to the `updatePetInStore` func:

```
func updatePetInStore(ctx context.Context, psc *psclient.
Client, pet *petstorev1.Pet, pbPet *pb.Pet) error {
    pbPet.Name = pet.Spec.Name
    pbPet.Type = petTypeToProtoPetType(pet.Spec.Type)
    pbPet.Birthday = timeToPbDate(pet.Spec.Birthday)
    if err := psc.UpdatePets(ctx, []*pb.Pet{pbPet}); err !=
nil {
```

```
            return errors.Wrap(err, "failed to update the pet in
the store")
    }
    return nil
}
```

When we update the pet in store, we use the fetched store pet and update the fields with the desired state from the Kubernetes `Pet` resource.

If at any point in the flow we run into an error, we bubble up the error to `Reconcile`, where it will trigger a re-queue of the reconciliation loop, backing off exponentially. The actions in `ReconcileNormal` are idempotent. They can run repeatedly to achieve the same state and in the face of errors will retry. Reconciliation loops can be pretty resilient to failures.

That's about it for `ReconcileNormal`. Let's look at what happens in `ReconcileDelete`:

```
// ReconcileDelete deletes the pet from the petstore and
removes the finalizer.
func (r *PetReconciler) ReconcileDelete(ctx context.Context,
pet *petstorev1.Pet) (ctrl.Result, error) {
    psc, err := getPetstoreClient()
    if err != nil {
        return ctrl.Result{}, errors.Wrap(err, "unable to
construct petstore client")
    }

    if pet.Status.ID != "" {
        if err := psc.DeletePets(ctx, []string{pet.Status.
ID}); err != nil {
            return ctrl.Result{}, errors.Wrap(err, "failed
to delete pet")
        }
    }

    // remove finalizer, so K8s can garbage collect the
resource.
    controllerutil.RemoveFinalizer(pet, PetFinalizer)
    return ctrl.Result{}, nil
}
```

In `ReconcileDelete` in the preceding code block, we get a pet store client to interact with the pet store. If `pet.Status.ID` is not empty, we attempt to delete the pet from the pet store. If that operation is successful, we will remove the finalizer, informing Kubernetes that it can then delete the resource.

You have extended Kubernetes and created your first CRD and controller! Let's give it a run.

To start the project and see your Kubernetes operator in action, run the following:

```
$ ctlptl create cluster kind --name kind-petstore
--registry=ctlptl-registry
$ tilt up
```

The preceding commands will create a `kind` cluster and a local **Open Container Initiative** (**OCI**) image registry, enabling you to publish images locally rather than to an external registry. Tilt will start at the command line. Press the *spacebar* to open the web view of `Tilt.dev`. Once you do, you should see something like the following:

Figure 14.2 – Tilt's All Resources web view

Wait for each of the services on the left panel to turn green. Once they are, it means that the pet store operator and Service have deployed successfully. If you click on one of the Services listed on the left, it will show you the log output for that component. `petstore-operator-controller-manager` is your Kubernetes controller. Next, we are going to apply some pets to our Kubernetes cluster and see what happens.

Let's first look at the pet samples we are going to apply. The samples are in `config/samples/petstore_v1alpha1_pet.yaml`:

```
---
apiVersion: petstore.example.com/v1alpha1
kind: Pet
metadata:
  name: pet-sample1
spec:
  name: Thor
  type: dog
  birthday: 2021-04-01T00:00:00Z
---
apiVersion: petstore.example.com/v1alpha1
kind: Pet
metadata:
  name: pet-sample2
spec:
  name: Tron
  type: cat
  birthday: 2020-06-25T00:00:00Z
```

We have two pets, `Thor` and `Tron`. We can apply them with the following command:

```
$ kubectl apply -f config/samples/petstore_v1alpha1_pet.yaml
```

That should have replied that they were created, and you should then be able to fetch them by running the following command:

```
$ kubectl get pets
NAME           AGE
pet-sample1    2m17s
pet-sample2    2m17s
```

We can see that we have two pets defined. Let's make sure they have IDs. Run the following command:

```
$ kubectl get pets -o yaml
apiVersion: petstore.example.com/v1alpha1
kind: Pet
metadata:
  finalizers:
  - pet.petstore.example.com
  name: pet-sample2
  namespace: default
spec:
  birthday: "2020-06-25T00:00:00Z"
  name: Tron
  type: cat
status:
  id: 23743da5-34fe-46f6-bed8-1f5bdbaabbe6
```

I've omitted some noisy content from the preceding code, but this is roughly what you should see. Tron has an ID generated from the pet store service; it was applied to the Kubernetes `Pet` resource status.

Now, let's test our reconciliation loop by changing the name of `Thor` to `Thorbert`:

```
$ kubectl edit pets pet-sample1
```

This will open your default editor. You can go and change the value of `Thor` to `Thorbert` to cause a new reconcile loop.

You should see something similar to this output in your browser, with Tilt in the pet store operator logs:

```
[manager] 1.6466368389433222e+09    INFO    controller.pet
finding pets in store    {"reconciler group": "petstore.
example.com", "reconciler kind": "Pet", "name": "pet-sample1",
"namespace": "default", "pet": "Thorbert", "id": "cef9499f-
6214-4227-b217-265fd8f196e6"}
```

As you can see from the preceding code, `Thor` is now changed to `Thorbert`.

Finally, let's delete these pets by running the following command:

```
$ kubectl delete pets --all
pet.petstore.example.com "pet-sample1" deleted
pet.petstore.example.com "pet-sample2" deleted
```

After deleting the resources, you should be able to check back in Tilt and see the log output reflecting that the `delete` operations succeeded.

In this section, you learned to build an operator from scratch, extended the Kubernetes API with a custom resource that reconciled state to an external Service, and used some really useful tools along the way.

Summary

In this chapter, we learned how to use Go to deploy and manipulate resources in Kubernetes. We built upon that knowledge to extend Kubernetes with our custom `Pet` resources and learned how to continuously reconcile the desired state of our pets with the state of the pet store. We learned that we can extend Kubernetes to represent any external resources and that it provides a robust platform to describe nearly any domain.

You should be able to take what you learned in this chapter and apply it to automate interactions with Kubernetes resources and extend Kubernetes to natively expose your own resources through the Kubernetes API. I bet you can think of some services and resources at your company that you would like to be able to manage by simply applying some YAML to your Kubernetes cluster. You are now empowered with the knowledge to solve those problems.

In the next chapter, we will learn about using Go to program the cloud. We'll learn how to mutate cloud resources using Go client libraries to interact with cloud service provider APIs, and how to use those cloud services and infrastructure after we've provisioned them.

15
Programming the Cloud

You've probably heard the saying *the cloud is just someone else's computer*. While it is somewhat true, it is also wildly off target. Cloud service providers offer virtual machines running in their data centers that you can use in exchange for money, so in that way, you are using someone else's computer. However, it misses the bigger picture of what a cloud service provider is. A cloud service provider is a collection of hundreds of application-hosting, data, compliance, and computing infrastructure services that run in hundreds of data centers across the globe and are exposed through a fully programmable API.

In this chapter, we will learn how to interact with a cloud API using Microsoft Azure. We'll start by learning a bit about the nature of the APIs, including how they are described and where to find additional documentation about them. We'll learn the fundamentals of identity, authentication, and authorization. We'll then apply what we have learned in a set of examples using the Azure SDK for Go to build cloud infrastructure and utilize other cloud services.

By the end of the chapter, you will be equipped with the knowledge to work effectively with Microsoft Azure and will have gained the transferable skills to work with other cloud service providers.

We will cover the following topics in this chapter:

- What is the cloud?
- Learning the basics of the Azure APIs
- Building infrastructure using Azure Resource Manager
- Using provisioned Azure infrastructure

Technical requirements

This chapter will require the following tools:

- Go
- The Azure CLI: `https://docs.microsoft.com/en-us/cli/azure/install-azure-cli`
- Code files downloaded from GitHub: `https://github.com/PacktPublishing/Go-for-DevOps/tree/rev0/chapter/15`

What is the cloud?

The scale of capital investment in the Amazon, Microsoft, and Google cloud physical computing infrastructure is monumental. Imagine the investment needed to build 200+ physical data centers with multiple redundant power and cooling systems, featuring state-of-the-art physical security. These centers are resilient in the face of a natural disaster. Even then, you are just scratching the surface.

These data centers require one of the largest interconnected networks on the planet to link them together. All of that infrastructure won't function without vast amounts of power and cooling, preferably from sustainable sources. For example, Azure has been carbon-neutral since 2012 and is committed to being carbon-negative by 2030. When people talk about hyper-scale cloud, they are talking about the planet-scale operations of these cloud service providers.

Ever wonder what it would be like to visit one of these data centers? For example, to access an Azure data center, there are multiple levels of security you must go through. You must first request access to the data center and provide a valid business justification. If access is granted, when you arrive at the data center's permitter access point, you'd notice the panoply of cameras, tall steel fences, and concrete surrounding the perimeter. You'd verify your identity and pass to the building entrance. At the building entrance, you'd be greeted by security officers who will once again verify who you are using two-factor authentication with biometrics. Upon passing biometric scanning, they'd guide you to the specific section of the data center where you have been approved to operate. As you proceed to the data center floor, you'd pass in and out through a full-body metal detection screening to ensure that you don't leave with anything you shouldn't. Security at these data centers is taken very seriously.

Still think this sounds like *someone else's computer*?

The physical infrastructure of cloud service providers is awe-inspiring. However, we should change our focus from the scale of cloud service provider operations to how cloud services are exposed to developers. As we mentioned initially, cloud service providers expose the functions of the cloud through APIs, which developers can use to manage infrastructure and applications running on the cloud. We can use these APIs to build applications that can leverage hyper-scale cloud infrastructure to become planet-scale.

Learning the basics of the Azure APIs

Now that we know the path to programming the cloud is through APIs, let's learn a bit more about them. It's important to establish some background on how a large system of APIs comes together to form a consistent programmatic interface. We will also learn where you can find code and documentation when you run into challenges.

In this section, we are going to discuss how the major clouds define APIs and produce **Software Development Kits** (**SDKs**) for programming against the cloud APIs. We will learn where to find these SDKs, and where to find documentation about the APIs and SDKs.

We will also learn about identity, **Role-Based Access Control** (**RBAC**), and **resource hierarchy** in Microsoft Azure. Finally, we'll create and log in to a free Azure account, which we will use in the subsequent sections to program the cloud.

A background on cloud APIs and SDKs

As we discussed in the previous section, cloud service providers expose APIs for management of and access to hundreds of services, spread across a vast number of regions. These APIs are commonly implemented using **Representational State Transfer (REST)** or **Google Remote Procedure Call (gRPC)**. Within each cloud service provider, there is likely an equal number of engineering teams building these APIs. It is imperative to provide a consistent representation of resources in these APIs so that, when viewed as a whole, each service provides similar behavior. Each cloud service provider takes its own approach to this problem. For example, at Microsoft Azure, the rule for defining REST APIs is codified by the **Microsoft Azure REST API Guidelines** (https://github.com/microsoft/api-guidelines/blob/vNext/azure/Guidelines.md). These rules provide guidance to service teams.

Developers don't usually use cloud APIs directly via HTTP but rather through the use of SDKs. These are collections of libraries that provide access to the APIs for a given language.

For example, Azure (https://github.com/Azure/azure-sdk-for-go), AWS (https://github.com/aws/aws-sdk-go), and Google (https://github.com/googleapis/google-api-go-client) all have Go SDKs for their clouds and many other languages. These SDKs do their best to eliminate the boilerplate code needed for programmatically accessing clouds' APIs, simplifying what the developer needs to write to program against them. Besides the documentation published by cloud providers, always remember that GoDocs are your friend. For example, the GoDocs for the Azure Blob storage service (https://github.com/Azure/azure-kusto-go) provide useful information for using the SDK.

These SDKs, for the most part, are generated based on machine-readable API specifications. When you have hundreds of services and multiple languages, it will not scale well to have an enormous number of humans writing SDKs by hand. Each cloud solves this problem in its own way.

For example, Microsoft Azure generates almost all of the Azure API reference documentation (https://docs.microsoft.com/en-us/rest/api/azure/) and SDKs using OpenAPI specifications in the Azure REST API Specs repository (https://github.com/Azure/azure-rest-api-specs). The entire process for producing documentation and generating SDKs is hosted on GitHub and powered by open source tools such as the AutoRest code generator (https://github.com/Azure/autorest).

> **Fun Note**
>
> One of this book's authors, David Justice, established this process at Azure and had the first commit to the Azure REST API Specs repository (`https://github.com/Azure/azure-rest-api-specs/commit/8c42e6392618a878d5286b8735b99bbde693c0a2`).

Microsoft Azure identity, RBAC, and resource hierarchy

To prepare us for interacting with the Azure API, we need to understand some basics – identity, RBAC, and resource hierarchy. **Identity** establishes the user, or principal, interacting with the API. RBAC defines what the identity can do within the API. The resource hierarchy describes the relationship between the resources in the Azure cloud. RBAC roles and rights describe what a principal can do with a given resource or resource hierarchy. For example, a user can be assigned the contributor rights to an Azure subscription and be able to mutate resources within that subscription.

Identities in Azure live in **Azure Active Directory (AAD)**. This is an enterprise identity and access management service. It provides single sign-on, multifactor authentication, and conditional access, among other features. Identities in AAD reside within one or more tenants. Tenants contain multiple identities. Identities can be user identities, which represent humans and have interactive authentication flows, or they can be service principals, which represent non-human identities such as applications that do not have interactive authentication flows.

The root of resources in Azure is an Azure subscription. A subscription is a logical container that contains Azure resource groups. Each resource such as a virtual machine, storage account or virtual network, resides within a resource group. A resource group is a logical entity that associates multiple Azure resources so that you can manage them as a single entity.

Identities are granted RBAC roles and rights to interact with Azure subscriptions and resources alike. You can think of AAD and Azure as separate systems that are bound together by RBAC rights and roles. We will not dive deeply into each RBAC role or right, but you can find more information about them in the Azure built-in roles documentation (`https://docs.microsoft.com/en-us/azure/role-based-access-control/built-in-roles`).

Now that we have some basic understanding of the cloud we will be working in, let's get started.

Creating an Azure account and accessing the API

To run the rest of the examples in this chapter, you will need an Azure account. If you do not have an Azure account, you can sign up for a free account with $200 of Azure credits (https://azure.microsoft.com/en-us/free/).

Once you have an account, log in with the Azure CLI:

```
$ az login
```

This command will log you into your Azure account and set the default context for your primary Azure subscription. By default, when you create an Azure account, your identity will be granted the owner role in the subscription. The owner role grants full access to manage all resources, including the ability to assign roles in Azure RBAC. To see what subscription is active, run the following command:

```
$ az account show
{
  "environmentName": "AzureCloud",
  "isDefault": true,
  "managedByTenants": [],
  "name": "mysubscription",
  "state": "Enabled",
  "tenantId": "888bf....db93",
  "user": {
      ...
  }
}
```

The preceding command output shows the name of the subscription and other details about the current context of the Azure CLI. In the following command, we will use the az CLI to directly interact with the Azure API:

```
az rest --method get --uri "/subscriptions?api-version=2019-03-01"
```

The preceding command will list the subscriptions your identity has access to via RBAC rights. Note that as part of the Azure REST API guidelines, all Azure APIs must be used with an `api-version` query parameter. This is enforced to ensure that API consumers can always rely on the stability of the request and response format for a specified `api-version`. The APIs are updated often, and without specifying the `api-version` query parameter of a given API, a consumer would possibly be subject to breaking changes in the API.

Next, let's run the same request using the `debug` flag:

```
az rest --method get --uri "/subscriptions?api-
version=2019-03-01" --debug
```

Executing any command with the Azure CLI using `--debug` will output the HTTP request details, showing output containing something similar to the following:

```
Request URL: 'https://management.azure.com/
subscriptions?apiversion=2019-03-01'
Request method: 'GET'
Request headers:
    'User-Agent': 'python/3.10.2 (macOS-12.3.1-arm64-arm-
64bit) AZURECLI/2.34.1 (HOMEBREW)'
    urllib3.connectionpool: Starting new HTTPS connection (1):
management.azure.com:443
urllib3.connectionpool: https://management.azure.com:443 "GET /
subscriptions?api-version=2019-03-01 HTTP/1.1" 200 6079
Response status: 200
Response headers:
    'Content-Type': 'application/json; charset=utf-8'
    'x-ms-ratelimit-remaining-tenant-reads': '11999'
    'x-ms-request-id': 'aebed1f6-75f9-48c2-ae0b-1dd18ae5ec46'
    'x-ms-correlation-request-id': 'aebed1f6-75f9-48c2-ae0b-
    'Date': 'Sat, 09 Apr 2022 22:52:32 GMT'
    'Content-Length': '6079'
```

This output is incredibly useful for seeing what was sent to the Azure API in HTTP. Also, note that the URI, `https://management.azure.com/...`, corresponds to **Azure Resource Manager** (**ARM**). ARM is a composite service composed of resource provider services for each resource in Azure and is responsible for mutating resources in it.

In this section, we learned about how the major clouds define APIs and produce SDKs for the APIs. We also learned specifically about Azure identities, RBAC, and resource hierarchies. This information may be specific to Azure, but all major clouds follow the same pattern. Once you learn how one of the clouds approaches **Identity and Access Management** (**IAM**), it's roughly transferable to other clouds. Lastly, we signed into an Azure account for use in subsequent sections and learned how to directly access the Azure REST API through the Azure CLI.

In the next section, we will use the Azure SDK for Go to mutate cloud infrastructure. Let's get started on programming the Azure cloud with Go.

Building infrastructure using Azure Resource Manager

Cloud APIs are bifurcated into two categories, the management plane and the data plane. The management plane is an API that controls the creation, deletion, and mutation of infrastructure. The data plane is an API exposed by provisioned infrastructure.

For example, the management plane would be used to create a SQL database. The data plane for the SQL database resource would be the SQL protocol for manipulating data and structure within the database.

The management plane is serviced by the cloud resource API, and the data plane is serviced by the API exposed by the provisioned service.

In this section, we will learn how to use the Azure SDK for Go to provision infrastructure in Azure. We will learn how to create and destroy resource groups, virtual networks, subnets, public IPs, virtual machines, and databases. The goal of this section is to build awareness of the Azure Go SDK and how to interact with ARM.

Azure SDK for Go

As we discussed in the previous section, cloud SDKs simplify the interaction between a given language and a cloud provider's API. In the case of Azure, we will be using the Azure SDK for Go (https://github.com/Azure/azure-sdk-for-go/) to interact with the Azure APIs. Specifically, we'll use the latest edition of the SDK (https://github.com/Azure/azure-sdk-for-go#management-new-releases), which has been redesigned to follow the Azure design guidelines for Go (https://azure.github.io/azure-sdk/golang_introduction.html). For the latest information about packages and docs, be sure to check out the Azure SDK Releases page (https://azure.github.io/azure-sdk/releases/latest/mgmt/go.html).

The code for this section is located in the GitHub code folder for this chapter https://github.com/PacktPublishing/Go-for-DevOps/tree/rev0/chapter/15.

Setting up your local environment

To run the code for this section, you will need to set up a **Secure Shell** (**SSH**) key and an .env file. Run the following commands from the ./chapter/15 directory of the repository:

```
$ mkdir .ssh
$ ssh-keygen -t rsa -b 4096 -f ./.ssh/id_rsa -q -N ""
$ chmod 600 ./.ssh/id_rsa*
```

This command will create a .ssh directory in ./chapter/15, generate an SSH key pair within that directory, and ensure that proper permissions are set on the key pair.

> **Note**
> The preceding command creates an SSH key that does not have a passphrase. We are only using this key pair as an example. You should provide a strong passphrase for real-world usage.

Next, let's set up a local .env file that we will use to store environmental variables used in the examples:

```
echo -e "AZURE_SUBSCRIPTION_ID=$(az account show --query 'id' -o tsv)\nSSH_PUBLIC_KEY_PATH=./.ssh/id_rsa.pub" >> .env
```

Now, this command will create an `.env` file that contains two environment variables, `AZURE_SUBSCRIPTION_ID` and `SSH_PUBLIC_KEY_PATH`. We derive the value for the Azure subscription ID from the Azure CLI's current active subscription.

Now that we have set up our local environment, let's build an **Azure virtual machine** that will run a `cloud-init` provisioning script and provide access using SSH via a public IP.

Building an Azure virtual machine

Let's get started by running the example, and then we'll delve into the code for building the infrastructure. To run the example, run the following command:

```
$ go run ./cmd/compute/main.go
Staring to build Azure resources...
Building an Azure Resource Group named "fragrant-violet"...
Building an Azure Network Security Group named "fragrant-violet-nsg"...
Building an Azure Virtual Network named "fragrant-violet-vnet"...
Building an Azure Virtual Machine named "fragrant-violet-vm"...
Fetching the first Network Interface named "fragrant-violet-nic-6d8bb6ea" connected to the VM...
Fetching the Public IP Address named "fragrant-violet-pip-6d8bb6ea" connected to the VM...
Connect with: `ssh -i ./.ssh/id_rsa devops@20.225.222.128`

Press enter to delete the infrastructure.
```

After running `go run ./cmd/compute/main.go`, you should see something similar to what is shown in the previous command block. As you can see from the output, the program built several bits of infrastructure, including an Azure resource group, network security group, virtual network, and virtual machine. We'll discuss every piece of infrastructure in more detail soon.

As the output states, you can also use SSH to access the virtual machine as described in the output. We'll use this to explore the provisioned state of the virtual machine to confirm that the `cloud-init` provisioning script ran as expected.

If you visit the Azure portal, you should see the following:

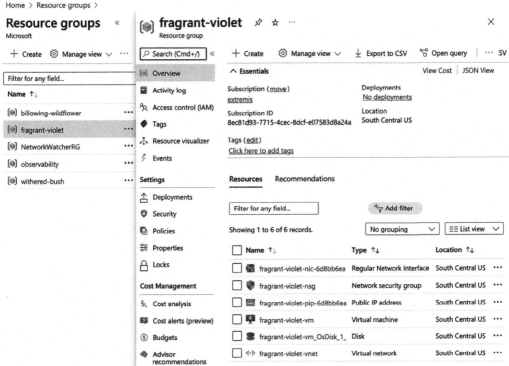

Figure 15.1 – The Azure portal virtual machine infrastructure

In the preceding screenshot, you can see the resource group as well as all of the infrastructure created. Next, let's look at the code that provisioned this infrastructure.

Provisioning Azure infrastructure using Go

In these examples, you will see how to build Azure API clients, probe for credentials for accessing APIs, and mutate infrastructure. Many of these examples use abbreviated error-handling behavior to keep the code as concise as possible for illustrative purposes. `panic` is not your friend. Please wrap and bubble your errors as appropriate.

Let's start with the entry point of go run ./cmd/compute/main.go and learn how to use Go to provision cloud infrastructure:

```go
func main() {
    _ = godotenv.Load()
    ctx := context.Background()
    subscriptionID := helpers.MustGetenv(
        "AZURE_SUBSCRIPTION_ID",
    )
    sshPubKeyPath := helpers.MustGetenv("SSH_PUBLIC_KEY_PATH")
    factory := mgmt.NewVirtualMachineFactory(
        subscriptionID,
        sshPubKeyPath,
    )

    fmt.Println("Staring to build Azure resources...")
    stack := factory.CreateVirtualMachineStack(
        ctx,
        "southcentralus",
    )

    admin := stack.VirtualMachine.Properties.OSProfile.AdminUsername
    ipAddress := stack.PublicIP.Properties.IPAddress
    sshIdentityPath := strings.TrimRight(sshPubKeyPath, ".pub")

    fmt.Printf(
        "Connect with: `ssh -i %s %s@%s`\n\n",
        sshIdentityPath, *admin, *ipAddress,
    )
    fmt.Println("Press enter to delete the infrastructure.")

    reader := bufio.NewReader(os.Stdin)
    _, _ = reader.ReadString('\n')
    factory.DestroyVirtualMachineStack(context.Background(), stack)
}
```

In the preceding code, we load environment variables in the local `.env` file using `godotenv.Load()`. In `main`, we create a new `VirtualMachineFactory` to manage the creation and deletion of Azure infrastructure. Once the infrastructure is created in `factory.CreateVirtualMachineStack`, we print the SSH connection details and prompt for user confirmation to delete the infrastructure stack.

Next, let's dive into the VM factory and see what is included in the VM stack:

```
type VirtualMachineFactory struct {
    subscriptionID  string
    sshPubKeyPath   string
    cred            azcore.TokenCredential
    groupsClient    *armresources.ResourceGroupsClient
    vmClient        *armcompute.VirtualMachinesClient
    vnetClient      *armnetwork.VirtualNetworksClient
    subnetClient    *armnetwork.SubnetsClient
    nicClient       *armnetwork.InterfacesClient
    nsgClient       *armnetwork.SecurityGroupsClient
    pipClient       *armnetwork.PublicIPAddressesClient
}
```

This code defines the structure of `VirtualMachineFactory`, which is responsible for the creation of and access to the Azure SDK API clients. We instantiate those clients using the `NewVirtualMachineFactory` func, as shown here:

```
func NewVirtualMachineFactory(subscriptionID, sshPubKeyPath
string) *VirtualMachineFactory {
    cred := HandleErrWithResult(azidentity.
NewDefaultAzureCredential(nil))
    return &VirtualMachineFactory{
        cred:           cred,
        subscriptionID: subscriptionID,
        sshPubKeyPath:  sshPubKeyPath,
        groupsClient:   BuildClient(subscriptionID, cred,
armresources.NewResourceGroupsClient),
        vmClient:       BuildClient(subscriptionID, cred,
armcompute.NewVirtualMachinesClient),
        vnetClient:     BuildClient(subscriptionID, cred,
armnetwork.NewVirtualNetworksClient),
        subnetClient:   BuildClient(subscriptionID, cred,
armnetwork.NewSubnetsClient),
        nsgClient:      BuildClient(subscriptionID, cred,
armnetwork.NewSecurityGroupsClient),
        nicClient:      BuildClient(subscriptionID, cred,
armnetwork.NewInterfacesClient),
```

```
                pipClient:       BuildClient(subscriptionID, cred,
armnetwork.NewPublicIPAddressesClient),
        }
}
```

This code builds a new default Azure identity credential. This credential is used to authenticate the client to the Azure APIs. By default, this credential will probe multiple sources for an identity to use. The default credential will probe for environment variables first, then it will attempt to use an Azure managed identity (`https://docs.microsoft.com/en-us/azure/active-directory/managed-identities-azure-resources/overview`), and finally, it will fall back to using the Azure CLI's user identity. For this example, we are relying on the Azure CLI identity to interact with the Azure APIs. This is convenient for development but should not be used for a deployed application or script. Non-interactive authentication requires either an Azure service principal (`https://docs.microsoft.com/en-us/azure/active-directory/develop/app-objects-and-service-principals`) or an Azure managed identity.

The VM factory builds each of the Azure API clients using `subscriptionID`, the credential, and the `New*` function for each of the clients. `BuildClient()` builds each client.

Now that we know how credentials and the API clients are instantiated, let's dive into the creation of infrastructure in `CreateVirtualMachineStack`:

```
func (vmf *VirtualMachineFactory) CreateVirtualMachineStack(ctx
context.Context, location string) *VirtualMachineStack {
        stack := &VirtualMachineStack{
            Location:    location,
            name:        haiku.Haikunate(),
            sshKeyPath:  HandleErrWithResult(homedir.Expand(vmf.
sshPubKeyPath)),
        }

        stack.ResourceGroup = vmf.createResourceGroup(ctx, stack.
name, stack.Location)
        stack.SecurityGroup = vmf.createSecurityGroup(ctx, stack.
name, stack.Location)
        stack.VirtualNetwork = vmf.createVirtualNetwork(ctx,
stack)
        stack.VirtualMachine = vmf.createVirtualMachine(ctx,
stack)
        stack.NetworkInterface = vmf.getFirstNetworkInterface(ctx,
stack)
```

```
        stack.PublicIP = vmf.getPublicIPAddress(ctx, stack)
        return stack
}
```

In the preceding code, we created the idea of a stack – a collection of related infrastructure. We created a new stack with a given location, a human-readable name, and the contents of the SSH public key path. Subsequently, we created each of the Azure resources needed to create a VM with public SSH access.

Let's explore each of the `create` and `get` funcs in `CreateVirtualMachineStack`:

```
func (vmf *VirtualMachineFactory) createResourceGroup(ctx
context.Context, name, location string) armresources.
ResourceGroup {
        param := armresources.ResourceGroup{
                Location: to.Ptr(location),
        }

        fmt.Printf("Building an Azure Resource Group named
%q...\n", name)
        res, err := vmf.groupsClient.CreateOrUpdate(ctx, name,
param, nil)
        HandleErr(err)
        return res.ResourceGroup
}
```

In the preceding code, `createResourceGroup` calls `CreateOrUpdate` on `groupsClient` to create an Azure resource group in the specified location. An Azure resource group is a logical container for Azure resources. We will use the resource group as a container for the rest of our resources.

Next, let's dive into the network security group creation function, `createSecurityGroup`:

```
func (vmf *VirtualMachineFactory) createSecurityGroup(ctx
context.Context, name, location string) armnetwork.
SecurityGroup {
        param := armnetwork.SecurityGroup{
                Location: to.Ptr(location),
                Name:     to.Ptr(name + "-nsg"),
                Properties: &armnetwork.
SecurityGroupPropertiesFormat{
                        SecurityRules: []*armnetwork.SecurityRule{
                                {
                                        Name: to.Ptr("ssh"),
```

```go
                        Properties: &armnetwork.SecurityRulePropertiesFormat{
                            Access:                 to.Ptr(armnetwork.SecurityRuleAccessAllow),
                            Direction:              to.Ptr(armnetwork.SecurityRuleDirectionInbound),
                            Protocol:               to.Ptr(armnetwork.SecurityRuleProtocolAsterisk),
                            Description:            to.Ptr("allow ssh on 22"),
                            DestinationAddressPrefix: to.Ptr("*"),
                            DestinationPortRange:   to.Ptr("22"),
                            Priority:               to.Ptr(int32(101)),
                            SourcePortRange:        to.Ptr("*"),
                            SourceAddressPrefix:    to.Ptr("*"),
                        },
                    },
                },
            },
        }

    fmt.Printf("Building an Azure Network Security Group named %q...\n", *param.Name)
    poller, err := vmf.nsgClient.BeginCreateOrUpdate(ctx, name, *param.Name, param, nil)
    HandleErr(err)
    res := HandleErrPoller(ctx, poller)
    return res.SecurityGroup
}
```

In the preceding code, we built an Azure network security group, which contains a single security rule to allow network traffic on port 22, enabling SSH access for the VM. Note that rather than calling `CreateOrUpdate`, we call `BeginCreateOrUpdate`, which issues PUT or PATCH to the Azure API and starts a long-running operation.

A long-running operation in Azure is one that – once the initial mutation is accepted – executes until it reaches a terminal state. For example, when creating a network security group, the API receives the initial mutation and then starts to build the infrastructure. After the infrastructure is ready, the API will indicate it is completed through the operation state or the provisioning state. `poller` takes care of following the long-running operation to completion. In `HandleErrPoller`, we follow the polling to completion and return the final state of the resource.

Next, let's explore the creation of the virtual network via `createVirtualNetwork`:

```
func (vmf *VirtualMachineFactory) createVirtualNetwork(ctx
context.Context, vmStack *VirtualMachineStack) armnetwork.
VirtualNetwork {
      param := armnetwork.VirtualNetwork{
         Location: to.Ptr(vmStack.Location),
         Name:     to.Ptr(vmStack.name + "-vnet"),
         Properties: &armnetwork.
VirtualNetworkPropertiesFormat{
            AddressSpace: &armnetwork.AddressSpace{
               AddressPrefixes: []*string{to.
Ptr("10.0.0.0/16")},
            },
            Subnets: []*armnetwork.Subnet{
               {
                  Name: to.Ptr("subnet1"),
                  Properties: &armnetwork.
SubnetPropertiesFormat{
                     AddressPrefix:            to.
Ptr("10.0.0.0/24"),
                     NetworkSecurityGroup: &vmStack.
SecurityGroup,
                  },
               },
            },
         },
      }
      fmt.Printf("Building an Azure Virtual Network named
%q...\n", *param.Name)
      poller, err := vmf.vnetClient.BeginCreateOrUpdate(ctx,
vmStack.name, *param.Name, param, nil)
      HandleErr(err)
      res := HandleErrPoller(ctx, poller)
```

```
        return res.VirtualNetwork
}
```

In the previous code block, we built an Azure virtual network for our VM. The virtual network is set up with a `10.0.0.0/16` **Classless Inter-Domain Routing (CIDR)** and a single subnet with a `10.0.0.0/24` CIDR. The subnet references the network security group we built in the previous code block, which causes the rules in the network security group to be enforced on the subnet.

Now that we have built the networking for our VM, let's build it via `createVirtualMachine`:

```
func (vmf *VirtualMachineFactory) createVirtualMachine(ctx
context.Context, vmStack *VirtualMachineStack) armcompute.
VirtualMachine {
        param := linuxVM(vmStack)

        fmt.Printf("Building an Azure Virtual Machine named
%q...\n", *param.Name)
        poller, err := vmf.vmClient.BeginCreateOrUpdate(ctx,
vmStack.name, *param.Name, param, nil)
        HandleErr(err)
        res := HandleErrPoller(ctx, poller)
        return res.VirtualMachine
}
```

There is not much to show for `createVirtualMachine()`. As you can see, the same pattern of resource creation through a long-running API invocation is applied in this code. The interesting bits are in `linuxVM()`:

```
func linuxVM(vmStack *VirtualMachineStack) armcompute.
VirtualMachine {
        return armcompute.VirtualMachine{
                Location: to.Ptr(vmStack.Location),
                Name:     to.Ptr(vmStack.name + "-vm"),
                Properties: &armcompute.VirtualMachineProperties{
                        HardwareProfile: &armcompute.HardwareProfile{
                                VMSize: to.Ptr(armcompute.
VirtualMachineSizeTypesStandardD2SV3),
                        },
                        StorageProfile: &armcompute.StorageProfile{
                                ImageReference: &armcompute.ImageReference{
                                        Publisher: to.Ptr("Canonical"),
                                        Offer:     to.Ptr("UbuntuServer"),
```

```
                SKU:        to.Ptr("18.04-LTS"),
                Version:    to.Ptr("latest"),
            },
        },
        NetworkProfile: networkProfile(vmStack),
        OSProfile:      linuxOSProfile(vmStack),
    },
    }
}
```

In `linuxVM`, we specify the location, name, and properties of the VM. In the properties, we specify the type of hardware we'd like to provision. In this case, we are provisioning a Standard D3v2 (you can read more about it at https://docs.microsoft.com/en-us/azure/virtual-machines/dv3-dsv3-series) hardware **Stock-Keeping Unit** (**SKU**).

We also specify our `StorageProfile`, which is used to specify the OS as well as the data disks we'd like attached to the VM. In this case, we specify that we'd like to run the latest version of Ubuntu 18.04. Both `NetworkProfile` and `OSProfile` are a little too complex to include in this function, so let's explore them individually in the following code block:

```
func networkProfile(vmStack *VirtualMachineStack) *armcompute.
NetworkProfile {
    firstSubnet := vmStack.VirtualNetwork.Properties.
Subnets[0]
    return &armcompute.NetworkProfile{
        NetworkAPIVersion: to.Ptr(armcompute.
NetworkAPIVersionTwoThousandTwenty1101),
        NetworkInterfaceConfigurations: []*armcompute.
VirtualMachineNetworkInterfaceConfiguration{
            {
                Name: to.Ptr(vmStack.name + "-nic"),
                Properties: &armcompute.
VirtualMachineNetworkInterfaceConfigurationProperties{
                    IPConfigurations: []*armcompute.
VirtualMachineNetworkInterfaceIPConfiguration{
                        {
                            Name: to.Ptr(vmStack.name +
"-nic-conf"),
                            Properties: &armcompute.
VirtualMachineNetworkInterfaceIPConfigurationProperties{
                                Primary: to.Ptr(true),
                                Subnet: &armcompute.
```

```
                    SubResource{
                                                        ID: firstSubnet.
ID,
                                                   },
                                                   PublicIPAddress
Configuration: &armcompute.VirtualMachinePublicIPAddress
Configuration{
                                                        Name:
to.Ptr(vmStack.name + "-pip"),
                                                        Properties:
&armcompute.VirtualMachinePublicIPAddressConfiguration
Properties{

PublicIPAllocationMethod: to.Ptr(armcompute.PublicIPAllocation
MethodStatic),

PublicIPAddressVersion:   to.Ptr(armcompute.IPVersionsIPv4),
                                                        },
                                                   },
                                               },
                                           },
                                       },
                                       Primary: to.Ptr(true),
                                   },
                               },
                           },
                       }
                   }
```

In `networkProfile()`, we create `NetworkProfile`, which specifies that the VM should have a single network interface using IPv4 and be exposed via a public IP. The network interface should be allocated on the subnet that we created in `createVirtualNetwork()`.

Next, let's explore the `OSProfile` configuration via `linuxOSProfile()` in the following code block:

```
func linuxOSProfile(vmStack *VirtualMachineStack) *armcompute.
OSProfile {
    sshKeyData := HandleErrWithResult(ioutil.ReadFile(vmStack.
sshKeyPath))
    cloudInitContent := HandleErrWithResult(ioutil.
ReadFile("./cloud-init/init.yml"))
```

```go
        b64EncodedInitScript := base64.StdEncoding.
EncodeToString(cloudInitContent)
    return &armcompute.OSProfile{
        AdminUsername: to.Ptr("devops"),
        ComputerName:  to.Ptr(vmStack.name),
        CustomData:    to.Ptr(b64EncodedInitScript),
        LinuxConfiguration: &armcompute.LinuxConfiguration{
            DisablePasswordAuthentication: to.Ptr(true),
            SSH: &armcompute.SSHConfiguration{
                PublicKeys: []*armcompute.SSHPublicKey{
                    {
                        Path:    to.Ptr("/home/devops/.ssh/authorized_keys"),
                        KeyData: to.Ptr(string(sshKeyData)),
                    },
                },
            },
        },
    }
}
```

In `linuxOSProfile`, we create an `OSProfile`, which includes details such as the admin username, computer name, and SSH configuration. Take note of the `CustomData` field used for specifying the Base64-encoded `cloud-init` YAML, which is used to run the initial configuration of the VM.

Let's explore what we are doing in the `cloud-init` YAML:

```
#cloud-config
package_upgrade: true
packages:
  - nginx
  - golang
runcmd:
  - echo "hello world"
```

Once the VM is created, the following `cloud-init` instructions are executed:

1. First, the packages on the Ubuntu machine are upgraded.
2. Next, the `nginx` and `golang` packages are installed via the **Advanced Package Tool** (**APT**).
3. Finally, `runcmd echos "hello world"`.

`cloud-init` is super-useful for bootstrapping VMs. If you have not used it previously, I highly recommend exploring it further (https://cloudinit.readthedocs.io/en/latest/).

We can verify `cloud-init` executed by accessing the VM using SSH and executing commands similar to the following. Remember, your IP address will be different than what is shown here:

```
$ ssh -i ./.ssh/id_rsa devops@20.225.222.128

devops@fragrant-violet:~$ which go
/usr/bin/go

devops@fragrant-violet:~$ which nginx
/usr/sbin/nginx

cat /var/log/cloud-init-output.log
```

As you can see, `nginx` and `go` have been installed. You should also see the APT mutations and *hello world* in `/var/log/cloud-init-output.log` on the provisioned VM.

You have provisioned and created an Azure VM and related infrastructure! Now, let's destroy the entire stack of infrastructure. You should be able to press *Enter* in the shell where you are running `go run ./cmd/compute/main.go`.

Let's see what happened when we called `factory.DestroyVirtualMachineStack`:

```
func (vmf *VirtualMachineFactory)
DestroyVirtualMachineStack(ctx context.Context, vmStack
*VirtualMachineStack) {
    _, err := vmf.groupsClient.BeginDelete(ctx, vmStack.name,
nil)
```

```
        HandleErr(err)
}
```

In `DestroyVirtualMachineStack`, we simply call `BeginDelete()` on the group's client, specifying the resource group name. However, unlike other examples, we do not wait for the poller to complete. We send the `DELETE HTTP` request to Azure. We do not wait for the infrastructure to be completely deleted; instead, we trust that the acceptance of `delete` means that it will eventually reach the deleted terminal state.

We have now built and cleaned up a stack of infrastructure using the Azure SDK for Go. We have learned how to create resource groups, virtual networks, subnets, public IPs, and VMs, and how a pattern can be extended to any resource in Azure. Additionally, these skills are applicable to each of the major clouds, not just Azure. AWS and GCP both have similar concepts and API access patterns.

In the next section, we'll build an Azure Storage account and learn a bit about using the data plane of a cloud service by uploading files and then providing constrained access to download those files.

Using provisioned Azure infrastructure

In the previous section, we built a stack of computing and networking infrastructure to illustrate how to manipulate cloud infrastructure. In this section, we will pair a provisioning infrastructure with the Azure control plane and use the infrastructure through the provisioned service's data plane.

In this section, we are going to build a cloud storage infrastructure. We will use Azure Storage to store files and provide constrained access to those files via shared access signatures (https://docs.microsoft.com/en-us/azure/storage/common/storage-sas-overview). We will learn how to use ARM to fetch account keys and use those keys to provide constrained access to storage resources.

Building an Azure Storage account

Let's get started by running the example, and then we'll delve into the code for building the infrastructure and using the provisioned storage account. To execute the example, run the following:

```
$ go run ./cmd/storage/main.go
Staring to build Azure resources...
Building an Azure Resource Group named "falling-rain"...
Building an Azure Storage Account named "fallingrain"...
```

```
Fetching the Azure Storage Account shared key...
Creating a new container "jd-imgs" in the Storage Account...
Reading all files ./blobs...
Uploading file "img1.jpeg" to container jd-imgs...
Uploading file "img2.jpeg" to container jd-imgs...
Uploading file "img3.jpeg" to container jd-imgs...
Uploading file "img4.jpeg" to container jd-imgs...

Generating readonly links to blobs that expire in 2 hours...
https://fallingrain.blob.core.windows.net/jd-imgs/img1.
jpeg?se=2022-04-20T21%3A50%3A25Z&sig=MrwCXziwLLQeepLZj
rW93IeEkTLxJ%2BEX16rmGa2w548%3D&sp=r&sr=b&st=2022-04-
20T19%3A50%3A25Z&sv=2019-12-12
...
Press enter to delete the infrastructure.
```

As you can see from the previous output, the example creates a resource group and a storage account, fetches an account key, and then uploads all of the images in ./blobs to the cloud. Finally, the example prints out URIs for each of the images using shared access signatures. If you click on one of those URIs, you should be able to download the image we uploaded to the storage account.

What happens when you try to download img1.jpeg without the query string – for example, using the https://fallingrain.blob.core.windows.net/jd-imgs/img1.jpeg link? You should get an access denied message.

Let's see how we can use Azure Storage to upload files and constrain access.

Provisioning Azure Storage using Go

In this example, we are going to provision an Azure resource group and an Azure Storage account. We are using abbreviated error-handling behavior to keep the code as concise as possible for illustrative purposes. As I said in the previous section, panic is not your friend. Please wrap and bubble your errors as appropriate.

Let's start with the entry point of Go run ./cmd/storage/main.go, and learn how to use Go to provision the storage account:

```
func init() {
        _ = godotenv.Load()
}

func main() {
```

```
        subscriptionID := MustGetenv("AZURE_SUBSCRIPTION_ID")
        factory := mgmt.NewStorageFactory(subscriptionID)
        fmt.Println("Staring to build Azure resources...")
        stack := factory.CreateStorageStack(
    context.Background(),
    "southcentralus",
)

        uploadBlobs(stack)
        printSASUris(stack)

        fmt.Println("Press enter to delete the infrastructure.")
        reader := bufio.NewReader(os.Stdin)
        _, _ = reader.ReadString('\n')
        factory.DestroyStorageStack(context.Background(), stack)
}
```

Similar to the VM infrastructure example in the previous section, we create `StorageFactory` using `NewStorageFactory()` and then use it to create and destroy the storage stack. In the middle, we call `uploadBlobs()` to upload the image files and `printSASUris()` to generate and print shared access signatures for each of the uploaded files.

Let's start by taking a look at how we provision the storage infrastructure:

```
type StorageFactory struct {
        subscriptionID  string
        cred            azcore.TokenCredential
        groupsClient    *armresources.ResourceGroupsClient
        storageClient   *armstorage.AccountsClient
}

func NewStorageFactory(subscriptionID string) *StorageFactory {
        cred := HandleErrWithResult(
    azidentity. NewDefaultAzureCredential(nil),
)
        return &StorageFactory{
                cred:           cred,
                subscriptionID: subscriptionID,
                groupsClient:   BuildClient(subscriptionID, cred,
    armresources.NewResourceGroupsClient),
```

```
            storageClient: BuildClient(subscriptionID, cred,
armstorage.NewAccountsClient),
        }
}
```

The storage factory looks similar to `VirtualMachineFactory` from the previous section. However, the storage factory only uses the resource group and storage clients.

Next, let's explore `CreateStorageStack()` to see how we create the Azure Storage account:

```
func (sf *StorageFactory) CreateStorageStack(ctx context.
Context, location string) *StorageStack {
    stack := &StorageStack{
        name: haiku.Haikunate(),
    }
    stack.ResourceGroup = sf.createResourceGroup(ctx, stack.
name, location)
    stack.Account = sf.createStorageAccount(ctx, stack.name,
location)
    stack.AccountKey = sf.getPrimaryAccountKey(ctx, stack)
    return stack
}
```

In the preceding code, we create a human-readable name for the stack, which we will use to name the resource group and the storage account. We then populate the stack fields with created resources.

I will not cover `createResourceGroup()`, as it was covered in the previous section. However, `createStorageAccount()` and `getPrimaryAccountKey()` are interesting. Let's explore what they do:

```
// createStorageAccount creates an Azure Storage Account
func (sf *StorageFactory) createStorageAccount(ctx context.
Context, name, location string) armstorage.Account {
    param := armstorage.AccountCreateParameters{
        Location: to.Ptr(location),
        Kind:     to.Ptr(armstorage.KindBlockBlobStorage),
        SKU: &armstorage.SKU{
            Name: to.Ptr(armstorage.SKUNamePremiumLRS),
            Tier: to.Ptr(armstorage.SKUTierPremium),
        },
    }

    accountName := strings.Replace(name, "-", "", -1)
```

```
    fmt.Printf("Building an Azure Storage Account named
%q...\n", accountName)
    poller, err := sf.storageClient.BeginCreate(ctx, name,
accountName, param, nil)
    HandleErr(err)
    res := HandleErrPoller(ctx, poller)
    return res.Account
}
```

In the preceding code, `createStorageAccount()` creates a new block blob, with premium tier performance, and a locally redundant Azure Storage account. Block blobs (https://docs.microsoft.com/en-us/rest/api/storageservices/understanding-block-blobs--append-blobs--and-page-blobs#about-block-blobs) are optimized for uploading large amounts of data and, as the name implies, are broken into blocks of arbitrary size. Locally redundant storage (https://docs.microsoft.com/en-us/azure/storage/common/storage-redundancy#locally-redundant-storage) means that each block is replicated 3 times within the same data center and is guaranteed to provide 99.999999999% (11 nines!) durability over a given year. Finally, the premium tier (https://docs.microsoft.com/en-us/azure/storage/blobs/scalability-targets-premium-block-blobs) of Azure Storage indicates that the storage account will be optimized for applications that consistently require low latency and high transaction throughput for block blob mutations.

Beyond the configuration of the storage account, provisioning is handled in a similar way to the rest of the resources we have provisioned thus far.

To generate shared access signatures for uploaded blobs, we need to acquire a storage account key that is provisioned when the storage account is created. Let's see how we can request the storage account keys:

```
func (sf *StorageFactory) getPrimaryAccountKey(ctx context.
Context, stack *StorageStack) *armstorage.AccountKey {
    fmt.Printf("Fetching the Azure Storage Account shared
key...\n")
    res, err := sf.storageClient.ListKeys(ctx, stack.name,
*stack.Account.Name, nil)
    HandleErr(err)
    return res.Keys[0]
}
```

In this code, we fetch the account keys by calling `ListKeys` on the storage client. We return the first account key returned.

Now that we have provisioned the storage infrastructure and fetched the storage account key, we are ready to use the storage service to upload files and provide constrained access to the files.

Using Azure Storage

Let's upload the files in `./blobs` to our storage account with the `uploadBlobs` func:

```go
func uploadBlobs(stack *mgmt.StorageStack) {
    serviceClient := stack.ServiceClient()
    containerClient, err := serviceClient.NewContainerClient("jd-imgs")
    HandleErr(err)

    fmt.Printf("Creating a new container \"jd-imgs\" in the Storage Account...\n")
    _, err = containerClient.Create(context.Background(), nil)
    HandleErr(err)

    fmt.Printf("Reading all files ./blobs...\n")
    files, err := ioutil.ReadDir("./blobs")
    HandleErr(err)
    for _, file := range files {
        fmt.Printf("Uploading file %q to container jd-imgs...\n", file.Name())
        blobClient := HandleErrWithResult(containerClient.NewBlockBlobClient(file.Name()))
        osFile := HandleErrWithResult(os.Open(path.Join("./blobs", file.Name())))
        _ = HandleErrWithResult(blobClient.UploadFile(context.Background(), osFile, azblob.UploadOption{}))
    }
}
```

In the preceding code, we create a service client to interact with the storage service client. With `serviceClient`, we can define a new storage container called `jd-imgs`. You can think of a storage container as an entity similar to a directory. After specifying the container, we call `create` to request the storage service to create the container. Once we have a container, we then iterate over each image in the `./blobs` directory and upload them using the block blob client.

Until this point, we have been using the Azure CLI identity as our credential for interacting with Azure services. However, when we instantiated `serviceClient`, we instead began using the Azure Storage account keys to interact with our storage account. Let's take a look at `ServiceClient()`:

```
func (ss *StorageStack) ServiceClient() *azblob.ServiceClient {
    cred := HandleErrWithResult(azblob.NewSharedKeyCredential(*ss.Account.Name, *ss.AccountKey.Value))
    blobURI := *ss.Account.Properties.PrimaryEndpoints.Blob
    client, err := azblob.NewServiceClientWithSharedKey(blobURI, cred, nil)
    HandleErr(err)
    return client
}
```

In the preceding code, we create a new credential using the storage account name and the value of the account key. We construct `ServiceClient`, using the blob endpoint for the storage account and the newly constructed shared key credential. The shared key credential will be used for all clients that derive from the service client.

Now that we have uploaded the files as block blobs, let's see how we can create signed URIs to provide constrained access:

```
func printSASUris(stack *mgmt.StorageStack) {
    serviceClient := stack.ServiceClient()
    containerClient, err := serviceClient.NewContainerClient("jd-imgs")
    HandleErr(err)

    fmt.Printf("\nGenerating readonly links to blobs that expire in 2 hours...\n")
    files := HandleErrWithResult(ioutil.ReadDir("./blobs"))
    for _, file := range files {
        blobClient := HandleErrWithResult(containerClient.NewBlockBlobClient(file.Name()))
        permissions := azblob.BlobSASPermissions{
            Read: true,
        }
        now := time.Now().UTC()
        sasQuery := HandleErrWithResult(blobClient.GetSASToken(permissions, now, now.Add(2*time.Hour)))
        fmt.Println(blobClient.URL() + "?" + sasQuery.Encode())
```

```
        }
}
```

We construct `ServiceClient` and establish a container client in the preceding code block. Then, we iterate over every file within the local `./blobs` directory and create a blob client.

The blob client has a helpful method called `GetSASToken`, which generates a shared access token given blob access permissions and a validity time span. In our case, we are granting read access that starts immediately and expires in 2 hours. To create a complete URI to access the blob, we need to combine the blob URL and the query string generated by the shared access token. We do that with `blobClient.URL()`, `"?"`, and `sasQuery.Encode()`. Now, anyone with the signed URI will have access to read the file.

In this final section, we built and used cloud storage infrastructure to store files and provide constrained access to those files by using shared access signatures. We learned how to fetch account keys and use them to provide constrained access to storage resources. Using these skills, you can combine permissions and other constraints to tailor access to your needs. Providing constrained access in this way is a powerful tool. For example, you can create a write-only URI to a blob not yet created, pass the URI to a client, and then have them upload a file without having access to any other files in the storage account.

Summary

Azure Storage is only one service out of hundreds that you can use to build applications in the cloud. Each cloud service provider has analogous storage services that operate in a similar way. The examples shown in this chapter are specific to Microsoft Azure, but they can be easily emulated for other clouds.

The Azure Storage example is useful for illustrating the separation between the management plane and the data plane of the cloud. If you look closely, you can observe a significant similarity in **Create, Read, Update, and Delete** (**CRUD**) resource operations using ARM in contrast to interacting with the Azure Storage service, container, and blob clients. Resource management is uniform within a cloud. The data plane for databases, storage services, and content delivery networks is rarely uniform and often exposed through purpose-built APIs.

Summary

In this chapter, we learned that the cloud is not just someone else's computer. The cloud is a planet-scale web of high-security data centers filled with computing, networking, and storage hardware. We also learned the fundamentals of identity, authentication, and authorization, with specifics drawn from Microsoft Azure. We briefly covered Azure RBAC and its relationship with AAD identities. Finally, we learned how to provision and use cloud resources using Microsoft Azure.

You should be able to take what you learned here and apply it to provisioning and using cloud services to achieve your goals. These skills were focused on Microsoft Azure, but the skills learned here are easily transferred to the AWS or Google clouds.

In the next chapter, we're going to explore what happens when software operates in less-than-perfect conditions. We will learn to design for chaos.

16
Designing for Chaos

Writing software that works in perfect conditions is easy. It would be nice if you never had to worry about network latency, service timeouts, storage outages, misbehaving applications, users sending bad arguments, security issues, or any of the real-life scenarios we find ourselves in.

In my experience, things tend to fail in the following three ways:

- Immediately
- Gradually
- Spectacularly

Immediately is usually the result of a change to application code that causes a service to die on startup or when receiving traffic to an endpoint. Most development test environments or canary rollouts catch these before any real problems occur in production. This type is generally trivial to fix and prevent.

Gradually is usually the result of some type of memory leak, thread/goroutine leak, or ignoring design limitations. These problems build up over time and begin causing problems that result in services crashing or growth in latency at unacceptable levels. Many times, these are easy fixes caught during canary rollouts once the problem is recognized. In the case of design issues, fixes can require months of intense work to resolve. Some rare versions of this have what I call a cliff failure: gradual growth hits a limitation that cannot be overcome by throwing more resources at the problem. That type of problem belongs to our next category.

That category is **spectacularly**. This is when you find a problem in production that is causing mass failures when a few moments ago everything was working fine. Cellphones everywhere start pinging alerts, dashboards go red, dogs and cats start living together—mass hysteria! This could be the rollout of a bugged service that overwhelms your network, the death of a caching service you depend on, or a type of query that crashes your service. These outages cause mass panic, test your ability to communicate across teams efficiently, and are the ones that show up in news articles.

This chapter will focus on designing infrastructure tooling to survive chaos. The most spectacular failures of major cloud companies have often been the results of infrastructure tooling, from **Google Site Reliability Engineering** (**Google SRE**) erasing all the disks at their cluster satellites to **Amazon Web Services** (**AWS**) overwhelming their network with infrastructure tool **remote procedure calls** (**RPCs**).

In this chapter, we will look at safe ways for **first responders** (**FRs**) to stop automation, how to write idempotent workflow tools, packages for incremental backoffs of failed RPCs, providing pacing limiters for rollouts, and much more.

To do this, we will be introducing concepts and packages that will be built into a generic workflow system that you can use to further your education. The system will be able to take requests to do some type of work, will validate the parameters are correct, validate the request against a set of policies, and then execute that work.

In this model, clients (which can be **command-line interface** (**CLI**) applications or services) detail work to be done via a protocol buffer and send it to the server. The workflow system does all the actual work.

We are going to cover the following main topics in this chapter:

- Using overload prevention mechanisms
- Using rate limiters to prevent runaway workflows
- Building workflows that are repeatable and never lost
- Using policies to restrict tools
- Building systems with an emergency stop

Technical requirements

This chapter has the same requirements as previous chapters, only adding the need to access the following GitHub repository: https://github.com/PacktPublishing/Go-for-DevOps/tree/rev0/chapter/16/workflow.

With that said, let's jump into our first chapter on using overload prevention mechanisms to keep our network and services healthy when problems occur.

Using overload prevention mechanisms

When you have a small set of services, misbehaving applications generally cause small problems. This is because there is usually an overabundance of network capacity to absorb badly behaving applications within a data center, and with a small set of services, it is usually intuitive to figure out what would cause the issue.

When you have a large number of applications running, your network and your machines are usually oversubscribed. **Oversubscribed** means that your network and systems cannot handle all your applications running at 100%. Oversubscription is common in networks or clusters to control costs. This works because, at any given time, most applications ebb and flow with network traffic, **central processing unit** (**CPU**), and memory.

An application that suddenly experiences some type of bug can go into **retry loops** that quickly overwhelm a service. In addition, if some catastrophic event occurs that takes a service offline, trying to bring the application back online can cause the service to go down as it is overwhelmed by requests that are queuing on all clients.

Worse is what can happen to the network. If the network becomes overwhelmed or when cloud devices have their **queries per second** (**QPS**) exceeded, other applications can have their traffic adversely affected. This can mask the true cause of your problems.

There are several ways of preventing these types of problems, with the two most common being the following:

- Circuit breakers
- Backoff implementations

Each of these prevention mechanisms has the same idea: when failures occur, prevent retries from overwhelming the service.

Infrastructure services are often an overlooked use case for these prevention mechanisms. Many times, we concentrate on our public services, but infrastructure services are just as important. If that service is critical and becomes overwhelmed, it can be difficult to restore it without manually touching other services to reduce load.

Let's have a look at one of the more popular methods: the **circuit breaker**.

Case study – AWS client requests overwhelm the network

AWS had an outage that affected AWS customers across the world when a misbehaving application began sending too much traffic across a network boundary between their customer network and their core network where AWS critical services live. This was restricted to their `us-east-1` region, but the effects were felt by their customers in multiple locations.

The problem was twofold, comprising the following factors:

- A misbehaving application sending too many requests.
- Their clients didn't back off on failure.

It is the second issue that caused the long failure. AWS had been doing the right thing in having a standard client for RPCs that invoked incrementing backoffs when requests failed. However, for some reason, the client library did not perform as expected in this case.

This means that instead of the load reducing itself as the endpoints became overwhelmed, they went into some type of infinite loop that kept increasing the load on the affected systems and overwhelmed their network cross-connects. This overwhelming of cross-connects disabled their monitoring and prevented them from seeing the problem. The result was they had to try reducing their network load by scaling back application traffic while trying to not affect the customer services that were still working—a feat I would not envy.

This case points to how important it is to prevent application retries when failures occur. To read more on this from Amazon, see the following web page: `https://aws.amazon.com/message/12721/`.

Using circuit breakers

Circuit breakers work by wrapping RPC calls within a client that will automatically fail any attempt once a threshold is reached. All calls then simply return a failure without actually making any attempt for some amount of time.

Circuit breakers have three modes, as follows:

- Closed
- Open
- Half-open

A circuit breaker is in a **closed** state when everything is working. This is the normal state.

A circuit breaker is in an **open** state after some amount of failures trip the breaker. When in this state, all requests are automatically failed without trying to send the message. This period lasts for some amount of time. It is suggested that this time be some set period and some randomness to prevent spontaneous synchronization.

A circuit breaker moves into a **half-open** state after some time in the open state. Once in the half-open state, some number of requests that are requested are actually tried. If some threshold of success is passed, the circuit breaker moves back into the **closed** state. If not, the circuit breaker moves into the **open** state again.

You can find several different circuit-breaker implementations for Go, but one of the most popular was developed at Sony, called **gobreaker** (https://github.com/sony/gobreaker).

Let's look at how we might use it to limit retries for **HTTP** queries, as follows:

```go
type HTTP struct {
    client *http.Client
    cb     *gobreaker.CircuitBreaker
}

func New(client *http.Client) *HTTP {
    return &HTTP{
        client: client,
        cb: gobreaker.NewCircuitBreaker(
            gobreaker.Settings{
                MaxRequests: 1,
                Interval:    30 * time.Second,
                Timeout:     10 * time.Second,
                ReadyToTrip: func(c gobreaker.Counts) bool {
                    return c.ConsecutiveFailures > 5
                },
            },
        ),
    }
}

func (h *HTTP) Get(req *http.Request) (*http.Response, error) {
    if _, ok := req.Context().Deadline(); !ok {
        return nil, fmt.Errorf("all requests must have a Context deadline set")
    }
```

```
        r, err := h.cb.Execute(
            func() (interface{}, error) {
                resp, err := h.client.Do(req)
                if resp.StatusCode != 200 {
                    return nil, fmt.Errorf("non-200 response
 code")
                }
                return resp, err
            },
        )
        if err != nil {
            return nil, err
        }
        return r.(*http.Response), nil
}
```

The preceding code defines the following:

- An HTTP type that holds both of these:
  - An `http.Client` for making HTTP requests
  - A circuit breaker for HTTP requests
- A `New()` constructor for our `HTTP` type. It creates a circuit breaker with settings that enforces the following:
  - Allows one request at a time when in the half-open state
  - Has a 30-second period where we are half-open after being in a closed state
  - Has a closed state that lasts 10 seconds
  - Enters the closed state if we have five consecutive failures
  - A `Get()` method on `HTTP` that does the following:
  - Checks that `*http.Request` has a timeout define
  - Calls the circuit breaker on our `client.Do()` method
  - Converts the returned `interface{}` to the underlying `*http.Response`

This code gives us a robust HTTP client wrapped with a circuit breaker. A better version of this might pass in the settings to the constructor, but I wanted it to be packed neatly for the example.

If you'd like to see a demo of the circuit breaker in action, you can see it here:

https://go.dev/play/p/qpG_13OE-bu

Using backoff implementations

A **backoff implementation** wraps RPCs with a client that will retry with a pause between attempts. These pauses get longer and longer until they reach some maximum value.

Backoff implementations can have a wide range of methods for calculating the time period. We will concentrate on exponential backoff in this chapter.

Exponential backoff simply adds delays to each attempt that increases exponentially as failures mount. As with circuit breakers, there are many packages offering backoff implementations. For this example, we will use https://pkg.go.dev/github.com/cenk/backoff, which is an implementation of Google's HTTP backoff library for Java.

This backoff implementation offers many important features that Google has found useful over years of studying service failures. One of the most important features in the library is adding random values to sleep times between retries. This prevents multiple clients from syncing their retry attempts.

Other important features include the ability to honor context cancellations and supply maximum retry attempts.

Let's look at how we might use it to limit retries for HTTP queries, as follows:

```
type HTTP struct {
    client *http.Client
}

func New(client *http.Client) *HTTP {
    return &HTTP{
        client: client,
    }
}

func (h *HTTP) Get(req *http.Request) (*http.Response, error) {
    if _, ok := req.Context().Deadline(); !ok {
        return nil, fmt.Errorf("all requests must have a Context deadline set")
    }

    var resp *http.Response
```

```go
        op := func() error {
                var err error
                resp, err = h.client.Do(req)
                if err != nil {
                        return err
                }
                if resp.StatusCode != 200 {
                        return fmt.Errorf("non-200 response code")
                }
                return nil
        }

        err := backoff.Retry(
                op,
                backoff.WithContext(
                        backoff.NewExponentialBackOff(),
                        req.Context(),
                ),
        )
        if err != nil {
                return nil, err
        }
        return resp, nil
}
```

The preceding code defines the following:

- An HTTP type that holds both of these:
  - An `http.Client` for making HTTP requests
  - An exponential backoff for HTTP requests
- A `New()` constructor for our `HTTP` type
- A `Get()` method on `HTTP`
- It also does the following:
  - Creates a `func()` error that attempts our request called `op`
  - Runs `op` with retries and exponential delays
  - Creates an exponential backoff with default values
  - Wraps that backoff in `BackOffContext` to honor our context deadline

For a list of the default values for `ExponentialBackoff`, see the following web page:

`https://pkg.go.dev/github.com/cenkalti/backoff?utm_source=godoc#ExponentialBackOff`

If you'd like to see a demo of this backoff in action, you can see it here:

`https://go.dev/play/p/30tetefu9t0`

Combining circuit breakers with backoff

When choosing a prevention implementation, another option is to combine a circuit breaker with backoff for a more robust implementation.

A backoff implementation can be set to have a maximum time in which retries are occurring. Wrapping that inside a circuit breaker to make any set of failed attempts to trigger our circuit breaker not only potentially reduces our load by slowing our requests, but we can also stop these attempts with our circuit breaker.

If you would like to see an implementation combining both, you can go to the following web page:

`https://go.dev/play/p/gERsR7fvDck`

In this section, we have discussed the need to have mechanisms to prevent overwhelming your network and services. We have discussed an AWS outage that was partially due to the failure of such mechanisms. You were introduced to the circuit-breaker and backoff mechanisms to prevent these types of failures. Finally, we have shown two popular packages for implementing these mechanisms with examples.

In our workflow engine, we will be implementing these prevention mechanisms for our **Google RPC (gRPC)** client to prevent issues talking to our server. You can see that here:

`https://github.com/PacktPublishing/Go-for-DevOps/blob/rev0/chapter/16/workflow/client/client.go`

In our next section, we will be looking at preventing workflows from executing too fast using rate limiters. It is important to enforce both pacing for workflows' actions and to prevent too many workflows of a type from executing at the same time.

Using rate limiters to prevent runaway workflows

DevOps engineers can be responsible for a service that is made up of dozens of microservices. These microservices can then number in the dozens to the tens of thousands of instances running in data centers around the globe. Once a service consists of more than a couple of instances, some form of rate control needs to exist to prevent bad rollouts or configuration changes from causing mass destruction.

Some type of a **rate limiter** for work with forced pause intervals is critical to prevent runaway infrastructure changes.

Rate limiting is easy to implement, but the scope of the rate limiter is going to depend on what your workflows are doing. For services, you may only want one type of change to happen at a time or only affect some number of instances at a time.

The first type of rate limiting would prevent multiple instances of a workflow type from running at a time; for example, you might only want one satellite disk erasure to occur at a time.

The second is to limit the number of devices, services, and so on that can be affected concurrently; for example, you might only want to allow two routers in a region to be taken out for a firmware upgrade.

For rate limiters to be effective, having a single system that executes actions for a set of services can greatly streamline these efforts. This allows centralized enforcement of policies such as rate limiting.

Let's look at the simplest implementation of a rate limiter in Go using channels.

Case study – Google satellite disk erase

In the early days, Google did not own all the data center space it does today—we were in a lot of rented space with a large number of machines. In some places, however, this was prohibitively expensive. To speed up connectivity in these places, we would rent small spaces that could have cache machines, terminate HTTP connections and backhaul the traffic to a data center. We called these **satellites**.

Google has an automated process for the decommissioning of machines. One part of this is called disk erase, whereby the machines have their disks wiped.

The software was written to grab a list of machines for a satellite and filter out other machines. Unfortunately, if you run it twice on a satellite, the filter is not applied, and your list of machines is all machines in every satellite.

Disk erase was very efficient, putting all machines in all satellites in disk erase at once before anything could be done.

For a more detailed breakdown, you can read `https://sre.google/workbook/postmortem-culture/`, where several **Site Reliability Engineers** (**SREs**) have provided more detail in the context of postmortems.

We can look at the filtering part of the code and discuss bad design, but there will always be badly written tools with bad inputs. Even if you currently have a good culture for code reviews, things slip by. During times of hypergrowth with new engineers, these types of problems can rear their ugly heads.

Some tools that are known to be dangerous in the hands of a small group of experienced engineers can be used quite safely, but new engineers without experience or ones lacking proper fear can quickly devastate your infrastructure.

In this case and many other cases, centralized execution with rate limiting and other mandatory safety mechanisms allow new people to write tools that may be dangerous but limited in their blast radius.

Channel-based rate limiter

A **channel-based rate limiter** is useful when a single program is handling the automation. In that case, you can make a limiter that is based on the size of a channel. Let's make a limiter that allows only a fixed number of items to be worked on at a time, as follows:

```go
limit := make(chan struct{}, 3)
```

We now have something that can limit the number of items that can be worked on.

Let's define a simple type that represents some action to be executed, as follows:

```go
type Job interface {
    Validate(job *pb.Job) error
    Run(ctx context.Context, job *pb.Job) error
}
```

This defines a `Job` that can do the following:

- Validate a `pb.Job` definition passed to us
- Run the job with that definition

Here is a very simplistic example of executing a set of jobs contained in something called a block, which is just a holder of a slice of jobs:

```go
wg := sync.WaitGroup{}
for _, block := range work.Blocks {
    limit := make(chan struct{}, req.Limit)
    for _, job := range block.Jobs {
        job := job
        limit <- struct{}{}
        wg.Add()
        go func() {
            defer wg.Done()
            defer func() {
                <-limit
            }()
            job()
        }()
    }
}
wg.Wait()
```

In the preceding code snippet, the following happens:

- We loop through a slice of `Block` inside the `work.Blocks` variable.
- We loop through a slice of `Jobs` in the `block.Jobs` variable.
- If we already have `req.limit` items running, `limit <- struct{}{}` will block.
- It executes our job concurrently.
- When our goroutine ends, we remove an item from our `workLimit` queue.
- We wait for all goroutines to end.

This code prevents more than `req.limit` items from happening at a time. If this were a server, you could make `limit` a variable shared by all users and prevent more than three items of work from occurring for all work that was happening in your system. Alternatively, you could have different limiters for different classes of work.

A note about that `job := job` part. This is creating a shadowed variable of `job`. This prevents the `job` variable from being changed inside our goroutine when the loop and the goroutine are running in parallel by making a copy of the variable in the same scope as the goroutine. This is a common concurrency bug for new Go developers, sometimes called the **for loop gotcha**. Here is a playground you can use to work through why this is necessary: `https://go.dev/play/p/O9DcUIKuGBv`.

We have completed the following example in the playground that you can play around with to explore these concepts:

`https://go.dev/play/p/aYoCTEFvRBI`

You can see a channel-based rate limiter in action in the workflow service inside `runJobs()` here:

`https://github.com/PacktPublishing/Go-for-DevOps/blob/rev0/chapter/16/workflow/internal/service/executor/executor.go`

Token-bucket rate limiter

Token buckets are normally used to provide burstable traffic management for services. There are several types of token buckets, the most popular being the standard token bucket and the leaky token bucket.

These are not normally deployed for an infrastructure tool, as clients tend to be internal and more predictable than external-facing services, but a useful type of a token bucket can be used to provide pacing. A standard token bucket simply holds some fixed set of tokens, and those tokens are refilled at some interval.

Here's a sample one:

```go
type bucket struct {
    tokens chan struct{}
}

func newbucket(size, incr int, interval time.Duration) (*bucket, error) {
    b := bucket{tokens: make(chan struct{}, size)}
    go func() {
        for _ = range time.Tick(interval) {
            for i := 0; i < incr; i++ {
                select{
                case <-b.tokens:
                    continue
```

```
                    default:
                    }
                    break
                }
            }
        }()
        return &b, nil
}

func (b *bucket) token(ctx context.Context) error {
        select {
        case <-ctx.Done():
            return ctx.Err()
        case b.tokens <-struct{}{}:
        }
        return nil
}
```

This preceding code snippet does the following:

- Defines a `bucket` type that holds our tokens
- Has `newBucket()`, which creates a new `bucket` instance with the following attributes:
- `size`, which is the total amount of tokens that can be stored
  - `incr`, which is how many tokens are added at a time
  - `interval`, which is how often to add to the bucket

  It also does the following:
  - Starts a goroutine that will fill the bucket at intervals
  - Will only fill to the max `size` value
- Defines `token()`, which retrieves a token:
  - If no tokens are available, we wait for one.
  - If a `Context` is canceled, we return an error.

This is a fairly robust implementation of a standard token bucket. You may be able to achieve a faster implementation using the `atomic` package, but it will be more complex to do so.

An implementation with input checking and the ability to stop a goroutine created with `newBucket()` can be found here:

https://go.dev/play/p/6Dihz2lUH-P

If we want, we could use a token bucket to only allow execution at some rate we define. This can be used inside a job to limit how fast an individual action can happen or to only allow so many instances of a workflow to happen within some time period. We will use it in our next section to limit when a particular workflow is allowed to happen.

Our generic workflow system has a token bucket package here:

https://github.com/PacktPublishing/Go-for-DevOps/blob/rev0/chapter/16/workflow/internal/token/token.go

In this section, we looked at how rate limiters can be used to prevent runaway workflows. We talked about Google's satellite disk erase as a case study on this type of event. We showed how channel-based rate limiters can be implemented to control concurrent operations. We talked about how a token bucket could be used to rate-limit a number of executions within a certain time period.

This section is also laying the foundation of how executing actions, defined as a job, will work in the workflow system example we are building.

Now that we have some ideas on how we can rate-limit actions, let's look at how we can develop repeatable workflows that cannot be lost by a client.

Building workflows that are repeatable and never lost

As DevOps engineers, we write tooling all the time. In small shops, many times, these are sets of scripts. In large shops, these are complicated systems.

As you may have gleaned from the introduction, I believe that tool execution should always occur in a centralized service, regardless of scale. A basic service is easy to write, and you can expand and replace it as new needs arise.

But to make a workflow service work, two key concepts must be true of the workflows you create, as follows:

- They must be repeatable.
- They cannot be lost.

The first concept is that running a workflow more than once on the same infrastructure should produce the same result. We called this **idempotency**, borrowing the computer science term.

The second is that a workflow cannot be lost. If a tool creates a workflow to be executed by a system and the tool dies, the tool must be able to know that the workflow is running and resume watching it.

Building idempotent workflows

Idempotency is a concept that if you make a call with the same parameters multiple times, you receive the same result. This is an important concept for writing certain types of software.

In infrastructure, we modify this definition slightly: an idempotent action is one that, if repeated with the same parameters and without changes to the infrastructure outside of this call, will return the same result.

Idempotency is key to making workflows that can be recovered when your workflow system goes down. Simple workflow systems can just repeat the entire workflow. More complicated systems can restart from where they left off.

Many times, developers don't think deeply about idempotency. For example, let's look at a simple operation to copy some content to a file. Here is a naive implementation:

```
func CopyToFile(content []byte, p string) error {
    return io.WriteFile(p, content)
}
```

The preceding code contains the following:

- A `content` argument that represents content for a file
- A `p` argument, which is the path to the file

It also does the following:

- Writes `content` to file at p

This initially appears to be idempotent. If our workflow was killed after `CopyToFile()` was called but before `io.WriteFile()` was called, we could repeat this operation, and it initially looks as though if we called this twice, we would still get the same result.

But what if the file didn't exist and we created it but did not have permissions to edit an existing file? If our program died before recording the result of io.WriteFile() but after the change has occurred, a repeat of this action would report an error, and because the infrastructure did not change, the action is not idempotent.

Let's modify this to make it idempotent, as follows:

```go
func CopyToFile(content []byte, p string) error {
    if _, ok := os.Stat(p); ok {
        f, err := os.Open(p)
        if err != nil {
            return err
        }
        h0 := sha256.New()
        io.Copy(h0, f)

        h1 := sha256.New()
        h1.Write(content)

        if h0.Sum(nil) == h1.Sum(nil) {
            return nil
        }
    }
    return io.WriteFile(p, content)
}
```

This code checks if the file exists and then does the following:

- If it exists and it already has the content, it doesn't do anything.
- If it doesn't, it writes the content.

This uses the standard library's sha256 package to calculate checksum hashes to validate if the content is the same.

The key to providing idempotency is often simply checking if the work is already done.

This leads us to a concept called three-way handshakes. This concept can be used in actions to provide idempotency when you need to talk to other systems via RPC. We will discuss how to use this concept in terms of executing workflows, but this can also be used in idempotent actions that talk to other services.

Using three-way handshakes to prevent workflow loss

When we write an application that talks to a workflow service, it is important that the application never loses track of workflows that are running on our service.

The three-way handshake is a name I borrowed from **Transmission Control Protocol (TCP)**. TCP has a handshake that establishes a socket between two machines. It consists of the following:

- **SYNchonize (SYN)**, a request to open a connection
- **ACKnowledge (ACK)**, an acknowledgment of the request
- SYN-ACK, an acknowledgment of the ACK

When a client sends a request to execute a workflow, we never want the workflow service to execute a workflow that the client doesn't know exists due to a crash of the client.

This can happen because the client program crashes or the machine the client is running on fails. If we sent a workflow and the service began executing after a single RPC, the client could crash after sending the RPC but before receiving an **identifier (ID)** for the workflow.

This would lead to a scenario where when the client was restarted, it did not know the workflow service was already running the workflow, and it might send another workflow that did the same thing.

To avoid that, instead of a single RPC to execute a workflow, a workflow should have a three-way handshake to do the following:

- Send the workflow to the service
- Receive the workflow ID
- Send a request to execute the workflow with its ID to the service

This allows the client to record the ID of the workflow before it executes. If the client crashes before recording the ID, the service simply has a non-running workflow record. If the client dies after the service begins execution, when the client restarts, it can check the status of the workflow. If it is running, it can simply monitor it. If it isn't running, it can request it to execute again.

For our workflow service, let's create a service definition that supports our three-way handshake using gRPC, as follows:

```
service Workflow {
    rpc Submit(WorkReq) returns (WorkResp) {};
    rpc Exec(ExecReq) returns (ExecResp) {};
    rpc Status(StatusReq) returns (StatusResp) {};
}
```

This defines a service with the following calls:

- `Submit` submits a `WorkReq` message that describes the work to be done.
- `Exec` executes a `WorkReq` previously sent to the server with `Submit`.
- `Status` retrieves the status of a `WorkReq`.

The content of the messages for these service calls will be discussed in detail in the next section, but the key to this is that on `Submit()`, `WorkResp` will return an ID, but the workflow will not execute. When `Exec()` is called, we will send the ID we received from our `Submit()` call, and our `Status()` call allows us to check the status of any workflow.

We now have the basic definition of a workflow service that includes a three-way handshake to prevent any loss of workflows by our clients.

In this section, we have covered the basics of repeatable workflows that cannot be lost by our clients. We covered idempotency and how this leads to repeatable workflows. We have also shown how a three-way handshake allows us to prevent a running workflow from becoming *lost*.

We have also defined service calls that we will use in the workflow system we are building.

Now, we want to look at how tools can understand the **scope of work** (**SOW**) being executed to provide protection against runaway tooling. To do this, let's explore building a policy engine.

Using policies to restrict tools

Rate limiting is great for preventing a bad tool run from wiping out a service when all items of work are equal. But not all items of work are equal, as some machine services are more important and fragile than others (such as your service's database systems). Also, machines or services may need to be put into logical groupings that can only happen in some limited amount. These could be broken up by sites, geographical areas, and so on.

This logic is generally specific to some set of work items. This bundling, which we will call a SOW, can be quite complex.

To safely do work, you must understand your scope. This might be how you can safely update database schemas for a particular service or how many route reflectors in a network region can be modified at a time.

To implement safety around a SOW, we will introduce the idea of policies. Policies will be used to check a set of work that is entering into the system for compliance. If it is not compliant, it will be rejected.

As an example, we will look at handling disk erasures similar to Google's disk erase case study. Here are some protections we will add:

- Only allow a single satellite disk erasure to happen every hour
- Rate-limit so that we can only erase five machines at a time
- Must pause for 1 minute after each five-machine erasure

To be able to make a policy engine, we must have a common way to define what kind of work will be executed, in what order, and with what concurrency.

We also want the tool engineers to only define the work to be done and submit it to a separate service that executes it. This allows for the centralization of control.

Let's define the service that could do that in gRPC.

Defining a gRPC workflow service

In the previous section, we talked about a service definition that defines our three-way handshake. Let's look at the arguments to those calls to see what our clients will send the workflow service, as follows:

```
message WorkReq {
    string name = 1;
    string desc = 2;
    repeated Block blocks = 3;
```

```
}

message WorkResp {
      string id = 1;
}

message Block {
      string desc = 1;
      int32 rate_limit = 2;
      repeated Job jobs = 3;
}

message Job {
      string name = 1;
      map<string, string> args = 2;
}
```

These messages are used to define the work that a client wants the server to execute and contain the following attributes:

- `WorkReq` message contains the name of the work and all `Block` messages that make up a workflow.
- The `Block` message describes a body of work in the workflow; each `Block` executes one at a time and has the following attributes:
  - Has a set of `Job` messages that describe the work to be done
  - At what concurrency to execute the work described by the `Job` messages
  - The Job message describes the server's Job type on the server to call and with which arguments.
- The `WorkResp` message returns the ID that refers to this `WorkReq`:
  - Uses `UUIDv1` IDs that encapsulate time into the ID so we know when it was submitted to the system
  - Uses that time mechanic to prevent execution if the `Exec()` RPC is not called in by some expiration time

Exec messages provide the ID you want to execute, as illustrated here:

```
message ExecReq {
    string id = 1;
}

message ExecResp {}
```

There are more messages and `enums` to allow for a `Status` call. You can find the complete protocol buffer definition here:

https://github.com/PacktPublishing/Go-for-DevOps/blob/rev0/chapter/16/workflow/proto/diskerase.proto

Now that we have messages to describe the work to be done, let's look at creating a policy engine.

Creating a policy engine

A policy checks our work to make sure some parameter is allowed. In our case, these parameters are inside a `pb.WorkReq` instance. We want policies to be generic so that they can be reused against multiple types of work described by a `pb.WorkReq`. Once defined, we will have a `policy.json` file that defines which policies are applied against a specifically named `pb.WorkReq`.

To make this work, each policy will need to receive the settings for the policy that should be applied to a specific workflow. Let's define two interfaces that describe a policy and its settings, as follows:

```
type Settings interface{
    Validate() error
}

type Policy interface {
    Run(ctx context.Context, name string, req *pb.WorkReq, settings Settings) error
}
```

`Settings` will always be implemented as some struct. Its `Validate()` method will be used to validate that the fields for that struct are set to valid values.

`Policy` runs our implementation against a `pb.WorkReq` with the settings provided.

Each `WorkReq` that is submitted will have a list of policies to apply. This is defined as follows:

```
type PolicyArgs struct {
    Name string
    Settings Settings
}
```

`Name` is the name of the policy to invoke. `Settings` are the settings for that invocation.

The configuration file will detail a set of `PolicyArgs` arguments to run. Each policy will need to be registered in the system. We are going to skip the registration method for policies, but this is where the policies are registered:

```
var policies = map[string]registration{}

type registration struct {
    Policy Policy
    Settings Settings
}
```

When a `pb.WorkReq` enters the system, we want to invoke those policies concurrently against that `pb.WorkReq`. Let's have a look at how that would work here:

```
func Run(ctx context.Context, req *pb.WorkReq, args
...PolicyArgs) error {
    if len(args) == 0 {
        return nil
    }

    var cancel context.CancelFunc
    ctx, cancel = context.WithCancel(ctx)
    defer cancel()

    // Make a deep clone so that no policy is able to make changes.
    creq := proto.Clone(req).(*pb.WorkReq)

    runners := make([]func() error, 0, len(args))
    for _, arg := range args {
        r, ok := policies[arg.Name]
        if !ok {
            return fmt.Errorf("policy(%s) does not exist", arg.Name)
```

```go
            }
            runners = append(
                runners,
                func() error {
                    return r.Policy.Run(ctx, arg.Name, creq, arg.Settings)
                },
            )
        }

        wg := sync.WaitGroup{}
        ch := make(chan error, 1)

        wg.Add(len(runners))
        for _, r := range runners {
            r := r
            go func() {
                defer wg.Done()
                if err := r(); err != nil {
                    select {
                    case ch <- err:
                        cancel()
                    default:
                    }
                    return
                }
            }()
        }
        wg.Wait()

        select {
        case err := <-ch:
            return err
        default:
        }

        if !proto.Equal(req, creq) {
            return fmt.Errorf("a policy tried to modify a request: this is not allowed as it is a security violation")
        }
```

```
        return nil
}
```

This preceding code defines the following:

- If the configuration for a `pb.WorkReq` has no policies, return.
- Create a `Context` object so that we can cancel policies being run on an error.
- Clone our `pb.WorkReq` so that it cannot be changed by a `Policy`.
- Make sure each `Policy` that is named actually exists.
- Run all our policies with the settings that we were given.
- If there is an error in any of them, record it and cancel all running policies.
- Make sure the copy of `pb.WorkReq` is the same as what was submitted.

We now have the main parts of a policy engine. The full engine can be found here:

https://github.com/PacktPublishing/Go-for-DevOps/blob/rev0/chapter/16/workflow/internal/policy/policy.go

The `Reader` type that is used to read our `policy.json` file where we define policies is detailed here:

https://github.com/PacktPublishing/Go-for-DevOps/blob/rev0/chapter/16/workflow/internal/policy/config/config.go

Let's look at writing a policy to be used by our engine.

Writing a policy

One of the most basic policies that you can define against a workflow is to limit which job types are allowed in that workflow.

This prevents some new type of work from being introduced into a workflow where no one has thought about policies that need to be applied to that `Job`.

For our first `Policy` implementation, let's write one that checks our `pb.WorkReq` to allow only `Job` types we have defined in our policy configuration. If we receive an unexpected `Job`, we reject the `pb.WorkReq`.

Let's define the settings for our `Policy`, as follows:

```
type Settings struct {
    AllowedJobs []string
}
```

```go
func (s Settings) Validate() error {
    for _, n := range s.AllowedJobs {
        _, err := jobs.GetJob(n)
        if err != nil {
            return fmt.Errorf("allowed job(%s) is not defined in the proto")
        }
    }
    return nil
}

func (s Settings) allowed(name string) bool {
    for _, jn := range s.AllowedJobs {
        if jn == name {
            return true
        }
    }
    return false
}
```

This preceding code contains the following:

- Our specific `Settings` that implement `policy.Settings`
- `AllowedJobs`, which are the names of the jobs we allow
- A `Validate()` method that validates the listed `Jobs` exist
- An `allowed()` method that checks a given name against what we allow
- It also uses our `jobs` package to do these checks

With these settings, a user can define a policy for any workflow in our configuration file that defines which `Job` types are allowed.

Let's define a type that implements the `Policy` interface as follows:

```go
type Policy struct{}

func New() (Policy, error) {
    return Policy{}, nil
}

func (p Policy) Run(ctx context.Context, name string, req *pb.WorkReq, settings policy.Settings) error {
```

```
        const errMsg = "policy(%s): block(%d)/job(%d) is a
type(%s) that is not allowed"

    s, ok := settings.(Settings)
    if !ok {
        return fmt.Errorf("settings were not valid")
    }

    for blockNum, block := range req.Blocks {
        for jobNum, job := range block.Jobs {
            if ctx.Err() != nil {
                return ctx.Err()
            }

            if !s.allowed(job.Name) {
                return fmt.Errorf(errMsg, blockNum, jobNum,
job.name)
            }
        }
    }
    return nil
}
```

This preceding code does the following:

- Defines our policy, which implements the `policy.Policy` interface
- Defines a `New()` constructor
- Implements the `policy.Policy.Run()` method
- Validates the `policy.Settings` value passed are the `Settings` for this `Policy`
- Loops through all our `req.Blocks` and gets our `Job` instances
- Checks each `Job` has an allowed name

We now have a policy we can apply to restrict `Job` types in a `pb.WorkReq`. This is how we could apply that in our configuration file to a workflow that does satellite disk erasures:

```
{
    "Name": "SatelliteDiskErase",
    "Policies": [
        {
```

```
                    "Name": "restrictJobTypes",
                    "Settings": {
                        "AllowedJobs": [
                                "validateDecom",
                                "diskErase",
                                "sleep",
                                "getTokenFromBucket"
                        ]
                    }
                }
            ]
        }
```

This policy has the following attributes:

- Is applied only to workflows called `"SatelliteDiskErase"`
- Has a single policy applied, `"restrictJobTypes"`, which we defined
- Allows only `Job` types called one of the following:
  - `"validateDecom"`
  - `"diskErase"`
  - `"sleep"`
  - `"getTokenFromBucket"`

You can see the full `Policy` implementation here:

https://github.com/PacktPublishing/Go-for-DevOps/blob/rev0/chapter/16/workflow/internal/policy/register/restrictjobtypes/restrictjobtypes.go

You can find other policies we have defined in directories here:

https://github.com/PacktPublishing/Go-for-DevOps/tree/rev0/chapter/16/workflow/internal/policy/register

You can see the policy configuration currently defined here:

https://github.com/PacktPublishing/Go-for-DevOps/blob/rev0/chapter/16/workflow/internal/policy/config/config.go

Cautions on policy engines

Before we move on, I would like to provide a word of caution.

Simplicity is the key to sustainable software. I define sustainable software as having the following attributes:

- Easy to debug
- Users can understand how to use it in a few hours at most

Policy engines can be amazingly effective in preventing major problems, acting as a secondary check on sanity to some set of actions. As with security, it should provide substantial benefits while only introducing a small burden.

Policy engines are easy to overdevelop, with the lofty goal of 100% protection while introducing a large amount of complexity and burden. Often, I will see policy engines that are not tightly coupled to a single workflow system. Instead, engineers will design a generic system that tries to deal with multiple tooling systems.

If your policy statements start to look like a programming language (`if` statements, loops, functions), you are moving toward complexity. As policy engines become generic, they become complex to deal with. If you need policy enforcement in multiple places, this is another warning sign.

Not all workflows can achieve safety with generic policies. When you have a complex workflow, feel free to design a policy that does deep checks for a single workflow. Keep your `if` statements, loops, and functions in your code, not your configuration.

I've seen engineers write lots of overcomplicated safety systems. Focus on providing guard rails that are easy to write and update while covering 80% of cases, not 100% of cases. With the division between software that creates a set of actions to run and a service that validates those actions against policies, you are unlikely to have a *disk-erase* type of event in the future, and importantly, you will be able to maintain velocity.

In this section, we have discussed what an SOW would be. To allow our workflow service to understand an SOW, to enforce it, we have designed a policy engine and created our first policy that can be applied to workflows submitted to our system.

Even with policies, something is going to go wrong. This could simply be a confluence of events that makes a normally safe operation unsafe. To be able to respond quickly to these types of events, let's look at introducing emergency-stop capabilities.

Building systems with an emergency stop

Systems are going to run amok. This is a simple truth that you need to come to terms with early in infrastructure tooling development.

When you are a small company, there is usually a very small group of people who understand the systems well and watch over any changes to handle problems. If those people are good, they can quickly respond to a problem. Usually, these people are the developers of the software.

As companies start to grow, jobs begin to become more specialized. The larger the company, the more specialized the jobs. As that happens, the first responders to major issues don't have the access or knowledge to deal with these problems.

This can create a critical gap between recognition of a major problem and stopping the problem from getting worse.

This is where the ability to allow first responders to stop changes comes into play. We call this an emergency-stop ability.

Understanding emergency stops

There are multiple ways to build an emergency-stop system, but the basics are the same. The software will check some data store that contains the name of the workflow you are executing and what the emergency-stop state is.

The most simplistic version of an emergency-stop system has two modes, as follows:

- `Go`
- `Stop`

The software that does any type of work would need to reference the system at intervals. If it cannot find itself listed or the system indicates it is in a `Stop` state, the software terminates, or if it is an execution system, it terminates that workflow.

More complicated versions of this might contain site information so that all tooling running at a site is stopped, or it might include other states such as `Pause`. These are more complicated to implement, so we will stick to this more simplistic form here.

Let's look at what an implementation of this might look like.

Building an emergency-stop package

The first thing we need to do is define what the data format will look like. For this exercise, we will make it **JavaScript Object Notation (JSON)** that will be stored on disk. The disk might be a distributed filesystem or a lock file in `etcd`. And while I'm using JSON here, this could be a single table in a database or a protocol buffer.

Let's define the status our workflows can have, as follows:

```
// Status indicates the emergency stop status.
type Status string

const (
    Unknown Status = ""
    Go Status = "go"
    Stop Status = "stop"
)
```

This defines a few statuses, as follows:

- `Unknown`, which means that the status was not set
- `Go`, which indicates the workflow can be executed
- `Stop`, which indicates the workflow should stop

It is key to know that any status that is not `Go` is considered `Stop`.

Now, let's define an emergency stop entry that can be converted to and from JSON, as follows:

```
type Info struct {
    // Name is the workflow name.
    Name string
    // Status is the emergency stop status.
    Status Status
}
```

This has the following fields:

- `Name`, which is a unique name for a workflow
- `Status`, which details the emergency-stop status for this workflow

Another key to an emergency-stop package is that every workflow must have an entry. If a check is made for an entry that is not named, it is treated as being set to Stop.

Now, we need to validate an entry. Here's how to go about this:

```
func (i Info) validate() error {
    i.Name = strings.TrimSpace(i.Name)
    if i.Name == "" {
        return fmt.Errorf("es.json: rule with empty name")
    }
    switch i.Status {
    case Go, Stop:
    default:
        return fmt.Errorf("es.json: rule(%s) has invalid Status(%s), ignored", i.Name, i.Status)
    }
    return nil
}
```

The preceding code does the following:

- Removes any spaces around a workflow name.
- If the Name value is empty, it is an error.
- If the Status value is not Go or Stop, it is an error.

We treat these errors as simply being that the rule doesn't exist. If a rule doesn't exist, then a workflow is considered in a Stop state.

We now need something that reads this emergency-stop file at intervals or receives notifications on changes. If a service cannot reach the datastore holding our emergency-stop information after some small amount of time, it should report a Stop state.

Let's make a Reader type that accesses our emergency-stop data, as follows:

```
var Data *Reader

func init() {
    r, err := newReader()
    if err != nil {
        panic(fmt.Sprintf("es error: %s", err))
    }
    Data = r
}
```

```
type Reader struct {
    entries  atomic.Value // map[string]Info
    mu       sync.Mutex
    subscribers map[string][]chan Status
}

func newReader() (*Reader, error) {...}

func (r *Reader) Subscribe(name string) (chan Status, Cancel) {...}
func (r *Reader) Status(name string) Status {...}
```

The preceding code does the following:

- Provides a `Data` variable that is the single access point for our `Reader` type
- Provides an `init()` function that accesses our emergency-stop data on program start
- Provides a `Reader` type that allows us to read our emergency-stop states
- Provides a `Subscribe()` function that returns status changes for a workflow and a `Cancel()` function that is called when you no longer want to subscribe
- Provides a `Status()` function that returns the status once
- Provides `newReader`, which is our `Reader` constructor

The full code is not provided here but can be located at the following link:

https://github.com/PacktPublishing/Go-for-DevOps/blob/rev0/chapter/16/workflow/internal/es/es.go

We only allow emergency-stop information to be accessed through `Data`, which is acting as a singleton. This prevents multiple instances from polling for the same data. I prefer having the singleton accessed through a variable to make it clear that a single instance exists.

We now have a package that can tell us our emergency-stop states. Let's look at how we can use this to cancel something.

Using the emergency-stop package

Now that we have a package that can read our emergency-stop data, let's show how we can use it, as follows:

```go
type Job interface{
    Run(ctx context.Context)
}

type Work struct {
    name string
    jobs []Job
}

func (w *work) Exec(ctx context.Context) error{
    esCh, cancelES := es.Data.Subscribe(w.name)
    defer cancelES() // Stop subscribing

    if <-esCh != es.Go { // The initial state
        return fmt.Errorf("es in Stop state")
    }

    var cancel context.CancelFunc
    ctx, cancel = context.WithCancel(ctx)
    defer cancel()

    // If we get an emergency stop, cancel our context.
    // If the context gets cancelled, then just exit.
    go func() {
        select {
        case <-ctx.Done():
            return
        case <-esCh:
            cancel()
        }
    }()

    for _, job := range w.jobs {
        if err := job(ctx); err != nil {
            return err
        }
    }
}
```

```
        return nil
}
```

This preceding code does the following:

- Creates a `Job` that executes some action we want to perform.
- Creates a `Work` type that executes some set of `Jobs`.
- Defines `Exec()`, which executes all `Jobs`.
- Subscribes to emergency stop with a given workflow name.
- If we don't start in the `Go` state, it returns an error.
- Executes a goroutine that calls `cancel()` if we receive a `Stop Status` type.
- Executes the Job instances held in work.jobs.

This is a simple example that uses a `context.Context` object to stop any `Job` that is executing when `cancel()` is called on our `context.Context` object. If we receive a state change with an emergency stop (which is always `Stop`), we call `cancel()`.

A more complete example of using the `es` package can be found in these two files:

- https://github.com/PacktPublishing/Go-for-DevOps/blob/rev0/chapter/16/workflow/internal/service/service.go
- https://github.com/PacktPublishing/Go-for-DevOps/blob/rev0/chapter/16/workflow/internal/service/executor/executor.go

An example `es.json` file that stores emergency-stop data can be found here:

https://github.com/PacktPublishing/Go-for-DevOps/blob/rev0/chapter/16/workflow/configs/es.json

You can see this integrated into our workflow system as part of our `Work.Run()` method at the following link:

https://github.com/PacktPublishing/Go-for-DevOps/blob/rev0/chapter/16/workflow/internal/service/executor/executor.go

Case study – Google's network backbone emergency stop

During an early postmortem for a network tooling problem, it was identified that on-call engineers responding to some major event needed a way to stop automations. At the time, we had a lot of small tools that could be executing against the network at any given time. An on-call engineer, recognizing a problem, had no good way of stopping other engineers from executing work or stopping a runaway program.

The first emergency-stop package was created from this postmortem and integrated into existing tooling. This worked by taking the tool's subscriber name and matching it against the **regular expressions** (**regexes**) contained in an emergency-stop file. This check would occur anytime the file changed or at the start of the execution of the tool.

This was used to stop several automations that were causing problems from growing out of control. However, the implementation was flawed for an organization growing at our rate.

First, it required that every tool developer integrate the emergency-stop package. As more teams outside the initial core team developed tools, they wouldn't know this was a requirement. This led to rogue tooling. And as Google developed its own network gear, tooling development spanned departments that didn't coordinate in many respects. This meant that many tools never had an emergency stop integrated or it was done in a separate system.

Even when an emergency stop was integrated into a tool, it was sometimes a flawed implementation that didn't work. Every integration relied on an engineer doing the right thing.

Finally, an emergency stop had an assumption of a `Go` state. So, if there was no rule listed that matched your subscriber ID, it was assumed it was in a `Go` state. This meant that many times, you had to just stop everything or had to dig through code to figure out a subscriber ID so that you could re-enable everything but the problem tool.

To solve these problems in our backbone, we centralized executions of our backbone work into a central system. This provided us with a single, well-tested emergency-stop implementation, and after a long audit, we switched the emergency-stop package to stop anything that didn't match a rule.

This provided our first responders the ability to stop backbone automation and tools during any major problem. If we found a problem tool, we could allow everything else to run except that tool until proper fixes were made.

In this section, you have learned what an emergency-stop system is, why it is important, how to implement a basic one, and finally, how to integrate an emergency-stop package into tooling.

Summary

This chapter has provided a basic understanding of how to write tooling that provides safety in the face of chaos. We have shown you how circuit breakers or exponential backoff can save your network and services from overload when unexpected problems occur. We have shown how rate-limiting automation can prevent runaway workflows before responders can react. You have learned about how tool scoping via a centralized policy engine can provide a second layer of safety without overburdening your developers. We have learned the importance of idempotent workflows to allow workflow recovery. And finally, we have conveyed how an emergency-stop system can be utilized by first responders by quickly limit damage to automation systems while investigating a problem.

At this time, if you haven't played with the workflow system that we have been developing, you should explore the code and play with the examples. The README.md file will help you get started. You can find this at the following link:

https://github.com/PacktPublishing/Go-for-DevOps/blob/rev0/chapter/16/workflow/README.md

Index

A

absolute pathing 126
ACKnowledge (ACK) 566
action 323
action semantic versioning
   managing 361-363
advanced CLI applications
   Cobra, using 211, 212
Advanced Packaging Tool
   (APT) 106, 245, 538
Alertmanager
   adding 308-313
   configuring 308-313
   reference link 308
Amazon Elastic Block Store
   (EBS) 403, 404
Amazon Machine Image (AMI)
   AWS source, setting up 404, 405
   build block, defining 406-411
   building 403, 404
   Packer build, executing 411, 412
   provisioners, adding 406-411
   reference link 403
AMD64 architecture 104

anonymous functions 31, 32
anonymous import 128
any 51
application I/O
   implementing 202
Application Programming Interface (API)
   about 176, 259
   accessing 522-524
APT on Ubuntu
   Linux, installing via 106
arm64 builds 104
arrays
   about 34
   using 34
authentication, authorization, and
   accounting (AAA) 266
AWS client requests
   overwhelming network 552
AWS Service Event
   reference link 552
AWS source
   setting up 404, 405
Azure account
   creating 522-524
   reference link 522

Azure Active Directory (AAD) 521
Azure APIs
　basics 519
Azure built-in roles
　reference link 521
Azure geography guidance
　reference link 451
Azure infrastructure
　provisioning, with Go 527-539
Azure Managed Identity
　reference link 530
Azure provider documentation
　reference link 453
Azure Resource Manager (ARM)
　used, for building infrastructure 524
Azure REST API
　reference link 520
Azure SDK for Go 525
Azure Service Principal
　reference link 530
Azure Storage
　provisioning , with Go 540-543
　using 544-546
Azure Storage account
　building 539, 540
Azure virtual machine
　building 526, 527

B

backoff implementation
　circuit breakers, combining with 557
　reference link 557
　using 555-557
base 124
basic chatbot
　building 371-376

basic flag error handling 206, 207
basic test file
　creating 82
basic value separation, using
　　　strings package
　about 135
　conversion, after reading
　　　whole file 135, 136
　line by line, converting 137, 138
　records, writing to CSV 138, 139
block blobs
　reference link 543
Block message 569
bufio package
　reference link 130
Buf tooling
　installation link 189
　reference link 187
build constraints
　reference link 234
built-in constraints 94, 95
bytes package
　reference link 130

C

call chain 79
cell 142
central processing unit (CPU) 264, 266
constructor pattern 48
change automations
　actions 248
　action validations 248
　designing 248
　global postconditions 248
　global preconditions 248

local postconditions 248
local preconditions 248
channel
　as event signal 72, 73
　used, for goroutine
　　communication 69, 70
channel-based rate limiter 559-561
ChatOps
　environment architecture 368
ChatOps service
　creating 370
Chipmunk
　case study 227, 228
circuit breakers
　closed state 552
　combining, with backoff
　　implementation 557
　half-open state 553
　open state 553
　reference link 555
　using 552-554
Classless Inter-Domain
　Routing (CIDR) 534
client binary
　creating 197, 198
client/server-distributed tracing
　with OpenTelemetry 287-295
client/server metrics
　with OpenTelemetry 299-307
cloud 518, 519
cloud APIs 520
cloud-init
　reference link 538
cloud resources
　defining 448-457
　provisioning 448-457
Cobra
　cancellation with 226, 227

code organization 212, 213
command package 215-219
optional Cobra generator 213, 214
using, advanced CLI
　applications 211, 212
code
　building, on machine 108
command package 215-219
comma-separated values (CSV) files
　about 134
　basic value separation, using
　　strings package 135
　encoding/csv package, using 139
　excelize, using 142
common format and MIME
　type for CSV files
　reference link 139
composite literal 38
concurrency
　goroutines, utilizing 65
concurrent job
　writing 249-258
concurrent programming 67
conditionals
　else 25, 26
　if statements 24, 25
　using 24
constants
　declaring 59, 60
　enumeration via 61
　utilizing 59
constraints 93, 94
constructors 48
container image release workflow
　creating 355-358
context
　best practices 81
　cancellation, honoring 77, 78

in standard library 78, 79
to pass values 79, 80
used, for communicating, timer state 76
used, for terminating, wait condition 76
using to handle canceling
  executions 221-225
context variables 319
continuous integration/continuous
  deployment (CI/CD) 231
continuous integration workflow
  building 328
controller 495, 500
correlation of telemetry 276
Create, Read, Update, Delete
  (CRUD) 447, 480
custom actions
  about 345
  action release management 348
  metadata 346, 347
  types 346
custom errors 57
custom flag types 204-206
custom Go GitHub Action
  action semantic versioning,
    managing 361-364
  creating 345
  optimizing 358-360
  publishing 360
  publishing actions 360, 361
  publishing, goals 361
  publishing, to GitHub Marketplace 364
custom providers
  building, resources 458
  publishing 474
  reference link 474
custom resource definitions (CRDs)
  about 497, 498
  conversion 499

defaulting 499
reference link 497
structured schema 499
validation 499
versioning 499
custom struct types 44

D

data
  adding 142-145
  reading, out of stream 120-122
  writing, into stream 122, 123, 130
  writing, to Postgres 170, 171
database/sql 164
data collection
  reference link 275
data migration, of orchestration system
  case study 177
data race 67
defer
  about 63, 64
  using 63
dereferencing pointer 41
dictionaries 37
Distributed Denial of Service
  (DDoS) attacks 227
distributed trace
  about 286
  instrumenting 286
  life cycle 286
  log entries, adding to spans 296
duck typing 12
Dv3 and Dsv3-series
  reference link 535
dynamically typed language 12

E

Elastic Container Service (ECS) 249
else statement
 about 25, 26
 else if 26
 if/else braces 26
embed filesystems 128
embed package
 reference link 130
emergency stop
 about 578
 used, for building systems 578
emergency-stop package
 building 579-581
 integrating, into tooling 584
 using 582, 583
encoding/csv package
 line by line, reading 140, 141
 line by line, writing 141
 using 139
encoding formats
 about 149
 Go field tags 149
 JavaScript Object Notation (JSON) 150, 151
 YAML encoding 158
enumerated type 61
enumeration
 via constants 61
enumerators
 printing 62
environment variables
 reference link 221, 226
error
 creating 54
 custom errors 57
 handling, in Go 54
 named errors, creating 56
 using 55
 wrapping 58, 59
escape analysis 42
essential tools
 availability, determining 231, 232
event
 about 318
 manual event 319
 multiple events 318
 scheduled event 319
 single event 318
 syntax 318
event handlers
 creating 377-385
event signal
 channel as 72, 73
event types
 reference link 375
Excel
 data, adding 142-145
 data summarization 145-147
 visualizations, adding 147, 148
excelize
 reference link 142
 using, when dealing with Excel 142
exec package
 binaries, executing with 232-239
 using 240
expect packages
 using, for complicated interactions 244-247
Expect Tool Command Language (TCL) language extension
 reference link 233
expression 320

F

fakes
  about 86
  creating, with interfaces 86-89
field tags 149
file content
  streaming 119
filepath
  functions 126
  joining 124
  splitting 125, 126
  using 124
filesystem
  walking 129
flag package 203, 204
floating-point 12
fmt.Printf() function 119
fmt.Println() function 119
for loop
  C style 21
  init statement, removing 21
  post statements, removing 22
for loop gotcha 561
FreeBSD 108
freepik
  URL 370
fs package
  reference link 130
Fully Qualified Domain Name (FQDN) 454
function closure 31
functions
  about 28, 29
  anonymous functions 31, 32
  multiple values, returning 29, 30
  named returns 29, 30
  variadic argument 30, 31
function scoped 17

G

generic function
  type, specifying when calling 98, 99
generics
  about 91
  gotchas 100, 101
  using 101
GitHub Actions
  basics 316
  building 323
  components, exploring 317
  triggering 323
GitHub Marketplace
  tweeter action, publishing to 364
GitHub releases 334
GitHub repository
  cloning 323
  creating 323
Git tag 335
Global Interpreter Lock (GIL)
  about 3, 227
  reference link 227
GNU Privacy Guard (GPG) 431
Go
  field tags 149
  installing 105
  installing, on machine 104
  used, for creating custom GitHub Action 345
  used, for provisioning Azure infrastructure 527-539
  used, for provisioning Azure Storage 540-543
Go 1.0.0 version 108
Go 1.7 78

Go 1.16 126
Go 1.17.5 version 108
Go 1.18 51
Go 1 and future of Go Programs
  reference link 108
gobreaker 553
Go compiler 104
Go compiler version
  compatibility 108
GoDoc 130
go.mod file
  creating 109, 110
Go modules 109
Google
  emergency stop 584
Google Remote Procedure Call (gRPC)
  about 64, 163, 520, 557
  features 198, 199
  reference link 64
Google satellite
  disk erase 558
Go package event
  reference link 375
Go Playground
  about 5-7
  URL 5
Go plugins for compiler
  installation link 189
Go program
  application, deploying into
    namespace 488
  ClientSet, creating 486, 487
  code 485, 486
  Ingress, creating on local
    host port 492, 493
  namespace, creating 487
  NGINX deployment, creating 488, 489

  pod logs, streaming for NGINX
    application 494, 495
  ready replica, waiting to match
    desired replica 490, 491
  Service to load-balance,
    creating 491, 492
  used, for deploying load-balanced
    HTTP application 483-485
GORM
  about 176
  reference link 176
goroutines
  channel 69, 70
  channels as event signal 72, 73
  mutexes 74
  receiving from channel 70, 71
  RWMutex 75
  select statement 71, 72
  sending to channel 70, 71
  synchronization 67
  utilizing, for concurrency 65
  WaitGroups 68, 69
  working 66
Goss
  Packer provisioner, adding 416-418
  spec file, creating 413-416
  used, for validating images 413
Go tooling
  installing, for macOS with
    package installer 104
GroupCache 130
gRPC client
  developing 186
  writing 190-192
gRPC server
  writing 192-195

gRPC service
  developing 186
  providing, inside company 199, 200
gRPC workflow service
  defining 568, 569

H

hashes 37
HashiCorp Configuration
    Language 2 (HCL 2) 403
heap 42
heap allocation 42
hello world application
  creating 110
  running 110
Homebrew
  macOS, installing via 104
  reference link 104
  updating 105
HyperText Transfer Protocol
    (HTTP) 260, 553

I

idempotent workflows
  building 564, 565
identifier (ID) 566
Identity and Access Management
    (IAM) 524
if statements 24, 25
images
  validating, with Goss 413
infinite loop
  creating 22
  loop brace 23
  loop control 22

Infrastructure as Code (IaC) 439
infrastructure, building with
    Azure Resource Manager
  about 524
  Azure SDK for Go 525
  Azure virtual machine,
      building 526, 527
  local environment, setting up 525
infrastructure specs
  applying, with Terraform 440-447
  initializing, with Terraform 440-447
init statement
  removing 21
input
  retrieving, from STDIN 209-211
input-output (I/O) 114
Instrumenting libraries
  reference link 276
integer 12
interface
  about 49, 50
  blank interface, defining 51
  defining 49, 50
  type assertion 51, 52
  used, for creating fakes 86-89
internally exported type 32
Internal packages
  reference link 32
Internet Protocol (IP) 236
io/fs 129, 130
io.fs filesystems 127
I/O interfaces 114, 115
io package
  reference link 130
io.Reader 121
isolation levels
  reference link 173

J

JavaScript Object Notation (JSON)
  about 149-157, 239, 403, 579
  file, marshaling to map 151, 152
  file, unmarshaling to map 151, 152
  large messages, marshaling 154-157
  large messages, unmarshaling 154-157
  structs, marshaling to 153, 154
  structs, unmarshaling to 153, 154
job
  about 321
  executing, on multiple platforms 321
  syntax 321
Job message 569
JSON functions and operators
  reference link 175
JSON Web Token (JWT) 183

K

KinD cluster
  creating 479
kubectl
  using, to interact with API 480, 481
kubectx
  reference link 483
Kubernetes
  building 500
  extending, with operators 495-497
  extending, with resources 495-497
Kubernetes API
  authentication 482, 483
  Group Version Kind (GVK)
    Namespace Name 481
  interacting with 479
  spec section 481
  status section 481

L

leveled logs
  with Zap 279, 280
lexer and parser
  versus regexes 378
Linux
  about 106
  installing, via APT on Ubuntu 106
  installing, via Snap on Ubuntu 106, 107
  installing, via tarball 107, 108
load-balanced HTTP application
  deploying, with Go program 483-485
local changes
  automating, with os/exec
    package 230, 231
local files
  reading 115, 116
  writing 116
locally redundant storage (LRS)
  reference link 543
lock 74
log entries
  adding, to spans 296
logs
  about 278
  correlating 295
  exporting, with OpenTelemetry 281, 282
  ingesting, with OpenTelemetry 281, 282
  OTel Collector configuration 282-285
  transforming, with
    OpenTelemetry 281, 282
log statement 278, 279
loop
  about 21
  infinite loop, creating 22

M

macOS
  installing, via Homebrew 104
  installing, with package installer 104
maps
  about 37
  declaring 37
  values, accessing 38
  values, adding 38
  values, extracting from 39
Marshal ()
  reference link 154
memfs 130
method of procedure (MOP) 231
methods
  type constraint with 95
metric event
  about 297
  client/server metrics, with
    OpenTelemetry 299-307
  example scenarios 297
  instrumenting 297
  life cycle 298, 299
  types 297
metrics abnormalities
  alerting 308
Microsoft Azure identity 521
Microsoft Azure REST API
    Guidelines 520
Microsoft Installer (MSI)
  used, for installing Windows 105
module
  updating 110
module directory
  creating 109, 110

multiple values
  returning 30
mustBool() 218
mustString() 218
mutex 74, 75

N

named errors
  creating 56
named returns 30
network
  AWS client requests overwhelming 552
network device
  rollouts 258
Network File System (NFS) 163
non-flag arguments
  accessing 208, 209
null values 169

O

Object-Relational Mappings (ORMs) 175
Open Authorization (OAuth) 81, 266
Open Container Initiative (OCI) 512
OpenFile() 118
OpenID Connect (OIDC) 80
OpenTelemetry
  about 273
  features 273
  logging, with context 278
  reference architecture 274
  used, for client/server-distributed
    tracing 287-295
  used, for client/server metrics 299-307
  used, for exporting logs 281, 282

used, for ingesting logs 281, 282
used, for transforming logs 281, 282
OpenTelemetry components
  automatic instrumentation 276
  correlation of telemetry 276
  language SDKs 276
OpenTelemetry Line Protocol (OTLP) 275
OpenTelemetry specification
  API 275
  data 275
  reference link 275
  SDK 275
OpenTelemetry tracing specification
  reference link 287
operators
  about 495
  used, for extending Kubernetes 496, 497
Ops service
  creating 370
  using 370, 371
orders of magnitude (OOM) 257
OS-agnostic filesystems 126
OS-agnostic pathing 123
os/exec package
  using, to automate local
    changes 230, 231
os package
  reference link 130
OS signals
  capturing 220, 221
  context, using to handle canceling
    executions 221-225
  handling 219
os.Stderr 119
os.Stdin 119
os.Stdout 119

OTel Collector
  about 275
  exporters 275
  processors 275
  receivers 275
outer scoped variable 19
overloaded operators 42
overload prevention mechanisms
  backoff implementations, using 555-557
  circuit breakers, using 552-554
  using 551
oversubscribed 551

P

package installer
  used, for installing macOS 104
packages
  about 7
  declaring 7, 8
  hello world program, writing 11, 12
  import and use rule 10
  importing 8, 9
  name conflicts 9
  using 9
package scoped 17
Packer
  customizing, with plugins 419
Packer build
  executing, to create image 411, 412
Packer builds, debugging
  reference link 435
Packer plugin
  ConfigSpec() function, defining 423
  configuration specification,
    defining 422, 423
  debugging 435

Packer, customizing with 419
Prepare(), defining 423, 424
Provision(), defining 424-430
provisioner configuration, adding 421
releasing 431, 432
testing 431
using, in build 433-435
writing 420
PagerDuty
　URL 310
panic
　about 64
　using 63
paths
　directories 124
　file 124
pet resource
　implementing 468-472
pet store
　Terraform provider, building 458
pet store data source
　implementing 464-468
pet store operator
　building 501
　initializing 501-514
pet store provider
　running 472-474
pet store Terraform provider 459-464
pointers
　about 39
　dereferencing 41
　function, creating copy of
　　arguments passed 40
　memory addresses 40
pointer-wrapped type 42
policies
　using, to restrict tools 568
　writing 573-576

policy engine
　cautions 577
　creating 570-573
Portable Operating System
　　Interface (POSIX) 319
Postgres
　data, writing to 170, 171
　installation link 164
Postgres database
　connecting to 164, 165
　querying 166-168
Postgres, running in local
　　Docker container
　reference link 164
Postgres-specific types 173-175
Postgres value types
　reference link 175
postmortem culture
　reference link 559
post statement
　removing 22
private types 32, 33
process identifiers (PIDs) 253
Prometheus guide for email configuration
　reference link 310
Prometheus Integration Guide
　reference link 310
protocol buffer compiler
　installation link 189
protocol buffers (proto)
　about 187, 188
　packages, generating 189, 190
　prerequisites 189
providers 447
provisioned Azure infrastructure
　using 539
provisioners
　reference link 406

public types 32, 33
publishing actions
   basics 360, 361

Q

queries per second (QPS) 551
Quote of the Day (QOTD) 179, 202

R

recover
   about 64, 65
   using 63
Redis 130
regular expressions (regexes)
   about 239, 584
   versus lexer and parser 378
relative pathing 126
release automation
   creating 336, 340, 341
   cross-platform binaries,
      building 337-339
   environmental setup 337
   for tweeter 335
   goals 335
   release notes, generating 339, 340
   triggering 336
   version injection, building 337-339
   workspace 337
release execution
   restricting 336, 337
release of tweeter
   creating 342-345
release workflow
   building 334
remote files
   reading 117, 118

Remote Procedure Call (RPC)
   64, 163, 178, 241
repeatable workflows
   building 563
REpresentational State Transfer (REST)
   about 58, 163, 251, 520
   for RPCs 178
resource hierarchy 521
resources
   used, for extending Kubernetes 495-497
REST API
   reference link 142
REST client
   developing 178
   task 179
   writing 179-183
RESTful API, developing with Go and Gin
   reference link 186
restrict tools
   policies, using 568
REST service
   developing 178
   providing, inside company 199, 200
   recommended practices 200
   writing 183-186
retry loops 551
Revel
   reference link 186
Role-Based Access Control (RBAC) 521
Role-Based Authorization
      Controls (RBAC) 503
Rosetta Code
   reference link 14
runaway workflows
   preventing, with rate limiters 558
run() method 254
runtime error 13

runtime package
  using 124
RWMutex 75

S

sandboxing 260
satellites 558
scalability targets for premium block blob storage accounts
  reference link 543
scope 17, 18
scope of work (SOW) 567
Secure File Transfer Protocol (SFTP) 177
Secure Shell (SSH) key
  setting up 525
select statement 71, 72
server binary
  creating 195, 196
Server Message Block (SMB) 163
Service Level Agreement (SLA) 3
Service Level Obligation (SLO) 3
shared access signatures (SAS)
  reference link 539
shorthand flags 208
Simple Network Management Protocol (SNMP) 378
single plugins 419
Site Reliability Engineering (SRE) 3, 199
Site Reliability Engineers (SRE) 230, 559
Slack
  reference link 386
Slack application
  creating 386-390
  running 391-394
slices
  about 35, 36

  using 34
  values, extracting from 36
Snap 106
Snap on Ubuntu
  Linux, installing via 106, 107
Software Development Kits (SDKs) 519, 520
spans
  log entries, adding to 296
spec section 481
SQL databases
  accessing 164
  data, writing to Postgres 170, 171
  null values 169
  Postgres database, connecting 164, 165
  Postgres database, querying 166-168
  Postgres-specific types 173-175
  storage abstractions 176, 177
  transactions 171-173
SSH authentication forms
  challenge-response authentication 241
  public key authentication 241
  username/password 241
SSH, in Go
  connecting, to another system 241-244
  using, to automate remote changes 240
SSH package
  reference link 240, 241
stack memory 42
standard library (stdlib) packages 8
standard output (stdout) 62
statement scoped 17
statically typed language 12, 13
status section 481
STDIN
  input, retrieving from 209-211
stdlib packages
  reference link 8

steps
    about 322
    for installing Go with action 322
    syntax 322
    with multiple line command 322
Stock-Keeping Unit (SKU) 535
storage abstractions 176, 177
strconv package
    reference link 116, 130
strings package
    reference link 130
    using, for basic value separation 135
struct GetReq 188
structs
    about 43
    custom type, declaring 44
    declaring 43
    field value, modifying 46, 47
    field value, modifying in method 47
    methods, adding to type 45
struct types
    type parameters, adding to 96-98
structured logs
    with Zap 279, 280
switch statements
    about 27
    exact match switch 27
    true/false evaluation switch 28
SYNchonize (SYN) 566
synchronization 67
synchronization primitive 74
system agent
    designing 259-262
    install, implementing 262, 263
    SystemPerf, implementing 264-267
    uses 259
    writing 259

systems
    building, with emergency stop 578

T

table-driven tests (TDTs) 82-86
tarball
    Linux, installing via 107, 108
Terraform
    about 439
    URL 439
    used, for applying infrastructure
        specs 440-447
    used, for initializing infrastructure
        specs 440-447
Terraform provider
    about 447
    building, for pet store 458
    URL 458
Terraform Registry
    URL 447
test, adding
    reference link 83
testing framework
    basic test file, creating 82
    fakes, creating with interfaces 86-89
    simple test, creating 83, 84
    table driven tests (TDT) 84-86
    utilizing 81, 82
testing packages
    reference link 90
three-way handshakes
    using, to prevent workflow loss 566, 567
token-bucket rate limiter 561, 562
traces
    correlating 295
transactions 171-173

Transmission Control Protocol
    (TCP) 492, 566
Transport Layer Security (TLS) 178, 266
tweeter
    release automation 335
tweeter action
    action metadata, creating 351, 352
    creating 349
    Dockerfile, defining 349-351
    Publishing, to GitHub Marketplace 364
    testing 353-355
tweeter command-line tool
    about 328
    avoidance 329
    cloning 328
    testing 328
tweeter continuous integration workflow
    about 330
    building 333, 334
    goals 329
    linting 333, 334
    matrix, entering 331, 332
    testing 333, 334
    triggering 330, 331
tweeter custom GitHub Action
    goals 348
    publishing, goals 361
Twitter developer credentials, set up
    reference link 363
two-factor authentication (2FA) 241
type assertion 51, 52
type constraint
    using 92, 93
    with methods 95
type conversion 51
type hints 13
type parameters
    about 91, 92

adding, to struct types 96-98
types
    about 12-14
    listing 14, 15
type ServeMux
    reference link 184
typical rollout
    canary phase 254
    general phase 254

U

Universal Resource Identifier (URI) 456
untyped constant 60

V

values
    accessing, in maps 38
    adding, in maps 38
    extracting, from maps 39
    extracting, from slice 36
    passing, on Context 79
variables
    declaring 15
    function, create and use rule 20
    redeclaration, avoiding in
        same scope 18, 19
    scopes 17
    shadowing 19
    statement, create and use rule 20
variables declaration
    long way 16
    shorter way 16
variable types 13, 14
variadic argument 30, 31
version output 104
virtual machines (VMs) 249

W

WaitGroup 68, 69
Windows
  installing, with MSI 105
workflow, GitHub Action
  about 317
  creating 324-327
  syntax 317
workflow loss
  preventing, with three-way
    handshakes 566, 567
workflow structure
  example 317
working directory 124
WorkReq message 569
WorkResp message 569

X

Xcode
  installation link 105
  installing 105
xlsx file
  using 142-145
X Window System (X11) 240

Y

Yet Another Markup Language (YAML)
  about 149, 158, 162
  file, marshaling to map 159
  file, unmarshaling to map 159
  structs, marshaling to 160-162
  structs, unmarshaling to 160-162

Z

Zap
  used, for leveled logs 279, 280
  used, for structured logs 279, 280
zero value 20

Packt.com

Subscribe to our online digital library for full access to over 7,000 books and videos, as well as industry leading tools to help you plan your personal development and advance your career. For more information, please visit our website.

Why subscribe?

- Spend less time learning and more time coding with practical eBooks and Videos from over 4,000 industry professionals
- Improve your learning with Skill Plans built especially for you
- Get a free eBook or video every month
- Fully searchable for easy access to vital information
- Copy and paste, print, and bookmark content

Did you know that Packt offers eBook versions of every book published, with PDF and ePub files available? You can upgrade to the eBook version at packt.com and as a print book customer, you are entitled to a discount on the eBook copy. Get in touch with us at customercare@packtpub.com for more details.

At www.packt.com, you can also read a collection of free technical articles, sign up for a range of free newsletters, and receive exclusive discounts and offers on Packt books and eBooks.

Other Books You May Enjoy

If you enjoyed this book, you may be interested in these other books by Packt:

Learning DevOps - Second Edition

Mikael Krief

ISBN: 9781801818964

- Understand the basics of infrastructure as code patterns and practices
- Get an overview of Git command and Git flow
- Install and write Packer, Terraform, and Ansible code for provisioning and configuring cloud infrastructure based on Azure examples
- Use Vagrant to create a local development environment
- Containerize applications with Docker and Kubernetes
- Apply DevSecOps for testing compliance and securing DevOps infrastructure
- Build DevOps CI/CD pipelines with Jenkins, Azure Pipelines, and GitLab CI
- Explore blue-green deployment and DevOps practices for open sources projects

The DevOps Career Handbook

John Knight, Nate Swenson

ISBN: 9781803230948

- Understand various roles and career paths for DevOps practitioners
- Discover proven techniques to stand out in the application process
- Prepare for the many stages of your interview, from the phone screen to taking the technical challenge and then the onsite interview
- Network effectively to help your career move in the right direction
- Tailor your resume to specific DevOps roles
- Discover how to negotiate after you've been extended an offer

Packt is searching for authors like you

If you're interested in becoming an author for Packt, please visit `authors.packtpub.com` and apply today. We have worked with thousands of developers and tech professionals, just like you, to help them share their insight with the global tech community. You can make a general application, apply for a specific hot topic that we are recruiting an author for, or submit your own idea.

Share your thoughts

Now you've finished *Go for DevOps*, we'd love to hear your thoughts! Scan the QR code below to go straight to the Amazon review page for this book and share your feedback or leave a review on the site that you purchased it from.

`https://packt.link/r/1801818894`

Your review is important to us and the tech community and will help us make sure we're delivering excellent quality content.

Download a free PDF copy of this book

Thanks for purchasing this book!

Do you like to read on the go but are unable to carry your print books everywhere?

Is your eBook purchase not compatible with the device of your choice?

Don't worry, now with every Packt book you get a DRM-free PDF version of that book at no cost.

Read anywhere, any place, on any device. Search, copy, and paste code from your favorite technical books directly into your application.

The perks don't stop there, you can get exclusive access to discounts, newsletters, and great free content in your inbox daily

Follow these simple steps to get the benefits:

1. Scan the QR code or visit the link below

`https://packt.link/free-ebook/9781801818896`

2. Submit your proof of purchase
3. That's it! We'll send your free PDF and other benefits to your email directly

Printed in Great Britain
by Amazon